FAST TRACK TO A 5

Preparing for the AP® Statistics Examination

To Accompany
Statistics: Learning from Data
1st and 2nd Editions
by Roxy Peck, Tom Short, and Chris Olsen

Joshua Wilkerson
Regents School of Austin, Austin, Texas

Vicki Greenberg
Kennesaw State University, Kennesaw, Georgia

Viva Hathaway
Norview High School, Norfolk, Virginia

Ed Moulton
Norview High School, Norfolk, Virginia

Australia •· Brazil •· Mexico •· Singapore •· United Kingdom •· United States

AP® is a trademark registered by the College Board, which is not affiliated with, and does not endorse, this product.

© 2019 Cengage Learning

WCN: 01-100-101

ALL RIGHTS RESERVED. No part of this work covered by the copyright herein may be reproduced, transmitted, stored, or used in any form or by any means graphic, electronic, or mechanical, including but not limited to photocopying, recording, scanning, digitizing, taping, Web distribution, information networks, or information storage and retrieval systems, except as permitted under Section 107 or 108 of the 1976 United States Copyright Act, without the prior written permission of the publisher.

National Geographic Learning/Cengage Learning is pleased to offer our college-level materials to high schools for Advanced Placement®, honors, and electives courses. To contact your National Geographic Learning representative, please call us toll-free at **1-888-915-3276** or visit us at **http://ngl.cengage.com**.

For permission to use material from this text or product, submit all requests online at **www.cengage.com/permissions**
Further permissions questions can be emailed to **permissionrequest@cengage.com**.

ISBN: 978-1-337-55891-4

Cengage Learning
20 Channel Center Street
Boston, MA 02210
USA

Cengage Learning is a leading provider of customized learning solutions with office locations around the globe, including Singapore, the United Kingdom, Australia, Mexico, Brazil, and Japan. Locate your local office at: **www.cengage.com/global**.

Cengage Learning products are represented in Canada by Nelson Education, Ltd.

To learn more about Cengage Learning Solutions, visit **www.cengage.com**.

AP® is a trademark registered by the College Board, which is not affiliated with, and does not endorse, this product.

Printed in the United States of America
Print Number: 01   Print Year: 2018

CONTENTS

About the Authors   vii

Preface   ix

Acknowledgments   x

Part I: Strategies for the AP® Examination   1

   Preparing for the AP® Statistics Examination   3
      What's in This Book   3
      Setting Up a Review Schedule   5
      Before the Exam   5

   Taking the AP® Statistics Examination   7
      Strategies for the Multiple-Choice Section   7
      Types of Multiple-Choice Questions   8
      Free-Response Questions   10
      Free-Response Sample Question   13

   A Diagnostic Test   15

      AP® Statistics Examination   15

      Answers to Diagnostic Test   29

      Calculating Your Score   43

Part II: A Review of AP® Statistics   45

   Chapter 1 Graphical Methods for Describing Data   47
      Qualitative Data: Bar Graphs, Circle Graphs, and Segmented Bar Graphs   48
      Quantitative Data: Stem-and-Leaf Displays, Frequency Distributions, and Histograms   52
      Bivariate Quantitative Data: Scatter Diagrams   58
      Graphical Methods for Describing Data: Student Objectives for the AP® Exam   59
      Multiple-Choice Questions   59
      Free-Response Problems   64
      Answers   65

   Chapter 2 Numerical Methods for Describing Data   69
      Describing the Center of a Data Set   69
      Describing Variability in a Data Set   72
      Summarizing a Data Set: Boxplots   76
      Interpreting Center and Variability: Empirical Rule and Z-Scores   78
      Numerical Methods for Describing Data: Student Objectives for the AP® Exam   81
      Multiple-Choice Questions   82
      Free-Response Problems   86
      Answers   87

Chapter 3 Summarizing Bivariate Data 91
The Correlation Coefficient 91
Linear Regression 95
Assessing the Fit of a Line 99
Nonlinear Relationships and Transformations 103
Summarizing Bivariate Data: Student Objectives for the AP® Exam 108
Multiple-Choice Questions 109
Free-Response Problems 114
Answers 116

Chapter 4 Collecting Data Sensibly 119
Collecting Data Sensibly 119
Sampling 120
Observational Studies 125
Experimental Design 125
Collecting Data Sensibly: Student Objectives for the AP® Exam 130
Multiple-Choice Questions 130
Free-Response Problems 134
Answers 135

Chapter 5 Probability 139
Chance Experiments and Events 139
Definition of Probability 142
Basic Properties of Probability 143
Conditional Probability 144
Independence 145
Simulation 146
Probability: Student Objectives for the AP® Exam 147
Multiple-Choice Questions 147
Free-Response Problems 151
Answers 152

Chapter 6 Random Variables and Probability Distributions 157
Random Variables 157
Probability Distributions for Discrete Random Variables 158
Continuous Random Variables 159
Mean and Standard Deviation of Random Variables 159
Binomial and Geometric Distributions 162
Normal Distributions 165
Random Variables and Probability Distributions: Student Objectives for the AP® Exam 171
Multiple-Choice Questions 171
Free-Response Problems 175
Answers 176

Chapter 7 Sampling Variability and Sampling Distributions 179
Statistics and Sampling Variability 179
The Sampling Distribution of a Sample Mean 180
The Sampling Distribution of a Sample Proportion 184
Sampling Variability and Sampling Distributions: Student Objectives for the AP® Exam 187
Multiple-Choice Questions 187
Free-Response Problems 191
Answers 192

Chapter 8 Estimation Using a Single Sample   197
　Point Estimation   197
　Large-Sample Confidence Interval for a Population Proportion   198
　Confidence Interval for a Population Mean   201
　Interpreting and Communicating the Results of Statistical Analyses   205
　Estimation Using a Single Sample: Student Objectives for the AP® Exam   207
　Multiple-Choice Questions   207
　Free-Response Problems   211
　Answers   212

Chapter 9 Hypothesis Testing Using a Single Sample   215
　Hypotheses and Test Procedures   215
　Errors in Hypothesis Testing   217
　Large-Sample Hypothesis Tests for a Proportion   218
　Hypothesis Tests for a Mean   222
　Power and Probability of Type II Error   226
　Interpretation of Results of Hypothesis Testing   227
　Hypothesis Testing Using a Single Sample: Student Objectives for the AP® Exam   228
　Multiple-Choice Questions   229
　Free-Response Problems   234
　Answers   235

Chapter 10 Comparing Two Populations or Treatments   239
　Inferences Concerning the Difference Between Two Population or Treatment Means Using
　　Independent Samples   240
　Inferences Concerning the Difference Between Two Population or Treatment Means Using Paired
　　Samples   245
　Large-Sample Inferences Concerning a Difference Between Two Population or Treatment
　　Proportions   249
　Interpreting and Communicating the Results of Statistical Analyses   254
　Comparing Two Populations or Treatments: Student Objectives for the AP® Exam   254
　Multiple-Choice Questions   255
　Free-Response Problems   260
　Answers   261

Chapter 11 The Analysis of Categorical Data and Goodness-of-Fit Tests   265
　Chi-Square Tests for Univariate Data   265
　Tests for Homogeneity and Independence in a Two-Way Table   271
　Interpreting and Communicating the Results of Statistical Analyses   274
　Categorical Data and Goodness-of-Fit Tests: Student Objectives for the AP® Exam   275
　Multiple-Choice Questions   275
　Free-Response Problems   280
　Answers   281

Chapter 12 Inference for Linear Regression and Correlation   285
　Simple Linear Regression Model   285
　Inferences about the Slope of the Regression Line   291
　Interpretation of Results of Hypothesis Testing   296
　Inference for Linear Regression and Correlation: Student Objectives for the AP® Exam   297
　Multiple-Choice Questions   297
　Free-Response Problems   301
　Answers   302

Part III: Practice Tests 307

    Practice Test I 309
        AP® Statistics Examination 309
        Answers 328
        Calculating Your Score 342

    Practice Test II 343
        AP® Statistics Examination 343
        Answers 364
        Calculating Your Score 378

Part IV: Equations and Constants 379

ABOUT THE AUTHORS

JOSHUA WILKERSON has taught for over 10 years, the last 5 of which have occurred at Regents School of Austin in Austin, Texas. He has taught AP® Statistics for the past 7 years, has served as a reader for the AP® Statistics exam, and has given multiple presentations on teaching AP® Statistics at the AP® Annual Conference. He holds a bachelor's degree in Mathematics from Texas A&M University and has recently completed a Ph.D. in Math Education from Texas State University. Joshua's dissertation focused on the benefits of service-learning projects in mathematics courses (specifically AP® Statistics) for cultivating a productive disposition in students.

VIVA HATHAWAY has taught AP® Statistics at Norview High School in Norfolk, Virginia, for the past 10 years of her 20-year career teaching high school mathematics. She received both bachelor's and master's degrees in mathematics from Bowling Green State University in Ohio. Viva has served as a reader for the AP® Statistics exam and routinely makes presentations on AP® Statistics at the annual meeting of the National Council of Teachers of Mathematics. In addition, she teaches statistics as an adjunct professor for Saint Leo University. Viva is also a recipient of the Presidential Award for Excellence in Mathematics and Science for the state of Virginia. Besides teaching statistics and geometry at Norview High School, Viva serves on local and national committees regarding mathematics in secondary education.

VICKI GREENBERG has taught mathematics for over 16 years and statistics for over 7 years. She currently teaches mathematics at Kennesaw State University in Kennesaw, Georgia, and AP® Statistics at the University of California, Irvine as part of its online high school extension program in Irvine, California, and has served as Assistant Director for the school's AP® Summer Institutes. She holds a bachelor's degree in Mathematics from the University of North Carolina at Greensboro and a master's degree in Mathematics Education from Georgia State University. She is a reader for the AP® Statistics exam and a regular presenter at local and regional AP® Summer Institutes. Her educational interests include creating hands-on and technology-infused activities to enhance her students' understanding of mathematics and statistics. In her spare time, Vicki enjoys photography, travel, baseball, football, and playing with her two children, two cats, and two dogs.

ED MOULTON is a teacher of dual enrollment calculus, AP® Calculus support, and Honors Algebra 2 at Norview High School in Norfolk, Virginia. Before coming to Norview High School, he co-taught the AP® Statistics Class at Dunbar High School in Baltimore, Maryland. Ed holds a bachelor's degree in Mathematics from Duke University and a master's degree in Arts and Teaching from Johns Hopkins University.

Preface

The field of statistics is relevant to nearly every career you will encounter. As such, most college majors will require at least a cursory knowledge of statistics. Statistics is an integral tool used in the fields of medicine, genetics, business, mathematics, engineering, psychology, sociology, education, and political science as well as a vast majority of other careers not mentioned. Because of this, we believe this course is critical for well-educated people to be successful in their careers.

Dealing with statistics in each field of study can vary depending on the subject matter. However, the basic statistical principles are the same in all fields and all majors. Thus, the study of AP® Statistics will allow you the unique opportunity to be well prepared for virtually any college major you choose. The statistician uses mathematics to crunch numbers appropriately, but the science of statistics is found in what happens once a set of values is calculated. After these numerical values are obtained, the statistician tries to answer the question "what does this mean" by delving into connections between what one might expect to see in similar scenarios. Through the scientific use of experimental design, data analysis, probability theory, and inference testing, our decisions become critical to a vast number of careers in our world.

We hope this guide will help you successfully navigate the waters of an introductory statistics course as well as give you the ability to apply these concepts to your future studies. Hopefully, some of you will find such an interest in this field that you consider changing your career plans to become a statistician! We trust that you will find this guide to be a useful aid in your preparation for and success on the AP® Statistics exam.

Joshua Wilkerson

Viva Hathaway

Vicki Greenberg

Edward Moulton

ACKNOWLEDGMENTS

I would like to thank my amazing wife Laura for all of her love and support. I am also very grateful to my employer, Regents School of Austin, for allowing me the opportunity not only to teach AP® Statistics but also the freedom to infuse it with my passion for service-learning. Thanks to Julie Allen at Cengage for approaching me with this project and to all of the reviewers, editors, and professionals who contributed to this work.

Joshua Wilkerson

I would like to dedicate this to my four wonderful granddaughters who keep me moving with their excitement. I want to thank my husband, Bill, for always pushing me to go beyond my comfort zone. Without this encouragement, I most likely would never have fallen in love with statistics in the first place. Thanks to my colleague Linda for keeping me real in analyzing data and my classes. Finally, without my mentor, Bill Speer, I would most likely not be as involved in mathematics. Thanks to you all! You're great! My thanks also to the reviewers, Brendan Murphy and Chris Olsen, as well as to all those involved in the editing and final production of this work.

Viva Hathaway

I would like to thank my wonderful husband for his support and encouragement during the writing and revision of this book. Thanks also to my mentor, Paul Myers, for me to discover my love for statistics and continuously challenging me to grow as a teacher and person. In addition, I greatly appreciate the support, suggestions, patience, organizational skills, and occasional nudges of Craig Leonard. Many thanks to the reviewers, Brendan Murphy and Chris Olsen, the editors, and the other professionals who contributed to the publication of this work.

Vicki Greenberg

I would like to acknowledge my late father and thriving mother, both of whom dedicated their lives to teaching undergraduate math and computer science. My thanks also to the reviewers, Brendan Murphy and Chris Olsen, the editors, and the other professionals who contributed to the publication of this work.

Ed Moulton

Part I

Strategies for the AP® Exam

Preparing for the AP® Statistics Examination

Advanced Placement® Statistics is an exciting, practical course that is also very challenging academically. It is designed to help the student delve deeply into the methods and concepts of the appropriate use and analysis of research. Whether you are taking AP® Statistics in a classroom or online, this year will prove to be both challenging and intellectually stimulating as you progress in your study of statistical analysis, inference, and experimental design.

The closer the school year gets to May, the more intimidating the looming Advanced Placement® test may seem. Learning how to take all the information you have learned this year and apply it in a way that will demonstrate your expertise can be very overwhelming at times.

The best way to achieve success on any AP® exam is to master it, rather than let it master you. If you think of these tests as a way to demonstrate how well your mind works, you will have an advantage—attitude does help.

This book is designed to put you on a fast track to a successful score. *Focused* review and practice time will help you master the examination so that you can walk in better prepared, more confident, and ready to do well on the test.

What's in this Book

This book is keyed to *Statistics: Learning from Data,* first and second editions, by Roxy Peck, Tom Short, and Chris Olsen. Because this book follows the College Board Topic Outline for AP® Statistics, it is compatible with other statistics textbooks as well; we have designed this book to help students prepare for this exam irrespective of the text being used. This book is divided into three sections. Part I offers suggestions for preparing for the exam, from signing up to take the test and having the correct calculators to writing a complete response for each free-response question. Part I ends with a diagnostic test that will help you determine which sections may need more focus as you prepare for the exam. The diagnostic test is designed in the same format as the Advanced Placement® Examination, with 40 multiple-choice questions and six free-response questions that follow the College Board Topic Outline.

The diagnostic test should help you identify the areas where you need the most practice; to make this easier for you, the content areas for each problem are noted. In reviewing the answers to the diagnostic test, you will be able to recognize gaps in your knowledge by noting when there are groups of questions from the same content area that gave you trouble. Page references with each answer will allow you to go to the textbook and review the content

---

AP® is a trademark registered by the College Board, which is not affiliated with, and does not endorse, this product.

area where you need to focus your attention. You will also be able to analyze your responses to the free-response questions to identify weaknesses that may exist in conveying your written response to the AP® Statistics test readers.

Part II consists of 12 review sections that encompass the four content areas covered by the AP® Statistics examination. Each of these corresponds to a key topic in the College Board content outline. The percentages below indicate the approximate proportion of exam questions devoted to each of the four content areas.

Review Section 1	Exploring Data	Exploratory Analysis 20–30%
Review Section 2	Numerical Methods for Describing Data	
Review Section 3	Summarizing Bivariate Data	
Review Section 4	Collecting Data Sensibly	Planning and Conducting a Study 10–15%
Review Section 5	Probability	Probability 20–30%
Review Section 6	Random Variables and Probability Distributions	
Review Section 7	Sampling Distributions	
Review Section 8	Estimation Using a Single Sample	Statistical Inference 30–40%
Review Section 9	Hypothesis Testing Using a Single Sample	
Review Section 10	Comparing Two Populations or Treatments	
Review Section 11	Categorical Data and Goodness of Fit Tests; Chi-Square Tests	
Review Section 12	Inference for Linear Regression and Correlation	

The review sections are **not** intended to be a substitute for a textbook and class discussions; they offer review and help you prepare further for the exam. Each review section also has the textbook sections listed for further review if, as you prepare for the exam, you find a topic that needs more study. At the end of each review section, you will find 15 multiple-choice and two free-response questions based on the content of that section. Again, you will find page references with each answer directing you to the appropriate discussion on each point in the first and second editions of *Statistics: Learning from Data*.

Part III offers two complete AP® Statistics examinations. At the end of each test, you will find the answers, explanations, and references to the first and second editions for the 40 multiple-choice and six free-response questions. Part IV contains formulas and tables useful for solving the problems you will encounter in the AP® Statistics exam.

SETTING UP A REVIEW SCHEDULE

If you have been steadily doing your homework and keeping up with the coursework, you will be in good shape. The key to preparing for the examination is to begin as early as possible; don't wait until the exam is just a week or two away to begin your studying. But even if you've done all that—or if it's too late to do all that—there are other ways to pull it all together.

To begin, read Part I of this book. You will be much more comfortable going into the test if you understand how the test questions are designed and how best to approach them. Then, take the diagnostic test and see where you stand.

Set up a schedule for yourself on a calendar. If you begin studying early, you can chip away at the review sections in Part II. You'll be surprised—and pleased—by how much material you can cover if you devote a half hour per day of study for a month or so before the test. Look carefully at the sections of the diagnostic test; if you missed a number of questions in one particular area, allow more time for the review sections that cover that area of the course. The practice tests in Part III will give you more experience with different kinds of multiple-choice questions and the wide range of free-response questions.

If time is short, reading the review sections may not be your best course of action. Instead, skim through the review sections to refamiliarize yourself with the main ideas. Spend the bulk of your time working on the multiple-choice and free-response questions at the end of each review. This will give you a good idea of your understanding of that particular topic. Then take the tests in Part III.

If time is really short, go straight from Part I to Part III. Taking practice tests repeatedly is one of the fastest, most practical ways to prepare.

BEFORE THE EXAM

By February, long before the exam, you should make sure that you are registered to take it. Many schools take care of the paperwork and handle the fees for their AP® students, but check with your teacher or the AP® coordinator to be certain that you are on the list. This is especially important if you have a documented disability and need testing accommodations. If you are studying AP® independently, call AP® Services at the College Board for the name of an AP® coordinator at a local school who will help you through the registration process.

The evening before the exam is not a great time for partying—nor is it a great time for cramming. If you like, look over class notes or skim through your textbook, concentrating on the broad outlines rather than the small details of the course. You might also skim over the AP® Statistics approved formula sheets one last time to remind yourself of the formulas you can check during the test if you need to confirm your idea, and skim through the book and read the AP® Tips. This is a great time to get your things together for the next day. Sharpen a fistful of number 2 pencils with good erasers; be sure your calculator is in good working order with either spare or extra batteries in case you have a malfunction of some sort; check out your watch and make sure the alarm is off if it has one; pack a healthy snack for the break like a piece of fruit, granola bar, and bottled water; make sure you have whatever identification is required as well as the admission ticket. Then relax and get a good night's sleep.

On the day of the examination, it is wise to eat breakfast—studies show that students who eat a healthy breakfast before testing generally do better. Be careful not to drink a lot of liquids, thereby necessitating a trip to the bathroom during the test. Breakfast will give you the energy you need to power you through the test—and more. Remember, cell phones and other electronic devices, other than your approved calculator(s), are not allowed in the testing room. You will spend some time waiting while everyone is seated in the right room for the right test. That's before the test has even begun. With a short break between Section I and Section II, the statistics exam lasts well over 3 hours. Be prepared for a long test time. You don't want to be distracted by hunger pangs.

Be sure to wear comfortable clothes; take along a sweater in case the heating or air-conditioning is erratic. Be sure to wear clothes you like—everyone performs better when they think they look better.

You have been on the fast track. Now go get a 5!

Taking the AP® Statistics Examination

The AP® Statistics exam has two sections: Section I consists of 40 multiple-choice questions; Section II contains six free-response questions. You will have 90 minutes to complete the multiple-choice portion. The exam is then collected, and you will be given a short break. Then, you have 90 minutes for the free-response questions. You should answer all six questions. Some AP® exams allow you to choose among the free-response questions, but statistics is *not* one of them. Keep an eye on your watch and devote about 13 minutes to each of questions 1–5 and about 25 minutes on question number 6. Since question number 6 carries more weight on your overall score, you want to be sure to at least try the first couple of parts of this question. Please note that watch alarms are *not* allowed.

Below is a chart to help you visualize the breakdown of the exam:

Section	Multiple-Choice Questions	Six Free-Response Questions	
Weight	50% of the exam	50% of the exam (weighted as follows):	
		37.5% of exam	12.5% of exam
Number of Questions	40	Questions 1–5	Question 6
Time Allowed	90 minutes	90 minutes	
Suggested Pace	2 minutes per question	13 minutes per question	25 minutes for this question

Strategies for the Multiple-Choice Section

Here are some rules of thumb to help you work your way through the multiple-choice questions:

SCORING OF MULTIPLE CHOICE There are five possible answers for each question. There is no penalty on the AP® Statistics exam for wrong answers. You will simply not get credit for the wrong answer. Since there is no penalty for guessing, be sure to answer every question prior to the end of the 90

AP® is a trademark registered by the College Board, which is not affiliated with, and does not endorse, this product.

minutes allotted. This means, fill in a bubble for each of the 40 questions even if you have to guess to answer a question.

Find Questions You Know First Find questions you are confident of and work those first. (Generally, the easier questions appear first on the exam.) Then, return to the questions you skipped. Make a mark in the booklet on questions you are unsure of, then return to those questions later.

Read Each Question Carefully Pressed for time, many students make the mistake of reading the questions too quickly or merely skimming them. By reading each question carefully, you may already have some idea about the correct answer. You can then look for that answer in the responses. Careful reading is especially important in EXCEPT questions (see the next section that describes the types of multiple-choice questions).

Eliminate Any Answer You Know Is Wrong You can write on the multiple-choice questions in the test book. As you read through the responses, draw a line through every answer you know is wrong. This will help you in choosing correct solutions on questions you aren't sure about.

Read Each Response, Then Choose The Most Accurate One AP® examinations are written to test your precise knowledge of a subject. Sometimes there are a few answers that seem correct, but one of them is more specific and therefore the correct response.

Avoid Absolute Responses These answers often include the words "always" or "never." For example, the statement "the data **are** normal" is an absolute answer. Instead, look for the phrase, "the data appear to be approximately normal."

Mark And Skip Tough Questions If you are hung up on a question, mark it in the margin of the question book. You can come back to it later if you have time. Make sure you skip that question on your answer sheet as well. In the end, be sure to answer ALL questions prior to the end of the 90 minutes.

Types of Multiple-Choice Questions

There are various kinds of multiple-choice questions. Here are some suggestions for how to approach each one.

Classic/Best-Answer Questions

This is the most common type of multiple-choice question. It simply requires you to read the question and select the correct answer. For example:

1. A firm claims that the percentage of workers who express job satisfaction is higher than the 58% under the previous supervisors. Which of the following are the correct hypotheses to test this claim?
   (A) $H_0: \mu = 0.58, H_a: \mu > 0.58$
   (B) $H_0: p = 0.58, H_a: p > 0.58$
   (C) $H_0: \mu = 0.58, H_a: \mu < 0.58$
   (D) $H_0: p = 0.58, H_a: p < 0.58$
   (E) $H_0: p > 0.58, H_a: p < 0.58$

   ANSWER: B. This is the only correct answer as the data are categorical. The claim is about a population percentage, which is equivalent to a claim about a population proportion. The null is written as an equality statement and the alternative is a greater than statement since they claim the percentage has gone up since the change in supervisors.

EXCEPT QUESTIONS

In EXCEPT style questions, you will notice all of the answer choices but one are correct. The best way to approach these questions is to treat them as true/false questions. Mark a T or an F in the margin next to each possible answer. There should be only one false answer, and that is the answer you should select. For example:

1. A random sample selected from a population is helpful for all of the following reasons except
   (A) it tends to produce a group that is representative of the population.
   (B) it avoids selection bias.
   (C) it ensures that all members of the population have an equal chance of selection.
   (D) it allows generalization from the sample to the population.
   (E) it eliminates response bias.

   ANSWER: E. Response bias is a type of bias that comes about because of the way a survey question is written or the way in which it is asked, leading the subjects to a certain response. Selecting a random sample will not eliminate this type of bias.

ANALYSIS/APPLICATION QUESTIONS

These questions will require you to apply your knowledge of statistics to a given situation or problem. For example:

1. A farmer wants to see which of two types of corn seed (seed A and seed B) will yield more corn. He has 52 plots marked off and he can plant either type of seed in any of the plots. Half of the plots (those on the west side) are bordered by a forest. The plots on the east side are not bordered by forest. Which of the following methods is the best way to decide how the two seed types should be assigned to the 52 plots?
   (A) Number the plots 01–52 and put these numbers in a hat. Pull out 26 numbers to determine the plots used for seed A. The remaining plots get seed B.

(B) Number the plots 01–52 and go to a random digits table and locate two-digit numbers. The plots corresponding to the first 26 numbers get seed A and the rest will get seed B.
(C) Plant the 26 plots on the west side with seed A and the 26 east side plots with seed B.
(D) Divide the 52 plots into two groups consisting of the 26 near the forest and the 26 not near the forest. Number the plots near the forest 00–25 and put these numbers in a hat. Pull out 13 numbers to determine which plots would be planted with seed A; the remaining 13 plots would be planted with seed B. Repeat this process with those plots not near forest.
(E) Pair up a plot near the forest with one not near the forest. Number them 1 and 2 and put numbers in a hat. First number out gets assigned seed A and the other seed B. Repeat for all pairs.

ANSWER: D. This is the only correct solution, since the forest may influence the results. So in this case, half of the plots near the forest will get seed A and half will get seed B. The same will occur for those away from the forest. Answer E might seem like a reasonable approach at first, but it is possible that most of the plots near the forest could have the same seed type with this method.

FREE-RESPONSE QUESTIONS

There are six free-response questions that should all be answered. These six questions account for 50% of the final score you receive on this exam and are weighted as follows. The first five free-response questions combine to make up 75% of your free-response score and the sixth question, the investigative task, will account for the remaining 25% of the grade. This means the first five make up 37.5% and the investigative task makes up 12.5% of the entire test. So it is important to answer all questions as completely as possible.

These questions can cover multiple content areas. Each of the four major content areas of the AP® syllabus will be found in the free- response section. The following hints may help you prepare for this half of the exam.

You should start by quickly reading the six questions. As you are reading, you may want to make a quick note as to an idea you have on the subject of each question. Once you have done this, you should go to the easiest question you find in the first five questions. Answer it as completely as you can and then jump to question number 6, the investigative task.

Now spend a little time, but no more than about 15 minutes, working on the investigative task. Since this carries 25% of the weight for this portion of the test, it is very important that you take the time to at least attempt this task. While this task is intended to stretch you beyond the course, typically it will begin with one or two parts that should be familiar to an AP® Statistics student.

You should then go back and answer the remaining four questions. If time permits, you should reread and note any key phrases or points that are made in a given question. Once you have answered the questions, be sure you read the question again to ensure you have actually answered the question asked. Examination readers comment that sometimes students don't actually answer the question that is asked. While the information you give may be correct, if it doesn't answer the question, you won't get credit.

Don't assume any question is asking for a "cookie cutter" type response. The AP® readers who will review your answer will be reading for a correct answer in the context of the question, and not just a memorized phrase or explanation. In that light, also be sure to use statistical vocabulary correctly. If you are not sure about the correct vocabulary, it is permissible to use a short phrase in place of the word you are unsure about. Correct notation is also important. It won't hurt to define your notation for clarity, but be sure you are using the notation correctly. For example, students may lose credit for using notation for a statistic when they should be using parameter notation and vice versa.

You will have 90 minutes for this section of the exam, so watch your time. As a recommendation from the College Board, you should allow about 12 minutes for each of the first five questions and 25 minutes for the investigative task. Then, use the remaining 5 minutes to read over your responses. However, earlier we recommended only about 15 minutes to begin with for the investigative task. This allows you to plan once you have begun answering the last question. In either case, it is important you take a watch and keep a close eye on your time. You want to be sure you have enough time to answer the questions you know and that you don't get bogged down on any one question.

KEY POINTS TO ANSWERING FREE-RESPONSE QUESTIONS

In answering the free-response questions, it is important to note the word choices used in the questions. Focus your writing for the AP® Statistics Exam with these points in mind.

READ Carefully read the question and circle key phrases and comments you are to address. Watch for the specific wording and don't make assumptions about what you are being asked before completely reading the question.

CONTEXT Be sure to answer in the context of the problem. For a complete answer, you are required to write the conclusions and interpretations in context.

DEFINE You are expected to define any nonstandard symbols you use.

CORRECT NOTATION Be clear on parameter versus statistic notation when answering. For example, when discussing a mean value, use the correct population and sample notation in your written responses. A sample mean notation $\bar{x}$ will be considered incorrect if you are supposed to use a population mean notation μ.

VOCABULARY Use statistical vocabulary correctly. If you are unsure of the meaning of a statistical term, write a couple of sentences and either define the term or—better yet—let the sentences describe the concept and don't use the word.

CHECK ASSUMPTIONS Unless the question states that all assumptions are reasonable or have been checked, you should state and check assumptions whenever possible. Assumptions need to be checked or referred to as uncheckable when carrying out any hypothesis test or constructing any confidence interval.

ANSWER Did you actually answer the question? Be sure you have answered the question that was asked.

INTERPRET Be ready to justify your work in a variety of statistical ways. Know how to read printouts, graphical displays, and tables. Provide correct analysis and comparisons as required.

SCORING FREE-RESPONSE QUESTIONS

All six free-response questions will be scored using a holistic four-point scale. However, as stated earlier, question 6 will be weighted more heavily than questions 1 through 5. The four-point score is holistic in nature. This means the readers will consider your entire solution in addition to each of the parts. Therefore, it is important that you answer the question and not contradict yourself. You should NOT attempt more than one solution; the reader will read each solution and your score will be that of your weakest solution.

Keep in mind that both statistical knowledge and verbal communication are essential on the AP® Statistics exam. To score a 4 on a question, you must demonstrate that you are able to both correctly compute statistical values as well as properly interpret those values in the context of the question. The table on the next page provides some general guidelines regarding the differences between the scores of 0 to 4 on any individual free-response question. More specific guidelines can be found on the College Board website (https://apstudent.collegeboard .org/apcourse/ap-statistics) where you can download the PDF file of the course description.

Score	Statistical Knowledge (Be able to correctly use the statistical ideas and techniques.)	Communication (Demonstrate a clear and concise explanation of what work you performed and why.)
4	Demonstrates a complete understanding of the statistics and is able to perform correct statistical calculations. Even if you make minor arithmetic errors, the solution is plausible.	Your thoughts and explanations are correct, with all aspects of the explanation utilizing correct procedures, terminology, and appropriate conclusions, etc.
3	Able to demonstrate clear understanding of appropriate techniques but may have some minor gaps. Overall, this solution is substantially correct even if there are some mathematical errors.	Overall, the rationale in this solution is correct but there may be some missing assumptions, caveats, or even a bit unfinished in the final work. While there is a conclusion, it may be incomplete.
2	Has some parts correct but others have either misused or even possibly unreasonable answers. There is some understanding of the pieces yet little relationship demonstrated between them.	Vague or inappropriate explanations. May be missing components or diagrams needed for the explanation to be complete. Conclusions that are drawn are not complete.
1	Misuses the statistical components and develops unreasonable solutions. Very limited knowledge of statistics given. *(A score of 1 may be awarded if the reader can identity something relevant to the question posed even if you have not answered the question.)*	Response is jumbled, messy, unclear, or difficult to follow. It may not match the statistical work provided by the student. Fails to provide a conclusion or answer the question posed. Incorrect diagrams or displays.
0	Very little, if any, understanding of the statistical pieces needed for the problem	No strategy that will lead to a solution is communicated.

FREE-RESPONSE SAMPLE QUESTION

Free-response questions can differ in the number of parts as well as how much each part contributes to the overall question. Carefully analyze your final answer to make sure you have made a complete response by answering all of the parts of the question.

Be careful **not** to include parallel solutions (or two different answers to the same question). The AP® readers are instructed to score the weakest solution, so try not to lose points you have already scored because you doubt or contradict yourself. Be confident in your choice and cross out any dual answers that you don't want graded.

Here is an example of a free-response question that addresses hypothesis testing.

1. A party rental company rents out tents for large parties. These tents must be setup prior to the party. The company usually allows 28 minutes for set up but is now wondering if the mean time required to set up a tent is actually greater than 28 minutes. To answer this question, the company selects 34 past rentals at random from all its tent rentals and notes the time required to setup the tent for each of the selected rentals. The average set

up time for the sample of rentals was 35 minutes and the sample standard deviation was 6 minutes. Do these data provide convincing evidence that the mean tent setup time is greater than the 28 minutes that the company allows?

Hypothesis test questions can usually be answered in four parts.

PART I—STATE THE HYPOTHESIS.
$H_0: \mu = 28$ minutes, $\quad\quad \mu =$ average tent setup time
$H_a: \mu > 28$ minutes
$\alpha = .05$ $\quad\quad\quad\quad\quad\quad$ Since no alpha level given, we will use .05

PART II—IDENTIFY TEST AND ANY CONDITIONS OR ASSUMPTIONS THAT MUST BE MET.
Because the hypotheses are about a population mean and the population standard deviation is unknown, we consider a one-sample t test.

Assumptions
RANDOM SAMPLE—The 34 rentals were selected at random from all of the company's past tent rentals.
LARGE SAMPLE OR NORMAL POPULATION DISTRIBUTION—the sample size is large ($n = 34$).

PART III—CALCULATIONS
$$t = \frac{35 - 28}{\frac{6}{\sqrt{34}}} = 6.802, \text{ with } df = 33$$

$p = 4.64 \times 10^{-8} \approx 0$

PART IV—CONCLUSION: GIVE YOUR CONCLUSION BOTH IN CONTEXT AND LINKED TO ALPHA.
Because $0 < .05$, the null hypothesis is rejected. There is convincing evidence that the mean setup time for a party tent is greater than the 28 minutes allowed by the company.

The usual scoring guidelines for a hypothesis test question classify each of the four parts in the test as essentially correct, partially correct, or incorrect. A response that is judged to be essentially correct on all four parts would receive a score of 4.

More examples of free-response type questions and scoring guidelines are included in the sample exams and review sections that appear later in this book.

A Diagnostic Test

This diagnostic test will give you some indication of how you might score on the AP® Statistics Exam. Of course, the exam changes every year, so it is never possible to predict a student's score with certainty. This test will also help to pinpoint strengths and weaknesses on the key content areas covered by the exam.

AP® STATISTICS EXAMINATION
Section I: Multiple-Choice Questions
Time: 90 minutes
Number of Questions: 40

DIRECTIONS: Each of the following questions or incomplete statements is accompanied by five suggested answers or completions. Select the one that best answers the question or completes the statement.

1. If the average test score for one class of 30 students is 75.6 and the average test score for another class of 24 students is 68.4, what is the overall average for this test for all 54 students?
   (A) 71.5
   (B) 72
   (C) 72.4
   (D) 72.8
   (E) 74

2. A snake's length is approximately normal with a mean of 50 cm. What standard deviation would be necessary to ensure that 80% of the snake lengths are within 12 cm of the mean?
   (A) 4.687
   (B) 9.375
   (C) 2.344
   (D) 7.129
   (E) 14.259

3. A simple random sample of 150 students at a local high school was taken to estimate the proportion who like strawberry-flavored licorice. Ninety-five of the students in the sample liked strawberry licorice. What would be an appropriate setup for a 90% confidence interval? Assume conditions for inferences are met.

   (A) $0.63 \pm 1.96\sqrt{\dfrac{0.63(0.37)}{150}}$

   (B) $0.63 \pm 1.96\sqrt{\dfrac{0.63(0.37)}{95}}$

   (C) $0.63 \pm 1.645\sqrt{\dfrac{0.63(0.37)}{150}}$

   (D) $0.63 \pm 1.645\sqrt{\dfrac{0.63(0.37)}{95}}$

   (E) $0.63 \pm 1.645\sqrt{\dfrac{0.63(0.37)}{149}}$

AP® is a trademark registered by the College Board, which is not affiliated with, and does not endorse, this product.

GO ON TO NEXT PAGE

4. Amy is graduating in the spring from Howard University with a degree in accounting. AmeriGroup has offered her a job with a starting salary of $48,000 per year. How many standard deviations below or above the mean is her starting salary if the mean and standard deviation for intro level accounting positions are $47,500 and $1,470, respectively?
   (A) 0.17
   (B) 0.45
   (C) 0.34
   (D) 0.61
   (E) cannot be determined

5.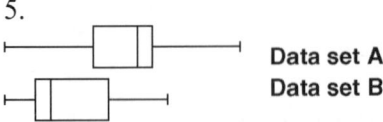

   Which of the following must be true for the two boxplots shown? (Although the scale is not shown, the two boxplots are drawn using the same numerical scale.)
   (A) The IQR of data set A is smaller than the IQR of data set B.
   (B) The lower quartile of data set A is greater than the upper quartile of data set B.
   (C) The ranges of data set A and data set B are equal.
   (D) The median of data set B is greater than the median of data set A.
   (E) There are more data in data set A than in data set B.

6. The given histogram was constructed using data on X = number of pets for a sample of 25 students. Which of the following is closest to the value of the mean of this data set?

   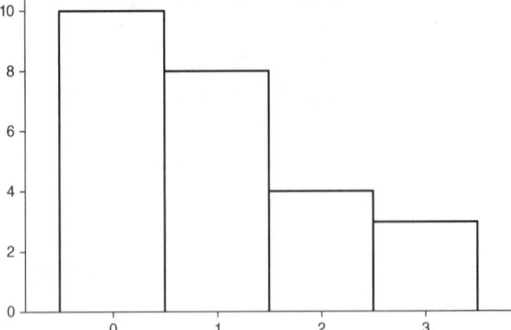

   (A) 0.5
   (B) 1.0
   (C) 1.5
   (D) 2.0
   (E) 3.0

7. To determine how students at a particular college feel about cigarette smoking in public places, all students at the college who chose to have their email address published in the college directory were sent an email with a link to an online survey. What is wrong with this sampling method?
   (A) Nothing, since students could go online to give their opinion.
   (B) Only smokers should have been surveyed.
   (C) They should have only sent the email to every 12th student in the directory.
   (D) This sampling method would result in a sample size that is too large.
   (E) Not all students would have an email listed in the student directory.

8. A cell phone company wants to know how happy their customers are with their service. The company sent a text message with a survey to every customer's phone. Out of the 100,000 customers, 42,000 replied. Based on the 42,000 responses, they concluded that their customers were highly satisfied. What type of bias should the company be worried about?
   (A) Selection bias
   (B) Response bias
   (C) Nonresponse bias
   (D) Measurement bias
   (E) There is no need to worry since all customers received the text message.

9. For employees of a large company, the correlation between x = years of experience and y = the pay increase is found to be $r = 0.74$. What would the correlation be if the y variable was years of experience and pay increase was the x variable?
   (A) −0.74
   (B) −0.28
   (C) 0.28
   (D) 0.74
   (E) The answer cannot be determined from the given information.

10. The following computer output was taken from a data set where the adult height was used to predict the wrist circumference.

	Coefficients	Standard Error	t Stat	P-value
Intercept	−2.13	0.4836	−4.40	0.048
Height	0.13	0.0073	17.3	0.003

R Square   0.993

Standard Error   0.082

Which of the following is the equation of the least squares regression line for this data set? Let $\hat{y}$ be the predicted wrist circumference.
   (A) $\hat{y} = 0.13 - 2.13$ (height)
   (B) $\hat{y} = -2.13 + 0.13$ (height)
   (C) $\hat{y} = 0.08 - 2.13$ (height)
   (D) $\hat{y} = 0.08 + 0.13$ (height)
   (E) $\hat{y} = 0.99 + 0.13$ (height)

GO ON TO NEXT PAGE

11. A study found the correlation between the heights of men and the heights of their biological sons to be $r = 0.71$. What is the approximate value of r^2 and what is its meaning?
    (A) $r^2 = 0.71$, it describes how well the least squares regression line fits the data.
    (B) $r^2 = 0.50$, it says that a son's height should be equal to $0.49 \times$ father's height
    (C) $r^2 = 0.84$, it is the ratio of father's height to son's height.
    (D) $r^2 = 0.50$, it is the proportion of the variability in sons' heights that can be explained by fathers' heights.
    (E) $r^2 = 0.84$, it is the proportion the son's height that is caused by father's height.

12. All but one of the following statements contain an error. Which of the following statements is correct?
    (A) A social scientist found a correlation of $r = -1.23$ between the weight of monkeys and their height.
    (B) The correlation coefficient for $x =$ political affiliation and $y =$ income was computed to be $r = 0.73$.
    (C) A psychology graduate student doing research found the correlation coefficient between gender and race to be $r = -0.81$.
    (D) The correlation coefficient for $x =$ amount of fertilizer and $y =$ yield was found to be $r = 0.58$.
    (E) The correlation coefficient between $x =$ the speed of a racing boat and $y =$ fuel consumption is found to be $r = 5.0$ mpg.

13. A new type of flame retardant created for clothing is ready for testing. There are two types of fabric that this retardant is to be tested on to see if it is better than the current substance used on these fabrics. There are 100 pieces of each type of fabric available for testing. Which of the following is the best method for assigning retardants to pieces of fabric?
    (A) Assign 100 pieces of each fabric to be tested with the new material.
    (B) Take one type of fabric first and number the 100 pieces 00–99. Using a random number table, find 50 different two-digit random numbers. The pieces of fabric corresponding to these numbers would get the new retardant and the remaining 50 get the old retardant. Repeat this process for the other fabric.
    (C) Take one type of fabric first and place the pieces of fabric in a stack. The first 50 pieces in the stack get the old retardant and the rest get the new retardant. Repeat this for the other fabric as well.
    (D) Put all 200 pieces of fabric in a stack with all of the pieces of the first type of fabric on the top of the stack. Select a piece and flip a coin. Heads get the old material and tails get the new material. Do this until 100 pieces have been assigned to one of the retardants. The rest of the pieces would get the other retardant.
    (E) Select one of the types of fabric (all 100 pieces) and flip a coin. If it comes up heads, then assign the old flame retardant to this fabric and the new to the other fabric.

14. Why would double-blinding be used in a study?
    (A) To make sure the researcher does not know who is getting which treatment.
    (B) To keep the subjects from knowing which treatment they are receiving.
    (C) To keep the subjects from communicating with each other since they don't know which treatment they are getting.
    (D) To keep the subjects from telling the researcher which treatment they received.
    (E) To keep the subjects and person measuring the response from influencing the outcome.

15. A lottery ticket is sold for $2 with the promise that someone will win this particular jackpot of $500. Only 1,000 tickets are sold. What are the expected winnings for someone who purchases a single ticket?
    (A) $500.00
    (B) $1.00
    (C) $0.50
    (D) –$1.00
    (E) –$1.50

16. Every year, 50% of all children miss at least 3 school days due to illness. Which of the following is closest to the probability that 216 or more children out of a random sample of 400 would miss at least 3 school days this year?
    (A) 0.00
    (B) 0.03
    (C) 0.05
    (D) 0.50
    (E) 0.95

17. Scores on a standardized test have a normal distribution with a mean of 20 and a standard deviation of 6. What is the approximate interquartile range of the test scores?
    (A) 4
    (B) 6
    (C) 8
    (D) 10
    (E) 24

18. A 90% confidence interval has been computed to estimate the mean height in centimeters of newborn babies. Which of the following is a correct interpretation of the confidence interval? Assume conditions for inferences are met.
    (A) 90% of all babies' heights would be within the interval.
    (B) The sample mean will be in this interval 90% of the time.
    (C) 90% of the time, the method used to construct the interval results in an interval that includes the true mean height of newborns.
    (D) Any baby with a height not contained within the interval is an outlier.
    (E) The true mean height of newborns is contained in this interval 90% of the time.

19. Each person in a random sample of 300 elementary school children in New York City was asked if he or she preferred outside recess in the morning. A 98% confidence interval for the proportion of New York elementary school children who prefer outside recess is (0.32, 0.46). Which of the following would be the 95% confidence interval computed from this sample data?
    (A) (0.30, 0.48)
    (B) (0.32, 0.42)
    (C) (0.31, 0.47)
    (D) (0.32, 0.50)
    (E) (0.33, 0.45)

20. A city official in a storm-damaged region of the United States believes that the percentage of homes with contaminated water is higher than the recently reported value of 9%. The city inspected 168 homes and found 23 homes with contaminated water. Is there enough evidence to conclude that the initial report of 9% is too low at the 0.05 significance level? Assume conditions for inference are met.
    (A) No, because the P-value = 0.017, which is smaller than α.
    (B) No, because the P-value = 0.034, which is bigger than α.
    (C) Yes, because the P-value = 0.017, which is smaller than α.
    (D) Yes, because the P-value = 0.034, which is bigger than α.
    (E) No, because the P-value = 0.14, which is larger than α

21. In a study of a random sample of 100 popular songs, the average length was found to be 3.2 minutes and the sample standard deviation was 0.04 minutes. Which of the following would be a true statement?
    (A) If we took another random sample of 100 popular songs, the average length for this sample would be 3.2 minutes and the standard deviation would be 0.04 minutes.
    (B) The sampling distribution of the sample mean song length would be approximately normal with a larger variance than that of the population.
    (C) The population standard deviation is likely to be larger than 0.04 minutes and the mean for the population will probably be smaller than 3.2 minutes.
    (D) The population standard deviation is likely to be smaller than 0.04 minutes and the population mean will probably be greater than 3.2 minutes.
    (E) The sampling distribution of sample mean song length is approximately normal, with a standard deviation that is likely to be smaller than 0.04.

Questions 22–24 refer to the following table, which is the probability distribution of x = the number of times a copy machine needs repair in a given month.

x	0	1	2	3	4	5
$P(x)$	0.12	0.18	0.23	0.20	0.14	0.13

22. A corporation must pay a service person at a rate of $50 per visit. On average, about how much should the company expect to pay per month for copy machine repairs?
    (A) $50.00
    (B) $59.75
    (C) $75.25
    (D) $100.00
    (E) $122.50

23. What's the probability the machine will need to be repaired at least once in a month?
    (A) 0.12
    (B) 0.18
    (C) 0.23
    (D) 0.70
    (E) 0.88

24. What is the standard deviation for the number of repairs the machine will need in a given month?
    (A) 1
    (B) 2.38
    (C) 2.45
    (D) 2.5
    (E) 5

25. Which of the following is not a property of a binomial experiment?
    (A) All trials are independent.
    (B) The outcome of each trial can be classified as success or failure.
    (C) The probability of success is the same for each trial.
    (D) There are a fixed number of trials.
    (E) Trials continue until a success occurs.

26. Dequarius decides to take a simple random sample from a population that is normally distributed. However, σ is not known. If his sample size is 20, and Dequarius wishes to compute a 95% confidence interval for the population mean, which formula would be correct? Assume conditions for inference are met.

    (A) $\bar{x} \pm 2.093 \dfrac{s}{\sqrt{20}}$

    (B) $\bar{x} \pm 2.093 \dfrac{s}{\sqrt{19}}$

    (C) $\bar{x} \pm 1.960 \dfrac{s}{\sqrt{20}}$

    (D) $\bar{x} \pm 1.960 \dfrac{s}{\sqrt{19}}$

    (E) $\bar{x} \pm 1.725 \dfrac{s}{\sqrt{20}}$

27. Marvin is planning to use a simple random sample of 30 to estimate a population mean. What would happen to the margin of error if he were to increase the sample size to 150?
    (A) The margin of error will increase.
    (B) The margin of error will decrease.
    (C) The margin of error will not be affected.
    (D) The margin of error will be multiplied by five.
    (E) There is not enough information to determine what will happen to the margin of error.

28. A video game company is interested in the proportion of people who currently play one of their online games who would be willing to pay for an enhanced version of the game. They plan to market the enhanced game if they are convinced that more than 40% of the current users would pay for the enhanced version. Which of the following correctly describes the company making a type I error?
    (A) Determining over 40% of users would pay for the enhanced version when they would not.
    (B) Determining that over 40% of users would not pay for the enhanced version when they would.
    (C) Failing to take a random sample.
    (D) Failing to enhance the video game.
    (E) Determining exactly 40% of users would buy the enhanced version.

29. A newspaper claims that the proportion of people using public transportation is 0.39. An environmental group disagrees, stating the proportion is smaller than what the newspaper claims. The environmental group plans to conduct a survey to support its position. What hypotheses should the environmental group test?
    (A) $H_0: p = 0.50, H_a: p > 0.50$
    (B) $H_0: p = 0.39, H_a: p \neq 0.39$
    (C) $H_0: P = 0.39, H_a: p > 0.39$
    (D) $H_0: P = 0.39, H_a: p < 0.39$
    (E) $H_0: P = 0.50, H_a: p \neq 0.50$

30. A scientist wants to use data from a survey of 1,000 randomly selected registered voters to determine whether there is a relationship between gender and whether or not a person voted in the last election. What is an appropriate test to use in this situation?
    (A) Chi-square goodness-of-fit test
    (B) Chi-square test of independence
    (C) Two-sample t-test
    (D) Two-sample z-test
    (E) One proportion z-test

GO ON TO NEXT PAGE

31. A researcher wants to study the effectiveness of two different medications for ADHD in children. Fifty boys and 50 girls who are diagnosed with ADHD have volunteered to participate in the study. Which of the following could cause the introduction of a confounding variable?
    (A) The subjects were not randomly selected.
    (B) For each child, a coin flip will determine which medication the child will receive.
    (C) The 50 girls will be given medication 1 and the 50 boys will be given medication 2.
    (D) Double blinding is used in the study.
    (E) No control group is used in the study.

32. The population {4, 6, 8, 10} has mean $\mu = 7$ and standard deviation $\sigma = 2.24$. If sampling is done with replacement, there are 16 different possible samples of size 2 that can be selected from this population. Each of these samples has a sample mean. For example, one of the samples is (8, 10), which has a mean of 9. The mean and standard deviation of the sampling distribution of the sample means are denoted by $\mu_{\bar{x}}$ and $\sigma_{\bar{x}}$, respectively. Which of the following statements is true?
    (A) $\mu_{\bar{x}} = 7$ and $\sigma_{\bar{x}} = 2.24$
    (B) $\mu_{\bar{x}} = 7$ and $\sigma_{\bar{x}} > 2.24$
    (C) $\mu_{\bar{x}} = 7$ and $\sigma_{\bar{x}} < 2.24$
    (D) $\mu_{\bar{x}} > 7$ and $\sigma_{\bar{x}} > 2.24$
    (E) $\mu_{\bar{x}} < 7$ and $\sigma_{\bar{x}} < 2.24$

33. A local storeowner wants to know if a new line of souvenir glass figurines is a better sales product than a line he has carried for years. To compare sales of the two products, he decides to keep track of sales of each item for a period of 1 month. He randomly assigns one item to the checkout lane and the other to the second aisle in the store. The new item is placed to the left of the checkout lane and the old item is randomly assigned to the second aisle. Is this a good study design?
    (A) Yes, because he has assigned the locations at random.
    (B) Yes, but the new item should be placed in the aisle and the old item by the register.
    (C) No, because a confounding variable of location within the store has been introduced.
    (D) Yes, because the new item will be seen more because it is by the register.
    (E) No, because 1 month is too short of a time to compare sales.

34. A weight loss group wants to see if a new program seems to be effective in helping individuals who want to lose weight. Nine individuals have been weighed before the program and then after 2 months on the program. The results are in the table below.

Subject	1	2	3	4	5	6	7	8	9
Before	150	182	118	197	208	215	134	107	168
After	151	180	118	203	206	216	133	105	170

What would be an appropriate set of hypotheses to use if the group wants to see if the program was effective for weight loss? Let μ_d = the true mean change in weight (before – after)
(A) $H_0: \mu_d = 0$, $H_a: \mu_d < 0$, $df = 8$
(B) $H_0: \mu_d > 0$, $H_a: \mu_d < 0$, $df = 17$
(C) $H_0: \mu_d = 0$, $H_a: \mu_d < 0$, $df = 9$
(D) $H_0: \mu_d = 0$, $H_a: \mu_d > 0$, $df = 8$
(E) $H_0: \mu_d > 0$, $H_a: \mu_d \neq 0$, $df = 17$

35. Which of the following actions will increase the power of a test?
I   Increasing the sample size
II Decreasing the sample size
III Increasing the significance level
IV Decreasing the significance level

(A) I only
(B) III only
(C) IV only
(D) I and III only
(E) II and IV only

36. In a particular town, 40% of the registered voters are registered as Democrats, 35% are registered as Republicans, and 25% are registered as Independents. What is the expected number of Independents in a random sample of 200 registered voters from this town?
(A) 20
(B) 25
(C) 40
(D) 50
(E) 75

37. A newspaper reported that based on a recent survey of reality show watchers, 58% of the people preferred the reality show *The Bachelor* to the reality show *Survivor*. The margin of error reported was ±4%. What does this ±4% mean?
(A) 4% of the reality TV watchers don't know what show they prefer.
(B) There is a 4% chance of error in these results from this particular sample.
(C) The results are based on 4% of the reality TV show watchers.
(D) The actual percentage who prefer *The Bachelor* to *Survivor* is probably somewhere between 54% and 62%.
(E) 54% to 62% of the population watches *The Bachelor*.

GO ON TO NEXT PAGE

38. Each person in a random sample of high school students was asked whether he or she takes vitamin C on a regular basis and whether he or she had a cold in the last 6 months. A chi-square test of independence resulted in a P-value of 0.37. What conclusion is reasonable based on the P-value? Assume conditions for inference are met.
    (A) There is an association between taking vitamin C and whether or not a person gets a cold.
    (B) The data prove that taking vitamin C and whether or not a person gets a cold are independent.
    (C) There is convincing evidence that there is an association between taking vitamin C and whether or not a person gets a cold.
    (D) There is convincing evidence that taking vitamin C and whether or not a person gets a cold are independent.
    (E) There is not convincing evidence that there is an association between taking vitamin C and whether or not a person gets a cold.

39. If a 95% confidence interval for the slope of a regression line were computed, what would it mean if the interval contained zero? Assume conditions for inference are met.
    (A) There is sufficient evidence to conclude that the slope of the true regression line is zero.
    (B) There is sufficient evidence to conclude that the slope of the true regression line is not zero.
    (C) There is insufficient evidence to conclude that the slope of the regression line is zero.
    (D) There is insufficient evidence to conclude that the slope of the regression line is not zero.
    (E) The slope of the population regression line is equal to zero.

40. A recent poll of 1,000 adults included 540 people who said they would be willing to give up television for the summer if they could be sure that doing so would result in weight loss. Assuming it is reasonable to regard this sample of 1,000 as a random sample of adult Americans, is there convincing evidence that a majority of adult Americans would be willing to do this? Assume conditions for inference are met.
    (A) Yes, since P-value < 0.01, we reject the null hypothesis.
    (B) Yes, since P-value > 0.01, we reject the null hypothesis.
    (C) Yes, since P-value > 0.05, we fail to reject the null hypothesis.
    (D) No, since P-value = 0.54, we fail to reject the null hypothesis.
    (E) No, because 0.54 is not enough larger than 0.50 to be convinced.

STOP

END OF SECTION I

IF YOU FINISH BEFORE TIME IS CALLED, YOU MAY CHECK YOUR WORK ON THIS SECTION. DO NOT GO ON TO SECTION II UNTIL YOU ARE TOLD TO DO SO.

SECTION II: FREE-RESPONSE QUESTIONS

Part A
Questions 1–5
Spend about 65 minutes on this part of the exam
Percent of Section II grade—75

DIRECTIONS: Show all your work. Clearly indicate the methods you use, as you will be graded on the correctness of the methods as well as the accuracy of your results and explanation.

1. Strep throat is a common infection among teenagers. It must be treated quickly to avoid serious complications. The Rapid Strep Test (RST) is a diagnostic test that may be performed by a doctor in his or her office. RST gives a false positive in about 4% of the healthy students and gives a negative result in about 20% of students who do have strep throat. Suppose there is a lot of strep throat going around, and 5% of the student body has been infected.
   (a) What is the probability that a student selected at random would test positive for strep throat if the RST is used? Show your work.
   (b) What is the probability that a child selected at random who tests positive for strep throat using the RST does not have the strep throat? Show your work.

2. *Aunt Pearl's Produce* grows fruits and vegetables for distribution to local grocery stores. The tomato field is located next to the trees in the apple orchard, meaning part of the tomato field gets more shade (the shady side) than the rest of the field (the sunny side). Sun and shade might affect tomato growth. The tomato field can accommodate 600 tomato plants, with 200 placed in the shady side and 400 placed in the sunny side. Larger tomatoes (greater than 2.5 inches in diameter) are considered more valuable since they can be sold for higher prices. Two brands of fertilizer are being considered for use in growing tomatoes and it is not known if one brand of fertilizer might produce larger tomatoes than the other brand of fertilizer.
   (a) You are asked to design an experiment to decide if there is a difference in the proportion of larger tomatoes produced for the two regions of the field. You can use 600 tomato plants that have been planted in the field described. Explain why it would be a good idea to incorporate blocking and describe the blocks you would use.
   (b) Describe the method you would use to assign a brand of fertilizer to each of the 600 tomato plants in the field using the table of random digits.
   (c) Using the random digits table provided below, pick the first two tomato plants for your study and tell where you are placing them.

75690	50177	50467	73999	60573	58156
06205	44401	01052	41856	75562	60464
05596	22931	85521	03730	12804	76697

GO ON TO NEXT PAGE

3. A local barbecue-cooking event consists of professional barbecue teams preparing three different types of meat: beef brisket, pork ribs, and chicken. The teams receive a score for each category of meat (on a scale of 1–25) and you can assume that team scores are independent across categories. The distributions of scores for each category are approximately normal.

	μ	σ
Beef Brisket	18.8	0.72
Pork Ribs	18.6	0.85
Chicken	19.4	0.78

(a) What are the mean and standard deviation for the score of a team competing in all three categories?
(b) What proportion of teams competing in all three categories score higher than 58.8 overall?
(c) What is the probability that two out of five teams competing in all three categories will score higher than 58.8 overall?
(d) What is the probability that a random sample of five teams competing in all three categories have a mean overall score higher than 58.8?

4. A cookie manufacturer sells two types of chocolate chip cookies, regular and fat free. The manufacturer claims that the fat-free cookies have, on average, the same number of chocolate chips as the regular cookies. A group of students wanted to test this claim. They counted the number of chips in a random sample of 20 regular cookies and in a random sample of 20 fat-free cookies. The data are summarized in the following dotplots.

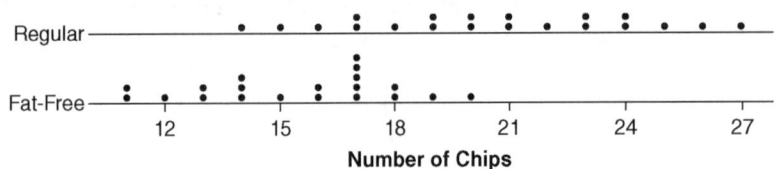

(a) Compare the distributions of number of chips for regular and fat-free cookies.
(b) What test should the students perform if they want to determine if there is convincing evidence against the manufacturer's claim? State the appropriate hypotheses.
(c) Would it be reasonable to test the hypotheses in part (b)? Explain why or why not.

5. LeRhonda and Nick want to consider the weights of *Snickers* fun-size candy bars to see if the advertised weight of 1 ounce is accurate. Eight candy bars are weighed. The weights (in ounces) were as follows:

0.99   0.97   0.98   0.96   1.01   1.03   0.99   1.02

(a) Assume that it is reasonable to consider this sample of eight bars as a random sample of all Snickers fun-size bars. Estimate the mean weight for Snickers fun-size bars using a 90% confidence interval.
(b) Based on your confidence interval from part (a), do you think that the manufacturer's advertised weight of 1 ounce is reasonable? Why or why not?
(c) Explain which error— a type I or type II error—could have occurred in part (b) and comment on the consequence of making this error.

SECTION II
Part B
Question 6
Spend about 25 minutes on this part of the exam
Percent of Section II grade—25

DIRECTIONS: Show all your work. Clearly indicate the methods you use, as you will be graded on the correctness of the methods as well as the accuracy of your results and explanation.

6. The Federal Bureau of Investigation (FBI) handles requests by law enforcement officers to gain top-secret clearance status. In years past, the requests were rarely granted. However, in recent years, more requests have been granted. The data below show the number of top-secret clearances granted by year.

Year	2001	2002	2003	2004	2005	2006	2007	2008	2009
# Top-Secret Clearances	8	57	102	136	258	317	489	743	1,823

Computer software was used to fit the least-squares regression line to these data, resulting in the output below.

```
Predictor        Coef          SE Coef         T            P
Constant        -342852        89460          -3.83         0.006
Year             171.22        44.62           3.84         0.006

S = 345.612          R - Sq = 67.8%      R - Sq(adj) = 63.2%
```

(a) What is the equation of the least-squares regression line?
(b) What is the residual value for the year 2006? Interpret this value.
(c) Based on the regression line, the predicted number of requests granted in the year 2020 is 3,012. Is this a good estimate to use? Explain.

(d) Below are a scatter diagram and a residual plot from the linear regression for these data. Based on these plots, an exponential model has been recommended as a better way to describe the relationship between number of requests granted and year. What aspect of these plots supports this recommendation?

(e) The recommended exponential model is given below.

$\hat{y} = 11.82(1.74)x$, where $\hat{y}$ is the predicted number of top-secret clearances and x is the number of years since 2000.

Use this model to find the residual in 2006. Interpret and compare this value to the value found in part (b).

(f) Here is the exponential model plotted with the data.

Explain why the exponential model is better than the linear model.

(g) Since the exponential model is better, can we use it to predict the number of requests granted in the year 2020? Why or why not?

END OF EXAMINATION

ANSWERS TO DIAGNOSTIC TEST

MULTIPLE-CHOICE ANSWERS

Using the table below, score your test.

Determine how many questions you answered correctly and how many you answered incorrectly. You will find explanations of the answers on the following pages.

1. C	9. D	17. C	25. E	33. C
2. B	10. B	18. C	26. A	34. D
3. C	11. D	19. E	27. B	35. D
4. C	12. D	20. C	28. A	36. D
5. A	13. B	21. E	29. D	37. D
6. B	14. E	22. E	30. B	38. E
7. E	15. E	23. E	31. C	39. D
8. C	16. C	24. B	32. C	40. A

ANSWERS AND EXPLANATIONS

MULTIPLE-CHOICE ANSWERS

1. **(C)** The combined average is calculated by $\frac{30(75.6)+24(68.4)}{54} = 72.4$
   (*Statistics: Learning from Data*, AP Edition, 1st ed. pages 133–135 and 143 / 2nd ed. pages 140–142 and 150–151).

2. **(B)** The upper z-score for a central area of 80% is 1.28. Values of snake lengths that are within 12 cm of the mean are those between 38 and 62. Using the upper value of 62, we get $z = \frac{62-50}{\sigma} = 1.28$ and solve for the value of σ. This results in $1.28 = \frac{62-50}{\sigma}$; $\sigma = \frac{62-50}{1.28} = 9.375$.
   (*Statistics: Learning from Data*, AP Edition, 1st ed. pages 160–162 / 2nd ed. pages 170–173)

3. **(C)** The z* for a 90% interval is 1.645 and the sample size of 150 is the denominator for the standard error calculation (*Statistics: Learning from Data*, AP Edition, 1st ed. pages 460–465 and 467–477 and 480–481 / 2nd ed. pages 475–480 and 482–493 and 497–498).

4. **(C)** Using $z = \frac{x-\mu}{\sigma}$, Amy can solve for her z-score. This would give $z = \frac{48000-47500}{1470} = 0.34$.
   (*Statistics: Learning from Data*, AP Edition, 1st ed. pages 160–162 / 2nd ed. pages 170–173)

5. **(A)** The IQR is equal to the width of the box in the boxplot, so the IQR for data set A is smaller than the IQR for data set B (*Statistics: Learning from Data*, AP Edition, 1st ed. pages 149–156 / 2nd ed. pages 158–165).

6. **(B)** Visually, you can estimate the mean of this data set to be close to 1 from the histogram, or you could also compute the mean if you wanted to by adding the 10 zeros, 8 ones, 4 twos, and 3 threes and then dividing by 25 (*Statistics: Learning from Data*, AP Edition, 1st ed. pages 133–135 and 143 / 2nd ed. pages 140–142 and 150–151).

7. **(E)** The use of the emails included in the directory would mean that only those who chose to be in the directory would be able to respond. This plan excludes students who are not in the directory and these students may be different in some way. The fact that they are not included in the survey may significantly alter the results (*Statistics: Learning from Data*, AP Edition, 1st ed. pages 13–21 / 2nd ed. pages 9–20).

8. **(C)** They should worry about nonresponse bias because the survey was returned by only 42% of the customers. The remaining 58% did not respond and if they had, the results may have been quite different since those 58% could differ in a specific way to the 42% (*Statistics: Learning from Data*, AP Edition, 1st ed. pages 13–21 / 2nd ed. pages 9–20).

9. **(D)** The interchanging of the x and y variables will not change the correlation (*Statistics: Learning from Data*, AP Edition, 1st ed. pages 182–193 / 2nd ed. pages 192–204).

10. **(B)** The slope of the line is found in the first column in the row with the named variable, height. The other coefficient value is the y-intercept (*Statistics: Learning from Data*, AP Edition, 1st ed. pages 198–206 / 2nd ed. pages 209–219).

11. **(D)** r^2 is calculated by squaring the correlation coefficient. It is defined as the proportion of the variability in the response variable that can be explained by the explanatory variable (*Statistics: Learning from Data*, AP Edition, 1st ed. pages 211–225 / 2nd ed. pages 223–239).

12. **(D)** Correlation has no units, so this will remove choice E. Also, the correlation must be between −1 and +1, which eliminates choice A. B and C both have at least one categorical variable and the correlation coefficient is for two numerical values (*Statistics: Learning from Data*, AP Edition, 1st ed. pages 182–193 / 2nd ed. pages 192–204).

13. **(B)** For the method in A, only the new fire retardant will be used. For the method described in C, there is no random assignment and if the first 50 pieces in the stack differ from the last 50 in the stack in some important way, this would be a problem. The method described in D will tend to produce an uneven distribution of fabric types for the two retardants. The method in part E results in retardant being confounded with fabric type.

The method described in B is the best choice (*Statistics: Learning from Data*, AP Edition, 1st ed. pages 24–38 / 2nd ed. pages 23–38).

14. (E) The subject as well as the person measuring the response would not know which treatment the subject is getting in order to keep this knowledge from influencing the study results (*Statistics: Learning from Data*, AP Edition, 1st ed. pages 24–38 / 2nd ed. pages 23–38).

15. (E) The probability of winning with a single ticket is 1/1000. Because the ticket costs $2, the possible amounts won are $498 (with probability 0.001) and –$2 (with probability 0.999). The expected amount won is then (498)(0.001) + (–2)(0.999) = –1.50 (*Statistics: Learning from Data*, AP Edition, 1st ed. pages 352–361 / 2nd ed. pages 367–378).

16. (C) This is a binomial probability with $n = 400$ and $p = 0.5$. This means we want $1 - P(x \leq 215)$. You can evaluate this using the following calculator command: 1 – binomcdf (400, 0.5, 215) or you can use the normal approximation to the binomial since $np > 10$ and $n(1 - p) \geq 10$ (*Statistics: Learning from Data*, AP Edition, 1st ed. pages 363–371/ 2nd ed. pages 402–410).

17. (C) The z-scores for a central area of 0.50 are $z = \pm 0.67$. The upper quartile is approximately 0.67 standard deviations above the mean and the lower quartile is about 0.67 standard deviations below the mean. The IQR is then about $2(0.67) - 1.34$ standard deviations or $(1.34 \times 6) = 8.04$ (*Statistics: Learning from Data*, AP Edition, 1st ed. pages 373–387 and 395–398 / 2nd ed. pages 380–394 and 412–415).

18. (C) A confidence interval uses a point estimate to generate an interval of plausible values for the true height of babies. Since it was a 90% interval, a method was used that will result in intervals that include the true mean height about 90% of the time (*Statistics: Learning from Data*, AP Edition, 1st ed. pages 467–474 and 581–587 / 2nd ed. pages 482–489 and 603–609).

19. (E) The 95% confidence interval will be narrower than the 98% confidence interval. It will also be centered in the same place as the 98% confidence interval, so the correct answer must be E (*Statistics: Learning from Data*, AP Edition, 1st ed. pages 460–465 and 467–477 and 480–481 / 2nd ed. pages 475–480 and 482–493 and 497–498).

20. (C) This will give a z test statistic of 2.12 and P-value = 0.017. Since 0.017 < 0.05, we reject the null hypothesis and have strong evidence that the earlier claim of only 9% is too low (*Statistics: Learning from Data*, AP Edition, 1st ed. pages 514–523 / 2nd ed. pages 530–539).

21. (E) For large samples, the sampling distribution is approximately normal with standard deviation equal to the population standard deviation divided by the square root of the sample size (*Statistics: Learning from Data*, AP Edition, 1st ed. pages 568–576 / 2nd ed. pages 590–598).

22. **(E)** The expected number of service calls is 2.45. This would mean that, on average, they should expect to pay (2.45)(50) = $122.50 per month (*Statistics: Learning from Data*, AP Edition, 1st ed. pages 352–361 / 2nd ed. pages 367–378).

23. **(E)** $P(x \geq 1) = 1 - P(x = 0) = 1 - 0.12 = 0.88$ (*Statistics: Learning from Data*, AP Edition, 1st ed. pages 273–276 and 278–287 / 2nd ed. pages 285–289 and 291–301).

24. **(B)** $\sigma = \sqrt{\sum(x_i - \mu)^2 \, p_i} = 2.38$ (*Statistics: Learning from Data*, AP Edition, 1st ed. pages 352–361 / 2nd ed. pages 367–378).

25. **(E)** Continuing trials until a success occurs is the property of a geometric situation (*Statistics: Learning from Data*, AP Edition, 1st ed. pages 363–371/ 2nd ed. pages 402–410).

26. **(A)** Because the population standard deviation is not known, a *t* interval should be used. The appropriate *t** value is based on 19 *df* and a central area of 0.95. (*Statistics: Learning from Data*, AP Edition, 1st ed. pages 578–588 / 2nd ed. pages 600–612).

27. **(B)** Increasing sample size decreases margin of error (*Statistics: Learning from Data*, AP Edition, 1st ed. pages 460–465 and 467–477 and 480–481 / 2nd ed. pages 475–480 and 482–493 and 497–498).

28. **(A)** A type I error is rejecting the null hypothesis when it is true. The null hypothesis would be that 40% of users would buy the enhanced version of the game and the alternative would be that over 40% (*Statistics: Learning from Data*, AP Edition, 1st ed. pages 502–505 / 2nd ed. pages 516–520).

29. **(D)** The alternative hypothesis is $p < 0.39$, as the group wants to determine if the actual proportion is less than the claimed proportion of 0.39 (*Statistics: Learning from Data*, AP Edition, 1st ed. pages 514–523 / 2nd ed. pages 530–539).

30. **(B)** The chi-square test for independence is designed to decide if there is an association between two categorical variables (*Statistics: Learning from Data*, AP Edition, 1st ed. pages 708–718 / 2nd ed. pages 716–728).

31. **(C)** If all the girls received medication 1 and all the boys received medication 2, we would not be able to distinguish the effect of the medication from a gender effect (*Statistics: Learning from Data*, AP Edition, 1st ed. pages 24–38 / 2nd ed. pages 23–38).

32. **(C)** The mean of the sampling distribution will be the same as the population mean but the standard deviation of the sampling distribution will be smaller than the population standard deviation because the standard deviation of the sampling distribution is the population standard deviation divided by the square root of the sample size (*Statistics: Learning from Data*, AP Edition, 1st ed. pages 568–576 / 2nd ed. pages 590–598).

33. **(C)** Since each is in a different location, the study has now introduced a confounding variable. A person may be more prone to last-minute shopping, for example, and thus choose the ones by the register more often (*Statistics: Learning from Data*, AP Edition, 1st ed. pages 13–21 / 2nd ed. pages 9–20).

34. **(D)** If the program is effective, the after weight should be less than the before weight. This would mean the before – after differences should tend to be greater than 0. Also, since this is a matched-pairs design, $df = n - 1 = 8$ (*Statistics: Learning from Data*, AP Edition, 1st ed. pages 633–639, 649–651, 672–674, and 679–682 / 2nd ed. pages 642–650).

35. **(D)** Increasing sample size is one way to increase power. Increasing the significance level decreases the probability of a type II error and increases power. So, both I and III increase power *(Statistics: Learning from Data*, AP Edition, 1st ed. pages 526–530 / 2nd ed. pages 543–547).

36. **(D)** The expected number is $200(0.25) = 50$ (*Statistics: Learning from Data*, AP Edition, 1st ed. pages 352–361 / 2nd ed. pages 367–378).

37. **(D)** The margin of error tells us that the sample percentage is expected to be within 4% of the actual population percentage. Therefore, the population percentage is probably between 54% and 62% (*Statistics: Learning from Data*, AP Edition, 1st ed. pages 460–465 and 467–477 and 480–481 / 2nd ed. pages 475–480 and 482–493 and 497–498).

38. **(E)** With a *P*-value as large as 0.37, we fail to reject the null hypothesis. There is no evidence of an association (*Statistics: Learning from Data*, AP Edition, 1st ed. pages 708–718 / 2nd ed. pages 716–728).

39. **(D)** Since the interval contains 0, it is plausible that the slope of the population least-squares regression line could be 0 (*Statistics: Learning from Data*, AP Edition, 1st ed. pages 748–756 / 2nd ed. pages 754–763).

40. **(A)** A one-proportion *z* test is appropriate for testing $H_0: p = 0.50$ versus $H_a: p > 0.50$. The *P*-value for this test is 0.006, which is very small and indicates that the null hypothesis should be rejected (*Statistics: Learning from Data*, AP Edition, 1st ed. pages 514–523 / 2nd ed. pages 530–539).

Free-Response Answers

1. (a) Those who test positive will consist of those who have strep and test positive and those who do not have strep but still test positive.

   $P(\text{have strep} \cap \text{test positive}) + P(\text{don't have strep} \cap \text{test positive})$

   $= P(\text{strep})P(\text{test positive} \mid \text{strep}) + P(\text{no strep})P(\text{test positive} \mid \text{no strep})$

   $= 0.05(0.80) + 0.95(0.04) = 0.078$

   This means that 7.8% of the students would test positive.

   It is helpful to diagram the probability as shown on the following page. This will also demonstrate that you are familiar with all the correct probabilities.

   ```
                          Tests positive
                              0.80
           Has strep
             0.05
                          Tests negative
                              0.20

                          Tests positive
                              0.04
        Does not have strep
             0.95
                          Tests negative
                              0.96
   ```

   (b) This is the conditional probability that a student doesn't have strep even though the student tested positive. The solution can be found as follows

   $P(\text{does not have strep} \mid B)$

   $= \dfrac{P(\text{does not have strep} \cap B)}{P(B)} = \dfrac{P(\text{does not have strep})P(B)}{0.078} = \dfrac{0.95(0.04)}{0.078}$

   $= 0.487$

   This means that 48.7% of those who test positive don't actually have strep.
   (*Statistics: Learning from Data*, AP Edition, pages 273–276, 278–287, and 290–299 / 2nd ed. pages 285–289, 291–301, and 304–314).

   Scoring Question 1:

   Each part of this problem can be scored as essentially correct (E), partially correct (P), or incorrect (I).

   Part (a) is scored
   E if the probability is correctly computed and supporting work is shown.

   P if a correct probability is given but no supporting work is shown OR if the probability computed only considers one of the two possible cases (testing positive and has strep or testing positive and does not have strep).

Part (b) is scored
E if the probability is correctly computed and supporting work is shown.

P if a correct probability is given but no supporting work is shown OR if the numerator in the conditional probability calculation is not correct but the computed probability is still reasonable (a number between 0 and 1).

Question 1 is scored a
4 if both parts are E
3 if one part is E and the other is P
2 if one part is E and one part is I OR if both parts are P
1 if one part is P and one part is I
0 if both parts are I

2. (a) Whether tomato plants are grown in the sunny side or the shady side might affect the proportion of larger tomatoes produced. Because the field consists of a sunny side and a shady side, we should use sides to create blocks. One block would consist of the 200 tomato plants planted on the shady side and the other block would consist of the 400 tomato plants planted on the sunny side.
(b) First assign fertilizer brand to each of the 200 tomato plants on the shady side. Number the tomato plants from 001 to 200. Read the table three digits at a time until you have 100 tomato plants chosen. Ignore duplicate numbers and the numbers 201–999 and 000. The 100 tomato plants chosen would get fertilizer brand A. The other 100 tomato plants would get fertilizer brand B. Repeat this process to assign a fertilizer brand to the 400 tomato plants on the sunny side. Number the tomato plants from 001 to 400. Read the table three digits at a time until you have 200 tomato plants chosen. Ignore duplicate numbers and the numbers 401–999 and 000. The 200 tomato plants chosen would get fertilizer brand A. The other 200 tomato plants would get fertilizer brand B.
(c) The tomato plants numbered 017 and 467 will be the first two assigned to fertilizer A in the shady area. 756, 905, and 750 are ignored.

75690	50177	50467	73999	60573	58156
06205	44401	01052	41856	75562	60464
05596	22931	85521	03730	12804	76697

(*Statistics: Learning from Data*, AP Edition, 1st ed. pages 24–38 / 2nd ed. pages 23–38).

Scoring Question 2:

Each part of this problem can be scored as essentially correct (E), partially correct (P), or incorrect (I).

Part (a) is scored
E if the sides are chosen as the blocks and the response states that the side may affect the proportion of larger tomatoes produced.

P if sides are chosen as blocks but the response is unclear in stating that the sides (shady or sunny) might be related to the proportion of larger tomatoes produced.

Part (b) is scored

 E if a correct method of assigning fertilizer brand at random to tomato plants is described and it is clear that this is done separately for each block (shady side and sunny side).

 P if a correct method of assigning fertilizer brand at random to tomato plants is described but it is not clear that this is done separately for each block OR if the blocking is clear but method does not include ignoring unused numbers and repeated numbers.

Part (c) is scored

 E if a correct method of selecting tomato plants is performed and this tomato plant is assigned a fertilizer brand and a field side.

 P if a correct method of selecting tomato plants is performed but the tomato plants are not assigned a fertilizer brand and a field side.

Question 2 is scored a
 4 if three parts are E
 3 if two parts are E and one part is P
 2 if two parts are E and one part is I OR one part is E and two parts are P OR if one part is E and one part is P and one part is I
 1 if three parts are P OR one part is E and two parts are I OR two parts are P and one part is I
 0 if one part is P and two parts are I OR three parts are I

3. (a) $\mu_{B+P+C} = \mu_B + \mu_P + \mu_C = 18.8 + 18.6 + 19.4 = 56.8$ points

    $\sigma_{B+P+C} = \sqrt{\sigma_B^2 + \sigma_P^2 + \sigma_C^2} = \sqrt{0.72^2 + 0.85^2 + 0.78^2} = \sqrt{1.8493} = 1.3599$ points

    (b) The desired probability is the area to the right of 58.8 under the normal curve with $\mu_{B+P+C} = 56.8$ and $\sigma_{B+P+C} = 1.3599$. The z-score is $z = \dfrac{58.8 - 56.8}{1.3599} = 1.47$. The area to the right of 1.47 under the standard normal curve is 0.0707. [Full credit can be awarded if the mean and standard deviation in (a) are incorrect but used in this calculation.]

    (c) This is a binomial situation where $n = 5$ and $p = .0707$.

    $p(x = 2) = \binom{5}{2}(0.0707)^2(1 - 0.0707)^{5-2} = 0.0401$

    (d) This refers to the sampling distribution of the sample mean. The desired probability is the area to the right of 58.8 under the normal curve with $\mu_{\bar{x}} = 56.8$ and $\sigma_{\bar{x}} = \dfrac{1.3599}{\sqrt{5}} = 0.6082$.

    The z-score is $z = \dfrac{58.8 - 56.8}{0.6082} = 3.289$. The area to the right of 3.289 under the standard normal curve is 0.0005.

    (*Statistics: Learning from Data*, AP Edition, 1st ed. pages 352–361, 363–371, 373–387, and 395–398 / 2nd ed. pages 367–378, 402–410, 380–394, and 412–415).

Scoring Question 3:

Each part of this problem can be scored as essentially correct (E), partially correct (P), or incorrect (I).

Part (a) is scored
    E if the mean and standard deviation are calculated correctly and supporting work is shown.

    P if the mean and standard deviation are calculated correctly but no supporting work is shown, OR if the mean is calculated correctly but the standard deviation is not calculated correctly.

Part (b) is scored
    E if the normal distribution is used to compute a correct probability and supporting work is shown. Note: Supporting work can consist of showing the computation of the z-score or of a sketch of the standard normal distribution with the appropriate area shaded.

    P if the normal distribution is used to compute a correct probability but no supporting work is shown.

Part (c) is scored
    E if a binomial situation is identified and correct probability is computed and supporting work is shown.

    P if a binomial situation is identified and correct probability is computed but no supporting work is shown.

Part (d) is scored
    E if a correct probability is computed using the standard deviation of the sampling distribution and supporting work is shown.

    P if a correct probability is computed using the standard deviation of the sampling distribution but no supporting work is shown OR an incorrect probability is computed using the incorrect standard deviation and supporting work is shown.

    Note: For parts (b) through (d), if the mean and standard deviation are incorrect in (a) but all work and answers for (b), (c), and (d) are correct based on the incorrect mean and standard deviation, (b), (c), and (d) are scored as correct.

Question 3 is scored a
    4 if four parts are E
    3 if three parts are E and one is P OR three parts are E and one is I OR two parts are E and two parts are P
    2 if two parts are E and one part is P and one part is I OR two parts are E and two parts are I OR one part is E and three parts are P OR one part is E and two parts are P and one part is I OR if four parts are P
    1 if one part is E and one part is P and two parts are I OR one part is E and three parts are I OR three parts are P and one part is I OR two parts are P and two parts are I
    0 if one part is P and three parts are I OR four parts are I

4. (a) Both of the distributions are approximately symmetric. The variability appears to be a little bit greater for regular cookies than for fat-free cookies (the range for regular cookies is 13 and the range for fat-free cookies is 11). The number of chips for regular cookies is centered at a higher value than number of chips for fat-free cookies. Neither distribution appears to have unusual observations.

   (b) We would perform a two-sample t test for population means. The claim is that the mean number of chips is the same for both types of cookies. Since no direction is implied, this would be a two-sided test with hypotheses
   $H_0: \mu_r = \mu_f$
   $H_a: \mu_r \neq \mu_f$
   where μ_r is the true mean number of chips for regular cookies and μ_f is the true mean number of chips for fat-free cookies.

   (c) The samples are independent random samples from their respective populations of cookies. The other condition required for the two-sample t test is that the samples sizes are large or that the population distributions are approximately normal. Because both sample sizes are less than 30, we need to look at the distributions. Both of the dotplots show distributions that are approximately symmetric and there are no outliers, so this condition is reasonable and it would be appropriate to carry out the two-sample t test.
   (*Statistics: Learning from Data*, AP Edition, 1st ed. pages 68–96, 618–627, 644–649, 672–674, and 679–682 / 2nd ed. pages 70–93 and 657–670).

Scoring Question 4:

Each part of this problem can be scored as essentially correct (E), partially correct (P), or incorrect (I).

Part (a) is scored
   E if the two distributions are compared on the basis of all three of shape, center, and spread.

   P if the distributions are compared on only two of shape, center, and spread OR if shape, center, and spread are described for both distributions, but no comparative statements are made.

Part (b) is scored
   E if the correct test is identified and correct hypotheses are given and if symbols other than μ_R and μ_F are used, they are correctly defined. Note: It is also correct to write the hypotheses in terms of the difference in means:
   $H_o : \mu_R - \mu_F = 0$ and $H_a : \mu_R - \mu_F \neq 0$.

   P if the correct test is identified and the null hypothesis is correct but the alternative hypothesis is one-sided.

Part (c) is scored
   E if the response says use of the t test is appropriate and mentions that independent random samples is reasonable and judges the normality conditions to be reasonable based on the given dotplot or on some other appropriate graphical display that is constructed and included in the response.

P if the response says use of the *t* test is appropriate and mentions that independent random samples are given and judges the normality conditions to be reasonable but does not link this judgment to a graphical display.

Question 4 is scored a
    4 if all three parts are E
    3 if two parts are E and the one is P
    2 if two parts are E and one part is I OR one part is E and two parts are P
    1 if three parts are P OR two parts are P and one part is I OR if one part is E and two parts are I
    0 if one or no parts are P

5. (a) Because we need to estimate a population mean and the population standard deviation is not known, we will use a one-sample *t* confidence interval.

    Check Assumptions
    1. We are told that it is reasonable to regard the sample as a random sample from the population of interest, so this condition is met.
    2. The sample size is not large, so we need to check to see if it is reasonable to assume the population distribution is approximately normal. A dotplot of the sample is

    The dotplot is approximately symmetric and there are no outliers, so it is reasonable to use the *t* confidence interval.
    Calculations:
    $\bar{x} = 0.994$
    $s = 0.024$
    $df = 8 - 1 = 7$
    $\bar{x} \pm t \cdot \dfrac{s}{\sqrt{n}} = (0.833, 1.155)$

    Interpretation:
    We can be 90% confident that the true mean weight of *Snickers* fun-size bars is between 0.833 ounces and 1.155 ounces.
    (b) Because 1 ounce is in the confidence interval, it is a plausible value for the population mean. There is no reason to think that the manufacturer's claim is not reasonable.
    (c) Based on the above interval, we have no evidence to conclude that the manufacturer's advertised weight is unreasonable. This is equivalent to the conclusion of failing to reject the null hypothesis of $\mu = 1$ ounce in a hypothesis test. Since we failed to reject the null hypothesis, we could have made a type II error in which the eight bars do not have a mean weight of 1 ounce but our test does not detect this fact. If the mean weight of candy bars is less than advertised, the company could lose customers for not giving them the advertised weight. If the mean weight of candy bars is more than advertised, the company loses money by including more chocolate than necessary. In either consequence, the company is losing money.
    (*Statistics: Learning from Data*, AP Edition, 1st ed. pages 502–505 and 578–588 / 2nd ed. pages 516–520 and 600–612).

Scoring Question 5:

Each part of this problem can be scored as essentially correct (E), partially correct (P), or incorrect (I).

Part (a) is scored as three parts
    E if the *t* confidence interval is identified by name or by formula and both conditions are verified.

    P if the *t* confidence interval is identified by name or by formula but it is not clear that both conditions are verified.

    E if the correct interval is given and supporting work is shown.

    P if the correct interval is given and supporting work is not shown OR the incorrect interval is given but correct supporting work is shown.

    E if a correct interpretation of the interval is given in context.

    P if a correct interpretation of the interval is given without context.

Part (b) is scored
    E if the response says that the manufacturer's claim is reasonable and justifies this based on the fact that 1 is in the computed interval.

    P if the response says the claim is reasonable but does not explicitly state that this is because 1 is in the interval.

Note: If the interval in part (a) is incorrectly computed, the response in part (b) must be consistent with the interval in part (a). Part (b) should be scored based on the interval in (a).

Question 5 is scored a
    4 if four parts are E
    3 if three parts are E and one is P OR three parts are E and one is I OR two parts are E and two parts are P
    2 if two parts are E and one part is P and one part is I OR two parts are E and two parts are I OR one part is E and three parts are P OR one part is E and two parts are P and one part is I OR if four parts are P
    1 if one part is E and one part is P and two parts are I OR one part is E and three parts are I OR three parts are P and one part is I OR two parts are P and two parts are I
    0 if one part is P and three parts are I OR four parts are I

6. (a) $\hat{y} = -342{,}852 + 171.2x$

    where $\hat{y}$ = predicted number of requests granted and x = year.

  (b) Predicted value for year 2006: $\hat{y} = -342852 + 171.22(2006) = 615.32$

    residual $= y - \hat{y} = 317 - 615.32 = -298.32$

    The least-squares regression line overpredicted the number of requests granted for 2006. The predicted number of requests granted was quite a bit larger than the actual number of requests granted.

(c) 2020 is far outside the range of the data (which only goes up to 2009). This is extrapolation; it would be unwise to use the line to predict number of requests granted for 2020.

(d) Both the scatter diagram and the residual plot show strong curved patterns, indicating that a linear model is not the best way to describe the relationship between number of requests granted and year. The pattern in the scatter diagram looks like an exponential curve, so it is reasonable to consider an exponential model.

(e) Predicted value for year 2006: $\hat{y} = 11.82(1.74)^6 = 328.03$

residual $= y - \hat{y} = 317 - 328.03 = -11.03$

The exponential model still overpredicts the number of requests granted for 2006, but the predicted number of requests granted is much closer to the actual number of requests granted than the prediction from the linear model.

(f) The exponential model does a better job of describing the relationship between number of requests granted and year in the scatter diagram than a line. The points in the scatter diagram fall much closer to the fitted exponential model than to any line.

(g) No. Even though the exponential model does a better job of describing the relationship for 2001 to 2009 than the least-squares regression line, it is still not a good idea to extrapolate this far outside the range of the data.

(*Statistics: Learning from Data*, AP Edition, 1st ed. pages 198–206, 211–225, and 231–246 / 2nd ed. pages 209–219, 223–239, and 245–263).

Scoring Question 6:

Part (a) is scored
  E if a correct equation for the least-squares regression line is given and variables are identified.

  P if a correct equation for the least-squares regression line is given but variables are not identified.

Part (b) is scored
  E if the predicted value and residual are correctly computed using the line from part (a) and the prediction is identified as an overprediction.

  P if the predicted value and residual are correctly computed using the line from part (a) but the prediction is identified as an underprediction OR the predicted value and residual are not correctly computed using the line from part (a) but the prediction is correctly identified as an over/underprediction based on the value calculated.

Part (c) is scored
  E if the response says it is not a good idea to use the least-squares regression line to make a prediction for 2020 and identifies extrapolation as the reason.

  P if the response says it is not a good idea to use the least-squares regression line to make a prediction for 2020 but does not identify extrapolation as the reason.

Part (d) is scored
> E if the response comments on the curved (or nonlinear) pattern in both plots.
>
> I otherwise

Part (e) is scored
> E if the predicted value and residual are correctly computed using the given exponential model and it is noted that the predicted value is closer to the actual value than the prediction from part (b).
>
> P if the predicted value and residual are correctly computed using the given exponential model but it is not noted that the predicted value is closer to the actual value than the prediction from part (b).

Part (f) is scored
> E if the exponential model is identified as providing a better fit with an appropriate explanation.
>
> P if the exponential model is identified as providing a better fit with an incomplete or missing explanation.

Part (g) is scored
> E if the response notes that even with the better exponential model, it is still not a good idea to predict outside the range of the data.
>
> I otherwise

Each part scored as E counts as 1 point and each part scored as P counts as ½ point to compute an overall score. Then Question 6 is scored a
> 4 if the overall score is 7 or 6.5
> 3 if the overall score is 6, 5.5, or 5
> 2 if the overall score is 4.5, 4, 3.5, or 3
> 1 if the overall score is 2.5, 2, 1.5, or 1
> 0 if the overall score is 0 or 0.5

CALCULATING YOUR SCORE

SECTION I: MULTIPLE-CHOICE QUESTIONS

[_____] × 1.25 = _____
Number Correct   Weighted Section I Score
(out of 40)   (do not round)

SECTION II: FREE-RESPONSE QUESTIONS

Question 1 _____ × (1.875) = _____
           (out of 4)   (Do not round)

Question 2 _____ × (1.875) = _____
           (out of 4)   (Do not round)

Question 3 _____ × (1.875) = _____
           (out of 4)   (Do not round)

Question 4 _____ × (1.875) = _____
           (out of 4)   (Do not round)

Question 5 _____ × (1.875) = _____
           (out of 4)   (Do not round)

Question 6 _____ × (3.1255) = _____
           (out of 4)   (Do not round)

Sum = _____
Weighted Section II Score
(Do not round)

COMPOSITE SCORE

_____ + _____ = _____
Weighted   Weighted   Composite Score
Section I Score   Section II Score   (Round to nearest
                                                whole number)

Composite Score Range	Approximate AP® Grade
68–100	5
53–67	4
40–52	3
29–39	2
0–28	1

Part II

A Review of AP® Statistics

1

GRAPHICAL METHODS FOR DESCRIBING DATA

Data are everywhere. You might be interested in data concerning the SAT® scores needed to get into specific colleges. When confronted with this or any other set of data, you might have questions about typical values, or whether or not the data are consistent with currently held beliefs. You might ask if this set of data is similar to a second set of data, or particular observations are unusual in the context of the data. In this review section, you will learn techniques for organizing and describing data using graphs and tables to better address these questions.

OBJECTIVES

- Use an appropriate graph to display qualitative data.
- Use an appropriate graph to display quantitative data.

Before we begin, we need to be able to distinguish between two different kinds of data: qualitative data and quantitative data. Qualitative data are not numerical and usually are the product of categorizing observations and counting the number of times each category occurs. Examples of qualitative data include hair color, phone number, make or model of a car, and gender. Qualitative data may also be referred to as categorical data. Quantitative data usually arise from a measurement. Examples of quantitative data include height, the age of a car, number of players on a sports team, and a person's salary. Quantitative data may also be referred to as numerical data.

EXAMPLE Decide if the following data sets are qualitative or quantitative.

(a) Heights of mothers
(b) Numbers on football player uniforms
(c) Number of years teachers have taught
(d) Colors on textbook covers

48 ❖ Chapter 1

SOLUTION:

(a) Height is quantitative.
(b) The number on a football player's uniform has no meaning as a number and so it is qualitative. There is nothing in the real world that would have any meaning corresponding to adding or subtracting or finding an average of the uniform numbers.
(c) The number of years teachers have taught is quantitative.
(d) The colors on textbook covers are qualitative.

QUALITATIVE DATA: BAR GRAPHS, CIRCLE GRAPHS, AND SEGMENTED BAR GRAPHS

(*Statistics: Learning from Data*, AP Edition, 1st ed. pages 58–68 and 101–107 / 2nd ed. pages 58–68 and 108–112)

Qualitative data are typically presented in a data table. Such is the case for the data given below on the state of residence for a sample of people attending a large music festival. Although we can glean some information from looking at the numbers, it is often easier to get a quick overall idea of the data from a picture.

One appropriate picture for qualitative data is a **bar graph**. A bar graph is shown below the data table. A correct bar graph has both axes labeled and an appropriate scale on the vertical axis. The numeric values above each bar are not necessary but provide a more precise value than could otherwise be estimated from the graph. The order of the states on the horizontal axis is arbitrary.

State	Relative Frequency
Georgia	0.163
Tennessee	0.131
South Carolina	0.146
Florida	0.154
North Carolina	0.132
Mississippi	0.132
Other States	0.20

SAMPLE PROBLEM 1 Three large bags of M&M candies were purchased: one bag of regular candies, one bag of peanut candies, and one bag of peanut butter candies. The color of each candy was recorded. The accompanying frequency distribution summarizes the data. Draw a comparative bar graph to represent the data and describe what the bar graph tells you about the color distributions.

Color	Regular	Peanut	Peanut Butter
Orange	165	120	112
Blue	135	106	88
Green	145	111	75
Yellow	103	98	64
Brown	92	71	51
Red	65	53	43

SOLUTION TO PROBLEM 1 Because the bags have different total numbers, we will convert the counts into percentages to make our comparisons easier (this is equivalent to working with relative frequencies). Below are the percentages for each type of candy and a comparative bar graph constructed using these percentages.

Color	Regular Percent	Peanut Percent	Peanut Butter Percent
Orange	23	21	26
Blue	19	19	20
Green	21	20	17
Yellow	15	18	15
Brown	13	13	12
Red	9	9	10

Color Distributions of M&M's

We can see from the comparative bar graph that the color distribution is similar in each of the three different types of M&M candies.

Another way to visually represent qualitative data is to use a **circle graph (or pie chart)**. A circle graph shows how a whole is divided into parts.

EXAMPLE Using the large bag of regular M&M candies referenced in the previous example, construct a pie chart to show the color distribution of the regular M&M's.

Solution

Color	Regular	Percent (%)	Central Angle Measure
Brown	92	13	47°
Yellow	103	15	53°
Red	65	9	33°
Blue	135	19	69°
Orange	165	23	84°
Green	145	21	74°

To find the percent column, you must first find the total number of M&M's that are in the bag: $92 + 103 + 65 + 135 + 165 + 145 = 705$. Then, find the percentage for each color by dividing the color count by the total count and then multiplying by 100. For example, the percentage of brown regular M&M's is $\left(\frac{92}{705}\right)(100) = 13\%$. To find the measure of the central angle that forms the piece of the pie chart, we multiply the percentage by 360°. For example, the brown sector has a central angle that measures $0.13 \times 360° \approx 47°$. Drawing circle graphs is much easier with software, and the use of such technology is strongly encouraged.

Regular M&M's Color Distribution

SAMPLE PROBLEM 2 Consider the following data. Does it make sense to draw a circle graph for these data on the percentage of people 25 years old and over with a bachelor's degree or more in 2005 in the southeastern states? Explain your reasoning.

State	Percent
Georgia	26.9
Tennessee	21.6
South Carolina	24.2
Florida	25.5
North Carolina	25.4
Alabama	19.8
Mississippi	21.9

SOLUTION TO PROBLEM 2 No, it does not make sense to construct a circle graph for these data. A circle graph shows how a whole group is divided into parts based on one characteristic. These data as a group do not represent a whole. The southern states are parts of the United States, but these seven states do not form a whole group in this problem. (One clue that a circle graph would be problematic is that the percentages add up to something different from 100%.)

An additional way to display qualitative data is a **segmented bar graph**. The segmented bar graph is similar to the circle graph from the previous example, but here each of the bars shows 100%. Within each bar you can see how the whole is divided into parts just as a circle graph.

EXAMPLE Each student in a random sample of 65 students at Westside High School is asked to name his or her favorite social networking site. Below is a summary of the data. Construct a segmented bar graph to display the data.

Favorite Site	Frequency
Instagram	35
Twitter	20
Facebook	7
Other Site	3

SOLUTION First, we convert the counts into percentages or relative frequencies. Here are the percentages for each category. The columns do not add up exactly to 100% because of rounding in computing the percentages.

Favorite Site	Percent
Instagram	54
Twitter	31
Facebook	11
Other Site	5

SAMPLE PROBLEM 3 The table below summarizes data on opinion regarding a change in public education in New York City under the present administration for a sample of New Yorkers who make less than $50,000 per year and a sample of New Yorkers who make over $50,000 a year. Construct segmented bar graphs to compare the opinions of New Yorkers with income under $50,000 and adults with income over $50,000.

Opinion	Under $50,000	Over $50,000
Satisfied	33	25
Not satisfied	52	62
Don't know	15	13

SOLUTION TO PROBLEM 3 Because both sample sizes are equal to 100, the percentages are equal to the frequencies in the given table so there is no need to compute them.

QUANTITATIVE DATA: STEM-AND-LEAF DISPLAYS, FREQUENCY DISTRIBUTIONS, AND HISTOGRAMS

(*Statistics: Learning from Data*, AP Edition, 1st ed. pages 68–96 / 2nd ed. pages 70–93)

There are many graphs that are useful in the display of quantitative data. Each graph has benefits and drawbacks. We will discuss the most common graphs for quantitative data here.

A **stem-and-leaf display** is an informative graph that shows each value in a set of data. Each data value is divided into a stem and leaf. Often (but not always), the leaf is the last digit of the data points (assuming they are rounded to the same decimal place) and the stem consists of the other digits. For example, if a data point were 3.07, 30 would be the stem and 7 the leaf.

EXAMPLE The grade point averages for 40 students are listed below. Make a stem-and-leaf display for these data.

2.0	3.2	2.8	1.8	0.9	4.0	3.4	2.9	3.6	0.8
3.1	2.1	2.4	2.3	1.6	1.6	4.0	3.1	3.2	1.8
2.2	2.2	1.7	0.5	3.6	3.4	1.9	2.0	3.0	1.1
3.0	4.0	4.0	2.1	1.9	1.1	0.5	3.2	3.0	2.2

SOLUTION The ones digit is the stem and the tenths digit is the leaf. So, the stems are 0, 1, 2, 3, and 4.

The first GPA given is 2.0; go to the stem of 2 and place 0 next to it. The next GPA is 3.2; go to the stem of 3 and place 2 next to it. The next GPA is 2.8; go to the stem of 2 and place 8 next to the 0 that is already there. Keep repeating this process until you have put every data value in the stem-and-leaf display. Be sure to include a key when you are done.

Student GPAs

0	9855	
1	866879191	
2	08914322012	Key:
3	246112640020	Stem = ones
4	0000	Leaf = tenths

The last step is to put the leaves in order from smallest to largest. (Note: This step is optional.)

Student GPAs

0	5589	
1	116678899	
2	00112223489	Key:
3	000112224466	Stem = ones
4	0000	Leaf = tenths

You may have noticed a drawback to stem-and-leaf displays: it is only reasonable to use with small data sets.

SAMPLE PROBLEM 4 The numbers of home runs that Sammy Sosa hit in each of his 18 years in major league baseball are listed below. Also listed are the numbers of home runs that Barry Bonds hit in the first 18 years of his major league baseball career. Construct a comparative (or back-to-back) stem-and-leaf display and comment on the similarities and differences in the distribution of home runs for the two players.

Sosa:	4	15	10	8	33	25	36	40	36
	66	63	50	64	49	40	35	14	21
Bonds:	16	25	24	19	33	25	34	46	37
	33	42	40	37	34	49	73	46	45

SOLUTION TO PROBLEM 4 The stems are the tens digit and the leaves are the ones digit.

Sosa's Homeruns		Bonds' Homeruns
84	0	
540	1	69
51	2	455
6653	3	334477
900	4	025669
0	5	
643	6	
	7	3

The distributions of homeruns are similar, with the centers in the 30s. The Sosa values are more variable than Barry Bonds'. Sammy Sosa did not seem to have any unusual seasons, whereas Barry Bonds had an unusual season (the one season where he hit 73 homeruns).

A **histogram** is another compact way to display larger data sets with ease.

EXAMPLE The grade point averages for 40 students are listed below. Construct a histogram to display the data. Then, describe the data set.

2.0	3.2	2.8	1.8	0.9	4.0	3.4	2.9	3.6	0.8
3.1	2.1	2.4	2.3	1.6	1.6	4.0	3.1	3.2	1.8
2.2	2.2	1.7	0.5	3.6	3.4	1.9	2.0	3.0	1.1
3.0	4.0	4.0	2.1	1.9	1.1	0.5	3.2	3.0	2.2

SOLUTION The first step is to decide on a scale. We might choose to look at GPAs grouped in intervals of 0.5 (for instance, 3.0–3.5) or in intervals of 1 (for instance, 3.0–4.0). Let's use 1 as the interval width. Now, construct a frequency (or relative frequency) table. Make sure that whenever a GPA falls on the border of two different intervals, you make the same decision as to which bin it goes into. From here on, we will put those GPAs in the bin to the right (that is, 3.0 would not go in the 2.0–3.0 bin, it would be counted in the 3.0–4.0 bin).

GPA	Frequency	Relative Frequency
$0.0 \leq GPA < 1.0$	4	0.1
$1.0 \leq GPA < 2.0$	9	0.225
$2.0 \leq GPA < 3.0$	11	0.275
$3.0 \leq GPA < 4.0$	12	0.3
$4.0 \leq GPA < 5.0$	4	0.1

You can decide which you would like to show on the vertical axis—frequency or relative frequency (or equivalently, percent). The graphs will convey the same information.

The distribution of GPAs is unimodal and slightly skewed left. The typical value appears to be around 3.0. The GPAs appear to have a range of approximately 4. (We could find the exact range by looking at the raw data.)

AP® Tip

When commenting on what you see in a graphical display of quantitative data, you should address the following:
1. Center or typical value,
2. Spread or variability,
3. General shape, including number of peaks,
4. Unusual features (which include outliers, gaps, and clusters).

Notice the similarities between the histogram and the stem-and-leaf display constructed earlier. They are almost identical in the information they show. The main difference is that in a histogram we can no longer see the individual data points.

AP® is trademark registered by the College Board, which was not involved in the production of, and does not endorse, this product.

SAMPLE PROBLEM 5 Suppose the following data are the average SAT math scores for public high schools in Los Angeles. Construct a histogram of the average SAT math scores and describe the distribution.

509	493	501	516
506	494	503	519
505	497	504	518
498	500	506	520
497	500	508	518
496	501	511	515
494	501	512	515
493	502	511	515
492	501	514	
492	500	514	

SOLUTION TO PROBLEM 5

Average Score	Frequency	Relative Frequency
490 ≤ Average Score < 494	4	0.105
494 ≤ Average Score < 498	5	0.132
498 ≤ Average Score < 502	8	0.211
502 ≤ Average Score < 506	4	0.105
506 ≤ Average Score < 510	4	0.105
510 ≤ Average Score < 514	3	0.079
514 ≤ Average Score < 518	6	0.158
518 ≤ Average Score < 522	4	0.105

The distribution of the average math SAT scores is bimodal with scores concentrated around 500 and again at 515. The center is around 505 and the range is about 30. There do not appear to be any unusual average SAT math values.

A **cumulative relative frequency plot** (or ogive) shows the cumulative proportions of the data plotted against the interval endpoints.

EXAMPLE Use the data on the average SAT math score to construct a cumulative relative frequency plot.

Average Score	Frequency	Relative Frequency
490 ≤ Average Score < 494	4	0.105
494 ≤ Average Score < 498	5	0.132
498 ≤ Average Score < 502	8	0.211
502 ≤ Average Score < 506	4	0.105
506 ≤ Average Score < 510	4	0.105
510 ≤ Average Score < 514	3	0.079
514 ≤ Average Score < 518	6	0.158
518 ≤ Average Score < 522	4	0.105

SOLUTION The cumulative relative frequencies are shown below. To find a cumulative relative frequency for data value for an interval, you add the relative frequencies up to and including the relative frequency for that interval. For example, the cumulative relative frequency associated with 494 (the endpoint of the first interval) is 0.105. The cumulative relative frequency associated with 498 (the endpoint of the second interval) is $0.105 + 0.132 = 0.237$.

Average Score	Relative Frequency	Cumulative Relative Frequency
490 ≤ Average Score < 494	0.105	0.105
494 ≤ Average Score < 498	0.132	0.237
498 ≤ Average Score < 502	0.211	0.448
502 ≤ Average Score < 506	0.105	0.553
506 ≤ Average Score < 510	0.105	0.658
510 ≤ Average Score < 514	0.079	0.737
514 ≤ Average Score < 518	0.158	0.895
518 ≤ Average Score < 522	0.105	1

To construct the cumulative relative frequency plot, we graph the cumulative relative frequency against the endpoints of the intervals and then connect these points with line segments.

BIVARIATE QUANTITATIVE DATA: SCATTER DIAGRAMS

(*Statistics: Learning from Data*, AP Edition, 1st ed. pages 96–98 / 2nd ed. pages 101–103)

Bivariate data are data with two variables that are paired in some logical way. Typically, one variable is termed the explanatory variable and the other the response variable. The explanatory variable is placed on the x axis and the response variable is placed on the y axis. Unless there is the intention to use one variable as the basis for predicting the other variable (as in a regression setting), either variable can be designated as the response variable.

EXAMPLE It is well known that the frequency (chirps per minute) of crickets changes with the temperature. The following data show the temperatures (in degrees Fahrenheit) at 15 times when cricket chirps per 15 seconds were observed. Draw a scatter diagram of the data.

Temperature	89	72	93	84	81	75	70	82	69	83	80	83	81	84	76
Chirps	20	16	20	18	17	16	15	17	15	16	15	17	16	17	14

SOLUTION Since it seems more reasonable that temperature might affect the number of chirps, rather than the other way around, temperature is selected as the independent or explanatory variable and the number of chirps per 15 seconds is selected as the dependent variable.

GRAPHICAL METHODS FOR DESCRIBING DATA: STUDENT OBJECTIVES FOR THE AP® EXAM

- You should be able to construct and interpret a frequency table.
- You should be able to construct and interpret a bar graph and a comparative bar graph.
- You should be able to construct and interpret a circle graph.
- You should be able to construct and interpret a stem-and-leaf display and a back-to-back stem-and-leaf display.
- You should be able to construct and interpret a histogram.
- You should be able to construct and interpret a cumulative frequency plot.
- You should be able to construct and interpret a scatter diagram.

MULTIPLE-CHOICE QUESTIONS

1. Which of the following is a qualitative variable?
   (A) Number of dogs in a house
   (B) TV channel number
   (C) Shoe size
   (D) Number of songs played on a radio station in one hour
   (E) Number of songs stored on an iPod

2. Which variable is most likely skewed to the right?
   (A) Students' grades on an easy statistics test
   (B) Heights of male high school students
   (C) Number of goals scored in a soccer game
   (D) Ages of male high school students
   (E) Color of a student's car

Questions 3–6 refer to the following histograms:

3. Which of the variables has a skewed left distribution?
   (A) $x1$
   (B) $x2$
   (C) $x3$
   (D) $x4$
   (E) $x5$

4. Which of the variables would be described as mound-shaped and symmetric?
   (A) $x1$
   (B) $x2$
   (C) $x3$
   (D) $x4$
   (E) $x5$

5. Which of the variables is most likely the distribution of hair length of high school students?
   (A) $x1$
   (B) $x2$
   (C) $x3$
   (D) $x4$
   (E) $x5$

6. Which of the distributions is the most representative of the costs of properties on a Monopoly board? (The costs increase around the board and have a great amount of variability.)
   (A) $x1$
   (B) $x2$
   (C) $x3$
   (D) $x4$
   (E) $x5$

7. Which of the following are false statements about stem-and-leaf displays?
   I. They can be used to display both qualitative and quantitative variables.
   II. They are useful for both small and large data sets.
   III. One can easily see the shape of the distribution and unusual data values.
   (A) I only
   (B) III only
   (C) I and III
   (D) I and II
   (E) II and III

Average Tuition by Year

8. Consider the bar graph on average yearly tuition for public four-year universities. Which of the following is true?
   I. The graph is a segmented bar graph.
   II. Tuition increased less from 2006 to 2007 than in 2008 to 2009.
   III. Starting the vertical axis at $13,000 would result in a misleading picture.
   (A) II only
   (B) III only
   (C) II and III
   (D) I and II
   (E) I, II, and III

9. Which of the following are true statements about histograms?
   I. The vertical axis can be either frequencies or relative frequencies.
   II. They are particularly useful for large data sets.
   III. One can easily see the shape of the distribution and unusual data values.
   (A) I and II
   (B) I and III
   (C) II and III
   (D) I, II, and III
   (E) I only

10. Which of the following are true statements?
    I. For a given data set, histograms can appear to be different if interval widths used in the two histograms are different.
    II. For every bar graph, you can construct a circle graph with the same information.
    III. Every symmetric distribution is unimodal.
    (A) I and II
    (B) I and III
    (C) I, II, and III
    (D) I only
    (E) III only

Student Test Scores

5	13779
6	2
7	35789
8	2347778
9	1112455579

Key:
Stem = tens
Leaf = ones

11. Given the stem-and-leaf display, which of the following is true?
    (A) The mean would be a good description of a typical value for the data.
    (B) The distribution is positively skewed.
    (C) If 60 is passing, most students did not pass.
    (D) The distribution is mound shaped.
    (E) The range of the scores is about 50.

12. Given the comparative bar graph for favorite type of pet, which of the following must be true?
    (A) The percentage of women who prefer cats is higher than the corresponding percentage for men.
    (B) The number of male dog lovers in the data set is greater than the number of female dog lovers.
    (C) A high percentage of women prefer a pet other than cats or dogs.
    (D) About 30% of the people in the sample who prefer cats are male.
    (E) Almost half of the dog lovers are female.

Type of Car Driven

- Other 15.0%
- SUV 35.0%
- Truck 20.0%
- Sedan 30.0%

13. Given the circle graph for data on the type of car driven for a sample of students, which of the following must be true?
    (A) Students tend to drive cars made in the USA.
    (B) Most teachers do not drive trucks.
    (C) More students in the sample drove SUVs than all other types of vehicles combined.
    (D) A higher percentage of students drive SUVs than any other type of vehicle.
    (E) More students drive jeeps than trucks.

14. The most appropriate graph to display data collected to show the relationship between the number of TVs and the number of people in a group of randomly selected households is
    (A) a bar graph.
    (B) a scatter diagram.
    (C) a back-to-back stem-and-leaf display.
    (D) a histogram.
    (E) a cumulative frequency plot.

15. The most appropriate graph to display data on favorite food for the students in your statistics class is
    (A) a bar graph.
    (B) a scatter diagram.
    (C) a back-to-back stem-and-leaf display.
    (D) a histogram.
    (E) a cumulative frequency plot.

Free-Response Problems

1. The following cumulative frequency plot was constructed using data on number of siblings for each of the students in an AP® Statistics class. Construct a histogram to display the class data and describe the distribution.

Number of Siblings for Students in an AP® Statistics Class

Number of Siblings	Cumulative Percent
0	0.33
1	0.83
2	0.96
3	0.96
4	1

2. There are 200 students in the graduating class at a local high school. Construct a bar graph based on the data used to construct the circle graph below.

College Choice

- Other 6.0%
- Third Choice 15.0%
- First Choice 32.0%
- Second Choice 47.0%

Answers

MULTIPLE-CHOICE QUESTIONS

1. **(B)** The number of a TV channel acts to designate that certain channel and not measure the channel as being greater than or less than other channels (*Statistics: Learning from Data*, AP Edition, 1st and 2nd eds. page 58).

2. **(C)** A soccer game typically has a low number of goals scored with only occasional high scoring games. Therefore, most data will be concentrated on the left side of a histogram with a few data points skewing the distribution to the right (*Statistics: Learning from Data*, AP Edition, 1st ed. pages 86–87 / 2nd ed. pages 88–90).

3. **(B)** The variable $x2$ is mostly concentrated to the right on the histogram with a few data points skewing the distribution to the left (*Statistics: Learning from Data*, AP Edition, 1st ed. pages 86–87 / 2nd ed. pages 88–90).

4. **(C)** The variable $x3$ has a single peak and the right half of the data mirrors the left half of the data making it symmetric. (*Statistics: Learning from Data*, AP Edition, 1st ed. pages 86–87 / 2nd ed. pages 88–90)

5. **(E)** We expect hair lengths to be bimodal—one cluster for the females and another cluster for the males (*Statistics: Learning from Data*, AP Edition, 1st ed. pages 86–87 / 2nd ed. pages 88–90)

6. **(D)** The variable $x4$ displays the greatest amount of variability (*Statistics: Learning from Data*, AP Edition, 1st ed. page 78 / 2nd ed. page 81).

7. **(D)** Option I is false because a stem-and-leaf display can only be used for quantitative data. Option II is false because a stem-and-leaf plot becomes too tedious for large data sets, in which case a histogram is preferred (*Statistics: Learning from Data*, AP Edition, 1st ed. pages 72–76 / 2nd ed. pages 74–79).

8. **(C)** Option II is true because the tuition increase from 2006 to 2007 is less than $500, whereas the tuition increase from 2008 to 2009 is over $1,000. Option III is true because starting the vertical axis at $13,000 would dramatically alter the appearance in scale between tuition in 2005 and tuition in 2009 (*Statistics: Learning from Data*, AP Edition, 1st ed. pages 62–67 / 2nd ed. pages 62–68).

9. **(D)** All of the statements are true. A histogram can display either frequencies or relative frequencies, grouping data in bins is useful for large data sets, and the shape and variability of the data are easy to visualize. (*Statistics: Learning from Data*, AP Edition, 1st ed. pages 76–87 / 2nd ed. pages 79–90).

10. (D) Option I is true because of the area principle for histograms; altering the interval width would also alter the height of the bins making a comparison difficult (*Statistics: Learning from Data*, AP Edition, pages 76–87 / 2nd ed. pages 79–90).

11. (E) The range of a data set is the maximum minus the minimum. In this case: 99 – 51 = 48, which is roughly 50 (*Statistics: Learning from Data*, AP Edition, 1st ed. pages 72–75 and 135–136 / 2nd ed. pages 74–78 and 142).

12. (A) According to the comparative bar graph, over 50% of women prefer cats, whereas less than 20% of men prefer cats (*Statistics: Learning from Data*, AP Edition, 1st ed. pages 65–67 / 2nd ed. pages 66–68).

13. (D) SUV accounted for 35% of responses which was larger than any other individual category. (*Statistics: Learning from Data*, AP Edition, 1st ed. pages 101–102 / 2nd ed. pages 108–109).

14. (B) A scatter diagram is the best way to display the relationship between two quantitative variables (*Statistics: Learning from Data*, AP Edition, 1st ed. pages 96–98 / 2nd ed. pages 101–103).

15. (A) Students' favorite food would be a qualitative variable, and a bar graph is the only option presented for displaying qualitative data (*Statistics: Learning from Data*, AP Edition, 1st and 2nd eds. pages 58–60).

FREE-RESPONSE PROBLEMS

1. First, find the percentage associated with each interval. For the interval 0 to 1, the percentage is 0.33. For the interval 1 to 2, the percentage is 0.83 – 0.33 = 0.5. For the interval 2 to 3, the percentage is 0.96 – 0.83 = 0.13. For the interval 3 to 4, the percentage is 0.96 – 0.96 = 0. For the interval 4 to 5, the percentage is 1 – 0.96 = 0.04. Here is the fully labeled histogram.

The distribution is skewed right and unimodal. The center appears to be between 1 and 2 siblings. The range is 4 siblings. There do not appear to be any unusual features (*Statistics: Learning from Data*, AP Edition, 1st ed. pages 76–90 / 2nd ed. pages 79–93).

2. Use the percentages given in the circle graph to determine the bar heights.

Seniors Attending College

(*Statistics: Learning from Data*, , 1st ed. pages 62–65 and 101–102 / 2nd ed. pages 62–66 and 108–109)

2

NUMERICAL METHODS FOR DESCRIBING DATA

Now we will focus on summarizing data by describing the overall shape, center, and spread of a set of data. This will allow us to compare distributions of data as well as make predictions based on the data we have.

OBJECTIVES

- Compute and interpret measures of center.
- Calculate and interpret measures of spread within a data set.
- Use measures of center and spread to compare two or more sets of data.

DESCRIBING THE CENTER OF A DATA SET

(*Statistics: Learning from Data*, AP Edition, 1st ed. pages 133–135 and 143 / 2nd ed. pages 140–142 and 150–151)

Two key measures of center are the mean and median. Measures of center give a single numerical value (sometimes called a *point* estimator) that is representative of the data set. This value gives us a "typical" value for the data set. Figuring out what is "typical" within a data set helps us in making decisions about the population as a whole. Both mean and median provide key information about the data set.

MEAN

The **mean** is the arithmetic average of any quantitative data set. This measure gives a value that represents the data by adding up all the numbers and dividing by the total number of observations in the data set. For example, if there were 20 observations, you would divide the sum by 20.

$$\bar{x} = \frac{\sum x}{n}$$

where $\bar{x}$ is the sample mean, $\sum x$ is the sum of all values in the data set, and n is the number of values in the data set.

To use this formula, add all of the values in the data set. Then divide this sum by the total number of observations in the data set.

> EXAMPLE Let's take a set of ages collected from a class of nontraditional night students in an Introductory Statistics course at a local university. The 18 ages were as follows:
>
> 46, 29, 44, 30, 47, 30, 31, 31, 39, 27, 25, 45, 40, 38, 48, 29, 42, 27
>
> To calculate the mean, add all the values and divide by 18.
>
> $$\frac{\begin{pmatrix} 46+29+44+30+47+30+31+31+39+ \\ 27+25+45+40+38+48+29+42+27 \end{pmatrix}}{18} = 36$$
>
> SOLUTION For these data, the average age is 36.

The sample mean $\bar{x}$ is commonly used to make inferential decisions about the population mean μ in the later units of AP® Statistics.

An important consideration regarding the mean is its sensitivity to any change in the data entries. No matter how small the change, the mean will also be affected. In the class age data from the example above, assume that the age of 25 was supposed to be a 35. In this case, the mean would now be 36.56 years of age.

$$\frac{(46+29+44+\ldots+29+42+27)}{18} = 36.56$$

Even a change of one year would affect the mean. So, an outlier or extreme value will pull the mean even further away from the rest of the data set. This sensitivity to change makes the mean a nonresistant point estimator.

The mean is a single number that represents a typical value in the data set. This allows us to use the mean to represent the data. For example, if three people with an average age of 41 are in a room and a 22-year-old walks in, we can still calculate the new mean. Since the average age of the first three is 41, then the sum of the first three folks would be 123 (3(41) = 123). Now, add 22 to this sum and divide by four individuals. The new mean would be 36.25.

MEDIAN

The **median** is another measure of the center of a data set. Here, the center is measured by placing all the data entries in numerical order (from smallest to largest or largest to smallest) and then identifying the middle value. Should there be an even number of entries, then the median is the average of the middle two values.

EXAMPLE Again, utilizing the university age data given in the prior example, the median calculation is computed by placing all the numbers in order and then finding the middle value. In the example, since there were 18 entries, the 9th and 10th values would be averaged.

25, 27, 27, 29, 29, 30, 30, 31, 31, 38, 39, 40, 42, 44, 45, 46, 47, 48

$$\text{median} = \frac{31+38}{2} = 34.5$$

Unlike the mean, the median is resistant to changes (or outliers) within the data set. Because the median is based on the ranked ordering of the numbers, an outlier doesn't affect it in the same way as the mean. Instead, the median maintains its place in the middle of the numerical set no matter how extreme an outlier value may be.

AP® Tip

A key strategy when analyzing data sets using the mean and median values is to compare two data sets using these values. It is important to state not just the numerical facts for each data set but also to stress what these values tell us. Questions on the AP® exam may ask you to state what the difference is between distributions of data. For example, consider two data sets A and B where both are roughly normal and have about the same spread. However, mean A is 6 and mean B is 4. It is not sufficient to just list these facts. You need to make a comparison. Here, you might say, "Distribution A is centered at 6 whereas distribution B is centered near 4. Since the mean in set B is lower than A, set B would tend to have lower overall values, on average, than set A."

SAMPLE PROBLEM 1 A student recorded the time (in seconds) required to travel from the first to the third floor in a school building on 10 separate occasions. Calculate the mean and median time and explain why these values are different.

39 32 28 36 40
37 34 36 29 37

Another student had found the mean of six trips to be 41 seconds. However, she forgot to include a seventh trip, which took her 55 seconds. What is the new mean for all seven of her trips?

SOLUTION TO PROBLEM 1 While the median is 36, the mean is 34.8 seconds. The difference in the two centers is based on their calculation. The median is the middle value, which in this case is the average of the fifth and sixth values of 36. However, the mean is being pulled to a lower value since 28 is smaller than the other values and far to the left of the rest of the values in the data set. The mean is sensitive to any numerical change, making the mean value smaller.

AP® is trademark registered by the College Board, which was not involved in the production of, and does not endorse, this product.

Since the mean is the numerical average, this value can be multiplied by the total number of entries and this will give a total number of seconds for all six trips. Then add 55 seconds to this total and divide by 7.

$$41 \times 6 = 246$$

$$\frac{246 + 55}{7} = \frac{301}{7} = 43 \text{ seconds}$$

QUALITATIVE DATA

We typically summarize qualitative data by the category relative frequencies. This calculation is based on the number of observations in a given category out of the total number of observations. If there are only two possible categories, one is often denoted as a "success" and the other as "failure." To find the sample proportion of successes, denoted by $\hat{p}$, compute

$$\hat{p} = \frac{\text{number of successes in the data set}}{\text{total number of observations}}$$

The notation $\hat{p}$ (or p-hat) is used for the sample proportion of successes and the population proportion of successes is denoted by p.

EXAMPLE If 12 students in an AP® classroom are female and there are a total of 20 students in all, then we say that the proportion of females is 0.60 or that 60% of the class is female. The meaning of "success" is arbitrary; but here we say that "success" is being female. The result would be written as a simple fraction.

$$\hat{p} = \frac{\text{number of successes}}{n} = \frac{12}{20} = 0.60$$

$$\hat{p} = \frac{\text{number of successes}}{n} = \frac{\text{number of females}}{n} = \frac{12}{20} = 0.60$$

In this scenario, the proportion of successes in the sample is 0.60. A sample proportion is often used to make inferences about the corresponding population proportion.

DESCRIBING VARIABILITY IN A DATA SET

(*Statistics: Learning from Data*, AP Edition, 1st ed. pages 135–140 and 144–147 / 2nd ed. pages 142–147 and 151–156)

While the center of a data set is important for describing what a typical value is, it does not give a complete picture of the data set. Two sets of data could have the same mean, for example, and yet look quite differently in terms of the overall spread of the values. Consider the following two sets of data.

Set A	Set B
10, 10, 11, 12, 12	2, 4, 11, 18, 20

In both cases, the mean is 11; however, a quick look at the dotplots reveals that data set B is more variable (spread out) than data set A.

Set A ———————•·•·•———————

Set B ———•·•———•———•·•———

A description of variability is also important information to have when looking at a set of data.

RANGE

The **range** is calculated by subtracting the minimum value from the maximum value in a data set. This point estimator describes variability in a quick and simplistic form. It is incomplete in giving information about the rest of the data set as it is calculated using only the two extreme observations of the entire data set. Consider the following two sets of data and their corresponding dotplots.

Set C	**Set D**
2, 10, 11, 12, 20	2, 4, 11, 18, 20

Set C ———•———•·•·•———•———

Set D ———•·•———•———•·•———

While both sets have the same range (20 – 2 = 18), data set C appears to have less overall variation than data set D. This is because data set C has more numbers tightly packed around the mean than those in data set D. These data sets demonstrate why it is important to look at more than just mean or median values. By taking variability into account, we have a better overall description of each data set. The range is one measure of variability, but as this example illustrates, it only gives a partial picture of the variation in values of a data set.

VARIANCE AND STANDARD DEVIATION

The most common way to measure variability is to use one of two statistics: the variance and standard deviation. Both the sample variance and the sample standard deviation take into account all the values within a data set and their individual distance from the sample mean. The standard deviation is calculated by taking the square root of the variance. Therefore, understanding variance will help us calculate standard deviation.

The **variance** for any set of sample data is calculated by subtracting the mean from each value in the data set to find its directed distance from the mean value. If these directed distances are all added together, they sum to 0 because some values are below the mean, yielding negative values and some are above the mean, yielding positive values. To get around this problem, the deviations are squared before adding. Then, the sum of these values is divided by $n - 1$. The formula for the sample variance, s^2, is shown on the next page.

$$s^2 = \frac{\sum(x-\bar{x})^2}{n-1}$$

Notice how squaring the $(x - \bar{x})$ values eliminates the negative quantities that lead to the deviations having a sum of 0. However, the squaring leads to a process of averaging "square units." To fix this, and get a more interpretable result, the square root of this value is taken and it returns the original units of measure. This value is known as the sample **standard deviation**.

$$s = \sqrt{\frac{\sum(x-\bar{x})^2}{n-1}}$$

In a very general sense, the standard deviation calculation allows the researcher to see how far a typical observation is from the mean. While some values will be closer to the mean and others farther away, this computation will be used to describe the typical (or average) distance from the mean value and allow the data analyst to compare data sets that have smaller versus larger deviation values.

By using both the measures of center and variability, different data sets can be compared and differences and similarities can be described. Unfortunately, the standard deviation, like the mean, is sensitive to the presence of extreme outlier values.

You will also notice that the formula for the variance uses a denominator of $n-1$ instead of n. While dividing by n will give you the average squared deviation for the data set, it is not very accurate when estimating the population variance.

AP® Tip

When asked to DESCRIBE a data set, you should always mention the *shape*, *center*, and *spread* of the data set and interpret this information in the context of the problem. You should also comment on any *unusual features* (such as outliers, gaps, or clusters).

INTERQUARTILE RANGE

The **interquartile range (IQR)** is a measure of variability that is helpful when there are extreme values present in the data set. The *IQR* is the range of the middle half of the data set. The *IQR* is resistant to outliers since any extreme values would be found below the lower quartile or above the upper quartile of the data set rather than in the middle of the data set. As with the median, to calculate the *IQR* place the data in ranked order. The median of the lower half of the data is the lower quartile, Q_1, and the median of the upper half of the data is the upper quartile, Q_3. Subtract Q_1 from Q_3 and this is the *IQR*. The formula is shown below.

$$IQR = Q_3 - Q_1$$

When using your graphing calculator to analyze a list of data, notice that simple one-variable summary statistics will include the values in a five-number summary (min, Q_1, median, Q_3, max). This will allow you to quickly make a boxplot as well as calculate the value of the *IQR*.

Note: In calculating Q_3: if there is an odd number of observations in the upper half of the data, the middle value will be Q_3; if there is an even number of observations in the upper half of the data, the average of the two middle values will be Q_3. The same is true for calculating Q_1.

EXAMPLE Recall the data set of 18 ages collected from a class of nontraditional night students in an Introductory Statistics course at a local university.

25, 27, 27, 29, **29**, 30, 30, 31, 31 | 38, 39, 40, 42, **44**, 45, 46, 47, 48

⇩ middle # of lower ½
$Q_1 = 29$

⇩ middle # of upper ½
$Q_3 = 44$

$44 - 29 = 15$
IQR = 15

SAMPLE PROBLEM 2 The following stem-and-leaf display summarizes data on the minutes it takes to get to work from home for 20 teachers at a regional rural high school in Virginia.

$1|3 = 13$ minutes to drive to work from home

0	1 2 5 6
1	0 1 3 5
2	1 2 4 7 8
3	2 4 9
4	3 6
5	8
6	
7	4

(a) Calculate the mean and median, and comment on the difference between these two values.

(b) Which measure would better represent a typical travel time for teachers at this school? Explain.

(c) Calculate the *IQR* for this data set.

SOLUTION TO PROBLEM 2

(a) The mean is 25.55 minutes and the median is only 23 minutes. The reason the mean is almost 3 minutes higher is that there is a very large observation (74 minutes) that is quite different from the other values in the data set. This value pulls the mean larger even though more than half the teachers take less than 30 minutes to get to work.

(b) The median, which is 23, is the better choice. The mean is being pulled up quite a bit due to the large value of 74 minutes as well as the 58 minutes, which make the value of the mean further from what seems typical for this data set.

(c) The *IQR* = 26. It was found by taking $Q_3 - Q_1$ (36.5 − 10.5). Since the upper half of the data has 10 values in it, Q_3 is the average of the middle two numbers.

$$Q_1 = \frac{10+11}{2} = 10.5 \text{ and } Q_3 = \frac{34+39}{2} = 36.5$$

Therefore,

$$IQR = 36.5 - 10.5 = 26$$

SUMMARIZING A DATA SET: BOXPLOTS

(*Statistics: Learning from Data*, AP Edition, 1st ed. pages 149–156 / 2nd ed. pages 158–165)

A nice way to present the data and get a quick idea of the data set's center, spread, and even the overall symmetry or skewness is with a **box-and-whisker plot** (or just boxplot for short). Boxplots are constructed using the five-number summary rather than each individual data value and present a quick summary of a distribution that shows center, spread, and outliers.

A boxplot is easy to draw and only requires five values to make. So even in a large set of data, there will only be five numerical values that we can see in the actual plot. These numbers are usually referred to as the "five-number summary" and consist of the following values.

$$\text{Minimum,} \quad Q_a, \quad \text{Median,} \quad Q_3, \quad \text{Maximum}$$

These values can be marked on a number line and a quick sketch is then made to look like a box with two whiskers as shown in the next diagram.

EXAMPLE Consider the mathematics and science departments at a local school and the ages of the teachers within these departments. Compare the ages of the two departments.

These boxplots were drawn using the same numerical scale. The two boxplots make it easy to see a few key things. First, while both graphs are box-and-whisker plots, in the Science Teacher plot, notice that the maximum value is displayed as a single dot, which marks it as an outlier. The boxplot allows us to see the outliers clearly and to quickly calculate if any such outliers may exist.

Next, we can look at the youngest and oldest teachers. The Science Department has the youngest as well as oldest teacher in the two departments, so the range of the Science Department is larger than the range of the Mathematics Department.

Now, focusing on center, the median ages (middle line of each box) seem to be approximately the same. The mean age, while not something that can be determined by just looking at the boxplot, will be pulled to the right of the median since the data in both departments appear to be skewed to the right.

We can also see skewness in boxplots. Each section of the boxplot represents 25% of the observations in the data set. With this in mind, you can think of each section as comparing the lowest 25% to upper 25% and note if either group is more tightly grouped than the other. For example, the smallest 50% of the ages in both departments seem to be pretty similar while the largest 50% of the ages are more spread out in both departments. In this case, the ages of the older 50% of the teachers are more variable than the ages of the younger 50%.

OUTLIERS

An **outlier** is a value that is unusual compared to other numbers in the data set. We will consider any observation that is beyond 1.5(IQR) from either Q_1 or Q_3 to be an outlier (see the example below). A nice way to think of this calculation is to look at the width of the box in a boxplot. Visualize a string of that length. Then make the string 1.5 times this box length. Now, place one end of the string at Q_1 and extend it to the left. Any observations that are beyond this 1.5 (box length) will be considered outliers. The same process is repeated at Q_3 to determine outliers at the upper end of the data set. We will now perform the calculations that implement this visualization.

> EXAMPLE Let's consider the length of time it takes Tiffany to apply highlight treatments to her clients at a local hair salon. The following 20 observations are recorded in minutes.
>
> | 11 | 12 | 13 | 14 | 16 | 16 | 17 | 18 | 19 | 21 |
> |----|----|----|----|----|----|----|----|----|----|
> | 21 | 22 | 22 | 23 | 24 | 26 | 28 | 33 | 36 | 49 |

To determine if there are outliers, we perform the following steps.

1. Find Q_1 and Q_3.
2. Calculate the $IQR = Q_3 - Q_1$
3. Compute 1.5(IQR).
4. Add this value to Q_3 and subtract this value from Q_1.
5. Any observations beyond these calculated values are considered outliers.

$Q_1 = 16$

$Q_3 = 25$

$IQR = 25 - 16 = 9$

$1.5(IQR) = 1.5(9) = 13.5$

$Q_1 - 1.5(IQR) = 16 - 13.5 = 2.5$

$Q_3 + 1.5(IQR) = 25 + 13.5 = 38.5$

Since there are no values below 2.5 minutes, there are no outliers on the lower end of Tiffany's coloring times. However, the maximum time of 49 minutes is beyond 38.5 minutes. This makes 49 minutes an outlier using this rule. This is also evident in the boxplot. Also notice the whisker on the right side stops at the last data point prior to 38.5, which is 36 minutes.

Interpreting Center and Variability: Empirical Rule, and z-Scores

(*Statistics: Learning from Data*, AP Edition, 1st ed. pages 160–162 / 2nd ed. pages 170–173)

The mean and standard deviation are both useful in describing a data set. However, using these values together can give additional information in terms of relative position of any particular observation within the data set. These strategies allow for an interpretation that not only takes into account the mean value but also the standard deviation by describing any individual observation in terms of the number of standard deviations it falls above or below the mean of the data set.

Empirical Rule

When a data set is roughly **normal**, its distribution has a mound, "bell shaped," appearance. Both of the data sets portrayed below are roughly normal as can be seen by the smooth curve over the top of each set.

While both examples are of different sets of data and Normal A looks a little skewed left, you can easily see that both would be considered roughly normal.

The characteristics common to all normal distributions allow us to say that on average, a set percentage of the data will fall within 1, 2, or 3 standard deviations of the mean. This rule, known as the **Empirical Rule**, states that for distributions that are approximately normal,

About 68% of the data lies within ±1 standard deviation of the mean,

About 95% of the data lies within ±2 standard deviations of the mean, and

About 99.7% of all the data lies within ±3 standard deviations of the mean.

The displays below are shaded to visually represent these areas.

SAMPLE PROBLEM 3 The commute times during rush hour traffic on a local interstate have a mean of 22 minutes and a standard deviation of 2 minutes. The data from repeated studies of this section of interstate suggest it is reasonable to consider the drive times to be approximately normally distributed.

(a) A local businessman claims his drive takes him 26 minutes. Draw this distribution and label it. Include the businessman's commute time.

(b) What percentage of commute times are between 20 and 24 minutes to work daily?

(c) What percentage of commute times are shorter than the time for the businessman in (a)?

SOLUTION TO PROBLEM 3

(a) Sketch a normal curve and locate a mean of 22 minutes at the center. Then mark off 3 standard deviation units above and below the mean. Add the standard deviation to the mean for each mark above and subtract the standard deviation for each mark below the mean as shown.

(b) The empirical rule says that approximately 68% of the observations are between 20 and 24 minutes. In other words, approximately 68% of the commutes on this section of interstate take 20–24 minutes.

(c) 97.5% of the commutes are at or shorter than 26 minutes. Since 95% of the observations are within 2 standard deviations of the mean (18–26 minutes), then 5% would be outside this range with 2.5% in each tail. So adding $0.025 + 0.95 = 0.975 = 97.5\%$.

CALCULATING Z-SCORES

Many times in data settings it is important to compare values that have been derived using different scales. One problem with such comparisons is the difficulty in comparing data from distributions that have different means and standard deviations. We can use the mean and standard deviation to convert any observation in a data set into standardized units. These standardized scores are called **z-scores**. They are simply the directed number of standard deviations away from the mean. Converting an observation into standardized units from the mean allows for comparison between two sets of data with different means and standard deviations. The calculation is made using the following equation.

$$z = \frac{x - \text{mean}}{\text{standard deviation}}$$

Once the z-score is found, the measures in different data sets can be compared by considering their relative standing.

> **SAMPLE PROBLEM 4** Consider once again the daily commute to work for a section of interstate that has a mean of 22 minutes and a standard deviation of 2 minutes. In the same community, the mean commute time on a noninterstate route is also normally distributed with a mean of 19.5 minutes and a standard deviation of 4.1 minutes.
>
> (a) Joey uses the interstate section to get to work and his commute takes 25 minutes. Calculate Joey's z-score.
>
> (b) Toyanda uses the noninterstate route to get to work and her commute takes 25.5 minutes. With this in mind, whose route is longer relative to the distribution of commute times for the respective routes?
>
> **SOLUTION TO PROBLEM 4**
>
> (a) $z_{Joey} = \dfrac{25 - 22}{2} = 1.5$
>
> (b) $z_{Toyanda} = \dfrac{25.5 - 19.5}{4.1} = 1.46$
>
> Since Joey's z-score is slightly larger than Toyanda's, this means he is farther above the mean than Toyanda. So here, Joey takes longer on his route than Toyanda relative to the other drivers on the same route. In other words, there was a higher percentage of commuters on Joey's route that had commute times that are less than his time.

PERCENTILES

Another way to describe a data point is to describe its relative standing, that is, where it is located compared to the other data points in the data set. **Percentiles** are exactly that—the percentage of observations that fall at or below that value. You have already worked with percentiles in this chapter; the median is the 50th percentile, Q_1 is the 25th percentile, and Q_3 is the 75th percentile.

SAMPLE PROBLEM 5 Let's revisit the length of time it takes Tiffany to apply highlight treatments to her clients at a local hair salon. The following 20 observations are recorded in minutes.

| 11 | 12 | 13 | 14 | 16 | 16 | 17 | 18 | 19 | 21 |
| 21 | 22 | 22 | 23 | 24 | 26 | 28 | 33 | 36 | 49 |

What percentile is 17 minutes? 90% of all Tiffany's highlight treatments are applied in less than what time?

SOLUTION TO PROBLEM 5

(a) 17 is the seventh observation when the 20 observations are ordered from smallest to largest. To find the percentile corresponding to 17 minutes, you divide its position by the total number of observations in the data set. So, 35% of all Tiffany's highlight treatments take 17 minutes or less to apply.

(b) We have a data set with 20 numbers. We want to determine how many numbers will represent 90% of the data set. $(.90)(20) = 18$. When the observations are ordered from smallest to largest, the 18th number will be our 90th percentile.

NUMERICAL METHODS FOR DESCRIBING DATA: STUDENT OBJECTIVES FOR THE AP® EXAM

- You should be able to compare measures of center and discuss differences in two or more data sets.
- You should be able to calculate sample variance and standard deviation.
- You should be able to discuss the similarities and differences in data sets based on variability.
- You should be able to calculate and use a five-number summary to draw a boxplot.
- You should be able to describe how to find the *IQR* from Q_1 and Q_3 values.
- You should be able to describe features of a data set using either a boxplot or a five-number summary.
- You should be able to identify outliers using the 1.5(*IQR*) rule.
- You should be able to draw and use a modified boxplot.
- You should be able to use the Empirical Rule as it relates to a data set that is approximately normal.
- You should be able to use a *z*-score to compare relative positions in data sets.

MULTIPLE-CHOICE QUESTIONS

1. Each of the boxplots shown contains 24 student scores on a recent test in two different classes. The boxplots are drawn using a common numerical scale. Which of the following must be true?

   (A) Class A had more people between the median and the lower quartile than Class B.
   (B) Class A and Class B both have the same number of people.
   (C) The distribution for Class A is somewhat symmetric, while the distribution for Class B is skewed right with a noticeable outlier as well.
   (D) The distribution for Class B is skewed left and has a noticeable outlier as well, while the distribution for Class A is somewhat skewed right.
   (E) The lower 25% of Class B are much more spread out than the lower 25% of Class A and the distribution for Class B skewed left.

Use the following scenario to answer Questions 2 and 3.

Heights of 250 men and 200 women were measured. The distribution of men's heights had a mean of 68" and a standard deviation of 3" while the distribution of women's heights had a mean of 65" and a standard deviation of 2.5". Both distributions were approximately normal.

2. Which of the following is true?
   (A) The percentage of women shorter than 62.5" is smaller than the percentage of men shorter than 65".
   (B) There is a higher percentage of women between the heights of 62.5" and 67.5" than men between the heights of 65" and 71".
   (C) More than one half of the men are taller than 68" while only one-fourth of the women are taller than 67.5".
   (D) Approximately 95% of the women have heights between 60" and 70" and approximately 95% of the men have heights between 62" and 74".
   (E) The percentage of men with heights between 68" and 71" and the percentage of women with heights between 65" and 67.5" is approximately 68%.

3. Which of the following is not a correct statement?
   (A) The men's heights have more variation than the women's heights.
   (B) The men's height distribution is more skewed than the women's height distribution because the standard deviation for the men is greater than the standard deviation for the women.
   (C) On average, the men are taller than the women.
   (D) Since the standard deviation of the men's heights is larger than the standard deviation of the women's heights, you would expect the graphical display of the height distribution to be more spread out for men than for women.
   (E) Although more men were sampled, you can still expect about 68% of the women to be within one standard deviation of the mean.

4. A teacher found that the mean number of hours her 12 students spent studying for an AP® Statistics exam per week was 6.7.
   A new student from across town transferred in and reported studying 11 hours per week. What is the new mean?
   (A) 7.6 hours
   (B) 7.0 hours
   (C) 6.7 hours
   (D) 8.9 hours
   (E) 8.3 hours

5. A small department at university is seeking faculty raises. The university claims the pay for faculty in the department is comparable to other departments on campus, but the department claims that they are paid less. The university and the department both based their statements on a measure of "typical" salary using data that included salary information for all faculty and administrators at the university. Administrator salaries tend to be much higher than faculty salaries. Which of the following best explains their differing interpretations of the same data?
   (A) The university compared the mean salary for the department to the mean salary of all faculty and administrators and the department also used the means for its comparison but made an error in the calculation.
   (B) The university compared the median salary for the department to the median salary of all faculty and administrators while the department used the means for its comparison.
   (C) The university compared the mean salary for the department to the mean salary of all faculty and administrators while the department used the medians for its comparison.
   (D) The university compared the median salary for the department to the median salary of all faculty and administrators while the department used the modes for its comparison.
   (E) The university compared the mode salary for the department to the mode salary of all faculty and administrators while the department used the means for its comparison.

6. Two data sets have the same variance. What must be true about the data sets?
   (A) Both data sets have the same standard deviation.
   (B) Both data sets have roughly the same shape.
   (C) If one data set contains an outlier, the other data set also contains an outlier.
   (D) Both data sets have the same *IQR*.
   (E) Both data sets have the same range.

7. Which measures are considered to be not resistant to outliers in the data set?
   (A) Mean, standard deviation, and interquartile range
   (B) Median, interquartile range, and variance
   (C) Mean, variance, interquartile range, and median
   (D) Median, range, and standard deviation
   (E) Mean, variance, and standard deviation

8. A teacher collects the time it takes for students to get to school and calculates the summary statistics. She later discovers that she made a mistake and recorded the shortest time wrong. Even after she corrected her mistake, the observation was still the shortest time. Which statistics will change and which will remain the same?
   (A) The mean, standard deviation, and range will not change but the median and *IQR* will change.
   (B) The median and *IQR* will not change but the mean, standard deviation, and range will change.
   (C) The median and mean will not change but the *IQR*, standard deviation, and range will change.
   (D) The standard deviation, range, and *IQR* will not change but the mean and median will change.
   (E) All of the summary statistics will change.

Use the following boxplots to answer Questions 9 and 10.

9. Which boxplot corresponds to the following histogram?

   (A) A
   (B) B
   (C) C
   (D) D
   (E) E

10. Which boxplot corresponds to the following histogram?

    (A) A
    (B) B
    (C) C
    (D) D
    (E) E

11. Which of the following are true statements?
    I. Variance is smaller when extreme outliers are present.
    II. The interquartile range (*IQR*) describes spread in the middle 50% of the data.
    III. The standard deviation gives relative position of a value from the mean.
    (A) I only
    (B) II only
    (C) I and II
    (D) II and III
    (E) I, II, and III

12. A group of 15 workers on an assembly line have a mean completion time of 15.2 minutes per part. A second group of 21 workers on a second assembly line have a mean completion time of 16.8 minutes per part. What is the mean time for the combined group of workers?
    (A) 0.89 minutes
    (B) 1.81 minutes
    (C) 16.0 minutes
    (D) 16.13 minutes
    (E) 32.0 minutes

13. The distribution of heights of 150 students is approximately normally distributed with a mean of 65 inches and a standard deviation of 2.5 inches. Which of the following intervals would contain approximately 102 student heights?
    (A) 57.5"–62.5"
    (B) 57.5"–72.5"
    (C) 60"–70"
    (D) 62.5"–67.5"
    (E) 65"–72.5"

14. A 2-year study of high school students in the 1980s measured the times to complete a 1-mile run. The mean for boys was 460 seconds and the standard deviation was 55 seconds. The mean for girls was 591 seconds and the standard deviation was 70 seconds. Darnell ran the mile in 394 seconds and Christina ran the mile in 500 seconds. Which student actually performed better when compared to high school students of the same gender?
    (A) Darnell performed better with a z-score of −1.2 being further to the right of Christina's z-score of −1.3 on a normal distribution.
    (B) Christina performed better with a z-score of −1.3 being further to the left of Darnell's z-score of −1.2 on a normal distribution.
    (C) Darnell performed better with a z-score of −1.3 being better than a z-score of −1.2 for a run time.
    (D) They both performed equally well within their groups, respectively.
    (E) These scores can't be compared to see who performed better because the means and standard deviations are different for males and females.

15. A study was conducted to investigate the length of time (in seconds) it took for a chocolate chip to melt in a person's mouth. Melt time was measured for each of 80 students who participated in the study. The five-number summary for the resulting data set was:

        12   29   35   38   41

    Approximately how many chips had a melt time between 12 and 29 seconds?
    (A) 6
    (B) 12
    (C) 17
    (D) 20
    (E) 40

FREE-RESPONSE PROBLEMS

1. Two AP® teachers recorded test scores on the district exam that was taken at the end of the first semester of the course. Both classes covered the same material prior to the first semester exam. The scores for each of the two classes are shown below.

    Teacher A   59, 86, 92, 42, 71, 73, 84, 78, 73, 78, 80, 75

    Teacher B   67, 68, 70, 55, 60, 95, 86, 72, 85, 80, 74, 59

    (a) Draw comparative boxplots that would allow you to compare the two score distributions.

    (b) Are there any outliers? Explain how you arrived at this answer.

    (c) Which class appears to have higher scores? Justify your response.

2. Shavonna will only eat the red M&M's from any bag of the candies. The dotplot below shows the count of red M&M's in 26 randomly selected bags of plain M&M's.

M&M's

[Dotplot showing counts of red M&M's from 0 to 20 on the x-axis labeled "Red"]

Comment on what Shavonna might expect in a typical bag based on these results. What is the approximate percentile rank for 15 red candies in a bag? How did you arrive at this percentile?

Answers

MULTIPLE-CHOICE QUESTIONS

1. **(E)** The outlier seen in Class B is further from the median as well and the boxplot shows left skew (*Statistics: Learning from Data*, AP Edition, 1st ed. pages 149–156 / 2nd ed. pages 158–165).

2. **(D)** Approximately 95% of the data in a normally distributed data set are within 2 standard deviations of the mean (*Statistics: Learning from Data*, AP Edition, 1st ed. pages 160–162 / 2nd ed. pages 170–173).

3. **(B)** This statement is incorrect because the standard deviation relates to the variability of the data and skewness is a description of shape (*Statistics: Learning from Data*, AP Edition, 1st ed. pages 160–162 / 2nd ed. pages 170–173).

4. **(B)** The mean is the average of all 12 students. 12(6.7) = 80.4. Then add the new student's hours to this value (80.4 + 11 = 91.4). Finally divide by 13 (*Statistics: Learning from Data*, AP Edition, 1st ed. pages 133–135 / 2nd ed. pages 140–142).

5. **(B)** The mean would be pulled larger by the higher administrator salaries, whereas the median would not be as sensitive to these salaries. So, if the department compared the mean salaries, the department mean would appear lower than the university mean (*Statistics: Learning from Data*, AP Edition, 1st ed. pages 133–135 and 143 / 2nd ed. pages 140–142 and 150–151).

6. (A) Since both data sets have the same variance, they will also have the same standard deviation. (*Statistics: Learning from Data*, AP Edition, 1st ed. pages 135–140 / 2nd ed. pages 142–147).

7. (E) These three measures are affected most by outliers in the data sets. The median and *IQR* are resistant to change when outliers and extreme values are present (*Statistics: Learning from Data*, AP Edition, 1st ed. pages 133–140 / 2nd ed. pages 139–147).

8. (B) Changing the minimum value as long as it remains the minimum value will change the mean, standard deviation, and range but will not change the median and *IQR* (*Statistics: Learning from Data*, AP Edition, 1st ed. pages 133–140 and 143–147 / 2nd ed. pages 139–147 and 151–156).

9. (C) The variability of the distribution assures us that there are no outliers (*Statistics: Learning from Data*, AP Edition, 1st ed. pages 149–156 / 2nd ed. pages 158–165).

10. (E) Of all the box plots with outliers, E is the one with outlier that is the "farthest out" compared to the rest of the distribution (*Statistics: Learning from Data*, AP Edition, 1st ed. pages 149–156 / 2nd ed. pages 158–165).

11. (B) The relative position is given by a *z*-score and is calculated using the standard deviation, but this is not the definition of standard deviation (*Statistics: Learning from Data*, AP Edition, 1st ed. pages 135–140 and 144–147 / 2nd ed. pages 142–147 and 151–156).

12. (D) $\dfrac{15.2 \times 15 + 16.8 \times 21}{36}$
(*Statistics: Learning from Data*, AP Edition, 1st ed. pages 133–135 / 2nd ed. pages 139–142).

13. (D) 102/150 = 68%. The Empirical Rule says about 68% of the data is within one standard deviation of the mean so 65 ± 2.5 is the correct answer (*Statistics: Learning from Data*, AP Edition, 1st ed. pages 160–162 / 2nd ed. pages 170–173).

14. (B) Christina's *z*-score is -1.3 and Darnell's is -1.2. In running, the faster time would be further to the left of the mean. In this case, Christina has the better run time when compared to high school girls (*Statistics: Learning from Data*, AP Edition, 1st ed. pages 160–162 / 2nd ed. pages 170–173).

15. (D) The five-number summary divides the data into quarters, with 25% of the data in each section. So, 25% of the 80 observations would be between the minimum (12) and the lower quartile (29) (*Statistics: Learning from Data*, AP Edition, 1st ed. page 151 / 2nd ed. page 159).

FREE-RESPONSE PROBLEMS

1. (a) The two boxplots are shown here. The scale should be labeled and the plots each marked with the correct teacher.
   (b) Yes. There is an outlier in Teacher A's class at 42. This was found by making the following calculations.

   $$IQR = Q_3 - Q_1 = 82 - 72 = 10$$
   $$1.5(IQR) = 1.5(10) = 15$$
   $$Q_1 - 1.5(IQR) = 72 - 15 = 57$$

   Any score smaller than 57 will be considered an outlier. So, 42 is an outlier.
   (c) While Teacher B has both a higher Q_3 and the highest score of 95, this teacher's scores are also more spread out. However, 75% of Teacher A's scores are above the value of 71 and only 50% of Teacher B's students are at or above this value. Teacher A appears to have better scores overall. Also, it should be noted that teacher A's students in the top 75% are tightly packed so this teacher's student scores are more consistent.

   (*Statistics: Learning from Data*, AP Edition, 1st ed. pages 149–156 / 2nd ed. pages 158–165)

2. A complete response to part (a) would include an appropriate response about the shape, center, and spread of the data in the context of red M&M's. A complete response to part (b) would show a simple calculation.
   (a) Based on these 26 bags, the distribution of red M&M's appears to be skewed left with a mean of about 11 and a median of 12. The range of counts of reds is 12, indicating that the number of red candies in a bag is quite variable. On average, it would appear that one should expect about 11–12 reds in a bag.
   (b) Since the count of 15 is the 23rd data entry of 26, it appears that the percentile rank is about 23/26 = 0.88. This means that 15 is about the 88th percentile.

   (*Statistics: Learning from Data*, AP Edition, 1st ed. pages 133–140 and 161–162 / 2nd ed. pages 139–147 and 172–173)

3

SUMMARIZING BIVARIATE DATA

In this section, we explore methods for describing relationships between two numerical variables and assessing the strength of such relationships. These methods allow us to use existing data to make predictions.

OBJECTIVES

- Discuss the strength of a linear relationship.
- Fit a line to bivariate data.
- Discuss the appropriateness of a linear model.
- Use transformations in describing nonlinear relationships.

THE CORRELATION COEFFICIENT

(*Statistics: Learning from Data*, AP Edition, 1st ed. pages 182–193 / 2nd ed. pages 192–204)

The **correlation coefficient** is a numerical assessment of the strength and direction of a linear relationship between two numerical variables. The correlation coefficient is given by

$$r = \frac{\sum z_x z_y}{n - 1}$$

This numerical value is between –1 and 1, inclusive ($-1 \leq r \leq 1$). A value of 1 indicates that the relationship is perfectly linear with a positive slope whereas a value of –1 indicates a perfect negative linear relationship (which almost never happens in the real world). A value close to 1 (or –1) describes a moderate to strong positive (or negative) linear relationship. A value close to 0 denotes a weak linear relationship or no linear relationship. The scatter diagrams below illustrate these relationships.

Strong Negative Relationship
$r \approx -0.88$

Moderate Negative Relationship
$r \approx -0.72$

Weak Negative Relationship
$r \approx -0.21$

No Relationship
$r \approx -0.04$

Moderate Positive Relationship
$r \approx -0.65$

Strong Positive Relationship
$r \approx -0.92$

Notice in a positive relationship that large values of y tend to be paired with large values of x, while in a negative relationship, large values of y tend to be paired with small values of x.

EXAMPLE Manatees are large marine mammals found along the coast of Florida. They are noted for their friendly nature, large size, and paddle-like flippers. Many manatees are injured or killed by collisions with powerboats each year. The table below shows data on the number of powerboat registrations (in thousands) and number of manatees killed by powerboats for the years 1977 to 2007.

Year	Powerboat Registrations	Manatees Killed
1977	447	13
1978	460	21
1979	481	24
1980	498	16
1981	513	24
1982	512	20
1983	526	15
1984	559	34
1985	585	33
1986	614	33
1987	645	39
1988	675	43
1989	711	50
1990	719	47
1991	681	53

Year	Powerboat Registrations	Manatees Killed
1992	679	38
1993	678	35
1994	696	49
1995	713	42
1996	732	60
1997	755	54
1998	809	66
1999	830	82
2000	880	78
2001	944	81
2002	962	95
2003	978	73
2004	983	69
2005	1010	79
2006	1024	92
2007	1027	73

Describe the relationship between the number of powerboat registrations (in thousands) and number of manatees killed by powerboats.

SOLUTION The linear relationship between the number of powerboat registrations and the number of manatees killed is relatively strong and positive.

Boat Registrations & Manatees

LinReg
y=a+bx
a=-40.64127672
b=0.1250058039
r²=0.8969714055
r=0.9470857435

BE CAREFUL!

You must look at a scatter diagram before interpreting the correlation coefficient. You can fit a straight line to any bivariate quantitative dataset regardless of the pattern shown in the scatter diagram. Do not assume that a correlation coefficient value near 1 or −1 means a strong linear relationship. A value of $r = 0.99$ doesn't necessarily mean the relationship *is* linear as there may be a strong curved pattern in the scatter diagram. Similarly, a value of $r = 0$ doesn't mean there is *no* relationship. You need to look at the scatter diagram before interpreting the value of r.

EXAMPLE The scatter diagram below displays a relationship where the correlation between x and y is 0.92. Clearly, this relationship is not linear, so the value of the correlation coefficient would not be interpreted as meaning a strong linear relationship for these data.

ASSOCIATION VERSUS CAUSATION

A strong association does not mean that x *causes* y. Correlation only measures the strength of the relationship between variables that have been assumed to be linearly related. For example, there is a strong positive linear relationship between ice cream sales and the number of swimming injuries at the beach. Increasing ice cream sales will not cause an increase in number of injuries. A more realistic theory is that another variable (in this case outside temperature) may cause both ice cream sales and swimming injuries to increase at the beach. When it is hot outside, people tend to buy more ice cream and more people are swimming at the beach (which unfortunately increases the number of swimming injuries).

SAMPLE PROBLEM 1 A college professor recorded the outside temperature and number of students absent from his statistics seminar for nine consecutive class meetings. Construct a scatter diagram of the data and describe the relationship between temperature and number of students absent.

Outside Temperature (°F)	60	62	63	65	67	71	72	74	75
Number of Students Absent	1	0	2	5	6	5	8	7	8

SOLUTION TO PROBLEM 1 The scatter diagram shows a strong, positive, and linear relationship between outside temperature and the number of absent students. The correlation coefficient, $r = 0.9026$, confirms that the relationship is strong and positive for this range of temperatures. A properly displayed scatter diagram will include labels on both axes.

LINEAR REGRESSION

(*Statistics: Learning from Data*, AP Edition, 1st ed. pages 198–206 / 2nd ed. pages 209–219)

One potential goal in analyzing bivariate quantitative data is to be able to use one variable, x, to predict the other variable, y. It is common to call the x variable the **explanatory variable** and the y variable the **response variable**. The linear relationship between x and y is expressed as

$$\hat{y} = a + bx,$$

where a is the y-intercept, b is the slope, and $\hat{y}$ is a predicted y value.

AP® Tip

On the AP® exam formula sheet, this equation is written as $\hat{y} = b_0 + b_1 x$, where b_0 is the y-intercept and b_1 is the slope.

AP® Tip

The calculator will give you both $y = ax + b$ and $y = a + bx$. You should be careful to use the equation form that is consistent with your text and the AP® formula sheet: $y = a + bx$.

There are many lines that could be drawn through a set of data. However, we are most interested in the line that in some sense minimizes the sum of vertical distances. That is, we want a line that gets as close to each of the points as possible. Any line that contains the mean point $(\bar{x}, \bar{y})$ will have a sum of the vertical distances equal to zero. There is only one line that minimizes the sum of the squared vertical distances: the **least squares regression line** (often abbreviated as LSRL). An illustration of the squared vertical distances is shown below.

AP® is a trademark registered by the College Board, which is not affiliated with, and does not endorse, this product.

Collection

$\hat{y} = -3.9 + 1.07x; r^2 = 0.90$
Sum of squares = 14.40

We write the LSRL as

$$\hat{y} = a + bx$$

The y has a "hat" to denote that the y value is a predicted value based on the value of x.

The slope of the LSRL is interpreted as "for a one-unit increase in x, the y increases (or decreases if the slope is negative) <u>on average</u> b units."

The intercept of the LSRL is interpreted as "when x equals zero, the y <u>is predicted to be</u> a." However, in many contexts, it does not make sense to interpret the value of a because an x value of 0 is not reasonable in that context or because 0 is far removed from the x values in the data set.

AP® Tip

Be sure to distinguish between actual data values and predicted values. In the above statements, the words "on average" and "predicted" accomplish this goal.

There is a clear relationship between the correlation between x and y and the slope of the LSRL:

$$b = r\left(\frac{s_y}{s_x}\right),$$

where r is the correlation coefficient, b is the slope of the LSRL, and s_x and s_y are the standard deviations of the x's and y's, respectively. This relationship shows that slope and correlation have the same sign: Either both are positive or both are negative since standard deviations are always positive.

Once we have found the LSRL, we can use it to make predictions. When making predictions using the LSRL, we need to stay within the given range of the x values. In the manatees example, we would only want to make predictions for x values between 447,000 and 1,027,000 boat registrations. Predictions based on values of x outside this range should be regarded as suspect and are less and less reliable the further away an x value is from the x values in the data set. Predicting beyond the range of the data values of x is called **extrapolation**.

EXAMPLE Use the Minitab regression output below for the manatee data to answer the following questions.

(a) What is the equation of the LSRL?

(b) What is the interpretation of the slope? Does it make sense to interpret the intercept in this context?

(c) What would you predict for number of manatees killed when 700,000 powerboats are registered?

```
Regression Analysis: Manatees versus Registrations

The regression equation is
Manatees = -40.6 + 0.125 Registrations

    Predictor       Coef    SE Coef        T        P
    Constant     -40.641      5.840    -6.96    0.000
Registrations  0.125006   0.007867    15.89    0.000
S = 7.87985       R-Sq = 89.7%    R-Sq(adj) = 89.3%
```

SOLUTION

(a) Notice in the printout that the equation of the LSRL is given. We can also get the equation of the LSRL from the numbers under the "Coef" (coefficient) column. The equation is $\hat{y} = -40.6 + 0.125x = -40.6 + 0.125x$, where x is the number of powerboat registrations in thousands and y is the number of manatees killed.

```
Regression Analysis: Manatees versus Registrations

The regression equation is
Manatees = -40.6 + 0.125 Registrations

    Predictor       Coef    SE Coef        T        P
    Constant     -40.641      5.840    -6.96    0.000
Registrations  0.125006   0.007867    15.89    0.000
S = 7.87985       R-Sq = 89.7%    R-Sq(adj) = 89.3%
```

(b) The slope of 0.125 means "for an increase of 1,000 in powerboat registrations, the number of manatees killed increases on average by 0.125 manatees."

The intercept means "when zero powerboats are registered, the LSRL predicts negative 40.6 manatee deaths." This has no real-world meaning. Since zero powerboats is far away from the range of the number of registered powerboats, our prediction of manatees killed when the number of powerboat registrations is 0 is extrapolation beyond the data. Furthermore, the intercept in this case does not have any practical meaning; we cannot have a negative number of manatee deaths.

(c) To predict the number of manatee deaths, we substitute 700 into the LSRL for x. (Remember that the data are in thousands, so we substitute 700 instead of 700,000.)

$$\hat{y} = -40.641 + 0.125006(700) = -40.641 + 87.5042 = 46.8632$$

If there are 700,000 powerboat registrations, our model predicts approximately 46.8632 manatees to be killed.

AP® Tip

Be sure to know how to read computer output. Know where you can find the statistics to answer the questions you might be asked. Some of the information on the computer output may be extraneous and you will not need this information nor are you expected to know what it means.

SAMPLE PROBLEM 2 Find the equation of the least squares regression line and interpret the slope in context. Then predict the number of students absent when the outside temperature is 70°F.

Outside Temperature (°F)	60	62	63	65	67	71	72	74	75
Number of Students Absent	1	0	2	5	6	5	8	7	8

The computer output is given here:

```
Predictor        Coef      SE Coef           T           P
Constant       -28.612       5.917       -4.84       0.002
Temp           0.49180      0.08719        5.64       0.001
1.36191       R-Sq = 82.0%         R-Sq(adj) = 79.4%
```

SOLUTION TO PROBLEM 2 From the computer output, the equation of the LSRL is

$$\text{Predicted NumAbsent} = -28.612 + 0.49180 \times \text{Temp}$$

The interpretation of the slope is that for a one-degree increase in outside temperature, the number of students absent is expected to increase by approximately 0.49 students. Note that the value of the intercept is an extrapolation in this context since outside temperature of zero is quite far away from the given outside temperatures. Predicting y when $x = 70$ gives

$$\hat{y} = -28.6120 + 0.4918(70) = -28.6120 + 34.426 = 5.814$$

When outside temperature is 70°F, our model predicts that 5.814 students will be absent.

Assessing the Fit of a Line

(*Statistics: Learning from Data*, AP Edition, 1st ed. pages 211–225 / 2nd ed. pages 223–239)

Once you have found the equation of the least squares regression line, you will want to assess how effectively this line summarizes the relationship between the two variables.

Residuals

A residual is the difference between an actual data value and the corresponding predicted or expected value. A residual indicates the distance to the LSRL and the direction; positive if the data value is above the LSRL or negative if the data value is below the LSRL.

EXAMPLE A positive residual and a negative residual are illustrated in the scatter diagram below.

Boat Registrations & Manatees

To calculate the residual for 1999, we first need to find the actual number of manatees killed in 1999 (look in the data table given earlier in this review section). We find the predicted number of manatees killed in 1999 using the LSRL.

Actual number of manatees killed = 82

Predicted number of manatees killed = –40.641 + 0.125(830) = 63.109

Residual = 82 – 63.109 = 18.891

This means that for the year 1999, our model underestimated the number of manatees killed by almost 19.

Likewise, for the residual in 1983,

Residual = 15 – (40.641 + 0.125(526)) = 15 – 25.109 = –10.109.

This means that for the year 1983, our model overestimated the number of manatees killed by approximately 10 manatees.

Residual Plots

To assess the overall fit of a line, one should look at a bigger picture—*all* of the residuals. A **residual plot** gives the big picture of how well our line fits the data.

A desirable residual plot is one that displays a random scatter of points. A residual plot that shows a distinct nonlinear pattern suggests that a different model would be a better choice for summarizing the data.

To create a residual plot, make a scatter diagram of the residuals versus the corresponding *x* values. When looking at a scatter diagram and a residual plot, take note of data points that are unusual compared to the rest of the data. An **influential point** is a data point that significantly changes the slope of the LSRL.

For our manatee example (residual plot shown above), we see what appears to be a random scatter of points until about 800,000 powerboat registrations (800 registrations on the graph) when we begin to see a curved pattern. The overall plot does not show an obvious curved pattern, although there is a hint of curvature for large registrations. Thus, we judge the LSRL to be an appropriate summary of the data.

THE COEFFICIENT OF DETERMINATION

The **coefficient of determination**, r^2, gives the proportion of variability in *y* that can be explained by the linear association with *x*.

$$r^2 = 1 - \frac{SSResid}{SST}$$

where *SSResid* is the sum of the squared residuals $\sum(y-\hat{y})^2$ and *SST* is the total sum of squares.

> EXAMPLE Suppose that your principal hires you, the new statistician extraordinaire, to predict the number of years your statistics teacher has been teaching. He could just ask her or look it up in his records but since he has hired you, he wants to put you to work. He tells you that you are allowed to collect data on one variable from a sample of 10 other teachers at your school. Here are the data you collect:
>
> | Teacher | 1 | 2 | 3 | 4 | 5 | 6 | 7 | 8 | 9 | 10 |
> |---|---|---|---|---|---|---|---|---|---|---|
> | Number of Years Teaching | 8 | 8 | 11 | 18 | 15 | 10 | 8 | 9 | 17 | 14 |
>
> You plot the data and find that the mean number of years teaching is 11.8 years. So, you tell the principal that you estimate your statistics teacher has taught for 11.8 years.

While you don't know how far off this prediction is, you could use the same method of prediction (using the sample mean $\bar{y}$ as the prediction) to make predictions for the 10 teachers in the sample. Because you know the actual y values for these teachers, you can compute the sum of the squared prediction errors to get a sense of how good this method of prediction is overall.

$$\sum(y-\bar{y})^2 = 135.6$$

Your principal comes back a few days later and tells you that he thinks you should collect data on a second variable for the same 10 teachers and see if you can improve your predictions. You decide that age might be related to number of years teaching, so you also collect data on age. You now have the following data:

Teacher	1	2	3	4	5	6	7	8	9	10
Age	30	36	35	41	37	33	31	34	39	39
Number of Years Teaching	8	8	11	18	15	10	8	9	17	14

The LSRL for the new data is where x is the teacher's age and y is the number of years teaching. In order to estimate the number of years your teacher has taught, you need to know her age. She tells you she is 33 years old. So, you tell the principal that you predict that your statistics teacher has taught for $\hat{y} = -21.7 + 0.944(33) = 9.452$ years.

Let's again measure the sum of squared prediction errors by using the LSRL to make predictions for the 10 teachers in the sample. The sum of the squared difference between actual number of years teaching and predicted number of years teaching is

$$\sum(y-\hat{y})^2 = 31.7373$$

How much better did the second method for making predictions do? Let's find the proportion reduction in the sum of squared prediction error achieved by adding the second variable. Remember that proportion change is found by dividing the change by the original value.

$$\frac{\text{change}}{\text{original value}} = \frac{135.6 - 31.7373}{135.6} = 0.7659$$

This is r^2! By using the LSRL to make predictions, we have achieved a 76.59% reduction in the sum of squared prediction errors. This can also be interpreted as meaning that 76.59% of the variability in number of years teaching is explained by the linear relationship created with age.

EXAMPLE We can also find the value of r^2 in computer regression output.

```
Regression Analysis: Manatees versus Registrations

The regression equation is
Manatees = -40.6 + 0.125 Registrations

   Predictor      Coef    SE Coef         T        P
    Constant   -40.641      5.840     -6.96    0.000
Registrations 0.125006   0.007867     15.89    0.000

S = 7.87935       R-Sq = 89.7%      R-Sq(adj) = 39.3%

Analysis of Variance

    Source      DF      SS       MS       F        P
Regression       1   15677    15677   252.48    0.000
Residual Error  29    1801       62
     Total      30   17477                    SSResid
                                              SST
```

AP® Tip

Notice that in the computer output, r^2 is given but not r. To find r, take the square root of r^2 and then look at the sign of the slope to determine the sign of r.

THE STANDARD DEVIATION ABOUT THE LEAST SQUARES REGRESSION LINE

The standard deviation about the least squares regression line is given by

$$s_e = \sqrt{\frac{SSResid}{n-2}}$$

Roughly speaking, s_e is a typical amount by which an observation deviates from the LSRL. Remember that the standard deviation for one variable data is a typical (or average) distance from the mean. Now for two variable data, we measure typical (or average) vertical distance from the LSRL.

> EXAMPLE From the printout, $s = 7.87985$, which means that a typical difference between the actual number of manatee deaths and the predicted number of manatee deaths is approximately 8 deaths.

```
Regression Analysis: Manatees versus Registrations
The regression equation is
Manatees = -40.6 + 0.125 Registrations

    Predictor        Coef      SE Coef          T        P
     Constant     -40.641        5.840      -6.96    0.000
Registrations    0.125006     0.007867      15.89    0.000

S = 7.87985         R-Sq = 89.7%      R-Sq(adj) = 89.3%
```
(S = 7.87985 is circled)

SAMPLE PROBLEM 3 Is the LSRL you found in Sample Problem 2 an appropriate model for the data?

Outside Temperature (°F)	60	62	63	65	67	71	72	74	75
Number of Students Absent	1	0	2	5	6	5	8	7	8

SOLUTION TO PROBLEM 3 The residual plot (shown below) shows a random scatter with no clear pattern and the data have a high r^2 value (82%). Thus, we believe that a linear model is an appropriate way to summarize the data.

[Residual plot with Residuals on y-axis and Outside Temperature on x-axis]

NONLINEAR RELATIONSHIPS AND TRANSFORMATIONS

(*Statistics: Learning from Data*, AP Edition, 1st ed. pages 231–246 / 2nd ed. pages 245–263)

Unfortunately, the relationship between two numerical variables is not always linear. When the residual plot shows a curved pattern, we should fit a curve to the data. A common method for fitting a curve to a nonlinear bivariate data is through the use of transformations.

> EXAMPLE The study of prehistoric birds depends on fossil information, which typically consists of imprints in stone of a prehistoric creature's remains. To study ancient ecosystems effectively it would be useful to know the actual mass of individual birds, but this information is not preserved in the fossil record. It seems reasonable that the biomechanics of birds is much the same today as in the past. For example, the relationship between the wing length and total weight of a bird today should be very similar to what it was in the distant past. The wing lengths of ancient birds can be obtained from the fossil record, but the weight cannot.

Data are available for some species of modern birds of prey and are given below. We will attempt to "predict" the total weight of a bird using the wing length.

Wing Length and Total Weight of Modern Species of Birds of Prey		
Bird Species	Wing Length (cm)	Total Weight (kg)
Gyps fulvus	69.8	7.27
Gypaetus barbatus grandis	71.7	5.39
Catharista atrata	50.2	1.70
Aguila chrysatus	68.2	3.71
Hieraeus fasciatus	56.0	2.06
Helotarsus ecaudatus	51.2	2.10
Geranoatus melanoleucus	51.5	2.12
Circatus gallicus	53.3	1.66
Buteo bueto	40.4	1.03
Pernis apivorus	45.1	0.62
Pandion haliatus	49.6	1.11
Circus aeruginosos	41.3	0.68
Circus cyaneus (female)	37.4	0.472
Circus cyaneus (male)	33.9	0.331
Circus pygargus	35.9	0.237
Circus macrurus	35.7	0.386
Milvus milvus	50.7	0.927

The regression equation is: $\widehat{\text{TotWeight}}$ predicted TotWeight = −6.87 + 0.173 WingLen.

Here is the scatter diagram of the data. It appears that the relationship between total weight and wing length might be best described by a curve rather than a line.

Scatterplot of TotWeight vs WingLen

The residual plot brings out the nonlinear nature of the data:

Scatterplot of Residuals vs WingLen

The residual plot clearly has a nonlinear pattern, so a linear model is not the most appropriate way to summarize the data. One way to analyze the data is to transform the data to make the pattern linear. Two common transformations are exponential transformations and power transformations.

If we believe the relation is **exponential**, we can "straighten the relationship" by substituting log y in the equation for y. Here is the scatter diagram of the data and residual plot after an exponential transformation.

Scatterplot of LogWeight vs WingLen

The regression equation for the transformed data is $\widehat{\text{LogWeight}}$ predicted LogWeight = −30 + 0.0290 WingLen.

Scatterplot of Resids vs WingLen

The transformation results in data that are linearly related. The random pattern in the residual plot for the transformed data (shown above) also confirms that an exponential model for the original data may be a more appropriate way to summarize these data.

EXAMPLE The home range of an animal (the area over which the animal typically travels) is a function of diet and energy consumption. The energy consumption is, in turn, typically a function of the animal's size. Data were gathered on 27 similar animal species and are presented in the table below.

| Body Weight versus Home Range for Representative Insectivorous Mammalian Species ||||||
Body Weight (g)	Home Range (Hectares)	Body Weight (g)	Home Range (Hectares)	Body Weight (g)	Home Range (Hectares)
1,000	180	142	0.1	210	1.2
3,900	110	100	20	58	0.3
11,600	87	66	0.1	45	0.1
2,400	4	21	2.9	700	10
780	31	20	0.4	100	0.3
1,260	240	5	0.2	3,800	25
270	30	10	0.4	4,500	78.5
3,400	64	3,300	3.5	20	0.4
8,300	100	200	5	1,200	1.8

Scatterplot of HomeRange vs BodWeight

The scatter diagram reveals that most of the animals have small values for body weight and home range, but a few have large values of body weight only or home range only. Thus, the linear model appears to be deficient. When distributions of both variables are skewed, a **power transformation** can be effective in linearizing the data. With a power transformation, we make the following transformations: We substitute $\log x$ for x and $\log y$ for y. Incredible as it might seem, these transformations result in a very nice linear fit:

Scatterplot of LogHR vs LogWght

The regression equation is predicted LogHR = −1.60 + 0.893 LogWght. The relation is not overly strong, as can be seen by considering the standard deviation of residuals and the coefficient of determination:

$$S = 0.734543 \quad R\text{--}Sq = 59.1\% \quad R\text{--}Sq(adj) = 57.4\%$$

However, the random scatter seen in the residual plot suggests modeling the relationship between $\log y$ and $\log x$ using a linear model is appropriate.

Scatterplot of RESI1 vs LogWght

SUMMARIZING BIVARIATE DATA: STUDENT OBJECTIVES FOR THE AP® EXAM

- You should be able to draw a scatter diagram with labeled axes.
- You should be able to interpret the sample correlation coefficient in context.
- You should be able to find the equation of the LSRL.

- You should be able to interpret the LSRL intercept in context.
- You should be able to interpret the LSRL slope in context, when appropriate.
- You should be able to use the LSRL to make a prediction.
- You should be able to calculate and interpret a residual in context.
- You should be able to assess linearity of a data set using a residual plot.
- You should be able to interpret the coefficient of determination in context.
- You should be able to interpret standard deviation of the residuals in context.
- You should be able to read computer regression output.
- You should be able to use transformations to linearize data (specifically exponential and power transformations).

MULTIPLE-CHOICE QUESTIONS

1. Which of the following pairs of variables would be expected to have a negative relationship?
   (A) GPA and height
   (B) Number of chores and weekly allowance
   (C) Number of hours spent studying and test grade
   (D) Number of miles driven and amount of gas remaining in the gas tank
   (E) Age and IQ

2. Given $\bar{x} = 3.8, s_x = 1.2, \bar{y} = 2.7, s_y = 0.5$, and $r = .64$. Find the equation of the LSRL.
   (A) $\hat{y}$ predicted $y = 2.7 + 3.8x$
   (B) $\hat{y}$ predicted $y = 2.7 + 1.563x$
   (C) $\hat{y}$ predicted $y = 1.687 + 0.267x$
   (D) $\hat{y}$ predicted $y = 2.7 + 0.267x$
   (E) $\hat{y}$ predicted $y = 1.687 + 1.563x$

3. Meg has a set of bivariate quantitative data with a correlation coefficient of $r = 0.83$. Elise has a data set with a correlation coefficient of $r = -0.83$. What can you conclude about the two sets of data?
   (A) The scatter diagrams for these two data sets both display a strong linear pattern.
   (B) In Meg's data, 83% of the data points are closely related.
   (C) In Elise's data, 83% of the variability in y can be explained by the linear association with x.
   (D) Meg's data is more linear than Elise's data.
   (E) Nothing can be concluded about the two data sets without looking at a scatter diagram.

4. Based on the scatter diagram below, which of the following is true?

Collection

(A) Point A is an outlier and an influential point.
(B) Point A is an outlier but not an influential point.
(C) Point A is not an outlier but is an influential point.
(D) Point A is neither an outlier nor an influential point.
(E) None of these are true.

5. Given the following Minitab output, which of the following is false?

```
Regression Analysis: y versus x

Predictor        Coef      SE Coef            T           P
Constant       -0.868        2.330        -0.37       0.716
       X      -1.6914        0.2342       -7.22       0.000
S = 4.34426       R-Sq = 80.0%      R-Sq(adj) = 78.5%
```

(A) 80% of the variability in y is explained by the linear relationship with x.
(B) Since $r = 0.898$, the linear relationship between x and y is linear, strong, and positive.
(C) As x increases by one unit, y decreases, on average, 1.6914 units.
(D) The intercept of the LSRL is –0.868.
(E) The equation of the LSRL is $\hat{y} = -0.868 - 1.6914x$ predicted $y = -0.868 - 1.6914x$.

6. Which of the following scatter diagrams could have created the following residual plot?

(A)
(B)
(C)
(D)
(E)

7. Two variables are exponentially related. The LSRL for transformed data is found to be $\hat{y} = 65.1 - 3.72x$. What is the predicted value of y when $x = 16.83$?
(A) 2.49
(B) 12.09
(C) 12.98
(D) 16.74
(E) 54.15

Questions 8–12 refer to the following set of data:

The early human ancestors were similar in shape to most large primates. The data below are average male hindlimb and forelimb lengths for different species of early hominins (humans and their ancestors). The relatively short hind limbs are thought to represent evolutionary specialization for vertical climbing.

Hindlimb and Forelimb Lengths	
Hindlimb Length (mm)	Forelimb Length (mm)
471	458
361	514
399	581
557	739
553	553
574	614
857	595
698	762

Computer output for a regression analysis relating the forelimb length to the hindlimb length is shown below:

```
The regression equation is
predicted ForeLen = 436 + 0.297 HindLen

Predictor        Coef      SE Coef           T          P
 Constant       435.8        135.9        3.21      0.018
 HindLen       0.2974       0.2349        1.27      0.252
S = 99.9009       R-Sq = 21.1%      R-Sq (adj) = 7.9%
```

The scatter diagram of the data is shown below:

Scatterplot of ForeLen vs HindLen

8. Which of the following is the correct interpretation of the slope of the LSRL?
   (A) An additional mm of forelimb length results in an increase in predicted hindlimb length of 435.8 mm.
   (B) An additional mm of hindlimb length results in an increase in predicted forelimb length of 435.8 mm.
   (C) An additional mm of hindlimb length results in an increase in predicted forelimb length of 0.297 mm.
   (D) An additional mm of forelimb length results in an increase in predicted hindlimb length of 0.297 mm.
   (E) None of the above statements are correct.

9. Which of the following is the correct interpretation of the intercept of the LSRL?
   (A) An additional mm of forelimb length results in an increase in predicted hindlimb length of 435.8 mm.
   (B) An additional mm of hindlimb length results in an increase in predicted forelimb length of 435.8 mm.
   (C) An additional mm of hindlimb length results in an increase in predicted forelimb length of 0.297 mm.
   (D) An additional mm of forelimb length results in an increase in predicted hindlimb length of 0.297 mm.
   (E) None of the above statements are correct.

10. Which of the following is a correct interpretation of the coefficient of determination?
    (A) 21.1% of the variability in forelimb length is explained by the linear relationship with hindlimb length.
    (B) 21.1% of the variability in hindlimb length is explained by the linear relationship with forelimb length.
    (C) 45.9% of the variability hindlimb length is explained by the linear relationship with forelimb length.
    (D) 45.9% of the variability in forelimb length year is explained by the linear relationship with hindlimb length.
    (E) The linear relationship between forelimb length and hindlimb length is strong and positive.

11. The predicted forelimb length of a hominid with a hindlimb length of 600 mm is
    (A) approximately 400 mm.
    (B) approximately 500 mm.
    (C) approximately 600 mm.
    (D) approximately 700 mm.
    (E) approximately 800 mm.

12. Which of the following is false?
    (A) This is a good model; the residual plot would show no distinct pattern.
    (B) The slope of the line and the correlation coefficient are both positive.
    (C) The standard deviation of the residuals indicates the scatter diagram is curved.
    (D) The data point corresponding to (557, 739) is an outlier.
    (E) The correlation coefficient indicates that the linear relationship between forelimb length and hindlimb length is not very strong.

13. Suppose that a scatter diagram of (log x, log y) has a coefficient of determination close to 1. Which of the following is true?
    (A) x and y also have a coefficient of determination close to 1.
    (B) A scatter diagram of x and y would show a linear relationship.
    (C) There is not a strong relationship between x and y.
    (D) Almost 100% of the variability in log y can be explained by the linear association with log x.
    (E) The value of the correlation coefficient between x and y would be close to 0.

14. A set of data has the following residual plot. Which of the following is true?

    I. A linear model is not an appropriate model for the data.
    II. The data show an exponential trend.
    III. The LSRL has a slope of 0.
    (A) I only
    (B) II only
    (C) III only
    (D) I and III only
    (E) I, II, and III

15. The correlation between x and y is 0.84. What is the correlation between $3x + 2$ and $5 - y$?
    (A) 0.84
    (B) 0.48
    (C) −0.84
    (D) −0.48
    (E) Cannot be determined without the original data

FREE-RESPONSE PROBLEMS

1. In a study of the growth of sparrows, data were gathered on the wing length (cm) and age (days) of 13 sparrows. A regression was performed with the following results:

Age (days)	Wing Length (cm)	Age (days)	Wing Length (cm)	Age (days)	Wing Length (cm)
3	1.4	9	3.2	15	4.5
4	1.5	10	3.2	16	5.2
5	2.2	11	3.9	17	5.0
6	2.4	12	4.1		
8	3.1	14	4.7		

The regression equation is predicted WingLength(cm) = 0.713 + 0.270 Age (days)

```
Predictor         Coef      SE Coef         T          P
  Constant       0.7131     0.1479        4.82      0.001
Age(days)        0.27023    0.01349      20.03      0.000

S = 0.218405     R-Sq = 97.3%      R-Sq(adj) = 97.1%
```

(a) What is the equation of the LSRL that relates wing length and age for these birds?

(b) Interpret the slope of the LSRL. Does it make sense to interpret the intercept in this context?

(c) What is the value of the correlation coefficient? What does the correlation coefficient tell you about the strength of the relationship in this context?

(d) Do you feel the LSRL would be useful in predicting the wing length of sparrows that are 100 days old? Explain?

(e) There are no observations with a wing length with age = 7 days. Based on the regression analysis, what wing length would be expected for 7-day-old sparrows?

2. In an AP® Statistics class, the teacher wanted to show the students that humans are not good at guessing or estimating quantities. She displayed a series of clear containers with different numbers of gumballs inside and asked each student to guess the number of gumballs in one of the containers. A large number of students participated in this study. The data were then used to produce the following computer regression output and residual plot.

```
Regression Analysis: Guessed Gumballs versus Actual
Gumballs
       Predictor         Coef     SE Coef        T          P
         Constant       28.52      46.80       0.61      0.543
Actual Gumballs        2.1690     0.1324      16.39      0.000
S = 140.344          R-Sq = 63.7%     R-Sq(adj) = 63.5%
```

Guessed Gumballs versus Actual Gumballs

(a) What is the equation of the LSRL for predicting guessed number of gumballs from actual number of gumballs?

(b) Comment on the appropriateness of a linear model for these data.

(c) After making his guess, one student counted 325 actual gumballs in the container he was shown. For this data point, the residual was determined to be 76.555. What was the student's guess for the number of gumballs in the container?

Answers

MULTIPLE-CHOICE QUESTIONS

1. (D) As miles driven increase, the amount of gas left in the gas tank decreases (*Statistics: Learning from Data*, AP Edition, 1st ed. pages 182–193 / 2nd ed. pages 192–204).

2. (C) Solving for the slope, we get: $(.64)(0.5/1.2) = 0.267$. Solving for the intercept, we get: $2.7 - (0.267)(3.8) = 1.687$. So, the equation of the LSRL is predicted $y = 1.687 + 0.267x$. (*Statistics: Learning from Data*, AP Edition, 1st ed. pages 198–206 / 2nd ed. pages 209–219)

3. (E) You must look at scatter diagrams before you can assess the linearity of each data set (*Statistics: Learning from Data*, AP Edition, 1st ed. pages 182–193 / 2nd ed. pages 192–204).

4. (A) Point A is an outlier since it has a large residual. Point A is an influential point since it appears to have heavily impacted the slope of the LSRL (*Statistics: Learning from Data*, AP Edition, 1st ed. pages 211–225 / 2nd ed. pages 223–239).

5. (B) Since the slope of the LSRL is negative, the correlation coefficient must also be negative (*Statistics: Learning from Data*, AP Edition, 1st ed. pages 182–193 / 2nd ed. pages 192–204).

6. (B) If the LSRL were added to the scatter diagram for option B, then the data points on the far left and far right would fall below the LSRL while the points in the middle would fall above the LSRL (*Statistics: Learning from Data*, AP Edition, 1st ed. pages 211–225 / 2nd ed. pages 223–239).

7. (B) $\ln \hat{y} = 2.4924$

    $\hat{y} = e^{2.4924} = 12.0903$

    (*Statistics: Learning from Data*, AP Edition, 1st ed. pages 231–246 / 2nd ed. pages 245–263)

8. (C) The slope of the LSRL should always be interpreted as for a one-unit increase in x, the y increases (or decreases if the slope is negative) on average b units. (*Statistics: Learning from Data*, AP Edition, 1st ed. pages 198–206 / 2nd ed. pages 209–219).

9. (E) The intercept of the LSRL is interpreted as "when x equals zero, the y is predicted to be a." (*Statistics: Learning from Data*, AP Edition, 1st ed. pages 198–206 / 2nd ed. pages 209–219).

10. (A) The coefficient of determination should be interpreted as meaning that $(r^2)\%$ of the variability in y is explained by the linear relationship

created with *x* (*Statistics: Learning from Data*, AP Edition, 1st ed. pages 211–225 / 2nd ed. pages 223–239).

11. (C) Predicted forelimb length is: 436 + 0.297 HindLen = 436 + 0.297(600) = 614.2 (*Statistics: Learning from Data*, AP Edition, 1st ed. pages 198–206 / 2nd ed. pages 209–219).

12. (C) The standard deviation of the residuals cannot provide any information about curvature in a scatter diagram (*Statistics: Learning from Data*, AP Edition, 1st ed. pages 211–225 / 2nd ed. pages 223–239).

13. (D) This follows from the definition of the coefficient of determination (*Statistics: Learning from Data*, AP Edition, 1st ed. pages 211–225 / 2nd ed. pages 223–239).

14. (A) The curved pattern in the residual plot shows that a linear model is not the most appropriate model (*Statistics: Learning from Data*, AP Edition, 1st ed. pages 211–225 / 2nd ed. pages 223–239).

15. (A) The correlation coefficient does not change after a linear transformation on *x* and *y* (*Statistics: Learning from Data*, AP Edition, 1st ed. pages 182–193 / 2nd ed. pages 192–204).

FREE-RESPONSE PROBLEMS

1. (a) Predicted Wing Length = 0.713 + 0.270 × Age
    (b) The slope of the LSRL is interpreted as meaning that on average, we expect the wing length to increase by 0.270 cm per day.
    Since sparrows are hatched from eggs somewhat fully developed, it is reasonable to interpret the intercept as the length at hatching, age 0 days. But we should be cautious about doing so because the smallest *x* value in the data set is 3 days.
    (c) $r = 0.986$; the linear relationship between wing length and age is strong and positive.
    (d) This equation should not be used to predict wing lengths far beyond the data. It is likely that in time growth would be slow, and that a different model would be appropriate over longer time spans.
    (e) WingLength (cm) = 0.713 + 0.270 Age (days)

    WingLength (cm) = 0.713 + 0.270 × 7

    $= 2.603$ cm.

    (*Statistics: Learning from Data*, AP Edition, 1st ed. pages 198–206 / 2nd ed. pages 209–219)

2. (a) Predicted guess of number of gumballs = 28.52 + 2.169x actual gumballs.
   (b) The residual plot does not show a discernable pattern, so a linear model is an appropriate model. The residual plot also shows that as the actual number of gumballs in a container increases, the LSRL is a less accurate predictor due to the increasing size of the residuals.
   (c) Since residual = actual – predicted, then actual = residual + predicted.

   actual = residual + predicted

   actual = 76.555 + (28.52 + 2.1690 × 325)

   actual = 76.555 + 733.445

   actual = 810

   The student guessed 810 gumballs in the container

(*Statistics: Learning from Data*, AP Edition, 1st ed. pages 211–225 / 2nd ed. pages 223–239)

4

COLLECTING DATA SENSIBLY

Data are used to make informed decisions in a variety of settings. But to be useful, data need to be collected in a sensible way. In this section, we look at data collections and discuss the kind of conclusions that can be drawn from statistical studies.

OBJECTIVES

- Distinguish between an experiment and an observational study.
- Identify the most common sampling methods.
- Choose an appropriate sampling method for an observational study.
- Identify different types of bias that arise in sampling situations.
- Know the characteristics of a well-designed experiment.
- Design an experiment to investigate the effect of an explanatory variable on a response.

COLLECTING DATA SENSIBLY

(*Statistics: Learning from Data*, AP Edition, 1st ed. pages 9–11 / 2nd ed. pages 5–7)

In order to make good statistical decisions, it is important to collect data that represent the group we want to make decisions about in our study. Representative data allow us to generalize the findings of our research to a larger population of interest. A well-designed experiment may allow us to identify causal relationships. A well-designed experiment with a representative sample allows us to talk about the likely causes and effects between the variables in the experiment and generalize to the population represented by the sample. Even when we are not trying to establish causal relationships, good sampling can help us identify likely relationships between variables in a larger population.

The first question to ask in the data collection process is, "what are we interested in knowing from the data?" There are two different approaches based on what type of information we want to glean and the type of data we need to gather. For example, if we want to know the average weight of 2-year-old calico cats, we would simply observe a collection of these cats and record the weights. This would be an **observational study** since we are only concerned with what already exists in the calico cat world. However, if we wanted to determine whether a new type of food would impact the weight of 2-year-old calico cats in a specific way, we would need to do more than observe. We would conduct an experiment using the new food type. We could discover how the new type of food impacts the weight of the cat by carefully studying the use of the new food type with our target population under very controlled conditions that allow us to rule out other influences on the weight of the cats besides the food itself. We would set up an experiment by manipulating the diet of the cats while attempting to keep values of other variables as similar as possible. We would need at least one comparison group of cats that is similar to the cats that are getting our food. Ideally, they would be similar in every relevant respect except that they would not get the new food. Of course, it would not work to have cats in the control group eat nothing. We would then be studying the difference between cats that eat something and cats that eat nothing. That would not tell us how our new food compares to other cat foods in causing weight gain in cats. We would need a different food for our comparison group. These two different diets are known as the treatments that we would study, since we would be giving some cats one food and other cats a different food. This is an **experiment** because we are imposing a treatment on the experimental subjects.

In an observational study as well as an experimental study, gathering a good sample is critical to making good judgments about the overall population we are interested in studying.

SAMPLING

(*Statistics: Learning from Data*, AP Edition, 1st ed. pages 13–21 / 2nd ed. pages 9–20)

Choosing a good sample is very important in the data collection process. It would be great if we could study the entire population. However, since this is typically not possible, and often not desirable, the researcher must rely on **sampling** in order to make decisions about the population. It is critical that we collect a sample in a way that makes it likely that the sample will be representative of the population. One way to achieve this is by selecting a random sample. Random sampling procedures help us minimize bias.

BIAS

There are several types of bias whose presence could result in a sample that is not representative of the actual population of interest and thereby prevent us from knowing if the findings of the study would apply to the population at large. In selecting a sample, the researcher should be mindful of the following types of bias and attempt to minimize them.

SELECTION BIAS Selection bias occurs if some elements in a population are systematically favored or excluded from participation. For example, if we want to know about the senior class but only survey students in 12th-grade English class, then seniors who do not have 12th-grade English or who skip their English class routinely will not be included in the sample. Their opinions may be missed completely because of this lack of inclusion. Our study would not tell us about the senior class—at best it tells us only about seniors taking senior English.

MEASUREMENT/ RESPONSE BIAS Measurement bias can occur in a couple of ways. First, if the wording of a question favors a particular response or outcome, this introduces bias. In addition, if measuring equipment is working improperly, then it is possible that the measurements are inaccurate.

NONRESPONSE BIAS This type of bias can occur if a group that would have altered the overall results had they participated does not respond to a survey. This happens often in surveys when people choose not to submit their responses. Diligence should be used to overcome these problems and to ensure there is no systematic bias arising from the failure of individuals to respond to the survey.

VOLUNTARY RESPONSE BIAS Some individuals may tend to have strong opinions on specific issue and they may tend to respond to surveys in a higher proportion. To help avoid this type of bias, it is important that individuals aren't simply allowed to volunteer to be participants.

> **AP® Tip**
>
> When considering whether bias may have occurred, it is helpful to ask three questions:
>
> 1. Could the question wording tend to lead to a certain response?
> 2. Was the sample chosen in a way that would tend to exclude some parts of the population?
> 3. Could the results have been impacted by missing responses from those who did not respond?
>
> If any of these problems occur, the results may not reflect characteristics of the population.

SAMPLE PROBLEM 1 Each of the following scenarios contains a potential source of bias. Identify and discuss the potential bias.

(a) Students in Algebra II were asked to choose their mathematics course for the following year based on the course descriptions given below.

AP® is trademark registered by the College Board, which was not involved in the production of, and does not endorse, this product.

1. Analysis is for hardworking students who will do their homework.

2. AP® Statistics involves exciting data analysis and fun activities.

3. Finite Mathematics is for students who aren't planning to take other mathematics courses or go to college.

(b) A phone survey was conducted to determine the need for afterschool help sessions at a local student center. Phone numbers were generated at random, and calls were made between the hours of 9 a.m. and 11 a.m.

SOLUTION TO PROBLEM 1

(a) The question wording may lead to response bias. It makes the AP® Statistics class sound more interesting than the others.

(b) The survey methodology may suffer from nonresponse bias. Since the survey will be done by phone, it systematically excludes anyone who doesn't have a phone. In addition, since the calls will occur during daytime hours, families in which all adults work may be missed and these individuals may be more likely to want such a service.

RANDOM SAMPLING

A **simple random sample** is chosen in a way that ensures that every different possible sample of a given size n from the population has an equal chance of being selected. A random sample can be selected with replacement or without replacement. If a chosen individual is not eligible to be chosen again, this is called sampling **without replacement**. If, however, the individual is chosen, then placed back in the group and can be selected again, this is called sampling **with replacement**.

EXAMPLE Suppose that five prizes are available. A sample of five students is to be elected to receive these prizes. The five winners will be chosen by pulling names out of a hat.

Without Replacement: If a person can only win one prize, once selected the name is removed and may not be drawn for additional prizes. This is sampling without replacement.

With Replacement: If we are going to pull a name out of the hat and then once the winner is given a prize we put the name back in the hat before drawing a name for the next prize, this is sampling with replacement.

Selecting a random sample can be done in a variety of ways. Some of the most common methods involve the use of a calculator, computer software, or a table of random digits. No matter which method is used, it is important that each individual in the population be identified and then that each of them has an equal chance of being chosen.

Here are some examples of methods for selecting a random sample of size 12 from a group of 100 individuals who have each been assigned a unique number between 1 and 100.

GRAPHING CALCULATOR: We would use the calculator to generate random integers between 1 and 100 and the first 12 distinct integers would be used to identify the individuals in the sample. On the TI-83 or TI-84 calculator, press "**randint(1,100)[enter]**". Continue pressing enter until we have 12 numbers. If we are sampling without replacement, we would ignore any duplicates that occur since we don't want to choose the same person more than once.

SOFTWARE: In this case, we will still generate 12 random integers but the manner in which this is done will be determined by the software package that is being used. It is very similar to using a calculator.

RANDOM DIGITS TABLE: Since we need 100 numbers, we would number the participants 00–99 (or 001–100). Next, using any random digits table, go to any line on the table and read the digits in pairs to form two-digit numbers. The first 12 distinct two-digit numbers you find on the table will be the participants. Again, any duplicates would be ignored and another two-digit number would be chosen if we are sampling without replacement.

AP® Tip

The AP® exam may require you to demonstrate that you know how to select a random sample using a random digit table. Be sure you know how to do this for the exam. Keep it simple and consider using the following strategies in choosing your participants.

10 or fewer participants—number 0–9 and read the table one digit at a time. (For, say, six participants, number 1–6 and ignore the digits 7–9 and 0 if they come up as well as any duplicates that occur.)

11–99 participants—number 00–99 and read the table two digits at a time. (Again, ignore numbers not needed or duplicates.)

101–999 participants—number 000–999 and read the table three digits at a time. (Again, ignore numbers not needed or duplicates.)

SAMPLE PROBLEM 2 There are 863 seniors at a large high school.

(a) Explain how you would use a random number table to select a random sample of 20 seniors.

(b) Using the random digits below, select your first five participants using the scheme in (a).

5 6 9 6 4	7 0 8 2 7	3 5 9 1 6	3 7 8 1 1	9 7 8 5 0
6 0 8 5 4	1 1 4 6 6	5 9 3 3 0	1 8 7 6 4	1 1 7 7 8
6 8 2 9 5	4 9 2 6 7	1 2 4 8 7	6 4 3 5 0	0 9 0 1 4

SOLUTION TO PROBLEM 2

(a) Number the seniors 001–863. Then, go to a randomly selected row of the random number table and select three-digit numbers from left to right. The seniors corresponding to the first 20 different three-digit numbers will be included in the sample. Any duplicates as well as numbers from 864 to 999 and 000 are to be ignored.

(b) The first five participants would be 569, 647, 082, 735, and 378. See the circled numbers below to follow the scheme used. Notice the number 916 was skipped as it does not correspond to one of the seniors.

```
56964    70827    35916    37811    97850
60854    11466    59330    18764    11778
68295    49267    12487    64350    09014
```

OTHER SAMPLING METHODS

There are other sampling strategies we might want to consider as alternatives to simple random sampling. For example, suppose a company has 58 male supervisors and 21 female supervisors. If five are going to be selected at random and interviewed about job satisfaction, it is possible to get all males or all females, which may not provide a fair measure of job satisfaction. In such a situation, we may want to consider a different sampling method.

STRATIFIED RANDOM SAMPLING. When a population of interest can be divided into homogenous subgroups that don't overlap (such as male/female or freshman, sophomore, junior, and senior), stratifying may help to ensure that each subgroup, called **strata**, is represented in the sample. In this case, a set number of individuals will be selected at random from each subgroup (stratum) so that each subgroup is represented in the sample.

CLUSTER SAMPLING. In cluster sampling, the population is divided into subgroups but instead of selecting a sample from each subgroup as in stratified sampling, a few of the subgroups are selected at random. For example, suppose that you want to know something about pillows that are packaged in crates of three dozen pillows per crate. If the manufacturer wanted to check the quality of nine dozen pillows, it would be easier to randomly select three of the crates at random and then study all of the pillows in these three crates. Here, each subgroup is representative of the population of interest.

SYSTEMATIC SAMPLING. This method works well if the population is easily arranged in a sequential order. We then randomly choose one of the first k individuals in the sequence and then we select every kth individual in the sequence from that starting point. For example, we might select one of the first 10 people to enter a store and then every 10th person who enters the store after that. Realize that this method does not result in a simple random sample unless the population starts out in a random order.

SAMPLE SIZE

It is a common misconception that a small sample cannot reflect the overall population well if the population is very large. However, this is not true. If the researcher chooses a sample carefully and uses random selection, the samples will most likely reflect population characteristics. Think of a spoonful of soup from a huge pot of soup—the spoonful is quite small compared to the entire pot but is representative of the soup. The key is to use a random sample.

OBSERVATIONAL STUDIES

(*Statistics: Learning from Data*, AP Edition, 1st ed. pages 9–11 / 2nd ed. pages 5–7)

When a researcher collects information (data) about a population without imposing any type of treatment, the study is called an observational study. In observational studies, it is important to select a sample that is representative of the population. This might be done by selecting a simple random sample or by selecting a stratified random sample.

> SAMPLE PROBLEM 3 A local school board wants to design a survey to see if more than 50% of the community would support increasing school funding by approving a local 1% tax on all restaurant purchases. The city has a large urban population as well as a smaller suburban population. How should the school board sample this community?
>
> SOLUTION TO PROBLEM 3 If the sample size is large, a simple random sampling plan would be fine and both groups (urban and suburban) should be represented in the sample. However, it would also make sense to stratify residents into urban and suburban strata and then select a random sample from each of these two strata.

EXPERIMENTAL DESIGN

(*Statistics: Learning from Data*, AP Edition, 1st ed. pages 24–38 / 2nd ed. pages 23–38)

Unlike observational studies, in an **experiment** the researcher imposes some treatment in order to see if there is an effect on some response variable. Researchers performing experiments must not only consider what information they would like to gather, but also a multitude of other variables that may cloud interpretation of the results of the study.

There are several key components to a well-designed experiment that will allow the researcher to attribute differences in the response to the treatment and generalize this finding to a broader population. A key difference between an experiment and an observational study is that in an experiment, the researcher assigns a treatment at random to experimental units.

Suppose a researcher wants to see if using a different type of food affects the weight of 2-year-old calico cats. The researcher will want to keep as many other outside variables as possible from changing to ensure that only the controlled diet would be responsible for any observed differences in weight between the experimental groups. Once the sample of cats is chosen for participation in the experiment, they would need to be randomly assigned to two groups. One group would get the old diet and the second group would get the new diet. The researcher would feed the cats and observe weight gain at the end of the study.

This is a very basic design that includes comparing the results of only two treatment groups. Let's take a look at the key information that must be included for a complete description of an experiment of this type.

First, include an explanation of what the experimental units for the experiment are in your description. Next, the subjects should be divided into two groups: old diet and new diet. This assignment must be random and the method of assignment should be clearly explained. Once assigned to treatments, the cats will be weighed prior to being placed on the controlled diets and after they have been eating the appropriate diet for a certain amount of time. In demonstrating this for the AP® exam, you can use a diagram to illustrate your design, but be sure to also include a written description of the important aspects of the design.

>EXAMPLE Suppose there are 80 calico cats available for an experiment to see if diet has an effect on weight gain.

The diagram would look like this:

```
                                          ┌─→ Old diet    ─→ Measure ─┐
                                          │   (40 cats)     weight    │
80 Calico  ─→ Weigh ─→ Random             │                 gain      │─→ Compare weight
cats          cats    assignment ─────────┤                            │   gain from the two
                                          │                            │   diets
                                          └─→ New diet    ─→ Measure ─┘
                                              (40 cats)     weight
                                                            gain
```

The accompanying statement should read as follows:

> *Number the cats 01–80. Then, select two-digit numbers from a designated row in a random number table. The first 40 different numbers chosen will identify the cats that receive old diet and the rest will receive new diet. Any numbers that are repeated or 81–99 and 00 will be skipped. The cats will be weighed at the beginning of the experiment and again after a specified time on the diet. Mean weight gain for the two diets will be compared to determine if there is a difference for the two diets.*

The plan for execution of the experiment is called the **design** of the experiment. The previous example illustrated simple design, but sometimes more complicated designs are required. For example, an experiment may include **blocking** to create similar groups for comparison, such as males and females. A **placebo** may also be included with human subjects. First, we will offer a few definitions and then we will look at different ways to describe and to diagram these other experimental designs.

BLOCKING. Divide the subjects into groups (called blocks) that contain some key common factors that may be related to the response, preventing us from concluding the changes are due just to the treatment, if they are not studied separately. For example, heart medication may have a different effect on men and women. With this noted, the subjects should first be divided into blocks by gender prior to randomly assigning subjects to the treatments.

CONTROL. A control group is a group that exists to provide a comparison with treatment group(s). For example, if there is an existing heart medication, the control group would continue taking this and doing all things as usual. This helps determine if the new medication is actually causing a change to occur.

PLACEBO. A placebo is given to disguise the identity of the treatment from experimental units that might react to this knowledge—such as humans. For example, one group might get a harmless sugar pill. This harmless pill is called a placebo. It looks just like the actual treatment. In the heart example, let's say there is not a current treatment for the particular condition of interest. In this case, a sugar pill of the same size and color would be given to the control group, so the researchers could see if the new drug actually works or if just having the idea of treatment is actually affecting the response.

REPLICATE. Replication involves applying the treatments to a number of different subjects within the experiment in order to have any extraneous effects "even out" in the long run. This implies that we have at least two experimental units for each treatment (and usually you would want more than two).

AP® Tip

Every experiment should include the following components:

- Randomization

- Imposing a treatment

- Control of any extraneous variables that might also affect the response (blocking is one example)

- Replication.

Be sure the AP® readers can see a clear indication of these four components in your written description of the experimental design.

SAMPLE PROBLEM 4 A pharmaceutical company has just developed a new medication for use with adults who are experiencing mild memory loss. Researchers have identified 500 women and 600 men who are experiencing some memory loss and who are willing to participate in this study. Currently, there is an older product on the market that seems to result in minor improvement in most patients. Design an experiment to evaluate the effect of this new medication.

SOLUTION TO PROBLEM 4

Since men and women may react differently to the drug, we will block on gender. Number the women 001–500. Then, go to the random number table and select three-digit numbers from a randomly selected row. The first 250 numbers chosen will determine which women are assigned to the new drug. The remaining 250 women will receive the old memory drug. Any numbers that are repeated or not in the range 001–500 on the random digits table will be skipped. Next, number the men 001–600. Again, start on a randomly selected line on the random number table and select three-digit numbers. The first 300 numbers will be the men assigned to the new drug while the remaining 300 will receive the old memory drug. Any repeats or numbers outside the range 001–600 on the random digits table will be discarded and another number will be chosen until we have the first 300 men assigned to the new treatment.

CONFOUNDING VARIABLES

As the researcher attempts to ensure that only the treatment is causing any difference in results to occur, close monitoring for potential **confounding variables** must always be considered. A confounding variable is one that wasn't considered a factor in the experiment but may be affecting the response variable. The presence of a confounding variable clouds the interpretation of the results of an experiment. If there are confounding variables, any differences in response for the treatment groups cannot be attributed solely to the treatments. If there are potentially confounding variables that are known, we attempt to eliminate their potential effect by holding them constant. We count on the random assignment of subjects to treatments to even out the effects of other potentially confounding variables. This is why random assignment to treatment groups is so important in the design of an experiment.

MATCHED PAIRS

One way to avoid many potentially confounding variables is by having the same subject try both treatments or find pairs of subjects that resemble each other. For example, if a vitamin is being compared, two women who are twins could be identified. Genetically, they are closely related so once identified, one woman would be randomly assigned to vitamin X and the other vitamin Y. Their results would be matched up and compared. Another type of matched pairs is a before and after study, where the response is measured before and again after some treatment. Blocking/matching is a very powerful experimental tool in controlling for confounding variables.

BLIND VERSUS DOUBLE BLIND

Finally, we consider the concept of blinding. **Blinding** occurs when the subjects or the person measuring the response do not know which treatment was received. As in the previous drug study, if the drugs look the same, then the participants receiving the old or new drug will not know which medication is the new drug or which drug they are receiving. **Double blinding** occurs when neither the subject nor the person measuring the response knows which treatment has been assigned. This can easily be accomplished by having the medications coded and given to the assistants that come in contact with the subject. The assistants know which bottle to give the participant, but have no knowledge of which treatment is in the bottle. The benefit here is that the research team will avoid making any comments to the subject that could lead toward biased results.

SAMPLE PROBLEM 5 A local clinic has found 30 volunteers willing to participate in a study involving a new treatment for anxiety. All 30 volunteers meet the necessary requirements of anxiety levels to participate.

(a) Explain how the subjects in the experiment could be blinded.

(b) How could double-blinding be accomplished?

(c) Could a placebo be added to this study? Explain.

SOLUTION TO PROBLEM 5

(a) Once the volunteers have been randomly assigned to either the old treatment or the new treatment, they would be given their medications each month. Both medications should look the same, so the patients wouldn't know if they were getting the old or the new treatment.

(b) To make this double-blind, it would be important that the individuals coming in contact with the patients and who evaluate the response to the treatment also not know which medication each patient received. This can easily be done by having the medications arrive with the patient's name on the bottle, so the individual administering the treatment and measuring the response wouldn't know whether the patient was receiving treatment A or B. The researcher in charge of gion.xperiment will know which patient received A or B and have all this information recorded.

(c) Yes. By simply adding a third group (that is, dividing the 30 subjects into three groups of 10), this could be done. The third group would also get a treatment but it would in fact be a harmless sugar pill that had no active ingredient.

AP® Tip

Stratification is to	Blocking is to
Observational Studies **as**	**Experimental Designs**
Strata are homogeneous groups, and because a random sample is selected from each stratum, all strata are represented in the sample.	Blocks are homogeneous groups and all treatments are tried within each block.

Collecting Data Sensibly: Student Objectives for the AP® Exam

- You should be able to determine if a study is an observational study or an experiment.
- You should be able to identify potential sources of bias and provide an explanation of the bias.
- You should be able to choose an appropriate sample for an observational study or an experiment.
- You should be able to describe an appropriate experimental design for a particular study.
- You should be able to use blocking to improve an experiment when warranted.
- You should be able to describe an appropriate sampling plan for a given observational study.
- You should be able to describe how to select a simple random sample using a random digits table, your calculator, or another method such as drawing names/numbers from a hat.
- You should be able to incorporate blinding and double blinding into an experimental design when appropriate.

Multiple-Choice Questions

1. A political polling group is interested in learning about the proportion of registered voters who favor a particular candidate for mayor. Their sampling plan may have introduced bias if
   (A) individuals were selected randomly to participate from a list of city-registered voters.
   (B) every 50th person on a list of registered voters was contacted and asked to identify who they would vote for in the upcoming election.
   (C) selected list of registered voters was first separated into two lists—one of males and one of females. Then individuals were selected at random from each of the two lists.
   (D) a survey was mailed to all registered voters and those who returned the survey make up the sample.
   (E) None of the above sampling plans creates the potential for bias.

2. Which of the following is not a necessary component of a well-designed experiment?
   (A) Imposing a treatment
   (B) Random assignment
   (C) Replication
   (D) Control of extraneous variables
   (E) Random selection of subjects

3. Which of the following is always problematic in a designed experiment?
   (A) No placebo is used.
   (B) Systematic sampling is used instead of random sampling to select subjects.
   (C) Subjects are not randomly assigned to treatments.
   (D) No control group is used.
   (E) Volunteers are randomly assigned to treatments.

4. A garden club wants to use a new fertilizer on its prize petunia patch in hopes of increasing the number of petunias produced per patch. A club member suggests they set up an experiment to see if this fertilizer is better than the fertilizer they have used in previous years. The patch can be divided into eight sections in order to run this experiment. Four of the sections receive more sun while the other four sections receive more shade. Which would be the best way to assign fertilizers to the sections for this study?
   (A) Number the sections 1–8 and randomly pick four numbers from a hat to receive the new fertilizer and the remaining four would get the old fertilizer.
   (B) Number the four sections in the sun 1–4 and randomly assign the new fertilizer to two sections and the old fertilizer to the other two sections. Repeat this process with the shady sections.
   (C) Randomly assign one fertilizer to the sunny sections and the other fertilizer to the shady sections.
   (D) Put the new fertilizer down in all eight sections, and then grow petunias. Once these are harvested, repeat the process in all eight sections but now with the old fertilizer.
   (E) Choose either the shady or the sunny sections to experiment with and randomly assign one fertilizer to the two sections and one to the other two sections.

5. What is the best reason to recommend the use of a placebo in an experiment?
   (A) When there are sufficient resources to warrant the use of a placebo
   (B) If the existing treatment is one that the researcher doesn't want to be included in the study
   (C) If the placebo can be used with animals for the appearance of an alternate treatment
   (D) When there isn't an existing treatment and you want to be sure that the effect seen is not due just to the fact that the subjects feel they are being treated
   (E) To make sure the placebo works before using it on other studies

6. Two variables are considered to be confounded if
   (A) they are both studied as part of the experiment.
   (B) their effects on the response variable cannot be separated.
   (C) more than one additional treatment group is included in the experiment.
   (D) the response variable is controlled by a placebo.
   (E) neither variable is related to the response variable.

7. The key difference between an observational study and an experiment is
   (A) the number of variables that are being studied.
   (B) the use of a randomized selection for participation.
   (C) the ability to replicate the study.
   (D) the creation of groups of homogenous subjects to study.
   (E) the assignment of treatments to experimental units.

8. Which of the following doesn't reflect some form of bias?
   (A) Choosing AP® students to survey regarding their GPA in order to estimate the average GPA in a school
   (B) Polling a group of potential voters outside a Republican campaign office in order to estimate the proportion of city residents who favor a particular candidate
   (C) Surveying people who work in the marketing department of a large corporation in order to assess employee satisfaction with management policies
   (D) Choosing a stratified random sample of juniors and seniors at a high school in order to estimate the proportion of juniors and seniors who plan to go on to college
   (E) Asking shoppers leaving a grocery store if they think groceries should cost less in order to estimate the proportion of city residents who think groceries cost too much

9. A church board wants to survey church members to see which times they prefer to have services. The board wants to ensure that members who have families attending as well as members who are single adults are represented in the sample. Which method will yield the best chance of getting a representative sample of their members' opinions?
   (A) Send a survey to a random sample of 50 members and ask them to return it in a self-addressed envelope that was sent with the survey.
   (B) Separate church membership into two lists: families and singles. Select a random sample from each of the two lists and contact the selected members for their opinion via phone, email, or interview after a service.
   (C) After a service, have a designated person survey every nth person as they leave the service.
   (D) Call a meeting of members and survey those who attend the meeting.
   (E) Send an email survey to a sample of members who have published their email addresses in the church directory.

10. Which of the following are true statements?
    I. Convenience samples are rarely useful.
    II. Every good experiment includes blocking.
    III. Experiments should always include a placebo.
    (A) I only
    (B) II only
    (C) I and II
    (D) I and III
    (E) I, II, and III

11. Why is double-blinding used in an experiment?
    (A) To avoid influencing the response by having knowledge of the treatment given
    (B) To insure that the treatments are randomly given to all subjects each time
    (C) To keep all subjects unaware of which treatment they are receiving
    (D) To avoid talking to the subjects at any time
    (E) To easily replicate an experiment in other environments

12. A car manufacturer is concerned about the time it is taking for batteries to be installed on the assembly line. The use of a new tool has been suggested to reduce time spent on this part of the assembly process. Which of the following would be the best way to establish if this new tool reduces battery installation time compared to the old tool?
    (A) Randomly assign pairs of two workers to perform the task. One would be assigned to use the old tool and the other worker to use the new tool.
    (B) Have day shift workers use the new tool and night shift workers use the old tool.
    (C) Have each worker use both tools for a day. Each worker would flip a coin to determine which tool would be used on the first day.
    (D) Randomly assign four workers one task to be performed for a month and then change to the other assembly task for a month.
    (E) Assign two different assembly lines of workers to use one of the tools and then compare the two lines.

13. Five thousand menopausal women are participating in a biofeedback regimen to see if this will help relieve the symptoms of menopause. Half of the women were randomly assigned to a group that received a biofeedback regimen while the other half were assigned to a control group and not given any treatment.
    This is an example of
    (A) an observational study.
    (B) a simple randomized comparison experiment.
    (C) a single-blind randomized comparison experiment.
    (D) a double-blind randomized comparison experiment.
    (E) a matched-pairs, double-blind randomized comparison experiment.

Questions 14–15 refer to the following experiment.

The mathematics department wants to see if the use of a software program will improve scores in geometry. The department has decided to set up a small experiment with 10 sections of geometry. Two teachers have volunteered to participate and use their sections of geometry. Ms. Smith is going to use the software alongside existing classroom materials while Mr. Jones is going to use the current classroom materials only. Each teacher will use five sections of geometry taught in periods 1 through 5. The students will be given a pretest as well as a posttest at the end of the course.

14. What are the treatments in this experiment?
    (A) Students taking the course
    (B) The time of day of the course
    (C) The teacher
    (D) Software or no software
    (E) Posttest results

15. What variable is confounded with the treatments in this experiment?
    (A) Students taking the course
    (B) The time of day of the course
    (C) The teacher
    (D) Software or no software
    (E) Posttest results

FREE-RESPONSE PROBLEMS

1. An athletic company has seen declining sales of its weight lifting gloves. Company executives feel that a competing company has a glove that lasts longer and hence gyms and stores are selling more of the competitors' product. To regain its market share, it has developed a newer material that it believes will outlast its current product. You have been called in to advise the executives in setting up and carrying out an appropriate study to determine if gloves made of the new fabric last longer than gloves made with the fabric currently in use.

   (a) There are 84 men and 56 women who are willing to participate in this study. Design an experiment that the company could use to determine if the new gloves last longer.

   (b) Is there a way to make this study double-blind? Justify your answer.

2. Ms. Partridge grows Japanese pears as well as Bosc pears for a living. She has learned of a new cross-pollination technique with another pear strain that may yield a larger, sweeter pear. Ms. Partridge has two of each type tree for use in this study and she would like to know whether cross-pollination with the Japanese pear trees or cross-pollination with the Bosc pear trees will yield a better fruit.

   (a) Describe how you would assign the four trees to four planting locations in a completely randomized design.

   (b) The actual plot of land she will use for this study is shown below. You notice that a stream runs along the northern edge of the land. Explain how you would assign the four trees to the four planting locations shown in the diagram.

   (c) What are some potential confounding variables that could affect the results of this study?

Answers

MULTIPLE-CHOICE QUESTIONS

1. **(D)** This sampling method introduces the possibility of nonresponse bias (*Statistics: Learning from Data*, AP Edition, 1st ed. pages 13–21 / 2nd ed. pages 9–20).

2. **(E)** Although desirable, random selection of subjects is not a requirement for a well-designed experiment. Many experiments use volunteers. Random assignment of subjects to treatments is critical (*Statistics: Learning from Data*, AP Edition, 1st ed. pages 24–38 / 2nd ed. pages 23–38).

3. **(C)** If subjects are not randomly assigned to treatments, the possibility of confounding variables makes it impossible to be sure that any differences in response are actually due to the treatments (*Statistics: Learning from Data*, AP Edition, 1st ed. pages 24–38 / 2nd ed. pages 23–38).

4. **(B)** It would be best to try each type of fertilizer in the various environmental conditions. This plan ensures that each fertilizer is in each type of environment (*Statistics: Learning from Data*, AP Edition, 1st ed. pages 24–38 / 2nd ed. pages 23–38).

5. **(D)** The purpose of a placebo is to offer a treatment that has no active ingredient but that makes the participants believe they are receiving a treatment. This will allow researchers to determine if the actual treatment being tested is working or if simply the idea of having a treatment is helping. Using a placebo is only important when the subjects in the experiment are people (*Statistics: Learning from Data*, AP Edition, 1st ed. pages 24–38 / 2nd ed. pages 23–38).

6. **(B)** Confounding is what occurs when a study is performed and the effects of some variables on the response variable can't be distinguished (*Statistics: Learning from Data*, AP Edition, 1st ed. pages 24–38 / 2nd ed. pages 23–38).

7. **(E)** In an experiment, the researcher applies a treatment. However, in an observational study, we are just observing what is or is not being done. The experiment allows for a cause and effect relationship to be discovered where an observational study cannot make such a discovery (*Statistics: Learning from Data*, AP Edition, 1st ed. pages 9–11 / 2nd ed. pages 5–7).

8. **(D)** This is the only choice without a clear bias in the initial design. Here, a sample of juniors and seniors will be chosen. The problem with A is the use of only an AP® class as they may tend to have higher GPAs. B is biased as one would expect folks outside a campaign office to more closely follow the views of that political party. C only includes those who work in marketing and there are other groups of company employees that would be excluded from the study. Finally, E is biased as shoppers may have a sense of buyer's remorse after just paying for their groceries (*Statistics: Learning from Data*, AP Edition, 1st ed. pages 13–21 / 2nd ed. pages 9–20).

9. **(B)** This choice has made an attempt to consider both types of members. Each of the other options potentially misses groups of individuals. For example, Choices A and D are problematic as there could be nonresponse bias (*Statistics: Learning from Data*, AP Edition, 1st ed. pages 13–21 / 2nd ed. pages 9–20).

10. **(A)** Convenience samples are problematic and should be avoided. Not all experiments require blocking or a placebo group—it depends on the nature of the experiment (*Statistics: Learning from Data*, AP Edition, 1st ed. 1st ed. pages 13–21 / 2nd ed. pages 9–20).

11. **(A)** The key purpose of a double-blind experiment is to avoid having knowledge of which treatment a particular subject received and possibly influence the response. This can sometimes occur if the subjects or the persons measuring the response know which treatment was received (*Statistics: Learning from Data*, AP Edition, 1st ed. pages 24–38 / 2nd ed. pages 23–38).

12. **(C)** While several of the methods would have pairs randomly assigned to either the old or the new tool for the results to be compared, only C is also attempting to control for the work and skill of an individual employee (*Statistics: Learning from Data*, AP Edition, 1st ed. pages 24–38 / 2nd ed. pages 23–38).

13. **(B)** This is an experiment where subjects are randomly assigned to one of two groups. Because one group receives a biofeedback regimen and the other does not, it is not possible to blind the subjects in this experiment (*Statistics: Learning from Data*, AP Edition, 1st ed. pages 24–38 / 2nd ed. pages 23–38).

14. **(D)** There are two treatments in this experiment—software and no software (*Statistics: Learning from Data*, AP Edition, 1st ed. pages 24–38 / 2nd ed. pages 23–38).

15. **(C)** Because one teacher has all of the software sections and the other teacher has all of the no-software sections, it will not be possible to distinguish the effect of the software from a teacher effect (*Statistics: Learning from Data*, AP Edition, 1st ed. pages 24–38 / 2nd ed. pages 23–38).

FREE-RESPONSE PROBLEMS

1. (a) Because men and women may lift weights differently, it makes sense to block on gender. It also makes sense in this setting to use a matched-pairs design, with each participant using one glove of each type. For the block consisting of the 84 males, number the men from 01 to 84. Then use a table of random digits or a random number generator to select 42 distinct two-digit numbers ignoring 00 and 85–99. These 42 men will receive a pair of gloves that uses the new fabric in the right-hand glove and the old fabric in the left-hand glove. The other 42 men will receive a pair of gloves with the old fabric used for the right-hand glove and the new fabric for the left-hand glove. This same process will be repeated for the women, except they will be numbered 01–56 and we will use random numbers to select 28 distinct two-digit numbers ignoring 00 and 57–99. These 28 women will receive a pair of gloves where the right glove is the new fabric and left glove is the old fabric and the other 28 women will receive a pair of gloves where the right glove is the old fabric and the left glove is the new fabric. See the diagram below to see this carried out and notice that the gloves will be compared by looking at the difference in wear for each person.

```
                              42   Right glove is              Compare
                         ┌──────── new fabric ── Measure ── difference in wear ──┐
            84 Males  Randomly                              for each person      │
         ┌──────────  assign                                                      │
         │              └──────── Left glove is ── Measure ── Compare             │
         │              42        new fabric                  difference in wear ─┤
Block on │                                                    for each person    │
gender ──┤                                                                       ├── Compile results
         │              28   Right glove is              Compare                  │
         │         ┌──────── new fabric ── Measure ── difference in wear ────────┤
         │ 56 Females Randomly                         for each person            │
         └────────── assign                                                       │
                        └──────── Left glove is ── Measure ── Compare             │
                        28        new fabric                  difference in wear ─┘
                                                              for each person
```

(b) Double-blinding is possible. Blinding the subjects would be accomplished by making sure the subjects don't know which glove is made with the new fabric and which is made with the old fabric. This will work if the materials look and feel the same and if they are handed out or assigned to subjects without them knowing the difference. Blinding the individual who is measuring the wear at the end of the 3 months is also possible. The gloves could be coded on the inside in a way that only the research team who will analyze the wear data would know what the code means.

(*Statistics: Learning from Data*, AP Edition, 1st ed. pages 24–38 / 2nd ed. pages 23–38)

2. (a) One way to randomize the four trees would be to number these 1–4 with 1 and 2 representing the Japanese pear trees and 3 and 4 the Bosc pear trees. Go to a planting location and roll a die. Place the corresponding tree in that location (roll again if a 5 or a 6 appears on the die). Repeat for the next planting locations and remember that any numbers corresponding to trees that have already been assigned a location should be ignored along with any 5's and 6's.

(b) Since there is a stream, there could be a difference in growing conditions close to the stream. In this case, you should block the two planting locations closest to the water (shaded sections) and randomly assign one of each type of tree to the locations in this block. Go to the top left shaded plot and flip a coin. If heads comes up, put in a Japanese tree. If tails comes up, put in Bosc. The other shaded plot will get the other type tree. Repeat for the unshaded region.

Ex: 1st flip = tails. Bosc tree goes here, so the Japanese tree will go here.

(c) A variety of confounding variables could be given to meet this part of the problem. A complete answer will include the confounding variable and why it confounds the results. The type of soil is a confounding variable. It is possible that the Japanese pear tree grows better in the type of soil that is on Ms. Partridge's farm. In this case, Japanese pear would give the better fruit but it is impossible to know if the cross-pollination or the soil is the cause of the better fruit. Other possible cofounding variables would include unknown health of the trees that are planted or any type of bug or animal that is a hindrance to one of the types of trees (that is, maybe local deer are drawn to the new Bosc cross-pollinated and they eat the fruit).

(*Statistics: Learning from Data*, AP Edition, 1st ed. pages 24–38 / 2nd ed. pages 23–38)

5

PROBABILITY

What is the chance you will be admitted to your first-choice university? How likely is it that Rory McIlroy will win the Masters Golf Tournament this year? What does it mean when the meteorologist on the evening news predicts rain with a 70% probability? Uncertainty surrounds us on a daily basis, but we still can make decisions based on available information. Understanding probability will help you to make well-informed decisions.

OBJECTIVES

- Be able to interpret probabilities as long-run relative frequencies.
- Understand the Law of Large Numbers in the context of probability.
- Be able to calculate the probability of an even using the complement, addition, and multiplication rules.
- Understand what it means to say that two events are independent.
- Be able to compute and interpret conditional probabilities.
- Be able to use simulation to estimate probabilities.

CHANCE EXPERIMENTS AND EVENTS

(*Statistics: Learning from Data*, AP Edition, 1st ed. pages 273–276 and 278–287 / 2nd ed. pages 285–289 and 291–301)

Consider a chance experiment where Sally is trying to decide what to have for dinner at the local diner. The limited menu includes three entrees: hamburger, pizza, and chef's salad; and two desserts: apple pie and carrot cake. Although we don't know what Sally's selections will be, if we know that Sally will choose one entree and one dessert, we can describe the complete set of possible outcomes.

The collection of all possible outcomes of a chance experiment is the **sample space** for the experiment. The sample space for the menu selection example consists of six outcomes.

1. {Hamburger, Apple Pie}
2. {Hamburger, Carrot Cake}
3. {Pizza, Apple Pie}
4. {Pizza, Carrot Cake}
5. {Chef's Salad, Apple Pie}
6. {Chef's Salad, Carrot Cake}

The sample space can also be illustrated using a tree diagram (shown below).

```
            ┌── Apple Pie
   Hamburger
            └── Carrot Cake

            ┌── Apple Pie
•── Pizza
            └── Carrot Cake

              ┌── Apple Pie
   Chef's Salad
              └── Carrot Cake
```

An **event** is any collection of outcomes from the sample space of a chance experiment. A **simple event** is an event consisting of exactly one outcome.

> EXAMPLE Consider a chance experiment where every year eight basketball teams compete in a basketball tournament. Suppose we are interested in the tournament outcome—the team that wins the tournament. The teams competing are:
>
> D = Duke Blue Devils V = Vanderbilt Commodores
>
> R = Rutgers Scarlet Knights T = Texas Longhorns
>
> M = Michigan Wolverines S = Southern Mississippi Golden Eagles
>
> G = Georgia Bulldogs B = Bradley Braves
>
> What is the sample space?
>
> SOLUTION The sample space is $\{D, R, M, G, V, T, S, B\}$.

In the previous example, each outcome is a simple event. A **compound event** is an event that is made up of two or more simple events. Three common types of compound events are unions, intersections, and complements.

The event <u>not A</u> consists of all outcomes that are not in event A. Not A is sometimes called the **complement** of A and is usually denoted by A^C, A', or $\overline{A}$.

The event <u>A or B</u> consists of all outcomes that are in at least one of the two events, that is, A or B consists of all outcomes that are in A or in B or in both of these. A or B is called the **union** of the two events, and is often denoted by $A \cup B$.

The event <u>A and B</u> consists of all outcomes that are in both of the events A and B. A and B is called the **intersection** of the two events, and is often denoted by $A \cap B$.

> EXAMPLE In the context of the basketball tournament, consider these events:
>
> P = a private school wins the tournament
>
> C = a school with a color in its name wins the tournament
>
> A = a school with an animal in its name wins the tournament

List the outcomes in each of the following events:

(a) the complement of A

(b) A or C

(c) A and C

SOLUTION

(a) The complement of A (the same as not A) consists of all schools that do not have an animal in its name: {D, R, V, B}. This solution is also shown visually in the Venn diagram below.

(b) The event A or C consists of all schools that have a color in its name, an animal in its name, or both a color and an animal in its name: {D, R, M, G, T, S}. This can be seen visually in the Venn diagram below by looking at all schools in either of the two circles or in both circles.

(c) The event A and C consists of all schools that have both a color and an animal in its name: {S}. This can be seen visually in the Venn diagram above by looking at all schools that are in both circles.

Events that have no common outcomes are said to be **disjoint** or **mutually exclusive**. The events P and A are disjoint events since the private schools are Duke and Vanderbilt and neither of these schools has an animal in its name.

Definition of Probability

(*Statistics: Learning from Data*, AP Edition, 1st ed. pages 267–276 / 2nd ed. pages 280–289)

Definition (Classical Approach)

If the outcomes in the sample space are equally likely, then for any event E, the probability of event E occurring, $P(E)$, is

$$P(E) = \frac{\text{number of outcomes in event } E}{\text{number of outcomes in the sample space}}$$

Note that it is only appropriate to use this approach to compute a probability if the outcomes in the sample space are equally likely.

> **Example** Paul practices the piano every morning. His repertoire consists of 8 classical pieces and 23 popular pieces. If he randomly selects one piece to play, what is the probability that it will be classical?
>
> **Solution** The sample space consists of the 31 pieces that Paul might play. Because he is selecting a piece at random, the outcomes in the sample space are equally likely. Let C = the event that a classical piece is chosen. Then since the number of outcomes in C is 8 and the total number of outcomes in the sample space is $8 + 23 = 31$, $P(C) = \frac{8}{31}$.

Law of Large Numbers

As the number of repetitions of a chance experiment increases, the relative frequency of the occurrence of an event approaches the true, or theoretical, probability of the event.

As an illustration, when we repeatedly spin the spinner shown below and calculate the relative frequency of landing in the shaded area, there is fluctuation over the short term but there is stability over the long term. Notice in the graph below that after a large number of spins, the relative frequency settles at about 0.75.

Definition (Relative Frequency Approach)

For any event E, the estimated probability of event E is

$$P(E) \approx \frac{\text{number of times } E \text{ occurs}}{\text{number of repetitions}}$$

The estimated probability should be close to the actual probability if the number of repetitions is large.

EXAMPLE Suppose we repeatedly flip a metal thumbtack to determine whether it will land with tip up or tip down. The results of the first 10 flips were:

Flip	1	2	3	4	5	6	7	8	9	10
Outcome	Down	Up	Down	Down	Up	Up	Up	Down	Down	Down

What is the estimated probability that the tack will land point up?

SOLUTION

Flip	1	2	3	4	5	6	7	8	9	10
Outcome	Down	Up	Down	Down	Up	Up	Up	Down	Down	Down
Cumulative Count of Ups	0	1	1	1	2	3	4	4	4	4
Relative Frequency of Ups	0	0.50	0.33	0.25	0.40	0.50	0.57	0.50	0.44	0.40

Notice that the estimated probability of event E is $P(E) = \frac{4}{10} = 0.40$.

The relative frequencies fluctuate quite a bit over the 10 repetitions, so it does not appear that the relative frequency has settled down yet. The law of large numbers says that if we continue this process so that we had many more repetitions, the estimated probability should be close to the actual probability.

BASIC PROPERTIES OF PROBABILITY

(*Statistics: Learning from Data*, AP Edition, 1st ed. pages 273–276 and 278–287 / 2nd ed. pages 285–289 and 291–301)

There are four basic rules of probability. They are:

1. For any event E, $0 \leq P(E) \leq 1$.

2. If S is the sample space for an experiment, $P(S) = 1$.

3. If two events are disjoint, then $P(E \text{ or } F) = P(E) + P(F)$.

    Two events are said to be disjoint if they cannot occur at the same time.

    [If two events are not disjoint, then $P(E \text{ or } F) = P(E) + P(F) - P(E \text{ and } F)$.]

4. For any event E, $P(E) + P(\text{not } E) = 1$.

   EXAMPLE A survey was taken in which students enrolled in AP® Statistics at a particular high school were asked what type of music they preferred most. The resulting data are shown in the table below.

Genre	Rock	Rap	Country
Number of Students	32	18	25

   If an AP® Statistics student at this school is selected at random, what is the probability that the student's preferred type of music is Rap or Rock?

   SOLUTION

   $$P(\text{Rap or Rock}) = P(\text{Rap}) + P(\text{Rock}) = \frac{32}{75} + \frac{18}{75} = \frac{50}{75} = \frac{2}{3}$$

   EXAMPLE Brett counted the change he had placed in the console of his car and found 7 quarters, 10 dimes, 4 nickels, and 9 pennies. If he randomly selects one coin, what is the probability it was *not* a penny?

   SOLUTION Using the complement rule (basic rule 4),

   $$P(\text{not Penny}) = 1 - P(\text{Penny}) = 1 - \frac{9}{30} = \frac{21}{30} = \frac{7}{10}$$

AP® Tip

When answering probability questions

1. Clearly define the event(s) of interest.
2. Use appropriate notation, that is, $P(X > 3)$ or $P(A \cap B)$.
3. When appropriate, illustrate your method with a Venn diagram or a tree diagram.
4. Show all relevant calculations.

CONDITIONAL PROBABILITY

(*Statistics: Learning from Data*, AP Edition, 1st ed. pages 290–299 / 2nd ed. pages 304–314)

In certain situations, knowing that one event has occurred will alter the probability that another event also occurred. For example, suppose your friend rolls one die. If your friend then tells you that the number showing is even, your assessment of the probability that the number rolled was a 2 would change from 1/6 to 1/3.

The **conditional probability** of event E given that event F has occurred, denoted by $P(E \mid F)$ is defined as

$$P(E \mid F) = \frac{P(E \text{ and } F)}{P(F)}$$

AP® is trademark registered by the College Board, which was not involved in the production of, and does not endorse, this product.

EXAMPLE Suppose that you have torn a tendon and are facing surgery to repair it. The orthopedic surgeon explains the risks to you. Infection occurs in 3% of such operations, the repair fails in 14%, and both infection and failure occur together in 1%. Find the probability that a randomly selected patient who has this surgery has a failed repair given that an infection occurred.

SOLUTION Let I = person gets an infection and F = the repair fails. Then, $P(I) = 0.03$, $P(F) = 0.14$, and $P(I \text{ and } F) = 0.01$.

$$P(F \mid I) = \frac{P(F \text{ and } I)}{P(I)} = \frac{0.01}{0.03} = 0.333$$

INDEPENDENCE

(*Statistics: Learning from Data*, AP Edition, 1st ed. pages 302–308 / 2nd ed. pages 318–323)

Two events E and F are said to be **independent** if $P(E \mid F) = P(E)$. In other words, this means that the occurrence of event F has not changed the probability of event E. If E and F are not independent, they are said to be **dependent** events.

MULTIPLICATION RULE FOR TWO INDEPENDENT EVENTS

The events E and F are independent if and only if $P(E \cap F) = P(E) \times P(F)$.

GENERAL MULTIPLICATION RULE

Given two events, E and F, $P(E \cap F) = P(E) \times P(F \mid E)$.

EXAMPLE Determine if events A and B are independent.

(a) $P(A) = 0.5$, $P(B) = 0.7$, $P(A \text{ and } B) = 0.3$

(b) $P(B \mid A) = 0.25$, $P(B \mid A') = 0.3$, $P(A) = 0.4$

(c) $P(A) = 2/3$, $P(B) = 1/2$, $P(A \text{ or } B) = 5/6$

(d) $P(A) = 0.5$, $P(\text{not } B) = 0.4$, $P(A \text{ or } B) = 0.9$

SOLUTION

(a) $P(A) = 0.5$, $P(B) = 0.7$, $P(A \text{ and } B) = 0.3$. $P(A) \times P(B) = 0.35$. Since $P(A) \times P(B) \neq P(A \text{ and } B)$, events A and B are not independent.

(b) $P(B \mid A) = 0.25$, $P(B \mid A') = 0.3$, $P(A) = 0.4$. This means that the occurrence (or lack of occurrence) of A changes the probability of B occurring. So since $P(B \mid A) \neq P(B \mid A')$, events A and B are not independent.

(c) $P(A) = 2/3$, $P(B) = 1/2$, $P(A \text{ or } B) = 5/6$. $P(A) \times P(B) = 1/3$. $P(A \text{ and } B) = P(A) + P(B) - P(A \text{ or } B) = 2/3 + 1/2 - 5/6 = 1/3$. Since $P(A) \times P(B) = P(A \text{ and } B)$, events A and B are independent. Note: Start with the formula $P(A \text{ or } B) = P(A) + P(B) - P(A \text{ or } B)$ and solve for $P(A \text{ and } B)$ to find the formula used above.

(d) $P(A) = 0.5$, $P(\text{not } B) = 0.4$, $P(A \text{ or } B) = 0.9$. $P(B) = 1 - P(\text{not } B) = 0.6$. $P(A) \times P(B) = 0.3$.

$P(A \text{ and } B) = P(A) + P(B) - P(A \text{ or } B) = 0.5 + 0.6 - 0.9 = 0.2$. Since $P(A) \times P(B) \neq P(A \text{ and } B)$, events A and B are not independent.

SIMULATION

(*Statistics: Learning from Data*, AP Edition, 1st ed. pages 317–323 / 2nd ed. pages 333–340)

Simulation is an artificial recreation of a random process to study its long-run behavior. Random digits are often used to carry out a simulation. Steps to perform a simulation using a random digit table include the following:

1. State the assumptions you are making about how the real-life situation works. Include any doubts you have about the validity of your assumptions.

2. Describe how you will use random digits to conduct one trial of a simulation of the situation. Show how you will assign a digit (or a group of digits) to represent each possible outcome. You can disregard some digits if necessary. Explain how you will use the digits to model the real-life situation. Describe what constitutes a single trial and what observation you will record.

3. Run the simulation a large number of times, recording the results in a frequency table.

4. Write a conclusion in context. Be sure to state that what you have computed is an estimated probability.

> EXAMPLE Suppose 70% of Beach High School students approve of a new uniform. You would like to estimate the probability that if five students are selected at random, all five approve of the new uniform. Use the list of random digits below to carry out 20 trials of simulation that would allow you to estimate this probability.
>
> 2039 2993 4362 6363 2914 4955 6364 5237 6456 5561
>
> 0176 2425 2968 3834 6077 4302 3499 9938 7231 2136
>
> 2161 1365 2764 7836 1584 2421 4247 2930 0783 9989
>
> 0407 1760 7048 1929 9034 0242 0753 4851 9465 0791
>
> SOLUTION Each student in the sample of five will be represented by a single random digit. Since 70% of students approve of the new uniform, let the digits 0 through 6 represent a student who approves of a new uniform and digits 7–9 represent a student who does not approve of the new uniform. A block of five random digits then represents a sample of five students. Count the number in the sample who approve (this is the number of digits in the block of 5 that are 0–6). Record whether or not all five students favor the new uniform. This is one trial. Repeat this process 19 more times to complete 20 trials. Notice that in this situation, repeated numbers are not ignored (in some problems, repeats symbolize a subject being chosen more than once and need to be ignored).

```
 2039    2993    4362    6368    2914    4955    6364    5237    6456    5561
  NO      NO     YES      NO      NO     YES     YES      NO     YES

 0176    2425    2968    3834    6077    4302    3499    9938    7231    2136
  NO      NO      NO      NO      NO     YES      NO      NO      NO     YES

 2161    1365    2764    7836    1584    2421    4247    2930    0783    9989
  YES     NO      NO      NO

 0407    1760    7048    1929    9034    0242    0753    4851    9465    0791
```

The estimated probability that all five selected students approve of the

$$\frac{\text{total number of yes trials}}{\text{total number of trials}} = \frac{6}{20} = 0.30.$$

PROBABILITY: STUDENT OBJECTIVES FOR THE AP® EXAM

- You should be able to interpret a probability in context.
- You should be able to interpret a long-run relative frequency as a probability.
- You should understand the concept of the law of large numbers.
- You should be able to calculate probabilities using the addition rule and the multiplication rule.
- You should be able to calculate and interpret a conditional probability.
- You should understand the concept of the independence.
- You should be able to determine whether or not two events are independent or not.
- You should be able to use simulation to estimate probabilities.

MULTIPLE-CHOICE QUESTIONS

1. In the fall of her senior year in high school, Carrie has begun to submit her college applications. Based on her research, she estimates the probability of her being admitted to the University of Georgia is 0.45, the probability of her being admitted to both the University of Georgia and Auburn University is 0.25, and the probability of her not being admitted to either is 0.10. What is her probability of being admitted to Auburn University?
   (A) 0.90
   (B) 0.45
   (C) 0.70
   (D) 0.20
   (E) 0.65

2. A recent survey of the employees at Aardvark Enterprises concerning their attitudes toward health care reform produced the following results.

		Type of Employee	
		Assembly Line Workers	Administrative Staff
Opinion on Health Care Reform	In Favor	127	13
	Opposed	42	31
	No Opinion	31	6

Considering only the employees who opposed health care reform, what is the probability that a randomly selected worker is on the administrative staff?

(A) $\dfrac{31}{73}$

(B) $\dfrac{31}{50}$

(C) $\dfrac{50}{250}$

(D) $\dfrac{31}{42}$

(E) $\dfrac{200}{250}$

3. The grade level breakdown at Bryans High School is as follows:

Freshman—32%, Sophomores—27%, Juniors—23%, Seniors—18%.

If a student at this school is selected at random, what is the probability the student is either a junior or a senior?
(A) 0.05
(B) 0.41
(C) 0.45
(D) 0.50
(E) 0.59

4. If $P(A) = 0.3$, $P(B) = 0.4$, and $P(\text{not } A \text{ and not } B) = 0.42$, are the events A and B disjoint? Are the events A and B independent?
(A) Disjoint; independent
(B) Not disjoint; not independent
(C) Disjoint; dependent
(D) Not disjoint; independent
(E) Cannot be determined

5. Each Saturday morning, Beau practices throwing pitches to his dad. His dad estimates the probability of any one pitch being a strike is 0.6. If pitches are independent, what is the probability that neither of Beau's next two pitches will be strikes?
   (A) 1.20
   (B) 0.48
   (C) 0.36
   (D) 0.16
   (E) 0

Questions 6–8 refer to the following information:

Suppose that 8% of all adults have a particular disease. Also suppose that a test for this disease returns a positive result for 96% of people who have the disease, but it also returns a positive result for 7% of people who do not have the disease.

6. What is the probability that a randomly selected adult has the disease and tests positive?
   (A) 0.0672
   (B) 0.0736
   (C) 0.0768
   (D) 0.08
   (E) 0.96

7. What is the probability that a randomly selected person tests positive for the disease?
   (A) 0.0768
   (B) 0.08
   (C) 0.1412
   (D) 0.144
   (E) 0.1536

8. If a person is selected at random and given the test and the test is positive, what is the probability that this person actually has the disease?
   (A) 0.0037
   (B) 0.0672
   (C) 0.0768
   (D) 0.1412
   (E) 0.5439

Questions 9–11 refer to the following information:

The 10,000 students at a polytechnic university were classified according to the type of program they were enrolled in (engineering, science, or mathematics) and their degree objective (B.S., M.S., or Ph.D.), as shown in the table below:

	B.S.	M.S.	Ph.D.	Total
Engineering	2142	1890	2268	6300
Science	368	432	800	1600
Math	882	630	588	2100
Total	3392	2952	3656	10000

9. What is the probability that a randomly selected student is in an M.S. program given that the student in not enrolled in a science program?
   (A) 0.0432
   (B) 0.0514
   (C) 0.2700
   (D) 0.3000
   (E) 1.0920

10. What is the probability that a randomly selected student is enrolled in a mathematics B.S. program?
    (A) 0.0882
    (B) 0.1606
    (C) 0.2600
    (D) 0.4200
    (E) 0.5492

11. What is the probability that a randomly selected student has a B.S. degree objective or is enrolled in an engineering program?
    (A) 0.2142
    (B) 0.3400
    (C) 0.6315
    (D) 0.7550
    (E) 0.9692

12. A weighted die is rolled 100 times and the results are given below. Find the estimated probability that, if this same die was rolled twice, the sum would be less than 4.

Number Shown	1	2	3	4	5	6
Frequency	15	10	6	9	30	30

    (A) 0.0150
    (B) 0.0300
    (C) 0.0375
    (D) 0.0525
    (E) 0.2100

Questions 13–14 refer to the following information:

Many fire stations handle emergency calls for medical assistance as well as those requesting firefighting equipment. A particular station says that the probability that an incoming call is for medical assistance is 0.85.

13. What is the probability that a call is not for medical assistance?
    (A) 0
    (B) 0.1275
    (C) 0.1500
    (D) 0.8500
    (E) 1

14. Assuming independence, calculate the probability that exactly one of the next two calls will be for medical assistance.
    (A) 0.0450
    (B) 0.2550
    (C) 0.7225
    (D) 0.8500
    (E) 0.9775

15. When we say that a coin is "fair," what does this mean?
    (A) That every occurrence of a head must be balanced by a tail in one of the next two or three tosses.
    (B) That if I flip the coin many, many times, the proportion of heads will be approximately one half, and this proportion will tend to get closer and closer to one half as the number of tosses increases.
    (C) That regardless of the number of flips, half will be heads and half will be tails.
    (D) Generally, the flips will alternate between heads and tails.
    (E) If a head is observed on the first four tosses, the probability of a tail on the fifth toss is greater than 50%.

FREE-RESPONSE PROBLEMS

1. At a certain high school, all students are required to take both physics and statistics. Suppose that the probability that a student earns an A in physics is one-fifth and that the probability that a student earns an A in statistics is one-fourth.
   (a) What is the probability that a student will earn an A in at least one of his or her physics or statistics courses if earning an A in physics and earning an A in statistics are INDEPENDENT?
   (b) What is the probability that a student will earn an A in at least one of their physics or statistics courses if the set of students who earn an A in physics is a subset of the set of students earning an A in statistics?
   (c) Now assume that of those who earned an A in physics, 90% of them also earned an A in statistics. Given that a student selected at random earned an A in statistics, what is the probability that student did *not* earn an A in physics?

2. A company has seven mathematicians on its staff, two of whom are women. The president of the company wonders what the probability of two or fewer female mathematicians on its staff is if there was no discrimination against women in the hiring process. Suppose that 40% of mathematicians are female.
   (a) Using the random digits below, carry out five trials of a simulation that could be used to estimate the probability of two or fewer females in a group of seven randomly selected mathematicians.
       88565 42628 17797 49376 61762 16953 88604 12724
       62964 88145 83083 69453 46109 59505 69680 00900
   (b) Based on your five trials from part (a), what is the estimated probability of two or fewer females in a group of seven randomly selected mathematicians?
   (c) Do you think your estimate in part (b) is likely to be very accurate? Explain.

Answers

MULTIPLE-CHOICE QUESTIONS

1. **(C)** Define the events: G = being admitted to Georgia, A = being admitted to Auburn. Given: $P(G) = 0.45$, $P(G \text{ and } A) = 0.25$, $P(\text{not } G \text{ and not } A) = 0.10$. Since $P(G) = 0.45$ and $P(G \text{ and } A) = 0.25$, then $P(G \text{ and not } A) = 0.20$ and since $P(\text{not } G \text{ and not } A) = 0.10$, then $P(G \text{ or } A) = 0.90$. Therefore, $P(A) = 0.70$ (*Statistics: Learning from Data*, AP Edition, 1st ed. pages 273–276 and 278–287 / 2nd ed. pages 285–289 and 291–301).

   ```
        G           A
      ┌─────┬─────┬─────┐
      │ 0.20│ 0.25│ 0.45│
      └─────┴─────┴─────┘
                      0.10
   ```

2. **(A)** Define events: O = oppose health care, A = administrative staff. Since there are 73 employees who oppose health care and 31 are on the administrative staff, $P(A \mid O) = \dfrac{31}{73}$ (*Statistics: Learning from Data*, AP Edition, 1st ed. pages 290–299 / 2nd ed. pages 304–314).

3. **(B)** Since the events junior and senior are disjoint, $P(\text{Junior or Senior}) = P(\text{Junior}) + P(\text{Senior}) = 0.27 + 0.18 = 0.41$ (*Statistics: Learning from Data*, AP Edition, 1st ed. pages 278–287 / 2nd ed. pages 291–301).

4. **(D)** Since $P(\text{not } A \text{ and not } B) = 0.42$, $P(A \text{ or } B) = 0.58$. Using the addition rule, $P(A \text{ and } B) = P(A) + P(B) - P(A \text{ or } B) = 0.3 + 0.4 - 0.58 = 0.12$. Since $P(A \text{ and } B) \neq 0$, A and B are not disjoint. Since $P(A) \times P(B) = P(A \text{ and } B)$, A and B are independent (*Statistics: Learning from Data*, AP Edition, 1st ed. pages 302–308 / 2nd ed. pages 318–323).

5. **(D)** $P(\text{not strike}) = .4$. Since pitches are independent of one another, $P(\text{not strike and not strike}) = P(\text{not strike}) \times P(\text{not strike}) = .4 \times .4 = .16$ (*Statistics: Learning from Data*, AP Edition, 1st ed. pages 302–308 / 2nd ed. pages 318–323).

In Problems 6–8, the following tree diagram may be helpful in keeping straight all of the possible probabilities.

```
         .08 ──── Disease ┬── .96 ──── Positive
        /                 └── .04 ──── Negative
  •────
        \                 ┌── .07 ──── Positive
         .92 ──── No Disease
                          └── .93 ──── Negative
```

6. **(C)** P(has disease and tests positive) = P(has disease) × P(tests positive | has disease) = $0.08 \times 0.96 = 0.0768$. Using the tree diagram, the top most branch represents P(has disease and tests positive).

```
         .08 ──── Disease ┬── .96 ──── Positive ──→ .08 * .96 = .0768
  •────                   └── .04 ──── Negative
```

(*Statistics: Learning from Data*, AP Edition, 1st ed. pages 302–308 / 2nd ed. pages 318–323)

7. **(C)** P(tests positive) = P(tests positive and has disease OR tests positive and does not have disease) = P(tests positive and has disease) + P(tests positive and does not have disease) = $(0.08 \times 96) + (0.07 \times 0.92)$ = 0.1412. Using the tree diagram, the two branches of interest end in a positive test result. This represents P(tests positive and has disease OR tests positive and does not have disease).

```
         .08 ──── Disease ┬── .96 ──── Positive ──→ .08 * .96 = .0768
        /                 └── .04 ──── Negative
  •────
        \                 ┌── .07 ──── Positive ──→ .92 * .07 = .0644
         .92 ──── No Disease
                          └── .93 ──── Negative
```

(*Statistics: Learning from Data*, AP Edition, 1st ed. pages 302–308 / 2nd ed. pages 318–323)

8. **(E)** P(has disease | tests positive) = P(has disease and tests positive) / P(tests positive) = 0.0768 / 0.1412 = 0.5439. The numerator and denominator here were found in the previous two problems (*Statistics: Learning from Data*, AP Edition, 1st ed. pages 302–308 / 2nd ed. pages 318–323).

9. **(D)** P(M.S. | engineering or math) = P(M.S. AND engineering or math) / P(engineering or math) = (0.1890 + 0.0630) / (0.63 + 0.21) = 252 / 0.84 = 0.3 (*Statistics: Learning from Data*, AP Edition, 1st ed. pages 302–308 / 2nd ed. pages 318–323).

10. **(A)** P(math and B.S.) = 882/10000 = 0.0882 (*Statistics: Learning from Data*, AP Edition, 1st ed. pages 302–308 / 2nd ed. pages 318–323).

11. **(A)** P(B.S. or engineering) = P(B.S.) + P(engineering) − P(B.S. and engineering) = 0.3392 + 0.6300 − 0.2142 = .7550 (*Statistics: Learning from Data*, AP Edition, 1st ed. pages 302–308 / 2nd ed. pages 318–323).

12. **(D)** P(sum less than 4) = P(1 and 1 OR 1 and 2 OR 2 and 1) = P(1 and 1) + P(1 and 2) + P(2 and 1) = 0.15 × 0.15 + 0.15 × 0.1 + 0.1 × 0.15 = 0525 (*Statistics: Learning from Data*, AP Edition, 1st ed. pages 302–308 / 2nd ed. pages 318–323).

13. **(C)** P(call is not for medical assistance) = 1 − (call is for medical assistance) = 1 − 0.85 = 0.15 (*Statistics: Learning from Data*, AP Edition, 1st ed. pages 302–308 / 2nd ed. pages 318–323).

14. **(B)** P(exactly one of two calls is for medical assistance) = P(first call is for medical assistance and the next call is not for medical assistance) + P(first call is not for medical assistance and the next call is for medical assistance) = (0.85 × 0.15) + (0.15 × 0.85) = 0.2550 (*Statistics: Learning from Data*, AP Edition, 1st ed. pages 302–308 / 2nd ed. pages 318–323).

15. **(B)** This is precisely what the Law of Large Numbers states will happen when a chance experiment is repeated a large number of times (*Statistics: Learning from Data*, AP Edition, 1st ed. pages 267–276 / 2nd ed. pages 280–289).

FREE-RESPONSE PROBLEMS

1. Given $P(\text{Physics}) = 0.2$ and $P(\text{Statistics}) = 0.25$
   $P(\text{Physics or Statistics}) = P(\text{Physics}) + P(\text{Statistics}) - P(\text{Physics and Statistics})$
   (a) Since the events are independent, $P(\text{Physics and Statistics}) = P(\text{Physics}) \times P(\text{Statistics})$.
   $P(\text{Physics or Statistics}) = P(\text{Physics}) + P(\text{Statistics}) - P(\text{Physics and Statistics}) = P(\text{Physics}) + P(\text{Statistics}) - (P(\text{Physics}) \times P(\text{Statistics})) = 0.2 + 0.25 - (0.2)(0.25) = 0.4$
   (b) Since the students getting an A in Physics are a subset of those students getting an A in Statistics, all students who make an A in Physics also make an A in Statistics. So, $P(\text{Physics and Statistics}) = 0.2$.
   $P(\text{Physics or Statistics}) = P(\text{Physics}) + P(\text{Statistics}) - P(\text{Physics and Statistics}) = 0.2 + 0.25 - 0.2 = 0.25$
   (c) $P(\text{A in Statistics}) = .25$. $P(\text{A in Physics AND A in Statistics}) = (0.2)(0.9) = 0.18$, making $P(\text{Not an A in Physics AND A in Statistics}) = 0.25 - 0.18 = 0.07$. $P(\text{Not an A in Physics} \mid \text{A in Statistics}) = P(\text{Not an A in Physics AND A in Statistics}) / P(\text{A in Statistics}) = 0.07/0.25 = 0.28$. A two-way table may be a helpful visual for this problem. Assume 100 students. From the given information, 20 total students will earn an A in Physics and 25 total will earn an A in Statistics. Since 90% of students who earn an A in Physics also earn an A in Statistics, that means 18 total students earned an A in both. This leaves $25 - 18 = 7$ students total who did not earn an A in Physics but did earn an A in Statistics. So, then $P(\text{Not an A in Physics} \mid \text{A in Statistics}) = 7/25 = 0.28$.

	A in Statistics	Not A in Statistics	Total
A in Physics	18		20
Not A in Physics	25 – 18 = 7		
Total	25		100

(*Statistics: Learning from Data*, AP Edition, 1st ed. pages 302–308 / 2nd ed. pages 318–323)

2. (a) Since 40% of mathematicians are female, let the digits 0–3 represent selecting a female mathematician and digits 4–9 represent selecting a male mathematician. A group of seven randomly selected mathematicians will be represented by seven digits in the random digit table. Count the number of female mathematicians and note whether two or fewer were women.
Do this five times.

88565	42628	17797	49376	61762	16953	88604	12724
1 female	2 females	1 female	3 females	2 females			

(b) In the five trials, four resulted in two or fewer women, so the estimated probability is 4/5 = 0.80.

(c) Because the estimate in part (b) is based on only five trials, it is not likely to be very accurate. Many more trials would need to be included in order for the estimated probability to be considered relatively accurate.

(*Statistics: Learning from Data*, AP Edition, 1st ed. pages 317–323 / 2nd ed. pages 333–340)

6

RANDOM VARIABLES AND PROBABILITY DISTRIBUTIONS

This chapter discusses the characteristics of random variables as well as the probability distributions used to describe the behavior of random variables.

OBJECTIVES

- Given a probability distribution, calculate probabilities for discrete and continuous random variables.
- Find the mean and standard deviation of a discrete random variable.
- Find the mean and standard deviation for linear combinations of random variables.
- Calculate probabilities of interest for binomial, geometric, and normal random variables.

RANDOM VARIABLES

(*Statistics: Learning from Data*, AP Edition, 1st ed. pages 337–338 / 2nd ed. pages 350–352)

A **random variable** is actually a function, one whose value depends on the outcome of a chance experiment. A **discrete** random variable is a function whose possible values consist of a set of individual points on the number line. For example, number of pets in a family would be a set of discrete values since the number of pets must be a whole number (0, 1, 2, 3, ...). A **continuous** random variable is one whose possible values consist of an entire interval on the number line. For example, the time it takes a student to get to school is a continuous random variable since time would include 5 minutes, 5.1 minutes, 5.01 minutes, or even 5.001 minutes. Sometimes the values of a continuous random variable are only measured to the nearest tenth or the nearest hundredth, but a continuous variable can theoretically take on any value in the interval. We will use variables, like x and y, to represent random variables.

A **probability distribution** for a discrete random variable is a model, typically represented as a table or a histogram, showing the probabilities associated with each of the possible values of the variable. These models help us study a variable's overall behavior and allow us to calculate probabilities based on the model. The probability distribution of a continuous random variable is represented by a curve and areas under the curve are interpreted as probabilities. We will use probability distributions to calculate probabilities for both discrete and continuous random variables.

PROBABILITY DISTRIBUTIONS FOR DISCRETE RANDOM VARIABLES

(*Statistics: Learning from Data*, AP Edition, 1st ed. pages 339–343/ 2nd ed. pages 353–357)

Since the possible values of discrete random variables are individual points, the probability distribution specifies a probability associated with each possible value. For example, consider the number of decorative coasters in sets sold by a souvenir store. The store sells coasters in sets of 2, 4, 6, and 8. In this case, the random variable being considered is x = *number of coasters in the coaster set sold*. Suppose that over the course of any summer tourist season, the probability of selling each size of coaster sets is as shown in the table below.

x	2	4	6	8
$P(x)$	0.10	0.35	0.5	0.05

The table shows that the probability of selling a set with six coasters is 0.50, while the probability of selling a set of two coasters is 0.10. This means that in the long run, about 50% of coaster sets sold will contain six coasters and about 10% will contain two coasters. Another way to display this information is as a histogram where the *x*-axis shows the values for number of coasters in a set and the *y*-axis is the probability associated with each size coaster set.

The histogram is an excellent visual representation of the probability distribution. Probability distributions for discrete random variables have the following properties:

1. For every value of x, $0 \leq P(x) \leq 1$
2. $\sum_{\text{all } x \text{ values}} P(x) = 1$
   (This means the sum of the probabilities always adds up to one.)

If the manager of the store wants to know the probability that a set of 2 or a set of 4 is sold, he or she would add the probabilities $P(x = 2) + P(x = 4) = 0.1 + 0.35 = 0.45$ since $P(x = 2)$ and $P(x = 4)$ are disjoint events.

CONTINUOUS RANDOM VARIABLES

(*Statistics: Learning from Data*, AP Edition, 1st ed. pages 345–350 / 2nd ed. pages 359–365)

Possible values of a continuous random variable consist of an entire interval along the number line. The height of an individual selected at random from some population is a continuous variable, even though we usually only measure it to the nearest inch or half of an inch. Since this is not just a set of discrete values, its behavior is described by a smooth curve, which is defined by some function $f(x)$. This function is called a density function. A density function has the following characteristics:

1. $f(x) \geq 0$ for all x values

2. The total area under the density curve is equal to 1

For a continuous random variable, the probability of observing a value in any particular interval is equal to the area under the density curve in that interval. The inclusion or exclusion of the endpoints of the interval will not change the associated probability. Unlike the discrete case, where including a single value might change the probability, in the continuous case, this isn't an issue. The diagram below shows a density function with a total area under the curve is equal to 1. For this distribution, $P(1 < x < 2)$ is the total area under the curve in the interval from 1 unit to 2 units. The probability of interest is the area of a rectangle with length 1 unit and height 0.4 units. It follows that $P(1 < x < 2) = 1(0.4) = 0.4$.

MEAN AND STANDARD DEVIATION OF RANDOM VARIABLES

(*Statistics: Learning from Data*, AP Edition, 1st ed. pages 352–361 / 2nd ed. pages 367–378)

The mean and standard deviation of a random variable (or equivalently of a probability distribution) are computed differently for discrete random variables and continuous random variables. In the AP® Statistics course, you are expected

160 ❖ Chapter 6

to be able to compute the mean and standard deviation given a discrete probability distribution. For continuous random variables, you do not need to be able to compute the mean and standard deviation (this involves the use of calculus), but you should be able to interpret the mean and standard deviation as measures of center and spread for values of the random variable.

Discrete Random Variables

The mean and standard deviation are useful in describing the behavior of a discrete random variable.

For any discrete random variable x,

$$\mu_x = \sum xP(x)$$

$$\sigma_x = \sqrt{\sigma_x^2} = \sqrt{\sum (x - \mu)^2 P(x)}$$

The mean of a random variable is also called the expected value of the random variable and denoted as $E(x)$.

> **Sample Problem 1** Recall the number of decorative coasters in sets sold by a souvenir store where x = number of coasters in the coaster set sold. Calculate the mean and standard deviation.
>
> | x | 2 | 4 | 6 | 8 |
> |--------|------|------|-----|------|
> | $P(x)$ | 0.10 | 0.35 | 0.5 | 0.05 |
>
> **Solution to Problem 1**
>
> $$\mu_x = \sum xP(x) = 2P(2) + 4P(4) + 6P(6) + 8P(8)$$
>
> $$= 2(0.1) + 4(0.35) + 6(0.5) + 8(0.05)$$
>
> $$= 5$$
>
> $$\sigma_x = \sqrt{\sigma_x^2} = \sqrt{\sum (x - \mu)^2 P(x)}$$
>
> $$= \sqrt{(2-5)^2 P(2) + (4-5)^2 P(4) + (6-5)^2 P(6) + (8-5)^2 P(8)}$$
>
> $$= \sqrt{(-3)^2 (0.1) + (-1)^2 (3.5) + (1)^2 (0.5) + (3)^2 (0.05)}$$
>
> $$= \sqrt{2.2}$$
>
> $$= 1.48$$

Notice the mean number of coasters in a set sold by the store would be 5; however, the store only sells them in sets of 4 or 6. As we have seen previously, the mean is an "average" value. The standard deviation of 1.48 coasters describes the variability in number of coasters in the coaster set sold over a long sequence of observations.

CONTINUOUS RANDOM VARIABLES

Computing the mean and standard deviation of a continuous random variable requires calculus. While you won't need to be able to do these calculations, you should be able to interpret the mean and standard deviation of a continuous random variable as measures of center and spread. As was the case with discrete random variables, the mean is the long-run average value and the standard deviation describes long-run variability in the values of the random variable.

MEAN, VARIANCE, AND STANDARD DEVIATION FOR LINEAR COMBINATIONS

It is also possible to define new random variables that are functions of other random variables. One such random variable is a linear combination of other known random variables. If we wish to calculate the mean of a random variable constructed as a linear combination of two or more random variables, $y = a_1 x_1 + a_2 x_2 + \ldots + a_k x_k$, we would use the following formula.

$$\mu_y = a_1\mu_1 + a_2\mu_2 + \ldots + a_k\mu_k$$

where the x_i's are random variables, the a_i's are constants, and μ_y is the mean of the data set.

> **EXAMPLE** Suppose that the weight of a student book bag is a random variable with a mean of 26 pounds with a standard deviation of 4 pounds. What is the mean total weight of seven students' book bags if x_i represents the weight of the ith book bag and the total weight y is $y = x_1 + x_2 + \ldots + x_7$?
>
> $$\mu_y = \mu_{x_1} + \mu_{x_2} + \ldots + \mu_{x_7}$$
> $$= 26 + 26 + \ldots + 26$$
> $$= 182$$

Finding the standard deviation of a linear combination of random variables requires a little more work. If the random variables in a linear combination are independent, then the standard deviation of $y = a_1 x_1 + a_2 x_2 + \ldots + a_k x_k$ is

$$\sigma_y = \sqrt{a_1^2\sigma_1^2 + a_2^2\sigma_2^2 + \ldots + a_k^2\sigma_k^2}$$

where the x_i's are independent random variables, the a_i's are numerical constants, and σ_y^2 is the variance of the data set.

The formula for the mean of a linear combination holds for any set of random variables, but the formula above for the standard deviation of a linear combination should only be used when the random variables are independent.

> **SAMPLE PROBLEM 2** A local high school requires seniors to take a comprehensive exam covering mathematics, science, and English prior to graduation. Each section is graded separately by a person who teaches the corresponding subject. The table below gives the mean and standard deviation for the time required to grade each section of the exam.

Subject	Mean Time per Test (in minutes)	Standard Deviation (in minutes)
Mathematics	5.2	0.4
Science	4.9	0.3
English	5.7	0.5

Since each exam contains all three sections, the total time required to score the exam is the sum of the times required to grade each section. Assuming that the time required to grade any one section is independent of the times required to grade the other two sections, what are the mean and standard deviation of the total time to grade an exam?

SOLUTION TO PROBLEM 2

Grading time $= x_M + x_s + x_E$, where x_M is the time to score the math section, x_s is the time required to score the science section, and x_E is the time required to score the English section.

$$\mu_{grading\ time} = 5.2 + 4.9 + 5.7 = 15.8 \text{ minutes}$$

$$\sigma_{grading\ time} = \sqrt{0.4^2 + 0.3^2 + 0.5^2} = \sqrt{0.16 + 0.09 + 0.25} = \sqrt{0.5} = 0.707$$

In this case, it will take an average of approximately 15.8 minutes to grade an exam. The standard deviation of total grading time is about 0.7 minutes, indicating that there is not much variability in exam grading times.

BINOMIAL AND GEOMETRIC DISTRIBUTIONS

(*Statistics: Learning from Data*, AP Edition, 1st ed. pages 363–371 / 2nd ed. pages 402–410)

There are two discrete probability distributions of major interest—the binomial distribution and the geometric distribution. Both of these distributions arise in situations where the experiment consists of a sequence of trials and where each trial can result in one of two possible outcomes. The outcomes are usually called success (S) and failure (F). If a chance experiment meets the requirements for either of these distributions, then we are able to use the binomial or geometric distribution to compute probabilities.

BINOMIAL DISTRIBUTIONS

A binomial experiment has the following characteristics:

- The experiment consists of a fixed number of trials, n.
- Each trial results in one of two possible outcomes, success (S) or failure (F).
- The n trials are *all* independent.
- The probability of success, p, is the same for each trial.

The random variable defined as $x =$ number of successes in a binomial experiment has a binomial distribution. Keep in mind that success doesn't necessarily mean "good"; it is the name given to the value of the outcome of the chance experiment in which we are interested.

For example, suppose we are interested in the number of students in a sample of 10 students who test positive for the H1N1 flu virus. Since a student will either test positive for the virus or not, we can think of the 10 students as 10 trials and each trial has two possible outcomes. To meet the independence criteria, we would need the events "student A tests positive" and "student B tests positive" to be independent. For this to be a binomial setting, we would also require a fixed probability that a randomly selected student has H1N1. Suppose that the county health department states that 18% of students will test positive for this virus. If we assume that 18% is a constant probability of a student testing positive, we have a binomial experiment.

Once we know that our random variable is binomial, a variety of probability questions can be considered.

The probability distribution of a binomial random variable is the **binomial probability distribution**.

$P(x) = P(x$ successes among n trials$)$

$$= \binom{n}{x} p^x (1-p)^{n-x}$$

where n = number of independent trials in a binomial experiment, p = probability of a success and $\binom{n}{x} = \dfrac{n!}{x!(n-x)!}$.

Suppose we want to know the probability that exactly 3 of the 10 students test positive for H1N1. Then $n = 10$, $p = 0.18$, and

$P(3) = P(x = 3)$

$$= \binom{10}{3} 0.18^3 (1 - 0.18)^{10-3}$$

$$= \dfrac{10!}{3!7!} 0.18^3 (0.82)^7$$

$$= 120(0.00583)(0.24929)$$

$$= 0.1744$$

The probability that exactly 3 of the 10 student test positive for the virus is 0.1744.

What is the probability that 3 or fewer of the 10 students test positive for the virus? In this case, the event of interest would "happen" if 3, 2, 1, or 0 students test positive. Here, we would compute each of the individual probabilities of success and then add these probabilities. (We can add them because the events are disjoint.)

$P(x \leq 3) = P(x = 0) + P(x = 1) + P(x = 2) + P(x = 3)$

AP® Tip

Remember that zero is a possible value for a binomial random variable.

To compute $P(x > 3)$, use $1 - P(x \leq 3)$.

To compute $P(x \geq 3)$, use $1 - P(x \leq 2)$.

AP® is a trademark registered by the College Board, which is not affiliated with, and does not endorse, this product.

Binomial probabilities can also be calculated using a graphing calculator using one of the **binomialpdf** or **binomialcdf** functions. The arguments entered on your calculator for each are shown below:

$P(x = \text{value})$: use pdf command **binompdf**(n, p, x)

```
NORMAL FLOAT AUTO REAL RADIAN MP
binompdf(10,.18,3)
              0.1744599437
```

$P(x \leq \text{value})$: use cdf command **binomcdf**(n, p, x)

```
NORMAL FLOAT AUTO REAL RADIAN MP
binomcdf(10,.18,3)
              0.911658903
```

Notice both arguments require the n, p, x values. The difference is that the *binompdf* calculates the probability for exactly three students test positive and *binomcdf* calculates the probability for three *or less* students test positive.

AP® Tip

The probability of "more than x" would be calculated on a graphing calculator using $1 - \text{binomcdf}(n, p, x)$.

Finally, if x has a binomial distribution, the mean and standard deviation of x are

$\mu_x = np$

$\sigma_x = \sqrt{np(1-p)}$

Refer to the earlier example of students testing positive for the H1N1 flu virus and find the mean and standard deviation.

$\mu_x = 10(0.18) = 1.8$

$\sigma_x = \sqrt{10(0.18)(0.82)} = 1.21$

GEOMETRIC DISTRIBUTION

A geometric experiment has the same properties as a binomial experiment with one exception. Instead of a fixed number of trials, a geometric experiment continues until the first success occurs.

- Each trial results in one of two possible outcomes, success (S) or failure (F).
- All trials are independent.
- Probability of success, p, is the same for each trial.

Then the random variable x = number of trials until the first success, including the first success trial, has a geometric distribution.

Using the example of the students testing positive for the H1N1 flu virus, in the geometric case we would continue to test students until we found the first student who tested positive. This is different from the binomial case because you could test one student and get a positive result or test many students before you had a positive result. The probability for a geometric random variable is

$$P(x) = (1-p)^{x-1} p$$

where x = number of trials until to first success and p = probability of success for each trial.

Recall that for the H1N1 flu virus example, the probability that any one student tests positive is 0.18. Suppose that we plan to continue to test students until one student tests positive. What is the probability that we would have to test two or fewer students before we find one who tests positive?

$$P(x=1) = (1-0.18)^{1-1}(0.18) = 0.18$$

$$P(x=2) = (1-0.18)^{2-1}(0.18) = 0.148$$

so $P(x \leq 2) = P(x=1) + P(x=2) = 0.18 + 0.148 = 0.328$

NORMAL DISTRIBUTIONS

(*Statistics: Learning from Data*, AP Edition, 1st ed. pages 373–387 and 395–398 / 2nd ed. pages 380–394 and 412–415)

Normal distributions are continuous probability distributions with a symmetric and unimodal density curve. Normal distributions are described by a mean and a standard deviation. One special case is the standard normal distribution, which has a mean of 0 and a standard deviation of 1.

Chapter 2 of this text (and chapter 6 of the textbook) introduced a standardized score known as a z score. This standardized score allows us to see the relative standing of any value within a distribution. The z score measures the number of standard deviations above or below the mean a value falls. For example, if $z = -1.32$, this would be a value 1.32 standard deviations below the mean. The shaded region in the picture shows the area corresponding to $P(z < -1.32)$.

One way to calculate this area is to look up the z score of interest on a "standard normal" table. Use the following steps.

- Read down the first column until you find the whole number and first decimal value (that is, to the tenths place). In this case, find −1.3.
- Next, read across this row until you are in the column of the second decimal value (that is, the hundredths place). For this example, go over to the 0.02 column.
- This is the area to the left of the z score (0.0934) and also the probability of observing a value less than or equal to the value of z used.

(this is a portion of a z table)

z*	0.00	0.01	0.02	0.03	0.04
−1.5	0.0668	0.0655	0.0643	0.0630	0.0618
−1.4	0.0808	0.0793	0.0778	0.0764	0.0749
−1.3	0.0968	0.0951	0.0934	0.0918	0.0901
−1.2	0.1151	0.1131	0.1112	0.1093	0.1075
−1.1	0.1357	0.1335	0.1314	0.1292	0.1271

Another way to calculate this would be to use your graphing calculator. In this case, depending on your calculator, you would enter the arguments as follows into the calculator.

normalcdf(lower bound, upper bound, $[\mu, \sigma]$)

where **normalcdf** is the command to find area under a normal curve, *lower bound* is the left endpoint of the region of interest, *upper bound* is the right endpoint of the region of interest, and $[\mu, \sigma]$ is the mean and standard deviation of the normal distribution if not using the standard normal distribution.

For this example, since the default values of μ and σ are for a standard normal distribution, we don't need to include the mean and standard deviation parameters. When entered, the calculator input returns the value shown below. Since the data are in standardized form, we need a lower boundary that will include the entire tail area in standard units. We used −5 since that will include the left tail to −5 standard deviations. We could have used other values such as −10, −100, as long as we choose a number far to the left.

```
NORMAL FLOAT AUTO REAL RADIAN MP
normalcdf(-5,-1.32)
              0.0934172853
```

The value returned is the area under the standard normal curve and to the left of a z score of −1.32. (A complete answer will include a well-labeled shaded picture as shown below.)

You will notice the area under the curve corresponds to the area from the left tail of this distribution up to the z score value. We can also solve problems to find the area between two z scores or even above a z score value. The notation and calculations we would use are shown here.

$$P(a < x < b) = P(a^* < z < b^*)$$

where z is a variable from a standard normal distribution and

$$a^* = \frac{a - \mu}{\sigma} \text{ and } b^* = \frac{b - \mu}{\sigma}$$

AP® Tip

You can use the graphing calculator to compute area in any interval (a, b). By using the command shown here, your calculator will return the probability of the area between the two boundaries given.

$$\text{normalcdf(lower bound, upper bound,}[\mu, \sigma])$$

You can either enter the lower bound and upper bound in terms of z scores (in which case you don't need to enter the values for μ and σ since the default values are 0 and 1, respectively) or you can use the original bounds (without transforming to z scores) and enter the appropriate values for μ and σ.

On the AP® exam, calculator syntax can be sufficient for demonstrating your work rather than using the mathematical formulas. To get full credit, you must identify each component of input into the graphing calculator syntax. For example: normalcdf (identify this number as lower bound, identify this number as upper bound, identify this number as mean, identify this number as standard deviation). Full credit is given if this is all the calculation presented and the answer is correct. This same standard of grading applies to other probability distributions as well.

Here are a few things to keep in mind when solving probability problems:

1. Often questions will ask for the probability that involves finding an area under a curve. In these questions, always draw the distribution, mark off the interval of interest, shade the appropriate area, and then find the desired probability.

2. Binomial distribution questions may ask for the probability of observing one possible value or a probability that involves a collection of possible values.

Watch for questions like $P(x < 3)$ vs. $P(x \le 3)$. In the first case, you do not include $x = 3$ in calculating the solution and in the second case you will include $x = 3$ in your calculations.

3. If the question involves some type of linear combination, you will need to first find the appropriate mean and standard deviation. The next sample problem involves this additional consideration.

SAMPLE PROBLEM 3 Recall the earlier example where time to grade an exam was the sum of the times required to grade each of three sections. Suppose that the time to grade each section has a normal distribution with the mean and standard deviation given below. Also suppose that the time to grade any one section of the exam is independent of the time to grade either of the other two sections.

Subject	Mean Time per Test (in minutes)	Standard Deviation (in minutes)
Mathematics	5.2	0.4
Science	4.9	0.3
English	5.7	0.5

We found earlier that

$$\mu_{grading\ time} = 5.2 + 4.9 + 5.7 = 15.8 \text{ minutes}$$

$$\sigma_{grading\ time} = \sqrt{0.4^2 + 0.3^2 + 0.5^2} = \sqrt{0.14 + 0.09 + 0.25} = \sqrt{0.5} = 0.707$$

We also know that the sum of normal random variables has a normal distribution. If the team's shortest grading time to date is 14.9 minutes, what is the probability that they grade a randomly selected exam in a shorter amount of time?

SOLUTION TO PROBLEM 3

$$P(x \le 14.9) = P\left(z \le \frac{14.9 - 15.8}{0.707}\right) = P(z \le -1.273) = 0.1015$$

To solve this in the calculator, you would use the command normalcdf(−10, −1.273). Alternatively, you can use the calculator to solve with the original values with the command normalcdf(−10,14.9,15.8,.707). If you choose the second option, make sure your picture reflects the actual values and not z scores.

CONVERTING A Z SCORE BACK TO AN X VALUE

Occasionally, we would like to convert a z score back to an x value if we know the z score or a related probability. This calculation is simple using the formula for a z score.

We can rewrite $z = \dfrac{x - \mu}{\sigma}$ to be $x = z\sigma + \mu$ using basic algebraic manipulation.

If you were interested in what score you would need to get to be in the 88th percentile on a test with a mean of 91 and standard deviation of 3, you would find the z score that goes with an area of 0.88 to the left of z and then solve the equation for x.

For an area of 0.88, look up the corresponding z score in the normal table or use the following command in your calculator.

invnorm(area to the left,[μ, σ])

where **invnorm** is the command to find an observation in a normal curve with area to the left of that value. [μ, σ] is the mean and standard deviation of the normal distribution if not using the standard normal distribution.

According to the calculator, invnorm(0.88) = 1.175; so $x = 1.175(3) + 91 = 94.5$.

Since it is probably safe to assume that scores on the test are whole numbers, you would need to score a 95 to be at the 88th percentile for the test.

NORMAL APPROXIMATIONS

Sometimes the normal distribution is used to approximate a discrete distribution, such as the distribution of the IQ of an individual or the number of trucks at a truck stop. When we say that discrete data are approximately normally distributed, we can use a normal distribution to compute probabilities. For example, suppose that the number of bags of groceries purchased on a military payday has a distribution that is approximately normal with a mean of 13 bags and a standard deviation of 2 bags. What is the probability that a randomly selected customer purchases 15 bags of groceries on a military payday? One way to answer this question is to approximate the probability of 15 bags using the area under the corresponding normal curve and between 14.5 and 15.5.

$$z_{14.5} = \frac{14.5 - 13}{2} = 0.75 \text{ and } z_{15.5} = \frac{15.5 - 13}{2} = 1.25$$

then

$$P(0.75 < z < 1.25) = 0.8944 - 0.7734 = 0.121$$

To solve this in the calculator, you would use the command normalcdf(.75,1.25). Again, the other option would be to use the original values with the command normalcdf(14.5,15.5,13,2).

The normal approximation may also be used to approximate binomial probabilities if the binomial distribution isn't too skewed. This approximation is appropriate when $np \geq 10$ and $n(1-p) \geq 10$. If this is the case, we can use the normal distribution with $\mu = np$ and $\sigma = \sqrt{np(1-p)}$ as an approximation of the binomial distribution. Notice that np is the number of successes and $n(1-p)$ is the number of failures. For this reason, these criteria are often called the success/failure condition.

> **SAMPLE PROBLEM 4** Suppose 40% of the people in a state support the use of traffic cameras. What is the approximate probability that a majority of the people in a random sample of 100 people in this state would favor the use of traffic cameras?
>
> **SOLUTION TO PROBLEM 4** The number in the sample that favors the use of traffic cameras is a binomial random variable with $n = 100$ and $p = 0.40$. Because $np = 10(0.40) = 40$ and $n(1-p) = 100(0.60) = 60$ are both greater than or equal to 10, it is appropriate to use a normal approximation. For the approximation, we would use the normal distribution with
>
> $$\mu = np = 100(0.40) = 40$$
>
> $$\sigma = \sqrt{np(1-p)} = \sqrt{100(0.40)(0.60)} = \sqrt{24} = 4.90$$
>
> We want the probability of a majority (more than half), which is more than 50 people. We would approximate this probability using the area under the normal curve and to the right of 50. Then
>
> $$P(x > 50) = P\left(z > \frac{50 - 40}{4.90}\right) = P(z > 2.04) = 0.021$$

$P(z > 2.04)$

Alternatively, you could use the calculator to solve $P(x > 50) = 0.021$ with the command normalcdf(50,1000,40,4.9).

RANDOM VARIABLES AND PROBABILITY DISTRIBUTIONS: STUDENT OBJECTIVES FOR THE AP® EXAM

- You will be able to calculate the mean and standard deviation of a discrete random variable.
- You will be able to use a given probability distribution to calculate probabilities.
- You will be able to find mean and standard deviations of a linear combination of random variables.
- You will be able to solve problems involving the binomial and geometric distributions.
- You will be able to use the normal distribution to compute probabilities.
- You will be able to use the normal approximation to the binomial distribution when appropriate.

MULTIPLE-CHOICE QUESTIONS

1. Air America Airways (AAA) tracks the number of delays per day for its jet fleet due to maintenance issues at a major airport.
Suppose that the probability distribution of x = number of delays on a randomly selected day is given in the table below.

x	0	1	2	3	4	5
$P(x)$	0.42	0.31	0.12	0.08	0.04	0.03

What is the probability that the airline has fewer than three delays due to maintenance at this airport on a randomly selected day?
(A) 0.08
(B) 0.12
(C) 0.15
(D) 0.85
(E) 0.93

2. Which of the following random variables is not continuous?
   (A) The amount of gasoline in a car
   (B) The time it takes to commute to work
   (C) Number of goals scored by a hockey team
   (D) Distance traveled by a police car in a day
   (E) Lifetime of a AAA battery

Questions 3–5 refer to the following set of data:

A store carries one brand of women's shoes in the following sizes and quantities based on customer demand.

3. The probability distribution of x is given in the table below.

x	5	6	7	8	9
$P(x)$	0.1	0.15	0.45	0.25	0.05

   What is the probability of finding a shoe smaller than a size 7?
   (A) 0.45
   (B) 0.25
   (C) 0.15
   (D) 0.70
   (E) 0.30

4. A woman is looking for only size 8 shoes. The sale bin contains 20 pairs of shoes. What is the mean and standard deviation for finding size 8 shoes?
   (A) $\mu = 2$, $\sigma = 0.1875$
   (B) $\mu = 2$, $\sigma = 3.75$
   (C) $\mu = 2$, $\sigma = 1.936$
   (D) $\mu = 5$, $\sigma = 0.1875$
   (E) $\mu = 5$, $\sigma = 1.936$

5. What is the probability that the woman from above finds exactly two pairs of size 8 shoes in the sale bin containing 20 pairs of shoes?
   (A) 0.25
   (B) 0.0913
   (C) 0.0625
   (D) 0.0669
   (E) 0.1339

6. Mr. Lopez teaches one statistics class. The girls have a semester average of 83 with standard deviation 9 and the boys have a semester average of 78 with standard deviation 6. Assuming that the students are all independent of one another, what is the standard deviation of the entire class?
   (A) 15
   (B) 10.8
   (C) 7.5
   (D) 3.9
   (E) 3

7. Which of the following is not a characteristic of a binomial experiment?
   (A) There are a fixed number of trials.
   (B) Trials continue until a success is observed.
   (C) Trials are independent.
   (D) The probability of success is the same in all trials.
   (E) There are only two possible outcomes for each trial, success or failure.

8. Thirty percent of a school district's students receive advanced scores on their state end-of-course assessment in mathematics. If you choose 25 students at random, what is the probability that more than 10 of these students received advanced scores on their assessment?
   (A) 0.3231
   (B) 0.1894
   (C) 0.0978
   (D) 0.9022
   (E) 0.0442

9. The time to make coffee at a local convenience store is normally distributed with a mean of 4.5 minutes and standard deviation of 6 minutes. What is the probability that it will take less than 3.5 minutes for a worker to make a pot of coffee?
   (A) 0.0478
   (B) 0.0984
   (C) 0.4522
   (D) 0.5873
   (E) 0.9522

10. Two independent observations of a random variable are made. If the random variable has a normal distribution with a mean of 75 and standard deviation of 9, what is the probability that the sum of these two observations is greater than 168?
    (A) 0.0787
    (B) 0.0228
    (C) 0.1587
    (D) 0.0013
    (E) 0.0001

11. Which of the following are true statements?
    I. The binomial distribution can always be approximated using a normal distribution.
    II. A normal distribution is defined by specifying its μ and σ.
    III. The standard deviation of the sum of two independent random variables is found by taking the square root of the sum of the individual variances.
    (A) I only
    (B) II only
    (C) I and II
    (D) II and III
    (E) I, II, and III

12. What is the approximate value of an observation that is in the 93rd percentile from a normal distribution with a mean of 86 and standard deviation of 8?
    (A) 102
    (B) 100
    (C) 98
    (D) 96
    (E) 94

13. If the height of a randomly selected woman is normally distributed with $\mu = 64.5$ inches and $\sigma = 2.5$ inches, approximately what proportion of women have heights between 65 and 67.5 inches?
    (A) 0.31
    (B) 0.88
    (C) 0.16
    (D) 0.14
    (E) 0.58

14. Suppose that 60% of all AP® students in a school district complete homework regularly. If eight AP® students from this district are chosen at random, what is the approximate probability that more than six of these students complete homework regularly?
    (A) 0.894
    (B) 0.791
    (C) 0.685
    (D) 0.315
    (E) 0.106

15. Two random variables X and Y are independent. The means and standard deviations are shown in the table below. Find the mean and standard deviation of $2X + Y$.

	μ	σ
X	6	0.5
Y	8	0.6

    (A) $\mu_{2X+Y} = 14, \sigma_{2X+Y} = 1.17$
    (B) $\mu_{2X+Y} = 14, \sigma_{2X+Y} = 0.78$
    (C) $\mu_{2X+Y} = 20, \sigma_{2X+Y} = 1.1$
    (D) $\mu_{2X+Y} = 20, \sigma_{2X+Y} = 0.78$
    (E) $\mu_{2X+Y} = 20, \sigma_{2X+Y} = 1.17$

FREE-RESPONSE PROBLEMS

1. A store catering to female preteens sells jeans in four sizes (0, 1, 2, and 3) corresponding to the waist measurements shown in the table below. These are the only sizes that the store carries.

Store Size	Waist Measurement
0	20 < waist < 22
1	22 < waist < 24
2	24 < waist < 26
3	26 < waist < 28

   Suppose that for female preteens, waist measurement is normally distributed with a mean of 24.4 inches and a standard deviation of 2.5 inches.

   (a) What proportion of female preteens will be unable to find jeans in this store?

   (b) What proportion of female preteens wear a size 2?

   (c) If 15 randomly selected female preteens are chosen, what is the probability that exactly five of them wear a size 2?

2. The time a car must wait for the light to change at an intersection depends on the type of intersection. Suppose that the wait time at major and the wait time at secondary intersections are approximately normal with the means and standard deviations given in the table below.

	Mean Wait Time (minutes)	Standard Deviation
Lights at Major Intersections	3.2 minutes	0.5 minutes
Lights at Secondary Intersections	2.5 minutes	0.7 minutes

   (a) How likely is it that Mario will have to wait for more than 4 minutes at a major intersection by his house?

   (b) Ella must travel through two major intersection lights and three secondary intersection lights on her way to work. Assuming that the wait times at these intersections are independent, what are the mean and standard deviation of her total wait time on the way to work?

   (c) What is the probability that Ella's total wait time will be less than 12 minutes?

Answers

MULTIPLE-CHOICE QUESTIONS

1. **(D)** Since x is a discrete random variable, the desired probability is the sum of the individual probabilities.

   $P(x < 3) = P(x = 0) + P(x = 1) + P(x = 2) = 0.42 + 0.31 + 0.12 = 0.85$

   Notice that $P(x = 3)$ is not included since the question asks for fewer than three delays (*Statistics: Learning from Data*, AP Edition, 1st ed. pages 339–343 / 2nd ed. pages 353–357).

2. **(C)** Possible values for number of hockey goals are discrete counts. This is the only noncontinuous variable given (*Statistics: Learning from Data*, AP Edition, 1st ed. pages 337–338 / 2nd ed. pages 350–352).

3. **(B)** Since this asks for $P(x \leq 7)$, this is $P(6) + P(5) = 0.10 + 0.15 = 25$ (*Statistics: Learning from Data*, AP Edition, 1st ed. pages 339–343 / 2nd ed. pages 353–357).

4. **(E)** $\mu = 20(0.25) = 5$. $\sigma = \sqrt{20(0.25)(0.75)} = 1.936$ (*Statistics: Learning from Data*, AP Edition, 1st ed. pages 352–361 / 2nd ed. pages 367–378).

5. **(D)** This is a binomial probability with $p = 0.25$ and $n = 20$. This probability can be evaluated using a graphing calculator using binompdf(20, 0.25, 2) or using the formula for binomial probabilities $\binom{20}{2} 0.25^2 (0.75)^{18} = 0.0669$

   (*Statistics: Learning from Data*, AP Edition, 1st ed. pages 363–371 / 2nd ed. pages 402–410).

6. **(B)** The standard deviation of $x + y$ is found by taking the square root of the sum of the variances. The calculation for this is

   $\sigma_{x+y} = \sqrt{\sigma_x^2 + \sigma_y^2}$, in this case, $\sigma_{x+y} = \sqrt{6^2 + 9^2}$ (*Statistics: Learning from Data*, AP Edition, 1st ed. pages 352–361 / 2nd ed. pages 367–378).

7. **(B)** Continuing trials until a success is observed is a characteristic of a geometric experiment (*Statistics: Learning from Data*, AP Edition, 1st ed. pages 363–371 / 2nd ed. pages 402–410).

8. **(C)** The desired probability is $P(x > 10)$, which can be found by computing $1 - P(x \leq 10)$ (*Statistics: Learning from Data*, AP Edition, 1st ed. pages 339–343 / 2nd ed. pages 353–357).

9. **(A)** This is the area under the normal curve with mean 4.5 and standard deviation 0.6 to the left of 3.5 minutes. $P(x < 3.5) = 0.0478$. This probability can be evaluated using a graphing calculator using normalcdf (−100,3.5,4.5,.6) or using the table for standard normal probabilities (*Statistics: Learning from Data*, AP Edition, 1st ed. pages 373–387 and 395–398 / 2nd ed. pages 380–394 and 412–415).

10. **(A)** $\mu = 75 + 75 = 150$

    $\sigma = \sqrt{9^2 + 9^2} = 12.728$

    $P(\text{sum} \geq 168) = P\left(z \geq \dfrac{168 - 150}{12.728}\right) = 0.0787$

    This probability can be evaluated using a graphing calculator using normalcdf(168,1000,150,12.728) or using the table for standard normal probabilities (*Statistics: Learning from Data*, AP Edition, 1st ed. pages 373–387 / 2nd ed. pages 380–394).

11. **(D)** The binomial distribution can only be approximated using the normal distribution if a sample is large enough so that $np \geq 10$ and $n(1-p) \geq 10$ (*Statistics: Learning from Data*, AP Edition, 1st ed. pages 395–398 / 2nd ed. pages 412–415).

12. **(C)** First find the z score that has an area to the left of 0.93 using the normal table or using the graphing calculator invnorm(.93) command. Finally, solve $1.48 = \dfrac{x - 86}{8}$ for x. This results in $x = 97.8 \approx 98$ (*Statistics: Learning from Data*, AP Edition, 1st ed. pages 373–387 / 2nd ed. pages 380–394).

13. **(A)** The area of interest is between the two x values, so find $P(x < 65)$ and subtract this from $P(x < 67.5)$. You can also use normalcdf(65,67.6,64.5,2.5) function on the graphing calculator (*Statistics: Learning from Data*, AP Edition, 1st ed. pages 373–387 / 2nd ed. pages 380–394).

14. **(E)** This is a binomial probability with $n = 8$ and $p = 0.60$. $P(x > 6) = P(7) + P(8)$. Another way to calculate the probability would be with $1 - P(x \leq 6) = 1 -$ binomcdf(8,.6,6) (*Statistics: Learning from Data*, AP Edition, 1st ed. pages 363–371 / 2nd ed. pages 402–410).

15. **(E)** The mean is $2(6) + 8 = 20$. The standard deviation
    $\sigma_{2X+Y} = \sqrt{2^2(0.5)^2 + (0.6)^2} = 1.17$ (*Statistics: Learning from Data*, AP Edition, 1st ed. pages 352–361 / 2nd ed. pages 367–378).

FREE-RESPONSE PROBLEMS

1. (a) Anyone with a waist measurement less than 20 inches or greater than 28 inches will not find jeans.

    $P(x < 20) + P(x > 28)$

    $= P\left(z < \dfrac{20 - 24.4}{2.5}\right) + P\left(z > \dfrac{28 - 24.4}{2.5}\right)$

    $= P(z < -1.76) + P(z > 1.44)$

    $= 0.0392 + 0.0749$

    $= 0.1141$

    or normcdf(−100,20,24.4,2.5) + normcdf(28,100,24.4,2.5)

(b)

[Calculator screenshot: NORMAL FLOAT AUTO REAL RADIAN MP / CALC INTEGRAL OVER INTERVAL / ∫f(x)dx=0.3024732 / [24,26]]

$$= P(24 < x < 26) = P\left(\frac{24-24.4}{2.5} < z < \frac{26-24.4}{2.5}\right) = 0.302 \approx 30\%$$

or normcdf(24,26,24.4,2.5)

(c) From part (b), we know that P(size 2) = 0.30. The desired probability is then a binomial probability with $n = 15$ and $p = 30$. Using the calculator, binompdf(15, 0.3, 5) = 0.206. This could also be calculated as $P(x=5) = \binom{15}{5}(0.3)^5(0.7)^{10}$.

(*Statistics: Learning from Data*, AP Edition, 1st ed. pages 363–371 and 373–387 / 2nd ed. pages 380–394 and 402–410.)

2. (a) $P(x > 4) = P\left(z > \dfrac{4-3.2}{0.5}\right) = P(z > 1.6) = 0.0548$ or

   normcdf(4,100,3.2,.5)

   (b) Ella's total wait time is the sum of the wait times for all five lights. Because the wait times are independent, the mean and standard deviation of Ella's total wait time are:

   $\mu_{time} = 2(3.2) + 3(2.5) = 13.9$ minutes

   $\sigma_{time} = \sqrt{0.5^2 + 0.5^2 + 0.7^2 + 0.7^2 + 0.7^2} = \sqrt{1.97} = 1.404$ min.

   (c) $P(x < 12) = P\left(z < \dfrac{12-13.9}{1.404}\right) = P(z < -1.353) = 0.088$

   or normcdf(–100,12,13.9,1.404). There is about an 8.8% chance that Ella's total wait time will be less than 12 minutes.

(*Statistics: Learning from Data*, AP Edition, 1st ed. pages 373–387 / 2nd ed. pages 380–394)

7

SAMPLING VARIABILITY AND SAMPLING DISTRIBUTIONS

When you take a sample, you have no idea if that sample is a perfect representation of the population of interest. You hope it is and you take careful steps to make sure you follow all of the rules of good sampling techniques. But simply due to the nature of how samples vary, each sample will be slightly different. Understanding how samples behave in repeated sampling will help us to truly appreciate the power of one sample. So in this section, we will consider sampling distributions and see how they describe the behavior of a sample statistic.

OBJECTIVES

- Understand that a sampling distribution describes the behavior of a sample statistic.
- Know the general properties of the sampling distribution of a sample mean, $\bar{x}$.
- Know the general properties of the sampling distribution of a sample proportion, $\hat{p}$.

STATISTICS AND SAMPLING VARIABILITY

(*Statistics: Learning from Data*, AP Edition, 1st ed. pages 433–436 / 2nd ed. pages 447–450)

What makes learning from sample data a challenge is that different samples from the same population give different results. For example, the average age at which a child learned to walk for one sample of 10 children would be different from the average age to walk for a different sample of 10 children. The value of the sample mean, $\bar{x}$, varies from sample to sample. To know what any one sample mean might tell us about the corresponding population mean, p, we need to understand this sampling variability. The sampling distribution of a sample statistic describes its behavior in repeated sampling.

THE SAMPLING DISTRIBUTION OF A SAMPLE MEAN

(*Statistics: Learning from Data*, AP Edition, 1st ed. pages 568–576 / 2nd ed. pages 590–598)

To help understand the sample-to-sample variability in the sample mean, consider taking sample after sample from a particular population and looking at the resulting sample means. We took 100 different random samples for size 5 from a normal population distribution with mean $\mu = 0$ and computed the sample mean for each sample. These 100 sample means were used to construct the top histogram in the figure below. Notice there is variability in the sample means, but the sample means tend to cluster around 0, the value of the population mean.

We repeated this process with samples of size $n = 10$ to produce the second histogram in the figure, samples of size $n = 20$ to produce the third histogram, and samples of size $n = 40$ to produce the bottom histogram. These histograms are approximations of the sampling distribution of $\bar{x}$ for the given sample sizes.

There are three characteristics of the previous graphs that we should note. First, all four sampling distributions appear to have a roughly normal shape. Second, the center for each histogram is approximately 0, the value of the population mean. Finally, the most interesting feature is that as the sample sizes increased, the overall spread decreased. In other words, as our sample size increased, $\bar{x}$ varies less from one sample to another and the $\bar{x}$ values tend to be closer to μ.

What if the population distribution is not normal? Would the sampling distribution of $\bar{x}$ still be described by these same three characteristics? Let's investigate by considering the population summarized in the histogram below. This population is skewed right and has a mean of $\mu = 1$.

Skewed right population

Now let's examine the approximate sampling distributions below. Each histogram was constructed using the sample means from 100 different random samples of size n from the skewed population. Notice the distributions appear to be centered at $\mu = 1$. As sample size increases, the sampling distribution becomes less and less spread out compared to the population. Finally, although the shape of the sampling distribution is skewed for small sample sizes, the sampling distributions become more symmetric and more closely resemble a normal distribution. For samples of size 30 or greater, the sampling distribution is considered approximately normal no matter what the shape of the population distribution.

[Histograms for n = 5, n = 10, n = 20, n = 30]

The fact that the sampling distribution of $\bar{x}$ is approximately normal in shape when the sample size is large, even when the population is not normal, is a consequence of a powerful theory known as the **Central Limit Theorem**. This theorem states that if n is sufficiently large, the sampling distribution of the sample mean will be approximately normal no matter what the shape of the population distribution.

There are two situations where we can count on the sampling distribution of $\bar{x}$ to be normal, or at least approximately normal:

1. If the population distribution is normal, the sampling distribution of $\bar{x}$ is normal for any sample size.

2. If the population distribution is not terribly skewed, then the sampling distribution of $\bar{x}$ will be approximately normal if $n \geq 30$.

GENERAL PROPERTIES OF THE SAMPLING DISTRIBUTION OF $\bar{X}$

Let $\bar{x}$ be the sample mean for a sample of size n from a population with mean μ and standard deviation σ, THEN

- $\mu_{\bar{x}} = \mu$
- $\sigma_{\bar{x}} = \dfrac{\sigma}{\sqrt{n}}$

This rule for the standard deviation of the sampling distribution of $\bar{x}$ is exact if we have an infinite population; otherwise, it's approximately correct with a finite population as long as no more than 10% of the population was included in the sample.

- If the population is normally distributed, the sampling distribution of $\bar{x}$ is normal for any sample size n.
- If the population distribution is not normal, the Central Limit Theorem states that for sufficiently large n, the sampling distribution of $\bar{x}$ is well approximated by normal distribution. A sample size of 30 or more is generally considered large enough.

These properties imply that if n is large or the population distribution is normal,

$$z = \frac{\bar{x} - \mu_{\bar{x}}}{\sigma_{\bar{x}}} = \frac{\bar{x} - \mu}{\frac{\sigma}{\sqrt{n}}}$$

has an approximately standard normal distribution.

SAMPLE PROBLEM 1 Suppose that the age at which children begin to walk on their own is normally distributed with a mean of 12 months and a standard deviation of 1.5 months. A sample of four babies is observed and the age when each of these babies began to walk is recorded.

(a) Describe the sampling distribution of $\bar{x}$ for samples of size 4.

(b) What is the probability that the mean age to walk for a random sample of four babies is between 11 and 12.5 months?

SOLUTION TO PROBLEM 1

(a) $\mu_{\bar{x}} = \mu = 12$

$\sigma_{\bar{x}} = \frac{\sigma}{\sqrt{n}} = \frac{1.5}{\sqrt{4}} = \frac{1.5}{2} = 0.75$

Because the population distribution of walking ages is normal, the sampling distribution of $\bar{x}$ is also normal.

(b) Because the sampling distribution of $\bar{x}$ is normal with a mean of 12 and a standard deviation of 0.75, we can use what we know about normal distributions to compute

$$P(11 \leq \bar{x} \leq 12.5) = P\left(\frac{11-12}{0.75} \leq z \leq \frac{12.5-12}{0.75}\right)$$

$$= P(-1.33 \leq z \leq 0.67)$$

$$= 0.7486 - 0.0918$$

$$= 0.6568$$

Rather than using normal tables, you could have used a graphing calculator to evaluate the desired probability:

```
NORMAL FLOAT AUTO REAL RADIAN MP
CALC INTEGRAL OVER INTERVAL
```

∫f(x)dx=0.6562962
[11,12.5]

Notice that the calculator gives a slightly different answer than the answer obtained using the normal table. This is due to rounding of the areas in the normal table.

THE SAMPLING DISTRIBUTION OF A SAMPLE PROPORTION

(*Statistics: Learning from Data*, AP Edition, 1st ed. pages 438–442 / 2nd ed. pages 453–458)

When the variable of interest in a population is categorical with just two possible categories, such as gender or whether or not a manufactured part is defective, we usually want to learn about the value of a population proportion. In this case, the sample proportion $\hat{p}$ is used to estimate the population proportion p. The statistic $\hat{p}$ varies from sample to sample, just as was the case for $\bar{x}$ for numerical data. The sampling distribution of $\hat{p}$ describes the sample-to-sample variability in the value of $\hat{p}$. For example, consider the histograms below. The first histogram was constructed using the $\hat{p}$ values from 100 random samples of size 10 drawn from a population with a proportion of successes of 0.34. The other histograms were constructed using sample sizes of $n = 25$, $n = 50$, and $n = 100$. Notice that the $\hat{p}$ values tend to cluster around the population proportion of $p = 0.34$ and that the variability in the approximate sampling distributions decreases as the sample size increases. Also notice that for the larger sample sizes, the sampling distribution of p is more nearly symmetric and has a shape that more closely resembles a normal distribution.

GENERAL PROPERTIES OF THE SAMPLING DISTRIBUTION OF $\hat{p}$

Let $\hat{p}$ be the proportion of successes in a random sample of size n from a population with a proportion of successes p. Then,

- $\mu_{\hat{p}} = p$
- $\sigma_{\hat{p}} = \sqrt{\dfrac{p(1-p)}{n}}$

  This rule for the standard deviation of the sampling distribution of $\hat{p}$ is exact if we have an infinite population; otherwise, it's approximately correct with a finite population as long as no more than 10% of the population was included in the sample.
- When n is sufficiently large and p is not too near 0 or 1, the sampling distribution of $\hat{p}$ is approximately normally distributed.

How large does n have to be in order for the sampling distribution of $\hat{p}$ to be approximately normal? It depends on the value of the population p. The further the population proportion gets from 0.5, the larger the sample size needs to be in order for the sampling distribution of $\hat{p}$ to be well-approximated by a normal distribution. The sampling distribution of p is approximately normal as long as n is large enough that $np \geq 10$ and $n(1-p) \geq 10$.

SAMPLE PROBLEM 2 Suppose that approximately 4% of American children have attention deficit/hyperactivity disorder (ADHD). A random sample of 100 American children will be selected.

(a) Describe the mean and standard deviation of the sampling distribution of $\hat{p}$, where $\hat{p}$ is the proportion of children in a sample with ADHD.

(b) What is the smallest sample size that would be large enough for us to think that the sampling distribution of $\hat{p}$ would be approximately normal?

SOLUTION TO PROBLEM 2

(a) $\mu_{\hat{p}} = 0.04$; $\sigma_{\hat{p}} = \sqrt{\dfrac{0.04(1-0.04)}{50}} = \sqrt{\dfrac{0.04(0.96)}{50}} = \sqrt{\dfrac{0.0384}{50}}$

$= \sqrt{0.000768} = 0.028$

(b) For the sampling distribution of $\hat{p}$ to be approximately normal, we want $np \geq 10$ and $n(1-p) \geq 10$. In this case, if we check both, we get $n(0.04) \geq 10$, so $n \geq 250$ and also $n(0.96) \geq 10$, so $n \geq 10.42$ or 11. Since both conditions must be met, the smallest sample size is 250 children.

SAMPLE PROBLEM 3 Suppose that 30% of the seniors at a large urban school drink soda on a typical school day. If a random sample of 49 students is selected from the seniors at this school, what is the probability that more than 37% of the students in the sample drink soda on a typical school day?

SOLUTION TO PROBLEM 3 To solve this problem we will

- Find the mean and standard deviation of the sampling distribution of $\hat{p}$.

$\mu_{\hat{p}} = 0.30$

$\sigma_{\hat{p}} = \sqrt{\dfrac{0.30(1-0.30)}{49}} = \sqrt{\dfrac{0.30(0.70)}{49}} = \sqrt{\dfrac{0.21}{49}} = \sqrt{0.0043} = 0.065$

- Verify that the sampling distribution of $\hat{p}$ is approximately normal. Since $np = 49(0.3) = 14.7 \geq 10$ and $n(1-p) = 49(0.7) = 34.3 \geq 10$, the sampling distribution of p is approximately normal.
- Use the normal distribution to calculate the probability of interest.

You can now evaluate the probability of interest, $P(\hat{p} \geq 0.37)$. Using a graphing calculator, we use normalcdf(0.37,0.99,0.3,0.065) and get 0.14.

The probability that more than 37% of the students in a random sample of size 49 drink soda on a typical school day is 0.14.

Sampling Variability and Sampling Distributions: Student Objectives for the AP® Exam

- You will be able to describe the sampling distribution of a sample mean.
- You will be able to describe the sampling distribution of a sample proportion.
- You will identify when the sampling distribution of $\bar{x}$ is normal or approximately normal.
- You will identify when the sampling distribution of $\hat{p}$ is approximately normal.
- You will use properties of the sampling distribution of a sample mean to compute probabilities.
- You will use properties of the sampling distribution of a sample proportion to compute probabilities.

Multiple-Choice Questions

1. The mean of a population is 83, and the standard deviation is 5. What are the mean and the standard deviation of the sampling distribution of $\bar{x}$ for samples of size 40?

   (A) 83 and $\dfrac{5}{40}$, respectively

   (B) $\dfrac{83}{40}$ and $\dfrac{5}{40}$, respectively

   (C) 83 and $\dfrac{5}{\sqrt{40}}$, respectively

   (D) $\dfrac{83}{\sqrt{40}}$ and $\dfrac{5}{\sqrt{40}}$, respectively

   (E) 83 and 5, respectively

2. Fifty recent house sales were randomly selected from all sales in a large urban community. The average home sale price for these 50 sales was $372,000. $372,000 is the value of a
   (A) proportion.
   (B) population.
   (C) parameter.
   (D) statistic.
   (E) sample.

3. A population has $\mu = 78$ and a standard deviation $\sigma = 4.8$. What would be the mean and standard deviation of the sampling distribution $\bar{x}$ for random samples of size 100 from this population?
   (A) $\mu_{\bar{x}} = 78$, $\sigma_{\bar{x}} = 0.048$
   (B) $\mu_{\bar{x}} = 78$, $\sigma_{\bar{x}} = 0.48$
   (C) $\mu_{\bar{x}} = 78$, $\sigma_{\bar{x}} = 4.8$
   (D) $\mu_{\bar{x}} = 78$, $\sigma_{\bar{x}} = 48$
   (E) $\mu_{\bar{x}} = 78$, $\sigma_{\bar{x}} = 480$

4. Which of the following statements is true?
   I. The mean of any sample is always equal to the mean of the population.
   II. The sampling distribution of the sample mean is approximately normal when the sample size is sufficiently large.
   III. As the sample size increases, the standard deviation of the sampling distribution of the sample mean decreases.
   (A) I only
   (B) II only
   (C) I and II
   (D) I and III
   (E) II and III

5. A population consisting of seven numbers has a mean of 8.5 and a standard deviation of 2.29. If random samples of size 3 are selected with replacement from this population, what can be said about the mean and standard deviation of the sampling distribution of x?
   (A) $\mu_{\bar{x}} = 8.5$ and the $\sigma_{\bar{x}} = 2.29$
   (B) $\mu_{\bar{x}} = 8.5$ and the $\sigma_{\bar{x}} > 2.29$
   (C) $\mu_{\bar{x}} = 8.5$ and the $\sigma_{\bar{x}} < 2.29$
   (D) $\mu_{\bar{x}} > 8.5$ and the $\sigma_{\bar{x}} = 2.29$
   (E) $\mu_{\bar{x}} < 8.5$ and the $\sigma_{\bar{x}} < 2.29$

6. Which of the following is a consequence of the Central Limit Theorem?
   (A) When n is sufficiently large, the sampling distribution of $\bar{x}$ is roughly approximated by the normal curve.
   (B) If the population distribution is normal, then the sampling distribution of $\bar{x}$ will also be normal when n is sufficiently large.
   (C) The shape of the sampling distribution will be the same as the shape of the population, but the sampling distribution will be less spread out than the population distribution.
   (D) The shape of the sampling distribution will be the same as the shape of the population, but the sampling distribution will be more spread out than the population distribution.
   (E) The sampling distribution will be centered at $\bar{x}$.

7. Each child in a random sample of 36 preschool children had his or her height measured. The sample mean height was 37.2 inches. Which of the following statements about the population of heights of preschool children is true?
   (A) The mean height of all preschool children is 37.2 inches.
   (B) The standard deviation of the heights of all preschool children is six times smaller than the sample standard deviation.
   (C) The standard deviation of the heights of all preschool children is six times larger than the sample standard deviation.
   (D) The distribution of heights of all preschool children is approximately normal since $n = 36 \geq 30$.
   (E) None of the above statements is true.

8. In a simple random sample of 1,000 Americans who purchased a car in 2010, 61% were satisfied with the service provided by the dealer from which they bought their car. In a simple random sample of 1,000 Canadians who purchased a car in 2010, 58% were satisfied with the service provided by the dealer from which they bought their car. How do the standard errors associated with these statistics compare?
   (A) The standard errors are about the same.
   (B) The standard error is much smaller for the Canadian percentage because the population of Canada is smaller than that of the United States and so the sample is a larger proportion of the population.
   (C) The standard error is much larger for the Canadian percentage because Canada has a lower population density than the United States. This means that Canadians tend to live further apart, which always increases sampling variability.
   (D) The standard errors are equal.
   (E) The standard errors cannot be compared because these are two different populations.

9. Suppose that the weights of packages of cheese are normally distributed with a mean of 8 ounces and a standard deviation of 0.2 ounces. A random sample of four packages of cheese is selected every 30 minutes and the sample mean weight is calculated. We would expect about 95% of the sample means to fall within what interval?
   (A) 7.6 to 8.4 ounces
   (B) 7.7 to 8.3 ounces
   (C) 7.8 to 8.2 ounces
   (D) 7.9 to 8.1 ounces
   (E) 8.1 to 8.4 ounces

10. It is believed that currently 37% of American homes have at least one flat screen television. Which of the following is true about the sampling distribution of $\hat{p}$ for random samples of size 150 American homes?

(A) $\mu_{\hat{p}} = 0.37$ and $\sigma_{\hat{p}} = \sqrt{0.37(0.63)}$

(B) $\mu_{\hat{p}} = 0.37$ and $\sigma_{\hat{p}} = \sqrt{(150(0.37)(0.63))}$

(C) $\mu_{\hat{p}} = 0.37$ and $\sigma_{\hat{p}} = 0.37(0.63)$

(D) $\mu_{\hat{p}} = 0.37$ and $\sigma_{\hat{p}} = \dfrac{0.37(0.63)}{150}$

(E) $\mu_{\hat{p}} = 0.37$ and $\sigma_{\hat{p}} = \sqrt{\dfrac{0.37(0.63)}{150}}$

11. Forty-three percent of the registered voters in a particular county are Democrats. A sample of 200 registered voters is selected at random. The approximate probability that more than 100 of the people in the sample are Democrats is
    (A) 0.463.
    (B) 0.388.
    (C) 0.038.
    (D) 0.023.
    (E) 0.012.

12. Suppose that 14% of the students at a university have a full-time job. If a random sample is to be selected from the students at this university, what is the smallest sample size for which it would be reasonable to think the sampling distribution of $\hat{p}$, the proportion in the sample who have full-time jobs, would be approximately normal?
    (A) 10 students
    (B) 11 students
    (C) 12 students
    (D) 71 students
    (E) 72 students

13. A news magazine claims that 30% of all New York City police officers are overweight. To investigate, the police commissioner plans to select a random sample of 200 police officers and determine the proportion in the sample who are overweight. Assuming that the 30% figure is correct, which of the following statements is true?
    (A) The sample proportion $\hat{p}$ will be 0.30.
    (B) The sample standard deviation will be $\sqrt{\dfrac{(0.30)(0.20)}{200}}$
    (C) The sample size is not large enough to sample proportion.
    (D) The sample standard deviation will be $\dfrac{0.30}{200}$
    (E) The sample proportion will probably be between 0.24 and 0.36.

14. A population has a mean of 27.3 and a standard deviation 20. What is the probability that the mean of a random sample of size 100 will be between 28.2 and 29.7?
    (A) 0.2113
    (B) 0.0500
    (C) 0.0000
    (D) 0.7887
    (E) 0.9500

15. A population has a proportion of successes of 0.2. Let $\hat{p}$ be the proportion of successes in a random sample from this population. How large would n have to be in order for the standard deviation of the sampling distribution of $\hat{p}$ to be less than 0.01?
    (A) 16
    (B) 64
    (C) 256
    (D) 1,600
    (E) 4,000

FREE-RESPONSE PROBLEMS

1. Suppose a company manufactures protective covers for smartphones. When the manufacturing process is working correctly, the diagonal lengths of the rectangular phone covers are approximately normally distributed with a mean diagonal length of 6 inches and a standard deviation of 0.02 inches. To make sure the machine is not producing covers that are too big or too small, each hour a random sample of 25 covers is selected and the sample mean diagonal length is calculated.

   (a) Describe the sampling distribution for sample mean diagonal length for a sample of 25 covers.

   (b) The company decides that it will shut down the machine if the sample mean is less than 5.99 inches or greater than 6.01 inches, since this indicates that some covers will be too small or too large for the smartphones and have to be discarded. Assuming the machine is working properly, what is the probability that a sample of size 25 will indicate the company needs to shut down the machine?

   (c) Which of the following results gives more convincing evidence that the machine needs to be shut down? Clearly explain your reasoning and justify your answer.

      1. Getting a single sample mean below 5.99 or above 6.01
                  OR
      2. Getting a single phone cover with a diagonal length over 6.04.

2. A Public Policy Polling survey was given in April of 2013 regarding conspiracy theories. The survey showed that 4% of people believe that shape-shifting lizard people "control our world by taking on human form and gaining political power to manipulate our societies." Assume this survey reveals the true percentage of the population that believe in shape-shifting lizard people controlling society and that you are going to test this claim in your local community

    (a) What sample size would you need in order to assume that the sampling distribution of $\hat{p}$, the proportion of people who believe in shape-shifting lizard people controlling society, is approximately normal?

    (b) Suppose you take a sample of 300 people. A local news agency has informed you that it will find the results of your survey interesting enough to run a story on if over 5% of people in the sample believe in shape-shifting lizard people controlling society. What is the probability of the local news running a story on your results?

Answers

MULTIPLE-CHOICE QUESTIONS

1. **(C)** The mean of the sampling distribution is equal to the mean of the population and the standard deviation of the sampling distribution is equal to the population standard deviation divided by the square root of the sample size (*Statistics: Learning from Data*, AP Edition, 1st ed. pages 568–576 / 2nd ed. pages 590–598).

2. **(D)** The average of $372,000 is computed from a sample of 50 homes; therefore, it is the value of a statistic (*Statistics: Learning from Data*, AP Edition, 1st ed. pages 433–436 / 2nd ed. pages 447–450).

3. **(B)** The mean of the sampling distribution is equal to the mean of the population and the standard deviation of the sampling distribution is equal to the population standard deviation divided by the square root of the sample size (*Statistics: Learning from Data*, AP Edition, 1st ed. pages 568–576 / 2nd ed. pages 590–598).

4. **(E)** Any particular sample mean is not necessarily equal to the population mean. However, the mean of the sampling distribution of $\bar{x}$ for random samples of size *n* will equal the population mean (*Statistics: Learning from Data*, AP Edition, 1st ed. pages 568–576 / 2nd ed. pages 590–598).

5. **(C)** The mean of the sampling distribution of $\bar{x}$ equals the mean of the population but the standard deviation of the sampling distribution will be smaller—it is the population standard deviation divided by the square root of the sample size (*Statistics: Learning from Data*, AP Edition, 1st ed. pages 568–576 / 2nd ed. pages 590–598).

6. (A) The Central Limit Theorem states that even in skewed populations, if the sample size n is sufficiently large, the sampling distribution will be well approximated by a normal distribution (*Statistics: Learning from Data*, AP Edition, 1st ed. pages 568–576 / 2nd ed. pages 590–598).

7. (E) The population mean and standard deviation are fixed and we don't expect the sample mean or the sample standard deviation to be exactly equal to μ and σ (*Statistics: Learning from Data*, AP Edition, 1st ed. pages 568–576 / 2nd ed. pages 590–598).

8. (A) The two standard errors are close: 0.000236 and 0.000244, respectively (*Statistics: Learning from Data*, AP Edition, 1st ed. pages 438–442 / 2nd ed. pages 453–458).

9. (C) Using the empirical rule, about 95% of the sample means will be within two standard deviations. The standard deviation from the sampling distribution of size 4 is 0.1 (*Statistics: Learning from Data*, AP Edition, 1st ed. pages 568–576 / 2nd ed. pages 590–598).

10. (E) Since $\mu_{\hat{p}} = \mu$ and $\sigma_{\hat{p}} = \sqrt{\dfrac{p(1-p)}{n}}$, $\mu_{\hat{p}} = 0.37$ and $\sigma_{\hat{p}} = \sqrt{\dfrac{0.37(0.63)}{150}}$.
(*Statistics: Learning from Data*, AP Edition, 1st ed. pages 438–442 / 2nd ed. pages 453–458).

11. (D) First, calculate the mean and standard deviation of the sampling distribution of $\hat{p}$. $\mu_{\hat{p}} = 0.43$, $\sigma_{\hat{p}} = \sqrt{\dfrac{0.43(0.57)}{200}} = 0.035$. With this information, now calculate the related area under the curve for more than 100 people in the sample to be democrats (or 100/200 = 0.50). Then, $P(\hat{p} > 0.5) = P(z > 2) = 0.0227$. This can also be found using normalcdf(0.5,0.99,0.43,0.035) (*Statistics: Learning from Data*, AP Edition, 1st ed. pages 438–442 / 2nd ed. pages 453–458).

12. (E) To ensure that $np \geq 10$, we need $n = \dfrac{10}{0.14} = 71.4$ students and to ensure that $n(1-p) \geq 10$, we need $n = \dfrac{10}{0.86} = 11.6$ students. In order to meet both conditions, at least 72 students should be included in the sample (*Statistics: Learning from Data*, AP Edition, 1st ed. pages 438–442 / 2nd ed. pages 453–458).

13. (E) The sampling distribution of the sample proportion will be approximately normal with mean 0.30 and standard deviation $\sqrt{\dfrac{0.3(0.7)}{200}} = 0.03$. About 95% of all possible random samples will have a value of $\hat{p}$. within two standard deviations of the mean or in the range $0.30 \pm 2(0.03)$ (*Statistics: Learning from Data*, AP Edition, 1st ed. pages 438–442 / 2nd ed. pages 453–458).

14. (A) The standard deviation of the sampling distribution is $\dfrac{\sigma}{\sqrt{n}} = \dfrac{20}{\sqrt{100}} = 2$.
Then, $P(28.3 \leq \bar{x} \leq 29.7) = P(0.45 \leq z \leq 1.20) = 0.2113$. This can also be found using the calculator command normalcdf(28.3,29.7,27.3,2) (*Statistics: Learning from Data*, AP Edition, 1st ed. pages 568–576 / 2nd ed. pages 590–598).

15. (D) This involves solving backward for *n*. Using the formula for the standard deviation of the sampling distribution of $\hat{p}$ gives the following:

$\sigma_{\hat{p}} = \sqrt{\dfrac{p(1-p)}{n}}$; now substitute and solve for *n*.

$$0.01 = \sqrt{\dfrac{0.2(0.8)}{n}}$$

$$0.01^2 = \dfrac{0.2(0.8)}{n}$$

$$\dfrac{0.0001}{1} = \dfrac{0.16}{n}$$

$$0.0001n = 0.16$$

$$n = \dfrac{0.16}{0.0001}$$

(*Statistics: Learning from Data*, AP Edition, 1st ed. pages 438–442 / 2nd ed. pages 453–458).

FREE-RESPONSE PROBLEMS

1. (a) $\mu_{\bar{x}} = \mu = 6$

    $\sigma_{\bar{x}} = \dfrac{\sigma}{\sqrt{n}} = \dfrac{0.02}{\sqrt{25}} = \dfrac{0.02}{5} = 0.004$

    Because the population distribution of phone covers is approximately normal, the sampling distribution of $\bar{x}$ is also approximately normal.

    (b) The probability of $\bar{x}$ being less than 5.99 inches or greater than 6.01 inches is equivalent to 1 minus the probability of $\bar{x}$ being between 5.99 and 6.01.

    $$1 - P(5.99 \leq \bar{x} \leq 6.01) = 1 - P\left(\dfrac{5.99-6}{0.004} \leq z \leq \dfrac{6.01-6}{0.004}\right)$$

    $$= 1 - P(-2.5 \leq z \leq 2.5)$$

    $$= 1 - 0.988$$

    $$= 0.012$$

    You can also use the calculator command
    1 − normalcdf(5.99,6.01,6,0.004)

(c) The probability of getting a single sample mean below 5.99 or above 6.01 was just computed to be 0.014. The probability of a single cover being greater than 6.04 is

$$P(x \geq 6.04) = P\left(z \geq \frac{6.04 - 6}{0.02}\right) = 0.0228$$

You can also use the calculator command normalcdf(6.04,1000,6,0.02).

Since the probability of getting a sample mean below 5.99 or above 6.01 is less than the probability of getting a single cover greater than 6.04, getting a sample mean below 5.99 or above 6.01 would provide stronger evidence that the machine needs to be shut down.

(*Statistics: Learning from Data*, AP Edition, 1st ed. pages 568–576 / 2nd ed. pages 590–598)

2. (a) In order for the sampling distribution of $\hat{p}$, the proportion of people who believe in shape-shifting lizard people controlling society, to be approximately normal, the following must be true:

$np \geq 10$ and $n(1 - p) \geq 10$

Since $p = 0.04$, which is less than $1 - p = 0.96$, focus on solving the inequality $np \geq 10$ to find the minimum sample size. Substituting $0.04n \geq 10$ gives $n \geq 250$.

(b) Since the sample size is over 250, the sampling distribution of $\hat{p}$ can be considered approximately normal.

Using a graphing calculator,

$$P(\hat{p} \geq 0.05) = normalcdf\left(0.05, 0.99, 0.04, \sqrt{\frac{0.04(0.96)}{300}}\right) = 0.188$$

The probability that the local paper picks up the story is 0.188 or 18.8%.

(*Statistics: Learning from Data*, AP Edition, 1st ed. pages 438–442 / 2nd ed. pages 453–458)

8

ESTIMATION USING A SINGLE SAMPLE

This section will cover methods for estimating a single population parameter. Since our goal is to estimate the population parameter of interest, making inferences based on a sample estimate will allow us to develop a set of plausible values for our population parameter.

OBJECTIVES

- Estimate a population mean or proportion using a point estimate.
- Construct and interpret a confidence interval estimate for a population proportion.
- Construct and interpret a confidence interval estimate for a population mean.
- Calculate the sample size needed in order to achieve a given bound on error.

POINT ESTIMATION

(*Statistics: Learning from Data*, AP Edition, 1st ed. pages 456–459 / 2nd ed. pages 470–473)

When we want to estimate some population characteristic, we will often use sample data to compute a single value, such as the sample mean $\bar{x}$. This value is called a point estimate of the population mean μ. Given a different sample, the sample mean would most likely be different—it is only an estimate of the value of μ. When estimating a population proportion, the usual point estimate is the sample proportion, $\hat{p}$. As an example, suppose a teacher wanted to estimate the proportion of student phone calls that are made to family members. Each student in a random sample of 100 students was asked whether the most recent call he or she made was to a family member. The teacher found that 29 of the students in the sample said the most recent call was to a family member. In this case, the sample proportion is $\hat{p} = 0.29$, and this is a point estimate of the proportion of calls made by all students to family members.

A statistic is said to be **unbiased** if, on average, the sampling distribution is centered at the true value of the population parameter. In other words, the average value of the statistic for all possible random samples of size *n* is equal to the value of the population parameter.

LARGE-SAMPLE CONFIDENCE INTERVAL FOR A POPULATION PROPORTION

(*Statistics: Learning from Data*, AP Edition, 1st ed. pages 460–465 and 467–477 and 480–481 / 2nd ed. pages 475–480 and 482–493 and 497–498)

Point estimates can be helpful in estimating a population characteristic; however, different samples would most likely yield different values. Instead of using just the point estimate, a better method is to present an entire interval of plausible values of the parameter. In this way, we are allowing for variation in the samples and yet offering a reasonable estimate of the population parameter. In the previous phone call example, we might report that the proportion of calls made to family members by students to be some value in an interval extending from 0.20 to 0.38. In this case, all values within that range would be considered plausible values for the proportion of calls made to family members by students. A narrow interval provides more precise information about the actual value of the population parameter, but at the same time, we want an interval for which we can be confident that the interval actually contains the correct value.

A **confidence interval** is an interval of reasonable values for the population parameter of interest based on the sample data. This interval is constructed with a prechosen confidence level. The **confidence level** specifies the success rate for the method used to construct the confidence interval. While in theory, the confidence level can be any percent; the most commonly used confidence levels are 90%, 95%, and 99%. No matter what level of confidence is set by the researcher, the meaning of the confidence level is the same: If the same method were used with a very large number of different random samples, in the long run, the confidence intervals generated would capture the true population characteristic the given percentage of the time. For example, if the confidence level were set at 90%, in repeated sampling, the intervals would capture the true value of the population parameter about 90% of the time.

Generating a confidence interval is relatively straightforward. We start with a point estimate. We use the point estimate as the center of the confidence interval. We then determine how far the interval should extend on either side of the point estimate.

The general form of any confidence interval includes three essential pieces.

$$\begin{pmatrix} \text{sample statistic} \\ \text{(point estimate)} \end{pmatrix} \pm (\text{critical value}) \begin{pmatrix} \text{standard deviation} \\ \text{of the statistic} \end{pmatrix}$$

In the case of proportions, the sample proportion p is the sample statistic. If the sample size is large (check $n\hat{p} \geq 10$ and $n(1-\hat{p}) > 10$), the sampling distribution of $\hat{p}$ is approximately normal. Notice that we are using $\hat{p}$ to estimate p. In this case, the critical value is found using the z distribution (the standard normal distribution) and depends on the desired confidence level. For a 95% confidence level, the critical value is found by finding the z value that corresponds to a central area of 0.95 under the z curve as shown below. For other confidence levels, adjust the central area.

For a 95% confidence level, the z critical value is 1.96. It follows that a 95% confidence interval for a population proportion is:

$$(\hat{p}) \pm (1.96) \begin{pmatrix} \text{standard deviation} \\ \text{of } \hat{p} \end{pmatrix}$$

Notice again that we are using $\hat{p}$ to estimate p in the calculation of the standard deviation of $\hat{p}$. When use $\hat{p}$ instead of p, we sometimes call it the standard error of $\hat{p}$.

Finally, as seen in the last section in this text (and in chapter 6 in the textbook), the estimated standard deviation of the sampling distribution of $\hat{p}$ is $\sqrt{\dfrac{\hat{p}(1-\hat{p})}{n}}$ resulting in $\hat{p} \pm (1.96)\sqrt{\dfrac{\hat{p}(1-\hat{p})}{n}}$

Returning to the example where 100 students were asked if the last phone call made was to a family member, a 95% confidence interval for the proportion of calls made to family members is

$$(0.29) \pm (1.96)\left(\sqrt{\dfrac{0.29(1-0.29)}{100}}\right) = (0.201, 0.379)$$

Note that the sample was a random sample from the population of interest, the sample size is large enough $(n\hat{p}) = 100(0.29) \geq 10$, $n(1 - \hat{p}) = 100(0.71) \geq 10$), and we assume that the sample size is less than 10% of the population size (it is reasonable to assume that there are more than $10(100) = 1{,}000$ students in the population). These are the three conditions that must be checked in order for this confidence interval for a population proportion to be appropriate.

The 95% confidence interval is (0.201, 0.379). Interpreting the interval, we would say that we are 95% confident that the true proportion of students' phone calls that are to family members is between 0.201 and 0.379. Instead of just having the point estimate of 0.29, we now have a range of reasonable values for the true proportion of students' phone calls that are to family members based on the sample data. This acknowledges the uncertainty in our original point estimate.

SAMPLE SIZE

The margin of error is defined to be the amount that we extend on either side of our point estimate. In other words, margin of error = (critical value) $\left(\sqrt{\dfrac{p(1-p)}{n}}\right)$.

Notice that the margin of error is related to sample size. Sometimes, it is useful to determine the sample size needed to achieve a particular margin of error. For example, if we wanted to achieve a margin of error of 0.05 with 95% confidence, we would want to solve $0.05 = (1.96)\sqrt{\dfrac{p(1-p)}{n}}$ for n. But there is a catch—we don't know the value of p and we haven't yet selected a sample, so we do not have a $\hat{p}$ to use as an estimate. A conservative approach is to use $p = 0.5$ in this equation. This results in a sample size that is large enough to achieve the desired margin of error no matter what the actual value of p. (This is because p is always between 0 and 1 and $p(1-p)$ is largest when $p = 0.5$.)

EXAMPLE Suppose that a cell phone company wants to estimate the proportion of calls made by students to contact family members. How large a sample would be needed to achieve a margin of error of 0.05 with 95% confidence?

$$0.05 = (1.96)\left(\sqrt{\dfrac{0.5(0.5)}{n}}\right)$$

Now, solve for n algebraically.

$$0.05^2 = (1.96)^2 \left(\sqrt{\dfrac{0.5(0.5)}{n}}\right)^2$$

$$0.0025 = \left(\frac{3.8416}{1}\right)\left(\frac{0.25}{n}\right)$$

$$\frac{0.0025}{1} = \frac{3.8416(0.25)}{n}$$

$$0.0025n = 3.8416(0.25)$$

$$n = \frac{3.8416(0.25)}{0.0025} = 384.16$$

So, we will need at least 385 students in the sample. Always round up to the next integer when making a sample size calculation to ensure you have the smallest sample size necessary to guarantee the required margin of error.

AP® Tip

To calculate a z confidence interval to estimate the population proportion

1. Verify (and state for the AP® Readers) that the necessary conditions are met.
   (a) The sample was a random sample from the population of interest.
   (b) The sample size is large. Check $n\hat{p} \geq 10$ and $n(1-\hat{p}) \geq 10$.
   (c) The sample size is less than 10% of the population size.
2. State the formula for a confidence interval with all of the corresponding numbers substituted in place of n, $\hat{p}$, and the z^* critical value.
3. Give the interval and interpret it in the context of the problem.

CONFIDENCE INTERVAL FOR A POPULATION MEAN

(*Statistics: Learning from Data*, AP Edition, 1st ed. pages 578–588 / 2nd ed. pages 600–612)

A confidence interval for a population mean has the same form as the confidence interval for a population proportion:

$$(\text{sample statistic}) \pm (\text{critical value})\left(\begin{array}{c}\text{standard deviation}\\ \text{of the statistic}\end{array}\right)$$

The sample statistic is the sample mean $\bar{x}$. When the sample is a random sample from the population of interest and either the sample size is large ($n \geq 30$) or the population distribution is approximately normal, the sampling distribution of $\bar{x}$ is approximately normal with a standard deviation of $\frac{\sigma}{\sqrt{n}}$.

There are two cases to consider depending on whether or not the population standard deviation σ is known.

AP® is a trademark registered by the College Board, which is not affiliated with, and does not endorse, this product.

If σ is known, a confidence interval for the population mean is

$$\bar{x} \pm (z \text{ critical value}) \frac{\sigma}{\sqrt{n}}.$$

The z critical value depends on the desired confidence level and is found in the same way as the confidence interval for a population proportion. Because it is rare that σ is known, the more commonly used interval is the one that follows.

If σ is not known, a confidence interval for the population mean is

$$\bar{x} \pm (t \text{ critical value}) \frac{s}{\sqrt{n}}.$$

The t critical value in the interval above is found using a t distribution rather than the standard normal distribution. The t distributions have a mound shape, similar to the z distribution, but t distributions are more spread out than the z distribution. A t distribution is characterized by a quantity known as degrees of freedom (df). As the degrees of freedom increase, the t distributions become more and more like the z distribution. Degrees of freedom is found by subtracting one from the sample size. This value will be needed to find the critical value for a confidence interval for a population mean.

The t critical value needed to compute the confidence interval can be found using the t distribution table (also provided during the AP® Statistics exam) or generated on your calculator. To use the table, find the degrees of freedom in the left-most column (remember, $df = n - 1$). Then follow this row over to the column that contains the critical values for the desired confidence level. The partial t table below shows t critical values for degrees of freedom equal to 8, 9, and 10. Keep in mind that the tail probability is the percent of the area to the left *outside* the interval you are seeking.

EXAMPLE If we want the t critical value for a 95% confidence interval and the sample size is 10, we would go down the first column to locate $df = n - 1 = 9$ and follow that row over to the column with 0.025 tail area for a 95% confidence level.

Tail probability p							
df	0.25	0.20	0.15	0.10	0.05	0.025	0.02
8	0.705	0.889	1.108	1.397	1.860	2.306	2.449
9	0.703	0.883	1.100	1.383	1.833	2.262	2.398
10	0.700	0.879	1.093	1.372	1.812	2.228	2.359
.	.	.	.	.	.	.	.
.	.	.	.	.	.	.	.
.	.	.	.	.	.	.	.
∞	0.674	0.841	1.036	1.282	1.645	1.960	2.054
	50%	60%	70%	80%	90%	95%	96%

Confidence Level C

Notice as the degrees of freedom increase, the critical values in any column of the table are getting closer to the critical value associated with the standard normal (z) distribution.

An alternative to reading the table is to use the capabilities of your graphing calculator. The argument required by the calculator is the area under the curve in the left tail up to the critical value and the *df*. The calculator will give the correct critical value, either the negative value or positive value, based on the area you enter into the argument. The only difference below is that one yields the left critical value (the negative critical value) and the other yields the right critical value (the positive critical value) as shown in the two calculator displays.

```
NORMAL FLOAT AUTO REAL RADIAN MP
invT(.025,9)
                    -2.262157158
```

```
NORMAL FLOAT AUTO REAL RADIAN MP
invT(.975,9)
                     2.262157158
■
```

Once the critical value is determined, the confidence interval is computed using

$$\bar{x} \pm (t \text{ critical value}) \frac{s}{\sqrt{n}}$$

where *t* critical value is based on $df = n - 1$.

Before using this confidence interval, be sure to check the two necessary conditions: (1) random sample from the population of interest and (2) large sample size or normal population distribution.

If the sample size is not large, we need to assume that the population distribution is approximately normal. This is reasonable when a dotplot or a boxplot constructed from the sample data is roughly symmetric and there are no outliers. One benefit of the *t* distributions over normal distributions is that the *t* distributions are robust. This means that the *t* distribution is still pretty accurate even when the sample size is less than 30.

EXAMPLE A cable TV company is interested in estimating the average time that customers must wait on hold when they call the company's customer support line. Twenty calls are selected at random from all calls made to the customer support line and the hold time is recorded for each call. The sample mean hold time was 10.5 minutes and the sample standard deviation was 1.1 minutes. A dotplot of the 20 hold times was approximately symmetric with no outliers. Estimate the mean hold time for customers calling the support line using a 90% confidence interval.

Because the population standard deviation is not known, we use the *t* confidence interval. First, we must verify that the conditions are met. The problem states that the sample is a random sample from our population of all calls. The sample size is not large (20 < 30), so we must be willing to assume that the population distribution of hold times is approximately normal. The actual sample data are not given here but we are told that the dotplot was approximately symmetric with no outliers, so it is reasonable to assume that the population of all calls is roughly normally distributed.

With a sample size of $n = 20$, $df = 19$. For a 90% confidence level, the t critical value is 1.729. This gives

$$\bar{x} \pm (t \text{ critical value}) \frac{s}{\sqrt{n}}$$

$$= 10.5 \pm (1.729)\left(\frac{1.1}{\sqrt{20}}\right)$$

$$= 10.5 \pm (1.729)(0.246)$$

$$= 10.5 \pm 0.426$$

$$= (10.08, 10.93)$$

We can now say that based on this sample, we are 90% confident that the true mean hold time is between 10.08 and 10.93 minutes. The 90% confidence level means that we used a method that will capture the true mean wait time about 90% of the time in repeated sampling.

AP® Tip

To calculate a t confidence interval to estimate the population mean

1. Verify (and state for the AP® Readers) that the necessary conditions are met.
   (a) The sample was a random sample from the population of interest.
   (b) The sample size is large ($n \geq 30$) or the population distribution is approximately normal. To decide if it is reasonable to think that the population distribution is approximately normal, look at a dotplot, histogram, or a boxplot. You want the plot to be reasonably symmetric with no outliers. You could also look at a normal probability plot—if the plot looks linear, normality is plausible.

2. State the formula for a confidence interval with all of the corresponding numbers substituted in place of n, $\bar{x}$, s, and the t critical value.

3. Give the interval and interpret it in the context of the problem.

As a final note, consider what happens if instead of using a 90% confidence level, we change to a 95% confidence level. Using the same information from the example above, the only change in the calculations would involve a change in the critical value. For a 95% confidence level, and $df = 19$, the t critical value is 2.093, resulting in

$$\bar{x} \pm (t \text{ critical value})\left(\frac{s}{\sqrt{n}}\right)$$

$$= 10.5 \pm (2.093)\left(\frac{1.1}{\sqrt{20}}\right)$$

$$= 10.5 \pm (2.093)(0.246)$$

$$= 10.5 \pm 0.515$$

$$= (9.98, 11.02)$$

Notice that this interval is wider than the 90% confidence interval. The higher confidence level comes at a price—a wider interval that is a bit less informative in terms of pinning down the value of the population mean.

> ### AP® Tip
>
> When computing a t confidence interval, don't forget to use $n - 1$ for df but still use n for the denominator of the standard error. A common AP® exam error is to use either n or $n - 1$ in both places.

INTERPRETING AND COMMUNICATING THE RESULTS OF STATISTICAL ANALYSES

(*Statistics: Learning from Data*, AP Edition, 1st ed. pages 467–474 and 581–587 / 2nd ed. pages 482–489 and 603–609)

Interpreting a confidence interval and the associated confidence level can be tricky. Here, wording is *everything*.

INTERPRETING THE CONFIDENCE INTERVAL

The confidence interval tells us that (based on the confidence level) we can be confident that the interval actually contains the actual value of the population characteristic. For example, for a 90% confidence interval for a population mean, you would say

> *I am 90% confident that the value of the population mean is contained within the interval (a, b).*

Of course, be sure to include appropriate context.

INTERPRETING THE CONFIDENCE LEVEL

A confidence level of 90% indicates that with *repeated sampling*, approximately 90% of the intervals constructed would contain the true value of the population characteristic being estimated. This does not mean that for every 100 times we sample, we will get exactly 90 intervals of the 100 that contain the truth. Rather, this is saying that if we continued to select random samples and to generate confidence intervals, approximately 90% of the intervals would actually contain the true population parameter. You would say something like

> *The method used to construct the intervals will capture the true population parameter about 90% of the time in repeated sampling.*

AP® Tip

To interpret a confidence interval, say something like

I am _____ % confident that the true value of the population _____ (proportion or mean) _____ (supply context here!) is contained within the interval (_____ , _____).

To interpret the confidence level, say something like

The method that was used to construct the interval will capture the true _____ (proportion or mean) about _____ % of the time in repeated sampling.

SAMPLE PROBLEM 1 The National Geographic Society conducted a study that included 3,000 respondents, ages 18–24, in nine different countries (*San Luis Obispo Tribune*, November 21, 2002). The society found that 10% of the participants could not identify their own country on a blank world map.

(a) Construct a 90% confidence interval for the proportion of people who can identify their own country on a blank world map.

(b) To what population would it be reasonable to generalize this confidence interval estimate?

SOLUTION TO PROBLEM 1

(a) We want a 95% z confidence interval for the proportion of people who can identify their own country on a blank world map. We assume that the sample was a random sample from all people aged 18–24 in the nine countries. The sample size is large enough since $n\hat{p}$ = 3000(0.10) = 300 ≥ 10, $n(1-\hat{p})$ = 3000(0.90) = 2700 ≥ 10. It is reasonable to assume that there are more than 10(3000) = 30000 people aged 18–24 in the nine countries.

$$(0.10) \pm (1.96)\left(\frac{\sqrt{0.10(1-0.10)}}{3000}\right) = (0.089, 0.111)$$

We are 95% confident that the true proportion of people aged 18–24 in the nine countries who can identify their own country on a blank world map is between 0.089 and 0.111.

(b) The population of interest is all people aged 18–24 in the nine countries.

SAMPLE PROBLEM 2 A real estate company in Colorado has noticed the housing market seems to be doing better in some markets than others. In order to help new home sellers set a price, it selected a random sample of 20 recent sales in Colorado and found the average selling price was $142,000 and the standard deviation was $4,000.

(a) Interpret the confidence level of 95%.

(b) Estimate the mean house price in Colorado.

SOLUTION TO PROBLEM 2

(a) The method used to generate the confidence intervals will capture the true mean housing price in Colorado about 95% of the time in repeated sampling.

(b) Since the standard deviation is from the sample, a t confidence interval will be constructed with 95% confidence. The sample is a random sample from all home selling prices. We must assume that the population distribution is approximately normal since we do not have the original data to check.

$$142000 \pm 1.729 \left(\frac{4000}{\sqrt{20}} \right), \text{ with } df = 19.$$

I am 95% confident that the true mean selling price of homes in Colorado is between $141,128 and $143,872.

ESTIMATION USING A SINGLE SAMPLE: STUDENT OBJECTIVES FOR THE AP® EXAM

- You will be able to calculate a point estimate of a population mean or a population proportion.
- You will be able to calculate a confidence interval for a population mean.
- You will be able to calculate a confidence interval for a population proportion.
- You will be able to find the required sample size for a given margin of error.
- You will be able to correctly interpret a confidence interval in context.
- You will be able to interpret the confidence level associated with a confidence interval.

MULTIPLE-CHOICE QUESTIONS

1. Which of the following is the z critical value for a 99% confidence level?
   (A) 2.33
   (B) 2.58
   (C) 2.97
   (D) 3.09
   (E) 3.29

2. Which of the following is a difference between a *t* interval and a *z* interval?
   (A) *z* intervals are used if you know the population standard deviation and *t* intervals are used when you do not know the population standard deviation.
   (B) *t* intervals are used if you know the population standard deviation and *z* intervals are used when you do not know the population standard deviation.
   (C) *t* intervals are used when the sample size is large and *z* intervals are used when the sample size is small.
   (D) *z* intervals are used when the population is not normally distributed.
   (E) *t* intervals can only be used when the sample size is large, whereas *z* intervals can be used for both large and small samples.

3. Assuming that the data came from a random sample from the population of interest, what other conditions must be met in order for the *z* interval to be an appropriate way to estimate a population proportion?
   I. $n \geq 30$ or the population distribution is approximately normal.
   II. The population size is at least 10 times greater than the sample size.
   III. The population standard deviation is known.
   IV. $n\hat{p} \geq 10$ and $n(1-\hat{p}) \geq 10$
   (A) I and III
   (B) III and IV
   (C) II and IV
   (D) I, II, and III
   (E) All of the above conditions must be met.

4. A researcher wants to find a confidence interval estimate of the mean time it takes to complete an order over the phone at a call center for a large retail company. He has selected a random sample of 18 orders and recorded the time to complete the order. The sample mean time was 4.27 minutes and the sample standard deviation was 0.78 minutes. Assuming the conditions needed for inference are met, which of the following is the appropriate 98% confidence interval?
   (A) $4.27 \pm 2.326 \left(\dfrac{0.78}{\sqrt{18}} \right)$
   (B) $4.27 \pm 2.054 \left(\dfrac{0.78}{\sqrt{17}} \right)$
   (C) $4.27 \pm 2.552 \left(\dfrac{0.78}{\sqrt{18}} \right)$
   (D) $4.27 \pm 2.567 \left(\dfrac{0.78}{\sqrt{18}} \right)$
   (E) $4.27 \pm 2.567 \left(\dfrac{0.78}{\sqrt{17}} \right)$

5. What size is needed to achieve a margin of error of 3% with 95% confidence when the population proportion of successes is 0.36?
   (A) 984
   (B) 983
   (C) 256
   (D) 255
   (E) 250

6. Which of the following would increase the width of a confidence interval?
   (A) Increasing the sample size
   (B) Decreasing the degrees of freedom
   (C) Decreasing the confidence level
   (D) Decreasing the standard deviation
   (E) Increasing the point estimate

7. In a sample of 64 children who received a new antibiotic for an infection, 52 of the children had positive results within 12 hours.
   Find a 95% confidence interval for the proportion of children with infections who will experience positive results within 12 hours when treated with the new antibiotic. Assume all conditions for inference are met.
   (A) 0.81 ± 0.096
   (B) 0.81 ± 0.080
   (C) 0.81 ± 0.071
   (D) 0.83 ± 0.079
   (E) 0.83 ± 0.094

8. The treatment records of a small Army hospital were examined for 49 randomly selected days. The number of patients treated was determined for each of these days. For this sample, the mean was 11.2 patients and the standard deviation was 3.6 patients. With what level of confidence can we say that the true mean number of patients treated per day is between 10.3 and 12.1?
   (A) 80%
   (B) 85%
   (C) 90%
   (D) 95%
   (E) 98%

9. What conditions are NOT necessary for a 95% t interval with a sample size of 9 to be valid?
   (A) The sample was selected randomly from the population of interest.
   (B) The population standard deviation is not known.
   (C) It is reasonable to assume that the population distribution is approximately normal.
   (D) $n\hat{p} \geq 10$ and $n(1-\hat{p}) \geq 10$
   (E) All of the above are necessary conditions.

10. A 98% confidence interval for a population mean is found to be 127 ± 18. Which of the following is a correct interpretation?
    (A) The probability that the true mean is contained in this interval is 0.98.
    (B) The probability that the sample mean is contained in this interval is 0.98.
    (C) The probability that another interval will give a true mean of 127 is 0.98.
    (D) If many different random samples of the same size are selected, about 98% of them will contain the true value of the population mean.
    (E) If many different random samples of the same size are selected, about 98% of them will contain the sample mean of 127.

11. Which of the following statements about the width of a confidence interval is true if the sample size is doubled?
    (A) The confidence interval is wider.
    (B) The confidence interval is narrower.
    (C) It will have no effect on the width of the confidence interval.
    (D) The width of the confidence interval will double.
    (E) The confidence interval will be half as wide.

12. You have been asked to compute a 96% confidence interval for a population mean. If the population standard deviation is known to be 7 and the sample size is 40, what critical value would be used in computing the interval?
    (A) 1.751
    (B) 1.960
    (C) 2.054
    (D) 2.122
    (E) 2.125

13. A community wants to see if there is enough support to hold a town children's festival. Forty two percent of 150 residents said they would participate in the event. What is the approximate standard error of $\hat{p}$?
    (A) 0.03
    (B) 0.24
    (C) 0.02
    (D) 0.04
    (E) 0.002

14. A large company wants to estimate the proportion of employees who would prefer a pay increase to an increase in retirement benefits using a 95% confidence interval. What sample size should be used in order to achieve a margin of error of 0.04 or smaller?
    (A) 156 employees
    (B) 157 employees
    (C) 307 employees
    (D) 600 employees
    (E) 601 employees

15. Based on a random sample of American adults, a consumer group states that 72% of American adults believe corporations are not concerned about public safety. They also reported a margin of error of 2 percentage points with 90% confidence. What does this mean?
    (A) If the poll were conducted again, the probability that 72% believe corporations are not concerned about safety is 0.90.
    (B) The probability that the proportion of adult Americans who believe corporations aren't concerned with public safety is between 70% and 74% is 0.90.
    (C) Between 88% and 92% of American adults believe corporations are not concerned with public safety.
    (D) About 90% of all random samples of the same size of American adults will result in a sample percentage that is within 2 percentage points of the actual population proportion.
    (E) About 90 out of every 100 samples of the same size of American adults will have between 70% and 74% who believe that corporations are not concerned with public safety.

FREE-RESPONSE PROBLEMS

1. Many of the trees in a national forest suffer from a virus that attacks the bark of the tree. Trees with this virus should be removed in order to minimize the risk to nearby trees. A random sample of 204 trees was selected and each selected tree was inspected. It was found that 28% of the trees in the sample had the virus.

   (a) Estimate with 95% confidence the proportion of trees with the virus.

   (b) Suppose that researchers want to keep the confidence level at 95%, but lower the margin of error to at most .05. How many *additional* trees need to be selected?

2. Ninety minutes are allowed for students to complete the multiple-choice section of a national exam. A random sample of 28 students selected from the students at a large high school took a practice exam and the time (in minutes) that it took each student to complete the multiple-choice section was recorded. The times are given below.

Time to Complete Multiple-Choice Section of a National Exam						
58	76	74	80	88	74	65
97	66	95	77	63	83	73
64	71	60	68	70	63	71
57	75	74	52	71	81	82

   (a) Construct and interpret a 90% confidence interval for the mean time to complete the multiple-choice section for students at this school.

   (b) Based on the confidence interval, do you think that 90 minutes is a reasonable amount of time to allow for the multiple-choice part of the test? Explain your reasoning.

Answers

MULTIPLE-CHOICE QUESTIONS

1. **(B)** Since the interval is 99%, we can either look up on a table the critical value for this (with a 0.005 area left and right of the interval) or use the calculator argument invnorm(0.005) or invNorm(0.995) (*Statistics: Learning from Data*, AP Edition, 1st ed. pages 460–465 and 467–477 / 2nd ed. pages 475–480 and 482–493).

2. **(A)** While there are conditions that must also be checked when running any confidence interval, a t interval is used rather than a z interval when we do not know the population standard deviation (*Statistics: Learning from Data*, AP Edition, 1st ed. pages 578–581 / 2nd ed. pages 600–603).

3. **(C)** The population size must be at least 10 times the sample size and a large sample size is required (so we need $n\hat{p} \geq 10$ and $n(1-\hat{p}) \geq 10$) (*Statistics: Learning from Data*, AP Edition, 1st ed. pages 460–465 and 467–477 / 2nd ed. pages 475–480 and 482–493).

4. **(D)** Since the standard deviation is from the sample, this is a t interval and will require a t critical value based on 17 degrees of freedom (*Statistics: Learning from Data*, AP Edition, 1st ed. pages 578–588 / 2nd ed. pages 600–612).

5. **(A)** $0.03 = 1.96\left(\sqrt{\dfrac{0.36(0.64)}{n}}\right)$; $0.0009 = 3.842\dfrac{0.2304}{n}$;

   $n = 3.842(256)$; $n = 984$ (*Statistics: Learning from Data*, AP Edition, 1st ed. pages 480–481 / 2nd ed. pages 497–498).

6. **(B)** A smaller degrees of freedom correspond to a smaller sample size and a larger t critical value, making the interval wider (*Statistics: Learning from Data*, AP Edition, 1st ed. page 476 / 2nd ed. page 491).

7. **(A)** $\frac{52}{64} \pm 1.96\sqrt{\dfrac{0.81(0.19)}{64}}$ (*Statistics: Learning from Data*, AP Edition, 1st ed. pages 460–465 and 467–477 / 2nd ed. pages 475–480 and 482–493).

8. **(C)** The 90% confidence interval is 11.2 ± 0.863 (*Statistics: Learning from Data*, AP Edition, 1st ed. pages 578–588 / 2nd ed. pages 600–612).

9. **(C)** $n\hat{p} \geq 10$ and $n(1-\hat{p}) \geq 10$ are the conditions for a z confidence interval to estimate a population proportion not a population mean (*Statistics: Learning from Data*, AP Edition, 1st ed. pages 578–588 / 2nd ed. pages 600–612).

10. **(D)** We have used a method that produces intervals that contain the true mean value about 98% of the time in repeated sampling (*Statistics: Learning from Data*, AP Edition, 1st ed. pages 467–474 and 581–587 / 2nd ed. pages 482–489 and 603–609).

11. **(B)** Since the sample size is found in the denominator, any increase in this value will make the width of the confidence interval smaller. However, doubling the sample size does not result in an interval that is half as wide (*Statistics: Learning from Data*, AP Edition, 1st ed. page 476 / 2nd ed. page 491).

12. **(C)** A z critical value would be used. 2.054 is the correct z critical value for a confidence level of 96% (*Statistics: Learning from Data*, AP Edition, 1st ed. pages 578–588 / 2nd ed. pages 600–612).

13. **(D)** The estimated standard error is

    $$\sqrt{\frac{\hat{p}(1-\hat{p})}{n}} = \sqrt{\frac{0.42(0.58)}{150}} = 0.0402$$

    (*Statistics: Learning from Data*, AP Edition, 1st ed. pages 460–465 and 467–477 / 2nd ed. pages 475–480 and 482–493).

14. **(E)** Solving $0.04 = 1.96\sqrt{\frac{0.5(0.5)}{n}}$ gives $n = 600.25$, which should be rounded up to 601 employees (*Statistics: Learning from Data*, AP Edition, 1st ed. pages 480–481 / 2nd ed. pages 497–498).

15. **(D)** The margin of error is the measure of how far off an estimate could be from the truth (*Statistics: Learning from Data*, AP Edition, 1st ed. pages 467–474 and 581–587 / 2nd ed. pages 482–489 and 603–609).

FREE-RESPONSE PROBLEMS

1. (a) We want a 95% z confidence interval for the proportion of trees in the national forest with the virus. The sample was a random sample from all trees in the forest. The sample size is large enough since $n\hat{p} = 204(0.28) = 57.12 \geq 10$ and $n(1-\hat{p}) = 204(0.72) = 146.88 \geq 10$. It is reasonable to assume that there are more than $10(204) = 2,040$ trees in the national forest. The 95% confidence interval is

    $$0.28 \pm 1.96\sqrt{\frac{0.28(0.72)}{204}} = (0.218, 0.341).$$

    I am 95% confident that the true proportion of trees that have the virus is between 0.218 and 0.341. The method used to construct this estimate will capture the true proportion of trees that have the virus about 95% of the time in repeated sampling.

    (b) Solving $0.05 = 1.96\sqrt{\frac{0.28(0.72)}{n}}$ gives $n = 309.79$, which should be rounded up to 310 trees total. Since 204 trees were already selected, this means an additional $310 - 204 = 106$ trees need to be selected.

    (*Statistics: Learning from Data*, AP Edition, 1st ed. pages 460–465 and 467–477 and 480–481 / 2nd ed. pages 475–480 and 482–493 and 497–498)

2. (a) The population standard deviation is not known, so a *t* interval will be constructed with 90% confidence. The sample is a random sample from all students at the large high school. Because the sample size is not greater than or equal to 30, we need to look at a plot of the sample data. Either a boxplot or normal probability plot would suffice. (Both are shown below.)

The boxplot is approximately symmetric with no outliers and the normal probability plot is relatively straight, so it is reasonable to think that the population distribution is approximately normal. The confidence interval is $72.4 \pm 1.701 \dfrac{10.77}{\sqrt{28}} = 72.4 \pm 4.1 = (68.3, 76.6)$.

I am 90% confident that the true mean time for students to complete the multiple-choice section is between 68.3 and 76.6 minutes.

(b) Based on the interval, we are confident that the mean time to complete the multiple-choice section is between 68.3 minutes and 76.6 minutes. Even though we expect about half of all students to take longer than the mean time (because we think that the population distribution of times is approximately normal), 90 minutes is quite a bit above the upper end of the confidence interval. So, 90 minutes seems like a reasonable amount of time.

(*Statistics: Learning from Data*, AP Edition, 1st ed. pages 578–588 / 2nd ed. pages 600–612)

9

Hypothesis Testing Using a Single Sample

Making decisions based on sample data helps us evaluate claims about a population. Researchers and analysts use hypothesis test methods in a variety of settings to evaluate a claim about a population characteristic. In this section, we will look at the basics of setting up and carrying out a hypothesis test using a univariate data set. Then, we will use this information to draw conclusions about some unknown population parameter. Finally, anytime we make a decision based on sample data, there is a risk of error, so we will discuss what types of errors might be made when testing hypotheses.

Objectives

- Correctly set up and carry out a hypothesis test about a population mean.
- Correctly set up and carry out a hypothesis test about a population proportion.
- Describe Type I and Type II errors in context.
- Understand the factors that affect the power of a test.

Hypotheses and Test Procedures

(*Statistics: Learning from Data*, AP Edition, 1st ed. pages 496–500 / 2nd ed. pages 510–515)

To evaluate a claim about a population, we perform a hypothesis test. The first step in carrying out a hypothesis test is developing the hypotheses. These are statements that will be used in the decision-making process. First, the researcher forms a hypothesis based on some initial claim. For example, suppose an auto manufacturer purchases off-road tires that are supposed to have a mean tread thickness of 0.3125 inches. The auto manufacturer will assume that the new tires have been manufactured as specified. After all, the tire company wouldn't stay in business for long if they didn't provide what they claim about the mean tread thickness. This initial assumption is called the **null hypothesis**. We write the null hypothesis as:

$H_0: \mu = 0.3125$, where H_0 stands for "the null hypothesis" and
μ is the population mean tread thickness for all tires of this type.

The auto manufacturer may suspect that there has been a change in the mean thickness of the tire tread, so it decides to check several of the tires. This leads the auto company to develop what is called an alternative hypothesis. The **alternative hypothesis** is a competing hypothesis and could be written in one of the following three ways:

$H_a: \mu \neq 0.3125$ inches *or*

$\mu < 0.3125$ inches *or*

$\mu > 0.3125$ inches

where H_a stands for "the alternative hypothesis."

Because the auto manufacturer suspects that the mean tread thickness has changed, but does not have a specific direction in mind, it would use $\mu \neq 0.3125$ inches as the alternative hypothesis.

No matter which alternative hypothesis the company uses, the hypothesis testing procedure only allows us to favor this alternative if there is strong evidence against the null hypothesis. This evidence would come from sample data. We would evaluate what we see in the sample to determine if the sample mean tire tread is just too far from the null hypothesis to be explained by just chance differences from sample to sample. This same reasoning is used in all hypothesis tests considered in the AP® Statistics course.

The null hypothesis is usually written as

H_0: some population characteristic = the hypothesized value

and the alternative hypothesis is written as one of the following:

H_a: some population characteristic ≠ the hypothesized value

H_a: some population characteristic < the hypothesized value

H_a: some population characteristic > the hypothesized value

EXAMPLE The marketing manager for an online computer game store targets the company advertising toward males because he believes that 75% of the company's purchases are made by men. The sales manager claims that the proportion of purchases made by females has increased; thus, the proportion of purchases made by men is now less than what the marketing manager believes. What null and alternative hypotheses would be used to test the sales manager's claim?

The appropriate hypotheses are shown below.

$H_0 : p = 0.75$

$H_a : p < 0.75$

where p = the true proportion of purchases made by males.

Notice that we will now use *p* to represent the parameter, since the hypotheses are about a population proportion.

The null and alternative hypotheses are written in terms of population characteristics. In this example, the alternative is written as "less than" since the sales manager's claim is that the proportion of purchases made by males is less than what the marketing manager believes.

ERRORS IN HYPOTHESIS TESTING

(*Statistics: Learning from Data*, AP Edition, 1st ed. pages 502–505 / 2nd ed. pages 516–520)

Now that we have an understanding of how to generate the null and alternative hypotheses, a **test procedure** will be used to decide if we should reject the null hypothesis. Test procedures are described in the next section. Once a decision is made after the test procedure is performed, there is a chance that the final decision is wrong. In other words, an error could have been made. There are two possible types of errors and they are called a Type I error and a Type II error.

Either types of error may occur when making a decision either to reject or to fail to reject the null hypothesis. For example, in the tire tread problem, if a decision is made to reject the null hypothesis, this could be a wrong decision that would cause the auto manufacturer to conclude that the tires did not meet specifications. However, if the decision was to *fail* to reject the null hypothesis, this could also be wrong and the auto manufacturer could end up using tires that do not meet specifications. In either case, a possible error exists that is potentially damaging in some way.

A **Type I error** is made if we reject the null hypothesis and the null hypothesis is actually true. Although the hypothesis test, based on probability, supports the decision, we are led to an incorrect inference about the population. This would amount to having strong enough evidence to conclude that the tires do not have a mean tread thickness of 0.3125 inches. The company would decide to return the tires, causing the tire manufacturer to lose money. If the tires actually meet specifications, the tire manufacturer lost money due to the decision error.

A **Type II error** is made if we fail to reject the null and in reality the null hypothesis is not true and should have been rejected. This type of error would amount to not having enough evidence to say the tires did not meet specifications. In this instance, the company would unknowingly use these tires. This error could mean that customers receive cars with faulty tires and this could cause a lawsuit for the company and potentially even the risk of loss of life for the customer.

Avoiding these errors is, of course, desirable. However, it isn't always possible to avoid making an error because we make decisions based on only a sample. What we can do is to try to keep the chance of these errors as small as possible.

We use the Greek symbol alpha (α) to denote the probability of a Type I error and the Greek symbol beta (β) to denote the probability of a Type II error. We can control the value of α by the significance level we select for the test. Type II error is more problematic as it is something that we can't control easily. The values of α and β are related—the smaller we make α, the larger β becomes, when all other things are equal. For this reason, we generally choose a significance level α that is the largest value that is considered an acceptable risk of Type I error. This will help control for the errors by keeping α small as well as controlling a bit for β.

LARGE-SAMPLE HYPOTHESIS TESTS FOR A PROPORTION

(*Statistics: Learning from Data*, AP Edition, 1st ed. pages 514–523 / 2nd ed. pages 530–539)

Next, we take the hypotheses we developed and systematically test them to decide whether or not to reject the null hypothesis. This process is known as a test procedure and the same basic procedure is used in the many different hypothesis tests learned in the AP® Statistics course. However, depending on the type of data that we have and the question of interest, there are different hypothesis tests. The first test we consider is a large-sample hypothesis test for a population proportion.

In this case, we are looking at categorical data that come from a single sample, such as the data on the proportion of customers who are male. In this situation, the data consist of observations on a categorical variable with two possible values—male or female.

Just as was the case with a confidence interval, the hypothesis test is based on the properties of the sampling distribution of the sample proportion $\hat{p}$. Recall that $\hat{p}$ is the sample proportion based on a random sample, then

1. $\mu_{\hat{p}} = p$

2. $\sigma_{\hat{p}} = \sqrt{\dfrac{p(1-p)}{n}}$ (as long as the sample size is less than 10% of the population size)

3. When n is large enough, the sampling distribution of $\hat{p}$ is approximately normal. To verify that the sample size is large enough, check to make sure that

$$np \geq 10$$

$$n(1-p) \geq 10$$

Once we have verified that the sample size is large enough, the sample is a random sample from the population of interest, and the sample size is less than 10% of the population size, we can proceed with the hypothesis test.

Using the properties of the sampling distribution of p, we can form a z test statistic:

$$z = \dfrac{\hat{p} - p}{\sqrt{\dfrac{p(1-p)}{n}}}, \text{ where } p = \text{population proportion}$$

In the computer game advertising example where we wanted to test H_0: $p = 0.75$ versus H_a: $p < 0.75$, we consider whether the sample proportion is enough smaller than the hypothesized proportion of 0.75 that the difference can't be explained just by sampling variability alone. To do this, we calculate the value of the z statistic using 0.75 (from the null hypothesis) as the value for p: $z = \dfrac{\hat{p} - 0.75}{\sqrt{\dfrac{0.75(1 - 0.75)}{n}}}$

If the null hypothesis is true, then this z statistic will have a standard normal distribution. If the value of the z statistic is a value that would be "unexpected" for a standard normal variable, we regard this as evidence that the null hypothesis should be rejected.

> **EXAMPLE** Suppose that the sales manager in the online computer game customer example selects a random sample of 423 previous customers and finds that 298 were males. The sample proportion is then $\dfrac{298}{423} = 0.70$. We can see that 0.70 is smaller than 0.75, but is it small enough to convince us that chance differences from sample to sample could not account for this difference? This is the question that is answered by a hypothesis test.
>
> First, let's check the assumptions needed. The sample was a random sample of all previous customers. We must assume that there are at least $10(423) = 4230$ previous customers. Finally, we check that the sample size is large enough, so we check $423(0.75) = 317.25 \geq 10$ and $423(1 - 0.75) = 105.75 \geq 10$.
>
> Since we met conditions, we can proceed to calculate the value of the z test statistic.
>
> $$\hat{p} = \dfrac{298}{423} = 0.704$$
>
> so we can now substitute into our test statistic
>
> $$z = \dfrac{0.704 - 0.75}{\sqrt{\dfrac{0.75(1 - 0.75)}{423}}} = -2.1615$$
>
> Because the conditions were met, we know that if H_0 were true, z has an approximately normal distribution. Using what we know about the standard normal distribution, we know that getting a z score more than +2 or less than −2 does not occur very often (only 5% of the time). Since our alternative hypothesis was "less than," we can compute the probability of observing a z value less than −2.16:
>
> $$P(z \leq -2.16 \text{ if } H_0 \text{ is true})$$
> $$= \text{area to the left of } z = -2.16$$
> $$= 0.0154$$
>
> In other words, a sample proportion as small as or smaller than 0.70 would happen only about 1.5% of the time due to random sampling variability if the population proportion really is 0.75. Based on this sample, it does seem unlikely that the null hypothesis is correct, so we

would *reject* the null hypothesis. The probability just computed is called a **P-value**.

If the P-value is small, we reject the null hypothesis. How small does the P-value have to be in order to reject H_0? This will depend on how large a risk of a Type I error we are willing to make. This level of risk is preset by the researcher and is known as the significance level of the test. It is denoted by α. For example, if we set $\alpha = 0.05$ (a very typical α value), this means we know that a result as extreme as what we saw in the sample could happen as often as 5% of the time if the null hypothesis is true, but we can live with a type I error occurring for about 5 out of 100 of all possible random samples.

AP® Tip

Once you have calculated the value of the test statistic and the associated P-value, compare the P-value to the value of α. If

P-value $\leq \alpha$, reject H_0.

P-value $> \alpha$, fail to reject H_0.

When writing a solution to a hypothesis test problem, make sure to explicitly compare the P-value to α. This shows you know how to link the P-value and α in making your decision. Then *always* state your conclusion in the context of the problem.

Finally, we note that there are three different computations of the P-value to consider; the computation chosen will depend on the alternative hypothesis. Here are the three possible situations that can occur.

Upper-tailed test:

$H_a : p >$ hypothesized value

P-value = area in upper tail

Calculated Z

Lower-tailed test:

$H_a : p <$ hypothesized value

P-value = area in lower tail

Calculated Z

Two-tailed test:

$H_a : p \neq$ hypothesized value

P-value = sum of area two tails

Calculated Z, −Z

AP® is a trademark registered by the College Board, which is not affiliated with, and does not endorse, this product.

Hypothesis Testing Using a Single Sample

> ## AP® Tip
> When performing a hypothesis test, make sure you show each key part.
> - Hypotheses and significance level
> - Conditions
> - Name or formula of test
> - Test statistic
> - P-value
> - Conclusion in context

SAMPLE PROBLEM 1 A local newspaper claims that only 25% of voters support a new tax. A city representative believes the true percentage is larger and takes a random sample of city residents eligible to vote to find out. He finds that 38 of 125 support the new tax. Does the sample support the claim at a 0.05% level?

SOLUTION TO PROBLEM 1 To solve this problem, we carry out a hypothesis test. All four parts of a hypothesis should be complete as shown.

HYPOTHESIS Let p represent the true population proportion of city residents eligible to vote that support the new tax,

$$H_0 : p = 0.25$$
$$H_a : p > 0.25$$
$$\alpha = 0.10 (given)$$

ASSUMPTIONS The sample is a random sample from all city residents eligible to vote. It is reasonable to assume that there are more than $10(125) = 1250$ city residents eligible to vote. The sample is large enough since $125(0.25) = 31.25 \geq 10$ and $125(1 - 0.75) = 93.75 \geq 10$.

TEST STATISTIC A z test will be used.

$$\hat{p} = \frac{38}{125} = 0.304, \quad z = \frac{0.304 - 0.25}{\sqrt{\frac{0.25(1-0.25)}{125}}} = 1.39, \text{ and } P\text{-value} = 0.082$$

CONCLUSION Since $0.082 > 0.05$, we fail to reject the null hypothesis. There is not convincing evidence that the true proportion of city residents eligible to vote who support the new tax is greater than 0.25.

> **AP® Tip**
>
> Using incorrect notation can lower your score on free-response questions. Remember to keep the different "*p*" notations straight.
>
> *P-value* This is a probability computed from the value of the test statistic. All hypothesis tests involve the use of a *P*-value to make a decision.
>
> *p* This is the notation used to denote the population proportion when we have categorical data.
>
> $\hat{p}$ Read as p-hat; it is used to denote the sample proportion.

HYPOTHESIS TESTS FOR A MEAN

(*Statistics: Learning from Data*, AP Edition, 1st ed. pages 591–602 / 2nd ed. pages 614–625)

Now that we have a handle on a hypothesis test for population proportions, let's consider hypothesis tests based on numerical data. With numerical data, we are usually interested in making inferences about a population mean. In chapter 8 of this book (and chapter 7 in the textbook) on confidence intervals, there were two types of intervals for estimating means, a *z interval* and a *t interval*. Which of these intervals is used in a particular situation is determined by whether we know the population standard deviation α or whether we have only the sample standard deviation s_x.

In either case, the hypotheses look very much like those of the hypothesis test for a population proportion. The difference is that now the hypotheses are in terms of the population mean, so the null hypothesis is

$$H_0: \mu = \text{hypothesized value}$$

where μ = the true population mean
and the alternative hypothesis is one of the following:

$$H_a : \mu \ne \text{hypothesized value}$$

$$H_a : \mu < \text{hypothesized value}$$

$$H_a : \mu > \text{hypothesized value}$$

The test statistic is based on either the *z* or the *t* test statistic shown below, depending on whether or not we know the population standard deviation.

If σ is known,

$$z = \frac{\bar{x} - \mu}{\frac{\sigma}{n}} = \frac{\bar{x} - \text{hypothesized value}}{\frac{\sigma}{n}}$$

and the *P*-value is computed as area under the *z* curve.

If σ is NOT known,

$$t = \frac{\bar{x} - \mu}{\frac{s_x}{\sqrt{n}}} = \frac{\bar{x} - \text{hypothesized value}}{\frac{s_x}{\sqrt{n}}}$$

and the *P*-value is computed as area under the *t* curve with $df = n - 1$.

It is very rare that the population standard deviation is known, so we will focus mainly on the *t* test statistic. Revisiting the earlier tire tread scenario, we can write the hypotheses, check assumptions, calculate the test statistic and P-value, and give a conclusion in context.

> EXAMPLE Trustworthy Tires sells its leading high-performance tire to a car manufacturer. The car manufacturer requires that the tires have a mean tread thickness of 0.3125. The car manufacturer thinks tires received from Trustworthy may be greater than 0.3125, because it has been finding that in some cars the tires are hitting parts of the wheel well area on bumps. In a random sample of 32 tires, it found the tire treads to have a mean of 0.3360 inches and a standard deviation of 0.094 inches.
>
> Since both these values came from the sample, we use the notation for sample statistics: $\bar{x} = 0.3360$ and $s_x = 0.094$. For this situation, let's look at the components that are common to all hypothesis tests.

HYPOTHESES

$H_0 : \mu = 0.3125$

$H_a : \mu > 0.3125$ (since the company suspects the mean tread is greater than the requirement of 0.3125)

let $\alpha = 0.05$.

ASSUMPTIONS

The assumptions that must be satisfied are the same as those for confidence intervals for a population mean.

We have a random sample from all tires. The sample size is large enough to assume the sampling distribution of $\bar{x}$ is approximately normal since $n \geq 30$.

TEST STATISTIC

$$t = \frac{\bar{x} - \text{hypothesized value}}{\frac{s_x}{\sqrt{n}}} = \frac{0.3360 - 0.3125}{\frac{0.094}{\sqrt{32}}} = 1.414$$

with $df = n - 1 = 32 - 1 = 31$

P-value $= 0.08$

Note that because the inequality symbol in the null hypothesis was greater than, the P-value is the area to the right of $t = 1.41$ under the t curve with $df = 31$.

CONCLUSION Since the *P*-value > α, we fail to reject the null hypothesis and conclude that there is not convincing evidence that the mean tread thickness of tires is greater than 0.3125 inches.

> ## AP® Tip
>
> When carrying out a hypothesis test for a population mean, whether or not you know the standard deviation of the population is what determines if you should use a *z* test or *t* test. Only use the *z* test when you are sure the standard deviation given is from the population. In the vast majority of hypothesis, test problems for a population mean the standard deviation of the population is unknown and a *t* test should be used.

Note that the steps in a hypothesis test about a population mean are the same as for the hypothesis test for a population proportion. What distinguishes the two tests is the type of data (numerical for means and categorical for proportions), the specific assumptions that must be checked, and the test statistic used for the test.

SAMPLE PROBLEM 2 A well-known brand of pain relief tablets is advertised to begin relief within 24 minutes. A random sample of 18 subjects suffering from the same type of headache pain were asked to record when they first notice relief after taking the pain relief tablet. The data gathered from this study are shown.

Time to Pain Relief (in minutes)								
25	24	27	23	25	22	25	25	24
27	24	23	26	28	25	24	26	23

Is there evidence that the mean pain relief time is longer than the advertised time? Test at the 0.05 significance level.

SOLUTION TO PROBLEM 2 To solve this problem, we carry out a *t* hypothesis test for a population mean. All four parts of a hypothesis test should be complete as shown.

HYPOTHESIS

With μ representing the population mean time to relief,

$$H_0 : \mu = 24$$
$$H_a : \mu > 24$$
$$\alpha = 0.05 \text{(given)}$$

ASSUMPTIONS

The 18 subjects are a random sample from the population of all people suffering from the same type of headache pain. Since there were only 18 subjects, we need to check to see if it is reasonable that the distribution of relief times in the population is approximately normal. A dotplot of the sample relief times is shown below. Since the dotplot is approximately symmetric and there are no outliers, it is reasonable to think that the population distribution of relief times is approximately normal.

Pain relief

[Dotplot showing Time on x-axis from 22 to 30]

TEST STATISTIC A t test will be used since we do not know the population standard deviation.

$$\bar{x} = 24.78 \text{ and } s_x = 1.59$$

$$t = \frac{24.78 - 23}{\frac{1.59}{\sqrt{18}}} = 2.072 \text{ with } df = 17$$

$$P\text{-value} = 0.027$$

CONCLUSION Since P-value $= 0.027 < 0.05$, we reject the null hypothesis in favor of the alternative hypothesis. There is convincing evidence that the true mean time to pain relief is greater than 24 minutes.

As a final note, should you be in the unusual situation where the population standard deviation σ is given, you would use the z test statistic and the associated P-value would be determined using the standard normal distribution. Otherwise, the process would be the same as the process illustrated in the example above.

> ### AP® Tip
>
> You will be required to provide complete answers to four key parts in every hypothesis test. Get in the habit of thinking in terms of these four pieces. If you chunk the information under each of these categories, you will have a better chance of remembering all aspects of any hypothesis test. The four pieces are
>
> 1. **State the hypotheses and define any symbols used in the hypotheses.**
>
> H_0 and H_a (correctly written with population parameters μ or p)
>
> α level
>
> 2. **Identify the test procedure by name or by formula. Check all assumptions (or conditions).**
>
>   The assumptions vary by test, but you should always state AND CHECK the assumptions appropriate for the test you are performing.
>
> 3. **Test statistic**
>
>   Show your z or t test statistic calculation.
>
>   Give the P-value associated with the value of the test statistic.
>
> 4. **Conclusion in context**
>
> $P \leq \alpha$, reject H_0.
>
> $P \geq \alpha$, fail to reject H_0.

POWER AND PROBABILITY OF TYPE II ERROR

(*Statistics: Learning from Data*, AP Edition, 1st ed. pages 526–530 / 2nd ed. pages 543–547)

While the AP® Statistics curriculum does not require you to calculate power, you are expected to know the factors that affect the power of a test. **Power** is the ability of the test to reject the null hypothesis when the null hypothesis is, in fact, false. There are four factors that are generally considered when thinking about power. First, increasing α will increase power. Although this seems like a fast fix, it is dangerous because the probability of a type I error will also increase. Another way to increase power is simply to increase the sample size, although this isn't always practical. The other two ways that increase power aren't really things that we can control, but it is helpful to know that they do to affect power. The variability in the population affects power; when the variability in the population is small, the power of the test is high. Also, the difference between the actual value of the population parameter and the hypothesized value affects power; the larger the difference between the two values, the power of the test is increased.

SAMPLE PROBLEM 3 Consider the earlier scenario of the online computer game customers. The sales manager was interested in deciding if the proportion of sales to males was less than the 0.75 claimed by the marketing manager. The appropriate hypotheses for this situation were:

$$H_0 : p = 0.75$$

$$H_a : p < 0.75$$

where p = the true proportion of purchases made by men

(a) Identify the type I error in this scenario *and* provide a possible consequence of this error.

(b) Identify the type II error in this scenario and provide a possible consequence of this error.

(c) What can be done to increase the power of this test?

SOLUTION TO PROBLEM 3

(a) A type I error would result if the hypothesis test concludes that the proportion of male customers is less than 0.75, when in fact this proportion is 0.75. A possible consequence of this error would be that the company might change its strategy of targeting males in its advertising, which might result in a decrease in sales.

(b) A type II error in this situation would occur when the hypothesis test concludes that there wasn't enough evidence to say that the proportion of male customers is less than 0.75 when this proportion really is less than 0.75. In this case, the company would probably continue to target males in its advertising, which might result in a loss of potential sales to female customers.

(c) One way to increase power would be to increase the significance level α of the test. However, this will also increase the chance of a type I error. Another way to increase power is to increase sample size.

INTERPRETATION OF RESULTS IN HYPOTHESIS TESTING

(*Statistics: Learning from Data*, AP Edition, 1st ed. pages 511–513 / 2nd ed. pages 526–529)

Once data have been gathered and an appropriate hypothesis test is carried out, the findings are typically shared with others interested in the outcome. In communicating results in journals and newspapers, it is not common to provide the same level of detail that you would want to provide in a solution to a hypothesis test question on the AP® exam. Some of the important things to conclude when reporting results are:

- *Hypotheses:* In either symbols or words, you need to clearly state both the null hypothesis and the alternative hypothesis.
- *Test Procedures:* Clearly state what test you used (large sample z test for proportions, and so on) and mention any assumptions that are necessary in order for this test to be appropriate.

- *Test Statistic:* Be sure to report the value of the test statistic as well as the associated *P*-value. This will allow the readers to know if they would draw the same conclusion given the sample data.
- *Conclusion in Context:* Be certain you have provided a conclusion in terms of the originally posed research question. This needs to include a comparison of the *P*-value to α. Simply stating that you reject the null hypothesis is *not* sufficient.

In many cases, the reported results only include a statement such as *P*-value < 0.05. This is common and tells the reader that the results of the test yielded a *P*-value smaller than 0.05, hence statistically significant. Journals may also use a standard method of coding where * means statistically significant results (their *P*-value was less than 0.05) and ** means very significant (their *P*-value was less than 0.01).

As you review published reports, be sure to look for the four key components you would report and ask yourself some questions about these pieces. What were the hypotheses they tested? Did they use an appropriate test for these? What was the associated *P*-value and what significance level was used? Also, were the conclusions reached consistent with the results of the test?

AP® Tip

In writing a conclusion for a hypothesis test, remember you are always either rejecting or failing to reject the null hypothesis. This means you either have convincing evidence in favor of the alternate hypothesis or that there is not enough evidence. You *never say that you accept the null hypothesis* because that implies strong evidence for the null hypothesis.

HYPOTHESIS TESTING USING A SINGLE SAMPLE: STUDENT OBJECTIVES FOR THE AP® EXAM

- You will be able to write the null and alternative hypothesis for a test about a population mean or a population proportion.
- You will be able to describe type I and type II errors in context.
- You will be able to describe a possible consequence of each type error in context.
- You will be able to carry out a test of hypotheses about a population mean.
- You will be able to carry out a test of hypotheses about a population proportion.
- You will be able to interpret the result of a hypothesis test in context.

MULTIPLE-CHOICE QUESTIONS

1. A psychologist reports that the result of a hypothesis test was statistically significant at the 0.05 level. Which of the following is consistent with this statement?
   (A) The P-value calculated was smaller than the significance level of 0.05.
   (B) The P-value calculated was larger than the significance level of 0.05.
   (C) The significance level calculated was larger than 0.05.
   (D) The significance level calculated was smaller than 0.05.
   (E) There was not enough information to make a decision.

2. A concrete learner is a student who learns best when various types of hands-on or manipulative activities are used to illustrate abstract concepts. Researchers have long believed that 60% of all students remain concrete learners until they are between 16 and 21 years of age. Each student in a random sample of 32 students age 17 to 19 was evaluated, and it was found that 24 of the 32 were concrete learners. Would it be appropriate to use the z test for a population proportion to test to determine if the proportion of all concrete learners in this age group is less than 0.60?
   (A) Yes. Since $32(0.6) = 19.2$ and $32(1 - 0.6) = 12.8$, we can proceed with the test.
   (B) Yes. Since 32 is larger than 30, the sample is sufficiently large and we can proceed with the test.
   (C) No. Since we do not know if the sample was a simple random sample, we cannot proceed with the test.
   (D) No. Since $32(0.05) = 1.6$, we do not have a large enough sample to proceed with test.
   (E) No. While 32 is larger than 30, it is so close to 30 and we don't know if the population distribution is normal.

3. A type I error occurs in which of the following situations?
   (A) H_a is rejected and the null hypotheses is true.
   (B) H_0 is not rejected and the null hypothesis is false.
   (C) H_0 is rejected and the null hypothesis is true.
   (D) The P-value is too small to reject the null hypothesis.
   (E) The α level is too small and so the null hypothesis is rejected.

4. A type II error occurs in which of the following situations?
   (A) H_0 is rejected and the null hypothesis is true.
   (B) H_0 is not rejected and the null hypothesis is false.
   (C) H_a is not rejected and the null hypothesis is false.
   (D) The P-value is too small to reject the null hypothesis.
   (E) The α level is too large and so the null hypothesis is rejected.

5. A graduate student at a private university wanted to study the amount of money that students at his university carried with them. A recent study reported that the average amount of money carried by college students is $31. He decides to collect data and carry out a test to see if there is evidence that the average is higher for students at his university. Which of the following describes a type II error in this context?
   (A) This would lead to the incorrect idea that students at his university, on average, spend more money each month than students at other universities.
   (B) This would lead to the incorrect idea that students at his university carry, on average, more than $31.
   (C) This would lead to the incorrect idea that students at his university carry, on average, less than $31.
   (D) This would lead to the incorrect idea that there was no reason to believe that students at his university carry, on average, more than $31.
   (E) This would lead to the correct idea that students at other campuses carry, on average, less than $31.

6. An animal rights group has been very supportive of a new silicon product that caps the nails on cats as an alternative to surgically declawing the pets. The company that makes the caps claims they last for an average of 69 days before needing to be replaced.
   Before publically endorsing the product, the animal rights group plans to collect data to see if there is convincing evidence that the mean time needed before replacement is actually less than what the company claims. Which of the following would be an appropriate pair of hypotheses for the animal rights group to test?
   (A) $H_0: \mu = 69$ days, $H_a: \mu > 69$ days
   (B) $H_0: \mu = 69$ days, $H_a: \mu < 69$ days
   (C) $H_0: \mu = 69$ days, $H_a: \mu \neq 69$ days
   (D) $H_0: \bar{x} = 69$ days, $H_a: \bar{x} > 69$ days
   (E) $H_0: \bar{x} = 69$ days, $H_a: \bar{x} < 69$ days

7. Neutering dogs is a common surgical practice. The mean time to recover from the general anesthetic used is 28 hours. A veterinarian believes that since changing to a new anesthetic, the mean recovery time is shorter than before. To investigate, she selects a random sample of 40 surgeries done with the new anesthetic and finds that the mean recovery time was 25 hours and the standard deviation was 2.5. She plans to use this sample data to test to see if there is evidence that the recovery time is shorter with the new anesthetic. Which of the following is the correct test statistic for this study? Assume conditions for inference have been met.

   (A) $z = \dfrac{25 - 28}{2.5}$, with $df = 39$

   (B) $t = \dfrac{25 - 28}{\frac{2.5}{\sqrt{39}}}$, with $df = 39$

   (C) $t = \dfrac{25 - 28}{\frac{2.5}{\sqrt{40}}}$, with $df = 39$

   (D) $t = \dfrac{25 - 28}{\frac{2.5}{\sqrt{40}}}$, with $df = 40$

   (E) $t = \dfrac{25 - 28}{\frac{2.5}{\sqrt{39}}}$, with $df = 40$

8. A recently published study reported that 63% of the nation's students have some type of structured homework study time. A school surveyed each student in a random sample of 83 students who attend the school and found that only 52% reported having a structured homework time. These data were used to carry out a hypothesis test to determine if there was evidence that the proportion of students at the school who had structured homework time was less that the proportion reported in the national study. Which of the following would be the test statistic for this test? Assume conditions for inference have been met.

(A) $z = \dfrac{0.52 - 0.63}{\sqrt{\dfrac{0.52(0.48)}{83}}}$

(B) $z = \dfrac{0.52 - 0.63}{\sqrt{\dfrac{0.52(0.48)}{82}}}$

(C) $z = \dfrac{0.52 - 50}{\sqrt{\dfrac{0.52(0.48)}{83}}}$

(D) $z = \dfrac{0.52 - 0.63}{\sqrt{\dfrac{0.63(0.37)}{83}}}$

(E) $z = \dfrac{0.52 - 0.63}{\sqrt{\dfrac{0.63(0.37)}{82}}}$

9. Bicycles purchased from a discount store come unassembled. The assembly instructions that come with the bicycle claim that the average assembly time is 30 minutes. A consumer group has received complaints from people who say that the assembly time was greater than the time claims. They decide to purchase 40 of these bikes and have asked 40 different people to assemble them. The consumer group believed that it was reasonable to regard these 40 people as representatives of the population of people who might purchase this bike. For this sample, they found that the assembly times had a mean of 34.2 minutes and a standard deviation of 8.6 minutes. Is there convincing evidence that the claimed average assembly time is too low? Test at the 0.05 significance level. Assume conditions for inference have been met.

(A) No, $z = 0.49$, P-value $= 0.312$.
(B) Yes, $t = 3.09$, $df = 39$, P-value $= 0.002$.
(C) Yes, $t = 3.05$, $df = 39$, P-value $= 0.004$.
(D) No, $t = 0.49$, $df = 39$, P-value $= 0.313$.
(E) Yes, $t = 3.05$, $df = 40$, P-value $= 0.002$.

10. The prom committee is thinking about changing the location of the prom. The new location is more expensive to rent, and for the increased cost to be reasonable, they would want to be fairly certain that more than 46% of the senior class would attend the prom. A survey of a random sample of 52 seniors found that 25 would attend if the site changed. Which of the following pairs of hypotheses should the prom committee test?
    (A) $H_0: \mu = 46\%$, $H_a: \mu > 46\%$
    (B) $H_0: \mu = 46\%$, $H_a: \mu \neq 48\%$
    (C) $H_0: p = 0.46$, $H_a: p > 0.46$
    (D) $H_0: p = 0.46$, $H_a: p \neq 0.46$
    (E) $H_0: p = 0.46$, $H_a: p < 0.46$

11. Which of the following is closest to the P-value associated with a two-tailed t test with 20 degrees of freedom if the value of the test statistic is 2.0?
    (A) 0.001
    (B) 0.01
    (C) 0.03
    (D) 0.05
    (E) 0.10

12. Which of the following statements is true?
    (A) The null hypothesis for a hypothesis test about a population proportion is $H_0: \hat{p} =$ hypothesized value.
    (B) For the z test to be an appropriate hypothesis test for a population proportion, the following condition must be met: $np \geq 10$ and $n(1-p) \geq 10$.
    (C) The standard deviation of the statistic $\hat{p}$ is $\sigma_{\hat{p}} = \sqrt{np(1-p)}$
    (D) The null hypothesis for a hypothesis test about a population proportion can be written as $H_0: \mu =$ hypothesized value written as a percent.
    (E) Sample size must be greater than or equal to 30.

13. A local group claims that more than 60% of the teens driving after 10 p.m. are exceeding the speed limit. It plans to collect data in hopes that a hypothesis test will provide convincing evidence in support of its claim. Which of the following is true about the hypotheses the group should test?
    (A) The null hypothesis states that less than 60% of the teens are exceeding the speed limit.
    (B) The null hypothesis states that more than 60% of the teens are exceeding the speed limit.
    (C) The alternative hypothesis states that less than 60% of the teens are exceeding the speed limit.
    (D) The alternative hypothesis states that less than or equal to 60% of the teens are exceeding the speed limit.
    (E) The alternative hypothesis states that more than 60% of the teens are exceeding the speed limit.

14. A study by a geological research team found that a new piece of equipment designed to measure the forces of an earthquake is not effective. It based this conclusion on data from a sample of 40 pieces of equipment and it carried out a test with $\alpha = 0.05$. The manufacturer of the equipment claims this study was flawed and that its equipment is good. The research team is considering carrying out a second study with the intention of increasing the power of the test. Which of the following would ensure an increase in the power of the test?
    (A) Move the equipment to three randomly chosen new locations.
    (B) Change $\alpha = 0.05$ to $\alpha = 0.02$.
    (C) Carry out a two-sided test instead of a one-sided test.
    (D) Increase the sample size to 60 pieces of equipment being tested.
    (E) Decrease the sample size to 20 pieces of equipment being tested.

15. Suppose that the mean height of women in the United States is 63.8 inches, with a standard deviation of 2.5 inches. A clothing designer feels that women who use their products may actually be taller on average. She selects a random sample of 70 women from all women who have previously purchased their clothing. What is the population of interest, and what test would the designer use to test her claim?
    (A) The population is all women in the United States and the appropriate test is a t test with $df = 70$.
    (B) The population is all women in the United States and the appropriate test is a z test with $\sigma = 2.5$.
    (C) The population is all women who have previously purchased the designer's clothing and the appropriate test is a t test with $df = 70$.
    (D) The population is all women who have previously purchased the designer's clothing and the appropriate test is a t test with $df = 69$.
    (E) The population is all women who have previously purchased the designer's clothing and the appropriate test is a z test with $\sigma = 2.5$.

FREE-RESPONSE PROBLEMS

1. A bridal gown industry publication claims that the nationwide average amount spent for a wedding gown is $1,012. A local bridal shop in an urban community has noticed its more expensive gowns are not selling well. Instead, the brides seem to be selecting only lower priced gowns or clearance gowns. The shop wonders if the average amount spent for a wedding gown is less than $1,012 for its customers. To investigate, it selected a random sample of 50 wedding gown sales. It found a sample mean of $985 and a standard deviation of $235.

   Is there convincing evidence that the average amount spent on a wedding gown at this shop is less than the national figure? Test using a 0.05 significance level.

2. A local school district believes that the proportion of seniors who are absent from school on the last day of school may be increasing. Over the past 5 years, 39% of the seniors have missed the last day. This year, the school district is considering a new reward program sponsored by local businesses where seniors who were at school on the last day would be entered in a drawing for an iPad. To see if this program might reduce the proportion of seniors who miss school on the last day, a random sample of 398 seniors from the school district was surveyed. Each student in the sample was asked if he or she planned to attend on the last day of class given the possibility of winning an iPad. Only 129 of the 398 seniors indicated that they would miss the last day of school. The school district would like to know if there is convincing evidence that the new program would reduce the number of seniors absent on the last day of school.

   (a) What hypotheses should the school district test?

   (b) Identify the appropriate test and verify that any conditions needed for the test are met.

   (c) Describe type I and type II errors in the context of this problem.

Answers

MULTIPLE-CHOICE QUESTIONS

1. **(A)** When a researcher says the results were statistically significant, it means the *P*-value was less than the set significance level (*Statistics: Learning from Data*, AP Edition, 1st ed. pages 511–513 / 2nd ed. pages 526–529).

2. **(A)** In a one-sample hypothesis test for proportions, one condition that is needed is $np \geq 10$ and $n(1 - p) \geq 10$. Notice these both use p and not $\hat{p}$ from the sample (*Statistics: Learning from Data*, AP Edition, 1st ed. pages 514–523 / 2nd ed. pages 530–539).

3. **(C)** By definition, a type I error occurs when the null hypothesis is rejected when it should not be rejected. This might happen when the *P*-value < significance level (*Statistics: Learning from Data*, AP Edition, 1st ed. pages 502–505 / 2nd ed. pages 516–520).

4. **(B)** A type II error will occur anytime you fail to reject the null when in fact the null is false. This might occur if the *P*-value > α (*Statistics: Learning from Data*, AP Edition, 1st ed. pages 502–505 / 2nd ed. pages 516–520).

5. **(D)** If a type II error was made, this means he failed to reject the null hypothesis. In this case, that would amount to saying there was not convincing evidence that the mean for his university was greater than $31 when in fact this is incorrect and the mean really is greater than $31 (*Statistics: Learning from Data*, AP Edition, 1st ed. pages 502–505 / 2nd ed. pages 516–520).

6. **(B)** Since the group is concerned if the caps last less than 69 days on average, the alternative hypothesis would be $\mu < 69$ days (*Statistics: Learning from Data*, AP Edition, 1st ed. pages 496–500 / 2nd ed. pages 510–515).

7. **(C)** Since we don't know σ, it must be a t test. Also, while $df = 39$, $n = 40$ is the value that is used in the test statistic calculation (*Statistics: Learning from Data*, AP Edition, 1st ed. pages 591–602 / 2nd ed. pages 614–625).

8. **(D)** In calculating the test statistic, the denominator uses the hypothesized value and sample size of 83 (*Statistics: Learning from Data*, AP Edition, 1st ed. pages 514–523 / 2nd ed. pages 530–539).

9. **(B)** A t test with 39 degrees of freedom would be used (*Statistics: Learning from Data*, AP Edition, 1st ed. pages 591–602 / 2nd ed. pages 614–625).

10. **(C)** This is a hypothesis test for a population proportion. The question of interest is whether the population proportion p is greater than 0.46 (*Statistics: Learning from Data*, AP Edition, 1st ed. pages 496–500 / 2nd ed. pages 510–515).

11. **(D)** The *P*-value is approximately 0.06, which is closest to 0.05 (*Statistics: Learning from Data*, AP Edition, 1st ed. pages 591–602 / 2nd ed. pages 614–625).

12. **(B)** Notice that choice A is written using $\hat{p}$ instead of p. All hypotheses are stated in terms of the population value, which would be p. Choice C is the standard deviation for a binomial random variable. The standard deviation of $\hat{p}$ is $\sqrt{\dfrac{p(1-p)}{n}}$ (*Statistics: Learning from Data*, AP Edition, 1st ed. pages 514–523 / 2nd ed. pages 530–539).

13. **(E)** Answer choices A, B, and D can be eliminated since the null hypothesis must include the equal case. Because the group wants to show support for then claim that *more* than 60% are speeding, the alternative hypothesis would be $p > 0.60$ (*Statistics: Learning from Data*, AP Edition, 1st ed. pages 496–500 / 2nd ed. pages 510–515).

14. **(D)** The easiest ways to increase power are either to increase the sample size or use a larger significance level (*Statistics: Learning from Data*, AP Edition, 1st ed. pages 526–530 / 2nd ed. pages 543–547).

15. **(E)** The designer is interested in the population of women who have previously purchased the designer's clothing and this is the rare case when the standard deviation of this population is known (*Statistics: Learning from Data*, AP Edition, 1st ed. pages 591–602 / 2nd ed. pages 614–625).

FREE-RESPONSE PROBLEMS

1. HYPOTHESIS

   $H_0 : \mu = \$1,012$

   $H_a : \mu < \$1,012$

   Where μ represents the true average amount spent for a wedding gown.

   $\alpha = 0.05$

   ASSUMPTIONS

   The problem states this was a random sample of wedding gown sales. Since 50 > 30, the sample is large enough for the one sample t test to be appropriate.

   TEST STATISTIC

   $\bar{x} = \$985$

   $s_x = \$235$

   $n = 50$

   $t = \dfrac{985 - 1012}{\dfrac{235}{\sqrt{50}}} = -0.081, \ df = 49$

   $p = 0.21$

   CONCLUSION

   Since the P-value of $0.21 > 0.05$, we fail to reject the null hypothesis. There is not convincing evidence that the average amount spent on a wedding gown at this shop is less than the national average of $1,012.

   (*Statistics: Learning from Data*, AP Edition, 1st ed. pages 591–602 / 2nd ed. pages 614–625)

2. (a) $H_0 : p = 0.39$ where p = true proportion of seniors skipping the last day of school

   $H_a : p < 0.39$

   (b) The appropriate test is a *one-sample z* test where

   $z = \dfrac{\hat{p} - p}{\sqrt{\dfrac{p(1-p)}{n}}}$

   The conditions of this test are (1) random sample from the population of interest, (2) the sample is less than 10% of the population, and (3) large sample size. The problem states that the sample was a random sample of seniors. It is questionable to assume that there are more than 10(398) = 3,980 seniors. Checking the conditions for large sample size: (398)(0.39) = 155 > 10 and (398)(0.61) = 243 > 10, so the sample size is large enough.

(c) A type I error would be that the iPad drawing would not actually reduce the proportion of seniors who miss the last day of school, but the school district thinks that it will and implements the drawing.

A type II error would be that the iPad drawing would in fact reduce the proportion of seniors who miss the last day of school, but the school district is not convinced of this and does not implement the drawing.

(*Statistics: Learning from Data*, AP Edition, 1st ed. pages 496–500 / 2nd ed. pages 510–515)

(*Statistics: Learning from Data*, AP Edition, 1st ed. pages 502–505 / 2nd ed. pages 516–520)

(*Statistics: Learning from Data*, AP Edition, 1st ed. pages 514–523 / 2nd ed. pages 530–539)

10

COMPARINGTWO POPULATIONS OR TREATMENTS

In this section, we will turn our attention to dealing with two populations or treatments. A typical question that arises involves how one treatment or population compares to another. This chapter deals with the inference methods used to answer this question.

OBJECTIVES

- Correctly set up and carry out a hypothesis test for the difference in two population or treatment means using independent or paired samples.
- Correctly set up and carry out a hypothesis test for the difference in two population or treatment proportions.
- Construct and interpret a confidence interval for a difference in two means.
- Construct and interpret a confidence interval for a difference in two proportions.

Inferences Concerning the Difference Between Two Population or Treatment Means Using Independent Samples

(*Statistics: Learning from Data*, AP Edition, 1st ed. pages 618–627, 644–649, 672–674, and 679–682 / 2nd ed. pages 657–670)

To begin, let's take a look at inference methods based on two **independent** samples. Independent samples are samples where knowing the individuals selected for one sample does not tell you anything about which individuals are selected into the other sample. In contrast, in paired samples, an observation from one sample is paired in some meaningful way with an observation in the other sample.

As we saw in the previous section of this book (and chapter 8 in the textbook), a hypothesis test can be consolidated into four key parts: hypotheses, assumptions, test statistic and computations, and a conclusion in context. Following this process, or **test procedure**, will be helpful in all other testing situations described in this course as well. The question of interest for a two independent sample procedure will be, "Are the two population means or proportions equal to each other or not?" However, since there are now two treatments or populations, it is important to define the symbols used to represent the populations or treatments. One way to manage this is by using subscripts to represent each population and sample separately. In the general notation shown, everything from the same population or treatment uses the same subscript.

Notation		Mean	Variance	Standard Deviation
Population or Treatment 1		μ_1	σ_1^2	σ_1
Population or Treatment 2		μ_2	σ_2^2	σ_2
	Sample Size	Mean	Variance	Standard Deviation
Sample from Population or Treatment 1	n_1	$\bar{x}_1$	s_1^2	s_1
Sample from Population or Treatment 2	n_2	$\bar{x}_2$	s_2^2	s_2

When working with independent samples, hypotheses that compare the means would be written as one of the following:

$$\mu_1 - \mu_2 = 0, \text{ which is the same as saying } \mu_1 = \mu_2$$

or if one mean were larger than the other, it would be written as

$$\mu_1 - \mu_2 > 0, \text{ which is the same as saying } \mu_1 > \mu_2 \text{ or}$$
$$\mu_1 - \mu_2 < 0, \text{ which is the same as saying } \mu_1 < \mu_2$$

When the samples are independent, the sampling distribution of the difference in sample means, $\bar{x}_1 - \bar{x}_2$, has a mean that is equal to the difference of the two population means. The variance of the sampling distribution of $\bar{x}_1 - \bar{x}_2$ is the sum of the two population variances.

Given this behavior, we get the following properties for the sampling distribution of $\bar{x}_1 - \bar{x}_2$:

If the random samples are selected independently, then

1. $\mu_{\bar{x}_1 - \bar{x}_2} = \mu_{\bar{x}_1} - \mu_{\bar{x}_2} = \mu_1 - \mu_2$

   so the sampling distribution of $\bar{x}_1 - \bar{x}_2$ will be centered around $\mu_1 - \mu_2$ making $\bar{x}_1 - \bar{x}_2$ an unbiased estimate for $\mu_1 - \mu_2$.

2. $\sigma^2_{\bar{x}_1 - \bar{x}_2} = \sigma^2_{\bar{x}_1} + \sigma^2_{\bar{x}_2} = \dfrac{\sigma_1^2}{n_1} + \dfrac{\sigma_2^2}{n_2}$ and $\sigma_{\bar{x}_1 - \bar{x}_2} = \sqrt{\dfrac{\sigma_1^2}{n_1} + \dfrac{\sigma_2^2}{n_2}}$

3. Finally, if both n_1 and n_2 are large or the population distributions are approximately normal, then both $\bar{x}_1$ and $\bar{x}_2$ are approximately normal and this implies that $\bar{x}_1 - \bar{x}_2$ is also approximately normal.

Simply interpreted, the general rules for two independent samples are

1. The mean value of a difference in means is the difference of the two individual mean values.
2. The variance of a difference in independent quantities is the sum of the two individual variances.

With this in mind, the statistic

$$z = \dfrac{(\bar{x}_1 - \bar{x}_2) - (\mu_1 - \mu_2)}{\sqrt{\dfrac{\sigma_1^2}{n_1} + \dfrac{\sigma_2^2}{n_2}}}$$

will have a standard normal distribution. However, because the values of σ_1^2 and σ_2^2 are rarely known, we will typically use a t statistic:

$$t = \dfrac{(\bar{x}_1 - \bar{x}_2) - (\mu_1 - \mu_2)}{\sqrt{\dfrac{s_1^2}{n_1} + \dfrac{s_2^2}{n_2}}}$$

$$**\, df = \dfrac{(V_1 + V_2)^2}{\dfrac{V_1^2}{n_1 - 1} + \dfrac{V_2^2}{n_2 - 1}}, \text{ where } V_1 = \dfrac{s_1^2}{n_1} \text{ and } V_2 = \dfrac{s_2^2}{n_2}$$

If you are using t table, the result for *df* should be truncated to get an integer for the degrees of freedom.

**You are not required to know this formula for degrees of freedom on the AP® exam. Instead, you are allowed to use the degrees of freedom that the calculator gives you. You are also allowed to use a conservative estimate for the degrees of freedom; this estimate is the smaller of $(n_1 - 1)$ and $(n_2 - 1)$.

TEST PROCEDURES

Once we have established that the two samples are independently selected, the null hypothesis of interest would be of the general form

H_0: $\mu_1 - \mu_2$ = some hypothesized value (very often, this value is 0)

We will follow the same basic hypothesis testing procedure as in previous chapters. Two key differences in comparing two populations will occur in the procedures. First, in the hypotheses and test statistic sections, there will be two populations and two sets of sample statistics used in the calculations and claims. Second, in the assumptions section, it is necessary to check assumptions with each sample.

A summary of the two-sample t test for comparing two population means is outlined in the steps below.

STATE THE HYPOTHESES

H_0: $\mu_1 - \mu_2$ = some hypothesized value

and the alternative hypothesis will be one of the following:

H_a: $\mu_1 - \mu_2$ > some hypothesized value

H_a: $\mu_1 - \mu_2$ < some hypothesized value

H_a: $\mu_1 - \mu_2$ ≠ some hypothesized value state the a level

ASSUMPTIONS

Random sample: Check that *both* samples are independent and came from a random sample from their respective populations of interest.

Large sample or normal population distributions: Again, check *both* samples to ensure that n_1 and n_2 are sufficiently large; if the samples sizes are not large, construct a plot to verify the plausibility that each population distribution is approximately normal.

TEST STATISTIC

Given $\bar{x}_1$, $\bar{x}_2$, s_{x_1}, s_{x_2}, n_1, n_2 then

$$t = \frac{(\bar{x}_1 - \bar{x}_2) - (\mu_1 - \mu_2)}{\sqrt{\frac{s_1^2}{n_1} + \frac{s_2^2}{n_2}}}$$

and

$$df = \frac{(V_1+V_2)^2}{\frac{V_1^2}{n_1-1}+\frac{V_2^2}{n_2-1}}, \text{ where } V_1 = \frac{s_1^2}{n_1} \text{ and } V_2 = \frac{s_2^2}{n_2}$$

(Note: If a t table is used, remember to truncate the df to an integer. You can also use the df that the calculator gives or the more conservative estimate of df can be used by using the smaller of either $(n_1 - 1)$ or $(n_2 - 1)$.)

CONCLUSION Once the test statistic and P-value are calculated, the P-value can be compared to the significance level, α. If the P-value $< \alpha$, there is sufficient evidence to reject the null hypothesis in favor of the alternative hypothesis. In other words, we would have sufficient evidence to say that the difference in the two means is not equal to the hypothesized value and favor whichever direction the alternative hypothesis claim takes.

SAMPLE PROBLEM 1 Students want to see if regular and low-fat chocolate chip cookies have the same number of chips in a cookie, on average. They suspect that the way low-fat cookies are made is by simply reducing the number of chips in each cookie. To test this theory, they selected random samples of cookies of each type and counted the number of chips in each cookie. Summary statistics are shown in the table below. Boxplots of the two samples were approximately symmetric with no outliers.

Cookie	Sample Size	Mean Chips	Standard Deviation
Regular	25	16.3	2.29
Low-Fat	25	15.2	3.25

Is there evidence that the mean number of chips for regular cookies is greater than the mean number for low-fat cookies?

SOLUTION TO PROBLEM 1 To answer this question, we will need to carry out an appropriate t hypothesis test for independent samples. The steps are shown here.

HYPOTHESES

H_0: $\mu_R - \mu_L = 0$, where μ_R = the true mean number of chips for regular chocolate chip cookies and μ_L = the true mean number of chips for low-fat chocolate chip cookies

H_a: $\mu_R - \mu_L > 0$ to test to see if regular cookies have more chips, on average, than low-fat cookies

$\alpha = 0.05$ (since no significance level is specified, we can choose a value.)

TEST: two-sample t test

ASSUMPTIONS

1. The samples were independent random samples from the populations (all regular chocolate chip cookies and all low-fat chocolate chip cookies).

2. The samples sizes are not greater than 30, but the problem states that the two boxplots were approximately symmetric with no outliers. So, it is reasonable to assume that the two population distributions are approximately normal.

TEST STATISTIC

$$t = \frac{(\bar{x}_1 - \bar{x}_2) - (\mu_1 - \mu_2)}{\sqrt{\frac{s_1^2}{n_1} + \frac{s_2^2}{n_2}}} = \frac{(16.3 - 15.2) - (0)}{\sqrt{\frac{2.29^2}{25} + \frac{3.25^2}{25}}} = \frac{(16.3 - 15.2) - (0)}{\sqrt{0.289 + 0.423}} = 1.33$$

$$df = \frac{(V_1 + V_2)^2}{\frac{V_1^2}{n_1 - 1} + \frac{V_2^2}{n_2 - 1}} = \frac{(0.289 + 0.423)^2}{\frac{0.289^2}{24} + \frac{0.423^2}{24}} = \frac{0.50694}{0.01096} = 46.3$$

P-value = 0.095

You could also give the results from the conservative degrees of freedom estimate: $df = 24$ and $p = 0.098$. Or you can report the calculator results: $t = 1.304$, $df = 46.38$, and $p = 0.099$. If you choose to report the calculator results, be sure to write the formula for the t test statistic with the numbers substituted. Whichever method you choose for the degrees of freedom, make sure you report the P-value that is associated with the degrees of freedom you choose.

CONCLUSION Since $0.095 > 0.05$, we fail to reject the null hypothesis. There is not convincing evidence that the mean number of chocolate chips in regular cookies is greater than the mean number in low-fat cookies.

POOLED T TEST

The pooled t test is used when it is known that the two population variances are the same $(\sigma_1^2 = \sigma_2^2)$. However, this rarely is known. So, unless there is reason to know the variances are the same, use an *unpooled* test. In the case of the AP® Exam, we advise you to always use the unpooled test when testing hypotheses about the difference in means using independent samples.

CONFIDENCE INTERVALS

A confidence interval can be used to estimate a difference in means. Similar to the one-sample interval, the two-sample interval would be calculated in the following manner.

$$\bar{x}_1 - \bar{x}_2 \pm (t \text{ critical value})\sqrt{\frac{s_1^2}{n_1} + \frac{s_2^2}{n_2}}$$

with

$$df = \frac{(V_1 + V_2)^2}{\frac{V_1^2}{n_1 - 1} + \frac{V_2^2}{n_2 - 1}}, \text{ where } V_1 = \frac{s_1^2}{n_1} \text{ and } V_2 = \frac{s_2^2}{n_2}$$

The same assumptions used for the two-sample t test still apply and need to be verified before computing the confidence interval. Remember, for a two-sample confidence interval for independent samples, both samples should be independent random samples from their respective populations of interest and both sample sizes must be sufficiently large or the populations approximately normal for the confidence interval to be appropriate.

We can also calculate a hypothesis test or confidence interval with two treatments from an experiment. The only difference is the random condition—in an experiment, we need treatments to be randomly assigned to subjects. Otherwise, the hypothesis test and confidence interval are calculated the same way.

INFERENCES CONCERNING THE DIFFERENCE BETWEEN TWO POPULATION OR TREATMENT MEANS USING PAIRED SAMPLES

(*Statistics: Learning from Data*, AP Edition, 1st ed. pages 633–639, 649–651, 672–674, and 679–682 / 2nd ed. pages 642–650)

The two-sample t test just described is used with two independent samples. However, sometimes there are other variables that should be considered. For example, tracking weight loss of individuals who are exercising versus those who are not may be confounded by the individual's caloric intake as well. So just having a mean weight loss for those who exercise and those who don't may not be the best comparison. However, if the two groups were *paired* by caloric intake, then the weight loss difference in the pairs could be calculated. This would allow us to see if the exercise had an effect on weight loss for individuals who ate roughly the same number of calories per day.

If the two sample sizes are the same, think about whether or not the samples are paired. If the sample sizes are different, then the samples cannot be paired samples. To perform the paired t test, you will use the same steps as for the one-sample t test where:

1. The hypothesis is based on the mean difference in the pairs (μ_d = hypothesized value where $d = x_1 - x_2$ for each pair in the data set).

2. $df = n - 1$, where the n is the number of pairs we have.

The paired t test is summarized in these simple steps.

Hypotheses

H_0: μ_d = hypothesized value, where μ_d = mean of the differences between all paired values of x_1 and x_2.

The alternative hypothesis will be either

H_a: μ_d > some hypothesized value

H_a: μ_d < some hypothesized value

H_a: μ_d ≠ some hypothesized value

state the α level

Test: paired t test

Assumptions

1. The samples are *paired*, and therefore, *not independent*.
2. The sample differences came from a random sample of population differences.
3. The sample size (number of differences) is large or it is reasonable to assume that the distribution of differences in the population is approximately normal.

Test Statistic

Given $\bar{x}_d$ = mean of the sample differences and s_d = standard deviation of sample differences

$$t = \frac{\bar{x}_d - \text{hypothesized value}}{\frac{s_d}{\sqrt{n}}}$$

and

$df = n - 1$, where n is the number of differences in the sample.

CONCLUSION As before, if the P-value < α, there is sufficient evidence to reject the null hypothesis in favor of the alternative hypothesis. We have sufficient evidence to reject the hypothesis that the mean difference equaled the hypothesized value. We use the same four steps as in the other hypothesis tests presented previously.

To better understand this procedure, let's reconsider the chocolate chip cookie scenario in the first part of this chapter. If you recall, we were given the mean number of chips in samples of 25 regular and low-fat cookies. Suppose that each student in the class counted the number of chips in one cookie of each type. Since everyone may count what constitutes a chip a little differently, a better way to analyze this data is to incorporate the pairing. The following sample problem uses the same set of data used for the two-sample test earlier, but instead of only having the means for each type of cookie, this data also contain information on the pairing. Notice how this test differs from the two-sample problem presented earlier.

SAMPLE PROBLEM 2 Twenty-five students counted the number of chocolate chips in a low-fat and a regular chocolate chip cookie and recorded the counts as seen in the table below. Prior to counting, each student flipped a coin to decide if he or she would count the regular or the low-fat cookie first. Is there evidence that, on average, regular chocolate chip cookies contain more chips than low-fat cookies?

R = the number of chips in regular chocolate chip cookies

L = the number of chips in low-fat chocolate chip cookies

d = Difference = R − L

Person	R	L	Diff	Person	R	L	Diff
1	20	17	3	14	21	14	7
2	17	13	4	15	17	11	6
3	12	10	2	16	13	16	−3
4	15	13	2	17	16	16	0
5	16	12	4	18	17	16	1
6	20	23	−3	19	15	15	0
7	15	16	−1	20	18	20	−2
8	19	18	1	21	14	12	2
9	18	16	2	22	13	15	−2
10	17	15	2	23	21	19	2
11	15	19	−4	24	12	10	2
12	18	18	0	25	15	13	2
13	13	12	1				

$\bar{x}_d = 1.12$, $s_d = 2.68$

SOLUTION TO PROBLEM 2 To answer this question, we need to carry out a hypothesis test. Since the samples are paired, we will use a paired t test.

HYPOTHESES

H_0: $\mu_d = 0$ where μ_d = the true difference in mean number of chips (regular − low-fat)

H_a: $\mu_d > 0$ since they want to know if regular cookies have more chips

$\alpha = 0.05$

TEST: paired t test

ASSUMPTIONS

1. The samples are paired.

2. The differences can be regarded as a random sample of differences from all differences between regular and low-fat chocolate chip cookies.

3. The sample size is only 25, which is not large. A normal probability plot (below) is reasonably straight and so it is reasonable to assume that the distribution of population differences is approximately normal.

chocolate chip cookies

— Normal Quantile = 0.373 Difference −0.42

TEST STATISTIC

$$t = \frac{\bar{x}_d}{\frac{s_d}{\sqrt{n}}} = \frac{1.12 - 0}{\frac{2.68}{\sqrt{25}}} = \frac{1.12}{\frac{2.68}{5}} = \frac{1.12}{0.536} = 2.09 \text{ and } df = n - 1 = 24$$

P-value = 0.024

CONCLUSION Since 0.024 < 0.05, we reject the null hypothesis in favor of the alternative hypothesis. There is reason to believe that the mean difference in chips is greater than zero, so there does appear to be more chocolate chips, on average, in regular cookies than in low-fat cookies.

What is important to notice in the sample problem given is that when using the differences instead of two independent samples, our conclusion changed significantly. Both tests used the same samples; however, the paired t test took the pairing into account. This illustrates why it is important to know which kind of data you are working with so that you can use the appropriate t test.

We can also calculate a hypothesis test or confidence interval with two paired treatments from an experiment. The only difference is the random condition—in an experiment, we need treatments to be randomly assigned to subjects. Otherwise, the hypothesis test and confidence interval are calculated the same way.

LARGE-SAMPLE INFERENCES CONCERNING A DIFFERENCE BETWEEN TWO POPULATION OR TREATMENT PROPORTIONS

(*Statistics: Learning from Data*, AP Edition, 1st ed. pages 542–548, 550–557, 674–676, and 682–684 / 2nd ed. pages 556–562, 564–572, and 573–580)

As we saw in the previous chapters, categorical data involve working with proportions instead of means. We also learned that a hypothesis test and confidence interval could be generated for this type of data. In this section, we will see how this concept can also be extended to compare two population proportions. For example, is the proportion of males who would be willing to pay an extra $300 to upgrade to a first-class airline seat equal to the proportion of females who would be willing to pay extra to upgrade? This question and others that involve comparing two population proportions can be answered using a two-proportion z test.

This test is based on the following properties of the sampling distribution of $\hat{p}_1 - \hat{p}_2$:

1. $\mu_{\hat{p}_1 - \hat{p}_2} = p_1 - p_2$, in other words, since the distribution of $\hat{p}_1 - \hat{p}_2$ is centered at $p_1 - p_2$, it is an unbiased estimator of $p_1 - p_2$

2. $\sigma^2_{\hat{p}_1 - \hat{p}_2} = \sigma^2_{\hat{p}_1} + \sigma^2_{\hat{p}_2} = \dfrac{p_1(1-p_1)}{n_1} + \dfrac{p_2(1-p_2)}{n_2}$

   $\sigma^2_{\hat{p}_1 - \hat{p}_2} = \sqrt{\dfrac{p_1(1-p_1)}{n_1} + \dfrac{p_2(1-p_2)}{n_2}}$

3. When the sample sizes are both large, the sampling distribution of $\hat{p}_1 - \hat{p}_2$ is approximately normal. This MUST be checked by verifying all of the following:

$$n_1 p_1 \geq 10 \qquad n_2 p_2 \geq 10$$
$$n_1(1 - p_1) \geq 10 \qquad n_2(1 - p_2) \geq 10$$

> ### AP® Tip
> It is not enough to just state the conditions—you must show that you have actually checked these conditions.

Once we have verified that the sampling distribution of $\hat{p}_1 - \hat{p}_2$ is roughly normal and the samples were random samples from their respective populations of interest, we can then calculate a test statistic:

AP® is a trademark registered by the College Board, which is not affiliated with, and does not endorse, this product.

$$z = \frac{(\hat{p}_1 - \hat{p}_2) - (p_1 - p_2)}{\sqrt{\dfrac{p_1(1-p_1)}{n_1} + \dfrac{p_2(1-p_2)}{n_2}}}$$

When the null hypothesis specifies $p_1 - p_2 = 0$, this simplifies to

$$z = \frac{\hat{p}_1 - \hat{p}_2}{\sqrt{\dfrac{p_1(1-p_1)}{n_1} + \dfrac{p_2(1-p_2)}{n_2}}}$$

The actual test procedure uses a slightly different denominator. Because the values of p_1 and p_2 are not known, the denominator cannot be computed. Because the null hypothesis H_0: $p_1 - p_2 = 0$ specifies that p_1 and p_2 are equal, we estimate this common value p_c as combined estimate of the common population proportion, using

$$p_c = \frac{n_1 \hat{p}_1 + n_2 \hat{p}_2}{n_1 + n_2} = \frac{\text{total successes in both samples}}{\text{total of the sample sizes}}$$

So given this information, we can now describe a two-proportion z test.

Hypothesis

H_0: $p_1 - p_2 = 0$

the alternative hypothesis will be one of the following:

H_a: $p_1 - p_2 \neq 0$
H_a: $p_1 - p_2 > 0$
H_a: $p_1 - p_2 < 0$

Assumptions

1. Independent random samples from their respective populations of interest
2. Large sample sizes. Verify

$$n_1 \hat{p}_1 \geq 10 \qquad n_2 \hat{p}_2 \geq 10$$
$$n_1(1 - \hat{p}_1) \geq 10 \qquad n_2(1 - \hat{p}_2) \geq 10$$

Test Statistic

$$z = \frac{\hat{p}_1 - \hat{p}_2}{\sqrt{\dfrac{p_c(1-p_c)}{n_1} + \dfrac{p_c(1-p_c)}{n_2}}}$$

This will allow us to find the related P-value using the standard normal distribution.

CONCLUSION Just like other hypothesis tests presented previously, the conclusion is based on comparing the *P*-value to α.

> ## AP® Tip
>
> In any hypothesis test for two samples, you MUST be sure to check the assumptions for *both* samples (and show your work). If you don't, you will not get credit for checking assumptions.
>
> A great way to be sure you have checked everything is to use a table to ensure that you have included a check for each of the samples on every assumption. Sketch something like the ones shown here and be sure you plug in the actual values or sketches as needed.
>
> | MEANS | | PROPORTIONS | |
> |---|---|---|---|
> | Sample 1 | Sample 2 | Sample 1 | Sample 2 |
> | Random sample? | Random sample? | Random sample? | Random sample? |
> | Is $n_1 > 30$? | Is $n_2 > 30$? | Verify large sample size | Verify large sample size |
> | If not, show a plot to see if normality is reasonable for population distribution | If not, show a plot to see if normality is reasonable for population distribution | Check: $n_1 p_1 \geq 10$ $n_1(1-p_1) \geq 10$ | Check: $n_2 p_2 \geq 10$ $n_2(1-p_2) \geq 10$ |

EXAMPLE An airline wishes to know if the proportion of passengers who would pay $300 extra to upgrade to a first-class airline seat is different for international flights than for flights within the United States. To investigate, they asked each person in a random sample of passengers on international flights and in a random sample of domestic flights if they would pay extra. The resulting data are summarized in the following table:

Flight Type	n	# Who Would Pay Extra	Proportion Who Would Pay Extra
International	99	73	$\hat{p}_i = \dfrac{73}{99} = 0.74$
Within United States	91	56	$\hat{p}_w = \dfrac{56}{91} = 0.62$

let $\hat{p}_i$ = sample proportion of international passengers who would pay extra.

$\hat{p}_w$ = sample proportion of passengers on flights within the United States who would pay extra.

Is there convincing evidence that the proportion of international passengers who would pay extra is greater different than the proportion for passengers on domestic flights within the United States? Use a significance level of 0.10. Would the conclusion be different if a significance level of 0.05 had been used?

Hypothesis

H_0: $p_i - p_w = 0$

H_a: $p_i - p_w \neq 0$

$\alpha = 0.10$

Assumptions

Samples are independent.
Sample of international passengers
  random sample from all international passengers

$$99\left(\frac{73}{99}\right) \geq 10$$

$$99\left(\frac{26}{99}\right) \geq 10$$

Sample of domestic passengers
  random sample from all domestic passengers

$$91\left(\frac{56}{91}\right) \geq 10$$

$$91\left(\frac{35}{91}\right) \geq 10$$

Test Statistic

$$\hat{p}_c = \frac{99\left(\frac{73}{99}\right) + 91\left(\frac{56}{91}\right)}{190} = 0.679$$

$$z = \frac{0.74 - 0.62}{\sqrt{\frac{0.679(0.321)}{99} + \frac{0.679(0.321)}{91}}} = 1.799$$

CONCLUSION At $\alpha = 0.10$: since $0.072 < 0.10$, we reject the null hypothesis and conclude that there is evidence that the proportion who would pay extra is different for international passengers than for domestic passengers. However, at $\alpha = 0.05$, since $0.072 > 0.05$, we fail to reject the null hypothesis and conclude that there is no evidence that the proportion who would pay extra is different for international passengers than domestic passengers.

> **AP® Tip**
>
> If a question does not specify a significance level, you can select one. Just be sure to state what you have chosen and then use it to reach a conclusion. (Note: 0.05 is often selected.)

A Confidence Interval

In some instances, it is more useful to estimate a difference rather than test a claim about the difference. A confidence interval can be used to estimate the difference between two population proportions. The conditions to be checked are the same as for the two-proportion z test: independent random samples and both sample sizes are large.

$$(\hat{p}_1 - \hat{p}_2) \pm (z \text{ critical value})\sqrt{\frac{\hat{p}_1(1-\hat{p}_1)}{n_1} + \frac{\hat{p}_2(1-\hat{p}_2)}{n_2}}$$

Using our previous example of international and domestic passengers who would be willing to pay extra for a first-class seat, let's generate a 90% confidence interval to estimate of the difference in population proportions. The assumptions were addressed in the hypothesis-testing example, so it is reasonable to proceed.

$$(\hat{p}_I - \hat{p}_D) \pm (z \text{ critical value})\sqrt{\frac{\hat{p}_I(1-\hat{p}_I)}{n_I} + \frac{\hat{p}_D(1-\hat{p}_D)}{n_D}}$$

$$= (0.74 - 0.62) \pm 1.645\sqrt{\frac{0.74(0.26)}{99} + \frac{0.62(0.38)}{91}}$$

$$= (0.011, 0.233)$$

Notice that the interval does not contain the value of zero. A difference of zero corresponds to the case of no difference in the population proportions. We are 90% confident that the proportion who would pay extra for a first-class seat is different for international passengers than for domestic passengers by somewhere between 0.011 and 0.233. We used a method that will capture the true difference 90% of the time in repeated sampling. This is consistent with what we found in the hypothesis test where $\alpha = .10$ since we rejected the null hypothesis.

Remember, we can also calculate a hypothesis test or confidence interval with two independent treatments from an experiment. The only difference is the random condition—in an experiment, we need treatments to be randomly assigned to subjects. Otherwise, the hypothesis test and confidence interval are calculated the same way.

Interpreting and Communicating the Results of Statistical Analyses

As we saw with the one-sample hypothesis tests, the conclusion is based on the P-value that is generated from our hypothesis test.

Hypothesis tests for two samples are widely used as many studies are designed to compare two populations or two treatments. With this in mind, there are several things to remember when reading descriptions of statistical studies. Make sure you ask yourself the following questions.

- Are only two groups being compared? If there are more, we will need a different method.
- Are the samples independent or paired?
- What are the hypotheses being tested?
- Is the test appropriate? In other words, have all the needed assumptions been checked and met?
- If a confidence interval is calculated, has it been correctly interpreted?
- What is the P-value and does it lead us to reject the null hypothesis?
- Are the conclusions made consistent with the test results?

If you keep these questions in mind as you read descriptions of statistical studies or carry out two-sample hypothesis tests, you will avoid many common mistakes.

Comparing Two Populations or Treatments: Student Objectives for the AP® Exam

- You will be able to write the null and alternative hypothesis for two-sample tests.
- You will be able to carry out a two-sample hypothesis test for a difference in means.
- You will be able to carry out a two-sample hypothesis test for a difference in proportions.
- You will be able to distinguish between independent samples and paired samples.
- You will be able to construct and interpret a confidence interval for a difference in population means.
- You will be able to construct and interpret a confidence interval for a difference in population proportions.

MULTIPLE-CHOICE QUESTIONS

1. Insurance companies charge higher monthly premiums for male drivers than female drivers between the ages of 16 and 25. Their rationale is that male drivers have more traffic violations than females. A consumer group believes this rationale is no longer appropriate. To investigate, a random sample of male drivers and a random sample of female drivers in the target age groups were selected. Each person was asked how many traffic violations he or she had received. The resulting data were used to compute the given summary statistics. A 98% confidence interval for the difference in population mean number of traffic violations is (−1.3, 1.5). Based on this confidence interval, is there evidence that the population means are different?
   (A) Yes. Since the interval contains zero, there is strong evidence that the mean number of traffic violations is greater for males than females.
   (B) No. Since the interval contains zero, it is plausible that the mean number of traffic violations is the same for males and females.
   (C) Yes. Since the interval does not contain zero, there is strong evidence that the mean number of traffic violations is greater for males than females.
   (D) No. Since the interval does not contain zero, there is insufficient evidence that the number of traffic violations is the same for males and females.
   (E) Yes. Since the interval is wider for positive numbers, there is evidence that the mean number of traffic violations is greater for males than females.

2. In a random sample of 300 elderly men, 65% were married, while in a random sample of 400 elderly women, 48% were married. Which of the following is the 99% confidence interval estimate for the difference between the proportion of elderly men and the proportion of elderly women who are married? Assume all conditions for inference are met.
   (A) 0.17 ± 0.073
   (B) 0.17 ± 0.096
   (C) 0.55 ± 0.067
   (D) 0.56 ± 0.067
   (E) 0.565 ± 0.096

3. Which of the following statements are *not* true?
   I. When samples are paired, a two-sample t test is appropriate.
   II. The degrees of freedom for a paired t test is $n - 1$, where n is the sum of the two sample sizes.
   III. A two-sample z-test is used to test hypotheses about $p_1 - p_2$ with large independent samples.
   (A) I only
   (B) II only
   (C) III only
   (D) I and II
   (E) I and III

4. Give the appropriate hypotheses for a research company that wants to see if there is a difference in the amount of vitamin D in a brand name multivitamin and generic brand multivitamin. Let μ_b be the true mean amount of vitamin D in the brand name multivitamin, μ_g be the true mean amount of vitamin D in the generic brand multivitamin, p_g be the true proportion of vitamin D in the generic brand multivitamin, and p_g be the true proportion of vitamin D in the generic brand multivitamin.
   (A) H_0: $\mu_b - \mu_g = 0$, H_a: $\mu_b - \mu_g > 0$
   (B) H_0: $\mu_b - \mu_g = 0$, H_a: $\mu_b - \mu_g < 0$
   (C) H_0: $\mu_b - \mu_g = 0$, H_a: $\mu_b - \mu_g \neq 0$
   (D) H_0: $p_b - p_g = 0$, H_a: $p_b - p_g > 0$
   (E) H_0: $p_b - p_g = 0$, H_a: $p_b - p_g \neq 0$

Questions 5–6 refer to the following set of data:

When a virus is placed on a tobacco leaf, small lesions appear on the leaf. To compare the mean number of lesions produced by two different strains of virus, one strain is applied to half of each of eight tobacco leaves, and the other strain is applied to the other half of each leaf. The strain that goes on the right half of the tobacco leaf is decided by a coin flip. The lesions that appear on each half are then counted. The data are given below. Assume all conditions for inference are met.

Leaf	1	2	3	4	5	6	7	8
Strain 1	31	20	18	17	9	8	10	7
Strain 2	18	17	14	11	10	7	5	6

5. What is the number of degrees of freedom associated with the appropriate t test for testing to see if there is a difference between the mean number of lesions per leaf produced by the two strains?
   (A) 6
   (B) 7
   (C) 8
   (D) 14
   (E) 15

6. Using a significance level of 0.01, is there statistical evidence that the mean number of lesions is different for the two strains? Let μ_1 be the true mean number of lesions from strain 1, μ_2 be the true mean number of lesions from strain 2, and μ_d be the true mean difference in number of lesions from strain 1 and strain 2.
   (A) Yes, H_0: $\mu_1 - \mu_2 = 0$, H_a: $\mu_1 - \mu_2 \neq 0$, P-value = 0.262
   (B) No, H_0: $\mu_1 - \mu_2 = 0$, H_a: $\mu_1 - \mu_2 \neq 0$, P-value = 0.262
   (C) No, H_0: $\mu_1 - \mu_2$, H_a: $\mu_1 \neq \mu_2$, P-value = 0.034
   (D) Yes, H_0: $\mu_d = 0$, H_a: $\mu_d \neq 0$, P-value = 0.034
   (E) No, H_0: $\mu_d = 0$, H_a: $\mu_d \neq 0$, P-value = 0.034

7. A new classroom strategy uses interactive technology to review information for a test. A random sample of 40 classroom teachers has been asked to use the technology with one of their classes and not with another class. The average test score for each class is then recorded for each teacher. Which would be the appropriate test to run to see if the technology helped?
   (A) One-sample z test for a population mean
   (B) One-sample z test for a population proportion
   (C) Two-sample t test for population means
   (D) Paired t test for population means
   (E) Two-sample z test for population means

8. Two independent samples were studied, resulting in the following summary statistics:

   $\bar{x}_1 = 10$, $s_{\bar{x}_1} = 2.1$, $n_1 = 108$ and $\bar{x}_2 = 15$, $s_{\bar{x}_2} = 2.9$, $n_2 = 78$

   Which of the following could be an appropriate test statistic for testing $H_0: \mu_1 - \mu_2 = 0$ where $\mu_{1 \text{ or } 2}$ is the true mean from population 1 or 2, respectively? Assume all conditions for inference are met.

   (A) $z = \dfrac{10-15}{\sqrt{\dfrac{2.1}{108} + \dfrac{2.9}{78}}}$

   (B) $z = \dfrac{10-15}{\sqrt{\dfrac{2.1^2}{108} + \dfrac{2.9^2}{78}}}$

   (C) $t = \dfrac{10-15}{\sqrt{\dfrac{2.1}{108} + \dfrac{2.9}{78}}}$

   (D) $t = \dfrac{10-15}{\sqrt{\dfrac{2.1^2}{107} + \dfrac{2.9^2}{77}}}$

   (E) $t = \dfrac{10-15}{\sqrt{\dfrac{2.1^2}{108} + \dfrac{2.9^2}{78}}}$

9. A soup manufacturer is deciding which company to use for his or her mushroom purchases. A random sample of 20 mushrooms for each company found 30% of the mushrooms from one company were damaged and 35% from the other company were damaged. What assumptions for the two-proportion z test would be a concern?
   I. We don't know that they are random samples from both companies.
   II. The samples may not be independent.
   III. The sample size is not large enough.
   (A) I only
   (B) II only
   (C) III only
   (D) I and II only
   (E) I, II, and III

10. In an experiment to test the effect of alcohol on fine motor skills, volunteers were randomly assigned to one of two groups, A and B. Everyone in group A drank 2 ounces of alcohol, and 20 minutes later everyone in both groups was timed on a manual dexterity test. The average completion times for the group A and B volunteers were 38 and 31 seconds, respectively. The 90% confidence interval estimate for the mean difference is (3,11). If μ_A and μ_B are the true mean completion times, respectively, for people who have and have not drunk 2 ounces of alcohol, which of the following statements is a reasonable conclusion? Assume all conditions for inference are met.
    (A) $\mu_A = \mu_B$ with probability 0.90
    (B) There is a 0.90 probability that $3 < \mu_A - \mu_B < 11$.
    (C) The interval (3,11) was calculated using a method that produces intervals that include $\mu_A - \mu_B$ for 90% of all possible random samples.
    (D) We are 90% confident that $\bar{x}_A - \bar{x}_B$ lies between 3 and 11 seconds.
    (E) Since zero is not in the interval, there is no evidence that there is a difference in mean completion times.

11. In a test of H_0: $\mu_1 - \mu_2 = 0$ versus H_a: $\mu_1 - \mu_2 > 0$, the value of the test statistic was $t = 2.34$ and the P-value was 0.01. What conclusion would be appropriate if $\alpha = 0.05$? Assume all conditions for inference are met.
    (A) There was not a significant difference in the population means.
    (B) There is convincing evidence that there is a difference in the population means.
    (C) There is convincing evidence that the mean for population 1 is greater than the mean for population 2.
    (D) The proportion of successes in population is greater than the proportion of successes in population 2.
    (E) There is convincing evidence that the mean for population 2 is greater than the mean for population 1.

Questions 12–13 refer to the following set of data:

Ten men and women were given a supplement for weight loss, and the number of pounds lost by each person was measured at the end of 1 month. The data are shown below. The investigators would like to know if there is evidence that the mean weight loss for men is greater than the mean weight loss for women.

Subject	1	2	3	4	5	6	7	8	9	10
Males	5	8	12	7	9	11	10	16	8	14
Females	4	9	8	6	11	7	8	12	10	13

12. Which of the following is an appropriate set of hypotheses if μ_m = the true mean weight loss for men, μ_w = the true mean weight loss for women, and μ_d = the true mean weight loss for the difference of men and women $(d = m - w)$?
    (A) H_0: $\mu_m - \mu_w = 0$, H_a: $\mu_m - \mu_w \neq 0$
    (B) H_0: $\mu_m - \mu_w = 0$, H_a: $\mu_m - \mu_w > 0$
    (C) H_0: $\mu_m - \mu_w = 0$, H_a: $\mu_m - \mu_w < 0$
    (D) H_0: $\mu_d = 0$, H_a: $\mu_d \neq 0$
    (E) H_0: $\mu_d = 0$, H_a: $\mu_d > 0$

13. Assuming that the conditions for inference are met, what would be an appropriate conclusion for a significance level of 0.10?
    (A) With $t = 1.62$, $df = 9$, and $p = 0.140$, we fail to reject the null hypothesis. There is no evidence of a difference in men's and women's mean weight loss.
    (B) With $t = 1.62$, $df = 9$, and $p = 0.140$, we reject the null hypothesis. There is evidence of a significant difference in men's and women's mean weight loss.
    (C) With $t = 1.62$, $df = 18$, and $p = 0.140$, we fail to reject the null hypothesis. There is no evidence of a difference in men's and women's mean weight loss.
    (D) With $t = 0.87$, $df = 17$, and $p = 0.197$, we fail to reject the null hypothesis. There is no evidence of a difference in men's and women's mean weight loss.
    (E) With $t = 0.87$, $df = 17$, and $p = 0.197$, we reject the null hypothesis. There is evidence of a significant difference in men's and women's mean weight loss.

14. A school district wishes to estimate the difference in the proportion of girls who purchase a school lunch and the proportion of boys who purchase a school lunch. Assuming that the conditions for inference are met, which of the following confidence intervals would be appropriate?
    (A) A one-sample t interval
    (B) A two-sample t interval
    (C) A paired t interval
    (D) A one-proportion z interval
    (E) A two-proportion z interval

15. Time spent studying in a typical week was recorded for each student in a random sample of juniors and a random sample of seniors in a large school district. A 95% confidence interval for the difference in mean time (junior − senior) was (7.4, 14.7). Which of the following is a correct interpretation of this interval? Assume that the conditions for inference are met.
   (A) I am 95% confident that the sample mean difference is between 7.4 and 14.7 minutes.
   (B) I am 95% confident that the true mean difference in time spent studying is between 7.4 and 14.7 minutes.
   (C) I am 95% confident that the difference in the proportion of students who study is between 7.4 and 14.7.
   (D) I know that 95 out of 100 times the mean difference in time is between 7.4 and 14.7 minutes.
   (E) 95% of the sample differences were between 7.4 and 14.7 minutes.

FREE-RESPONSE PROBLEMS

1. A local outreach organization offers a counseling program to help people with alcohol addiction. The participants who enter this program are given a survey prior to starting counseling and they are given the same survey after they have completed the counseling program. One survey question asks participants to report their frequency of alcohol consumption on a 1 to 5 scale with 5 being very frequent and 1 being very infrequent. The table below shows the responses of 13 randomly selected participants. Is there convincing evidence that the participants have reduced the frequency of their alcohol consumption after counseling?

Alcohol Use Frequency													
Participant	1	2	3	4	5	6	7	8	9	10	11	12	13
Before Program	2	5	4	3	4	2	3	4	5	2	1	1	1
After Program	1	1	0	2	1	1	1	2	3	2	0	2	3

2. A recent study reported that in a random sample of 248 women, 58 had changed their political affiliation since the last election. It also reported that 120 in a random sample of 387 men had changed political affiliation. The researchers would like to know if these data provide convincing evidence that the proportion changing political affiliation is greater for men than for women. Is there convincing evidence that the proportion changing political affiliation is greater for men than for women?

Answers

MULTIPLE-CHOICE QUESTIONS

1. **(B)** When a two-sample interval is computed, if the value of 0 is within that interval then there appears to be no difference in the two samples. Choice E is also incorrect as it was run as a one-sample confidence interval on males only (*Statistics: Learning from Data*, AP Edition, 1st ed. pages 618–627, 644–649, 672–674, and 679–682 / 2nd ed. pages 657–670).

2. **(B)** The difference between 0.65 and 0.48 is 0.17, making choice A or choice B the solution. Answer choice A is for a 95% interval (*Statistics: Learning from Data*, AP Edition, 1st ed. pages 542–548, 550–557, 674–676, and 682–684 / 2nd ed. pages 556–562, 564–572, and 573–580).

3. **(D)** If the samples are paired, the appropriate test is a paired *t* test, and $df = n - 1$ where *n* is the number of pairs (*Statistics: Learning from Data*, AP Edition, 1st ed. pages 633–639, 649–651, 672–674, and 679–682 / 2nd ed. pages 642–650).

4. **(C)** The researchers want to know if there is a difference in means. In this case, the alternative hypothesis would be two-sided (*Statistics: Learning from Data*, AP Edition, 1st ed. pages 618–627, 644–649, 672–674, and 679–682 / 2nd ed. pages 657–670).

5. **(B)** This is a paired *t* test, so $df = n - 1$ where *n* is the number of sample pairs (*Statistics: Learning from Data*, AP Edition, 1st ed. pages 633–639, 649–651, 672–674, and 679–682 / 2nd ed. pages 642–650).

6. **(E)** This would require a matched-pairs test. Each virus is being tested on the same tobacco leaf and that makes the samples paired. When *P*-value < α, there is strong evidence in favor of the alternative hypothesis. Choices A and B are incorrect as they use a test for independent samples. Finally, choice C is incorrect as it is the same as choice B with the hypotheses written in an alternative format (*Statistics: Learning from Data*, AP Edition, 1st ed. pages 633–639, 649–651, 672–674, and 679–682 / 2nd ed. pages 642–650).

7. **(D)** Each teacher is being assigned a class with which to use the technology and a class to not use the technology, so the samples are paired by teacher (*Statistics: Learning from Data*, AP Edition, 1st ed. pages 633–639, 649–651, 672–674, and 679–682 / 2nd ed. pages 642–650).

8. **(E)** This is a two-sample *t* test. Notice the denominator must be set up correctly (*Statistics: Learning from Data*, AP Edition, 1st ed. pages 618–627, 644–649, 672–674, and 679–682 / 2nd ed. pages 657–670).

9. **(C)** The sample size is not large enough to meet the conditions of the two-proportion *z* test (*Statistics: Learning from Data*, AP Edition, 1st ed. pages 542–548, 550–557, 674–676, and 682–684 / 2nd ed. pages 556–562, 564–572, and 573–580).

10. **(C)** Choice C is the only reasonable statement based on the confidence interval (*Statistics: Learning from Data*, AP Edition, 1st ed. pages 618–627, 644–649, 672–674, and 679–682 / 2nd ed. pages 657–670).

11. **(C)** Since the *P*-value is less than 0.05, the null hypothesis would be rejected in favor of the alternative $\mu_1 > \mu_2$ (*Statistics: Learning from Data*, AP Edition, 1st ed. pages 618–627, 644–649, 672–674, and 679–682 / 2nd ed. pages 657–670).

12. **(B)** The samples are independent since there is no indication that the male and female subjects are paired in any meaningful way. Finally, the alternative hypothesis is $\mu_m - \mu_w > 0$ since we are asking if the mean for men is greater than the mean for women (*Statistics: Learning from Data*, AP Edition, 1st ed. pages 618–627, 644–649, 672–674, and 679–682 / 2nd ed. pages 657–670).

13. **(D)** The appropriate test is based on two independent samples with the alternative being that mean loss for men is greater than mean loss for women. Choices A–C are incorrect as they use the test designed for paired data (*Statistics: Learning from Data*, AP Edition, 1st ed. pages 618–627, 644–649, 672–674, and 679–682 / 2nd ed. pages 657–670).

14. **(E)** The samples are independent and we are estimating the difference in population proportions (*Statistics: Learning from Data*, AP Edition, 1st ed. pages 542–548, 550–557, 674–676, and 682–684 / 2nd ed. pages 556–562, 564–572, and 573–580).

15. **(B)** Confidence intervals are estimates for true/population values. (*Statistics: Learning from Data*, AP Edition, 1st ed. pages 618–627, 644–649, 672–674, and 679–682 / 2nd ed. pages 657–670).

FREE-RESPONSE PROBLEMS

1. To answer this question, we will need to carry out a matched-pairs *t* test for population means. The steps are shown here.

Alcohol Use Frequency													
Participant	1	2	3	4	5	6	7	8	9	10	11	12	13
Before Program	2	5	4	3	4	2	3	4	5	2	1	1	1
After Program	1	1	0	2	1	1	1	2	3	2	0	2	3
Difference (After − Before)	−1	−4	−4	−1	−3	−1	−2	−2	−2	0	−1	1	2

HYPOTHESES

H_0: $\mu_D = 0$ where μ_D is the mean of the differences between all participants (After – Before).

(Note: The difference could also be calculated as Before – After)

H_a: $\mu_D < 0$

$\alpha = 0.05$

ASSUMPTIONS

1. The observations are independent assuming over 130 participants.
2. The participant responses were randomly selected.
3. The sample size is not greater than 30, so a normal probability plot of the differences must be constructed. Since the normal probability plot appears roughly linear, it is reasonable to assume the data come from an approximately normal population.

TEST STATISTIC We will use a matched-pairs t test for population means.

If you use the calculator, your work should look like this:

$$t = \frac{\bar{x}_d}{\frac{s_d}{\sqrt{n}}} = \frac{-1.38 - 0}{\frac{1.76}{\sqrt{13}}} = \frac{-1.38}{\frac{1.76}{\sqrt{13}}} = \frac{-1.38}{0.488} = -2.84 \text{ and } df = n - 1 = 12$$

P-value = 0.007

CONCLUSION Since $0.007 < 0.05$, we reject the null hypothesis in favor of the alternative hypothesis. There is convincing evidence that the participants have reduced their alcohol use frequency after the counseling program (*Statistics: Learning from Data*, AP Edition, 1st ed. pages 633–639, 649–651, 672–674, and 679–682 / 2nd ed. pages 642–650).

2. To answer this question, we will need to carry out a two-sample z test for population proportions. The steps are shown here.

   ### HYPOTHESES

   $H_0 : p_w - p_m = 0$

   $H_a : p_w - p_m < 0$

   where p_w and p_m are the true proportion of women and men changing affiliation, respectively.

   ### ASSUMPTIONS

   The samples were independently selected and both were random samples from their respective populations (all women and all men). Check to see that the samples sizes are large enough:

   $\hat{p}_w = \frac{58}{248} = 0.23$ $\hat{p}_m = \frac{120}{387} = 0.31$

   $248(0.23) > 10$ $387(0.31) > 10$

   $248(0.67) > 10$ $387(0.69) > 10$

   ### TEST STATISTIC

   The appropriate test is a two-sample z test for population proportions.

   $$\hat{p}_c = \frac{58 + 120}{248 + 387} = \frac{178}{635} = 0.28$$

   $$z = \frac{0.23 - 0.31}{\sqrt{\frac{0.28(0.72)}{248} + \frac{0.28(0.72)}{387}}} = -2.08$$

   P-value $= 0.018$.

   CONCLUSION Since $0.018 < 0.05$, we reject the null hypothesis. There is evidence that the proportion of men who changed political affiliation is greater than the proportion of women who did so (*Statistics: Learning from Data*, AP Edition, 1st ed. pages 542–548, 550–557, 674–676, and 682–684 / 2nd ed. pages 556–562, 564–572, and 573–580).

11

THE ANALYSIS OF CATEGORICAL DATA AND GOODNESS-OF-FIT TESTS

This section will explore inference for categorical data using chi-square test procedures. These procedures are used with univariate as well as bivariate data sets as long as the variables are categorical.

OBJECTIVES

- Carry out a chi-square goodness-of-fit test.
- Carry out chi-square tests for homogeneity of proportions and for independence.

CHI-SQUARE TESTS FOR UNIVARIATE DATA

(*Statistics: Learning from Data*, AP Edition, 1st ed. pages 694–705 / 2nd ed. pages 702–714)

In this section, we extend techniques for analyzing univariate categorical data sets. Here we can consider questions about variables that involve two or more categories. A chi-square test (χ^2) for univariate data allows us to test hypotheses about the proportions falling into the different categories for a categorical variable. We do this by looking at the frequencies observed in each of the categories and comparing them to what would be expected if a null hypothesis were true. The hypothesized proportions can be equal or they can be different for each category.

EXAMPLE A new donut shop plans to sell plain, strawberry, blueberry, and cinnamon donuts. They wonder if there is a preference for one of these types of donuts or if the same proportion of customers prefers each type. We will let

p_p = the true proportion of customers preferring plain donuts
p_s = the true proportion of customers preferring strawberry donuts
p_b = the true proportion of customers preferring blueberry donuts
p_c = the true proportion of customers preferring cinnamon donuts

We are interested in knowing if $p_p = p_s = p_b = p_c = 0.25$ or if there is evidence that these proportions are not all the same. To answer this question, a random sample of 60 customers is surveyed, and each person in the sample is asked which of the four donut types they prefer.

Instead of running a separate two-sample proportions test for each of the possible pairs of proportions, a chi-square test will allow us to decide if the proportions we have observed in our sample are significantly different from the hypothesized proportions. The chi-square goodness-of-fit test will allow us to test the following hypotheses:

H_0: $p_p = p_s = p_b = p_c$

H_a: not all of the proportions are equal to 0.25

(For chi-square tests, it is acceptable to state hypotheses in words on the AP® exam. The above null hypothesis would be written as "the true proportions of donut flavor preference is the same as the claimed proportions" or "the four types of donuts are equally preferred.")

To make the decision to reject or fail to reject the null hypothesis, the chi-square test will compare the number of responses observed in each category to what we would expect to see in each category if the null hypothesis is true. If the difference is too large, we reject the null hypothesis. Otherwise, we fail to reject the null hypothesis.

Data on a single categorical variable are usually summarized using a one-way frequency table. Returning to the previous example, suppose that the sample of 60 customers resulted in the data summarized in the table below. The table entries are observed frequencies or counts.

Types of Donuts Preferred				
	Plain	Strawberry	Blueberry	Cinnamon
Observed Count	13	12	16	19

These counts represent the number of times a person in the sample selected each particular donut type. *Expected* counts are calculated using the hypothesized proportions from the null hypothesis. In this example, all four hypothesized proportions are equal to 0.25, so if the null hypothesis is true, we would expect to see the same number preferring each type. We calculate expected counts by multiplying the sample size by each hypothesized proportion. The expected counts can now be entered into the table as shown here.

Types of Donuts Sold				
	Plain	Strawberry	Blueberry	Cinnamon
Observed Count	13	12	16	19
Expected Count	60(0.25) = 15	60(0.25) = 15	60(0.25) = 15	60(0.25) = 15

Now we are ready to calculate the value of the test statistic. This test statistic is called the χ^2 **goodness-of-fit test** statistic because it considers how well the observed values fit to what we expected if the null hypothesis were true.

$$\chi^2 = \sum \frac{(\text{observed cell count} - \text{expected cell count})^2}{\text{expected cell count}}$$

which is often abbreviated $\chi^2 = \sum \frac{(O-E)^2}{E}$

For the example problem, the value of this test statistic is

$$\chi^2 = \frac{(13-15)^2}{15} + \frac{(12-15)^2}{15} + \frac{(16-15)^2}{15} + \frac{(19-15)^2}{15}$$

$$= \frac{(-2)^2}{15} + \frac{(-3)^2}{15} + \frac{(1)^2}{15} + \frac{(4)^2}{15}$$

$$= \frac{4}{15} + \frac{9}{15} + \frac{1}{15} + \frac{16}{15}$$

$$= \frac{30}{15}$$

$$= 2$$

To find the associated *P*-value, we use a chi-square distribution with $df = k - 1$, where k is the number of categories of the categorical variable. The *P*-value is the area to the right of the computed test statistic value (the chi-square goodness-of-fit test is only an upper-tailed test). This area is found by referring to the chi-square table or by using a graphing calculator or other technology.

The chi-square table is similar to the *t* table. You locate the degrees of freedom in the leftmost column then read across the row to find the value of the χ^2 test statistic. If the value is between two columns, then the *P*-value is between the two corresponding tail probabilities.

Chi-Square Tail Probability ($\chi 2$)						
df	0.25	0.20	0.15	0.10	0.05	0.025
1	1.32	1.64	2.07	2.71	3.84	5.02
2	2.77	3.22	3.79	4.61	5.99	7.38
3	4.11	4.64	5.32	6.25	7.81	9.35
4	5.39	5.99	6.74	7.78	9.49	11.14
⋮	⋮	⋮	⋮	⋮	⋮	⋮

Our *df* = 3 and our χ^2 = 2.00. Since this χ^2 value is smaller than 4.11, we know the tail probability is greater than 0.25. Using any reasonable α level will result in a failure to reject the null hypothesis.

The only things that we have not yet discussed are the overall assumptions required for the chi-square goodness of fit test. The first assumption is that we have a random sample of observations of a categorical variable from the population of interest. In addition, the sample size must be large enough that the following conditions are met:

1. No expected counts are less than 1,
2. All of our expected counts should be ≥ 5 and if they are not,
3. No more than 20% of the expected counts are < 5.

Returning to the donut example:

Hypotheses

H_0: p_p = 0.25, p_s = 0.25, p_b = 0.25, p_c = 0.25

H_a: not all of the proportions are equal

We will use a significance level of 0.05 for this test.

Test and Assumptions

Test: Chi-square goodness-of-fit test

Assumptions:

1. The sample was a random sample of customers.
2. All expected counts are > 5 (see above).

TEST STATISTIC As seen earlier, the calculated test statistic for this test would be

$$\chi^2 = \frac{(13-15)^2}{15} + \frac{(12-15)^2}{15} + \frac{(16-15)^2}{15} + \frac{(19-15)^2}{15}$$

$$= \frac{(-2)^2}{15} + \frac{(-3)^2}{15} + \frac{(1)^2}{15} + \frac{(4)^2}{15}$$

$$= \frac{4}{15} + \frac{9}{15} + \frac{1}{15} + \frac{16}{15}$$

$$= \frac{30}{15}$$

with $df = 3$

Based on the table, the P-value is greater than 0.25.

We can also solve this problem using the calculator. Here is the work that would be shown:

$$\chi^2 = \frac{(13-15)^2}{15} + \frac{(12-15)^2}{15} + ... + \frac{(19-15)^2}{15} = 2 \text{ with } df = 3$$

$p = 0.572$

CONCLUSION Since P-value $> \alpha$, we fail to reject the null hypothesis. There is not convincing evidence that the four types of donuts are not equally preferred.

> ## AP® Tip
>
> For all chi-square tests, make sure to show the expected counts and verify that they are large enough.

SAMPLE PROBLEM 1 A music producer is interested in marketing a new artist via ads in movie theaters. The target age group is teenagers from 14 to 18 years of age. The company developing the advertisement has offered to run the ad in conjunction with the following types of movies: 20% of the time with comedies, 50% with dramas, and 30% with action films. However, the movie producer is not sure these percentages reflect the types of movies that teens attend. To investigate, each person in a random sample of teens was asked what type of movie they had seen most recently, resulting in the following data:

Movie Most Recently Watched by 90 Teens			
	Comedy	Drama	Action
Observed Count	36	32	21

Do these data provide convincing evidence that the proportions of teens watching the different types of movies are different than the proportions proposed by the company developing the ad? Use a significance level of 0.05.

SOLUTION TO PROBLEM 1

HYPOTHESIS

Let p_c = the true proportion of teens who watched a comedy, p_d = the true proportion of teens who watched a drama, and p_a = the true proportion of teens who watched an action film.

H_0: $p_c = 0.2$; $p_d = 0.5$; $p_a = 0.3$ (or the proportions of teens watching the different types of movies are the same as the proportions proposed by the company developing the ad)

H_a: at least one of the proportions of teens watching the various film types is not equal to the hypothesized proportion.

$\alpha = 0.05$

ASSUMPTIONS The problem states the teens were a random sample from all teenagers from 14 to 18 years of age.

All the expected counts are greater than or equal to 5 (see table below).

Movie Most Recently Watched by 90 Teens			
	Comedy	Drama	Action
Expected Counts	90(0.2) = 18	90(0.5) = 45	90(0.3) = 27

TEST STATISTIC

χ^2 Goodness-of-fit test:

$$\chi^2 = \frac{(36-18)^2}{18} + \frac{(32-45)^2}{45} + \frac{(21-27)^2}{27} = 23.09 \text{ with } df = 2$$

$p = 0.0000097$

CONCLUSION The P-value associated with $\chi^2 = 23.09$ and $df = 2$ is approximately 0.000. Since 0.000 < 0.05, there is strong evidence to reject the null hypothesis. There is strong evidence that at least one of the proportions is not equal to the proportion stated by the ad company.

Just as with the other hypothesis tests you have learned, it is important to address all parts of the test. Clearly conveying your understanding of the procedure will include:

- explaining the notation used,
- addressing all assumptions that are required for the test,
- demonstrating correct mechanics,
- and finally writing a conclusion in context.

As with the other tests you have learned, the mechanics can be done using a graphing calculator, but it is strongly recommended that you still show the initial setup. This lets the AP® Reader know you understand how to compute the value of the test statistic.

TESTS FOR HOMOGENEITY AND INDEPENDENCE IN A TWO-WAY TABLE

(*Statistics: Learning from Data*, AP Edition, 1st ed. pages 708–718 / 2nd ed. pages 716–728)

A chi-square test procedure can also be used with bivariate categorical data, which is usually displayed in a two-way frequency table. There are two different types of investigations that arise from this type of data. One type involves inferences about association between two different categorical variables being observed on a single sample. The other type involves comparing two or more populations or treatments when a single categorical variable is observed. The calculation procedure is the same for both types of investigation, but the primary question of interest is different.

TEST FOR HOMOGENEITY

In a **chi-square test for homogeneity**, we are interested in whether the proportions falling into each of the possible categories of a categorical variable are the same for all of the treatments or populations studied. In this case, the null hypothesis is that the distribution of the categorical variable is the same for each population or treatment.

EXAMPLE A snack manufacturer produces three types of chips in two different locations (Location A and Location B). Sometimes bags of chips are damaged in the packaging process. Each bag in a random sample of 45 bags of chips packaged at Location A and in a random sample of 30 bags of chips packaged at Location B was classified into one of three categories: no damage, minimal damage, and severe damage. The resulting data are summarized in the table below. The manufacturer was interested in determining if there was sufficient evidence to conclude that the proportions falling into each of the three damage categories is different for the two locations.

	No Damage	Minimal Damage	Severe Damage	Row Totals
Location A	15	18	12	45
Location B	8	12	10	30
Column Totals	23	30	22	75

To answer the question of interest, the hypotheses would be

H_0: The proportions falling into each damage category for the two locations are the same

H_a: The proportions falling into each damage category for the two locations are different

The assumptions that need to be are (1) the sample must be a random sample from the population of interest and (2) all expected counts must be at least 5.

The samples are random samples of bags of chips from the two locations.

The expected counts for a chi-square test of homogeneity are calculated using the following formula:

$$\text{expected count for a cell} = \frac{(\text{row total})(\text{column total})}{\text{table total}}$$

For example, the expected count for the cell of no damage and Location A is

$$\frac{(53)(23)}{76} = 16.04$$

A way to record these expected counts is either in a separate two-way table of just the expected counts or in parenthesis beside each observed count as shown in the table below. All of the expected counts are greater than or equal to 5.

	No Damage	Minimal Damage	Severe Damage	Row Totals
Location A	19 (16.04)	20 (18.13)	14 (18.83)	53
Location B	4 (6.96)	6 (7.87)	13 (8.17)	23
Column Totals	23	26	27	76

Degrees of freedom for the chi-square test of homogeneity is computed as follows:

$df = (r-1)(c-1)$ where r = number of rows and c = number of columns

Note that the total column and total row are not counted in computing degrees of freedom.

The chi-square test statistic that was used in the goodness-of-fit test is also used here.

χ^2 test for homogeneity

$$\chi^2 = \frac{(19-16.04)^2}{16.04} + \frac{(20-18.13)^2}{18.13} + \ldots + \frac{(13-8.17)^2}{8.17} = 6.5$$

with $df = (2-1)(3-1) = 2$

Notice that you do not need to show every term in the calculation of the test statistic—feel free to show more but do not show any less than what is shown above. Using the graphing calculator technology, you first enter a matrix of the observed counts and then run a chi-square test from the test menu. The calculator will automatically calculate the expected counts and store them in matrix[B].

```
NORMAL FLOAT AUTO REAL RADIAN MP
MATRIX[A] 2 ×3
[ 19  20  14 ]
[  4   6  13 ]




[A](1,1)= 19
```

```
NORMAL FLOAT AUTO REAL RADIAN MP
         χ²-Test
Observed:[A]
Expected:[B]
Color: BLACK
Calculate  Draw
```

```
NORMAL FLOAT AUTO REAL RADIAN MP
         χ²-Test
χ²=6.534131993
p=0.0381181018
df=2
■
```

Finally, since 0.038 < 0.05, we reject the null hypothesis. There is strong evidence that the proportions falling into each of the three damage categories is not the same for both locations.

TEST FOR INDEPENDENCE

The **chi-square test for independence**, also known as the chi-square test for association, is used to investigate if there is an association between two categorical variables. The calculations will proceed in the same manner as the test for homogeneity; however, we are actually looking to see if knowing the value of one variable provides information about the value of the other variable.

The χ^2 test for independence is extremely similar to the χ^2 test for homogeneity. The way you can tell the difference is how the sample(s) was collected. The χ^2 test for independence has *one* sample and each subject is categorized by two variables. The χ^2 test for homogeneity has *two* samples and each subject is categorized by one variable.

> EXAMPLE A car manufacturer has two production lines building three types of cars. An engineer is wondering if there is an association between the type of car and the production line that made the vehicle for cars that are found to have major defects. Each car in a random sample of 75 cars selected from all cars found to have major defects was classified according to the type of car and the production line that produced the car. The resulting data are given in the table below.
>
> | | Sedan | Wagon | Truck |
> |--------|-------|-------|-------|
> | Line A | 13 | 9 | 12 |
> | Line B | 18 | 12 | 11 |

Is there an association between car type and production line for cars with major defects? To answer this question, we use the chi-square test for independence.

Hypotheses

H_o: Production line and car type are independent.

H_a: Production line and car type are not independent.

$\alpha = 0.05$

Note that another acceptable way to write the hypotheses is

H_o: There is no association between production line and car type.

H_a: There is an association between production line and car type.

ASSUMPTIONS The sample was a random sample of cars with major defects.

The expected counts are all greater than or equal to 5 (see table below).

Expected Counts for Auto Errors			
	Sedan	Wagon	Truck
Line A	14.1	9.5	10.4
Line B	16.9	11.5	12.6

TEST STATISTIC Since this is a χ^2 test for independence, the calculations are

$$\chi^2 = \frac{(13-14.1)^2}{14.1} + \frac{(9-9.5)^2}{9.5} + \ldots + \frac{(11-12.6)^2}{12.6} = 0.63 \text{ with } df = 2$$

$p = 0.73$

CONCLUSION Since $0.73 > 0.05$, we fail to reject the null hypothesis. We do not have sufficient evidence of an association between car type and production line.

Notice, the steps in the chi-square hypothesis tests are the same as for all other tests: State hypotheses, identify the test by name or formula, check assumptions required for the test, calculate the value of the test statistic and the associated *P*-value, and write a conclusion in context that is linked to the *P*-value.

INTERPRETING AND COMMUNICATING THE RESULTS OF STATISTICAL ANALYSES

This particular set of tests involved writing our conclusions in terms that match the setting of the individual test. Each chi-square test is performed in a different setting depending on the data we have to work with. It is important to state which of the three chi-square tests you are using when carrying out one of these tests. The goodness-of-fit, homogeneity, and independence tests all have different hypotheses and conclusions. Be clear which test you are using.

CATEGORICAL DATA AND GOODNESS-OF-FIT TESTS: STUDENT OBJECTIVES FOR THE AP® EXAM

- You will be able to determine degrees of freedom for chi-square tests of goodness-of-fit, homogeneity, and independence.
- You will be able to calculate expected counts for chi-square tests of goodness-of-fit, homogeneity, and independence.
- You will be able to carry out chi-square tests of goodness-of-fit, homogeneity, and independence.
- You will identify the correct hypothesis for each of the three chi-square scenarios.
- You will be able to interpret conclusions in contest for chi-square tests of goodness-of-fit, homogeneity, and independence.

MULTIPLE-CHOICE QUESTIONS

1. Each car in a random sample of 200 cars sold in 2010 at a large car dealership was classified by color; sixty of the cars were white, eighty were blue, twenty were silver, and ten were red. What is the value of the chi-square statistic in a test of $H_0: p_w = p_b = p_s = p_r = 0.25$? Assume conditions for inference are met.
   (A) 18
   (B) 32
   (C) 50
   (D) 70
   (E) 110

2. Which of the following is not true of the χ^2 probability distribution?
   (A) For small degrees of freedom, the distribution is right skewed.
   (B) As the degrees of freedom increase, the χ^2 distribution approaches a normal distribution.
   (C) All of the area under a chi-square curve is associated with positive values.
   (D) The total area under the χ^2 curve is equal to one.
   (E) The mean of a chi-square distribution is 0.

3. There are four surgical methods currently being used to place medical implants in patients. After surgery, patients are monitored and their pain level is recorded as severe, moderate, or mild. What are the degrees of freedom for a test to determine if there is an association between surgical method and pain level?
   (A) 2
   (B) 3
   (C) 4
   (D) 6
   (E) 12

Questions 4–7 refer to the following set of data:

A group of AP® Statistics students wanted to see if plain, peanut, and almond M&Ms have the same color distribution. To test this, students took a random sample of each type of M&M and classified the candies in the sample by color. They plan to carry out a chi-square test to decide if there is evidence that the color distributions are not the same for the three types of M&Ms. Assume conditions for inference are met.

	Red	Blue	Yellow	Green	Orange	Brown
Plain	20	18	15	10	14	12
Peanut	8	6	8	25	5	7
Almond	7	11	10	12	10	9

4. What is the expected count for green peanut M&Ms?

   (A) $\dfrac{25}{47}$

   (B) 25

   (C) $\dfrac{59(47)}{25}$

   (D) $\dfrac{59(47)}{207}$

   (E) $\dfrac{25(47)}{207}$

5. What are the correct degrees of freedom for the appropriate test?
   (A) 206
   (B) 18
   (C) 10
   (D) 7
   (E) 4

6. What is an appropriate set of hypotheses?
   (A) H_0: There is no association between the type of M&M and color.
   H_a: There is an association between the type of M&M and color.
   (B) H_0: There is an association between the type of M&M and color.
   H_a: There is no association between the type of M&M and color.
   (C) H_0: The color proportions are the same for all 3 types of M&Ms.
   H_a: The color proportions are not the same for all 3 types of M&Ms.
   (D) H_0: The proportions of red M&Ms are the same for all 3 types of M&Ms.
   H_a: The proportions of red M&Ms are not the same for all 3 types of M&Ms.
   (E) H_0: The colors of M&Ms match a given distribution.
   H_a: The colors of M&Ms do not match a given distribution.

7. The value of the chi-square test statistic is 22.9. What conclusion would be reached in a test of the hypotheses of interest using a significance level of 0.05?
   (A) Fail to reject the null hypothesis and conclude there is strong evidence of an association.
   (B) Fail to reject the null hypothesis and conclude there is strong evidence that the color distributions are the same.
   (C) Fail to reject the null hypothesis and conclude there is not strong evidence that the color distributions are the same.
   (D) Reject the null hypothesis and conclude there is strong evidence of an association.
   (E) Reject the null hypothesis and conclude there is strong evidence that the color distributions are not the same.

8. A cupcake store manager believes that half of the cupcakes sold are chocolate and that the other half is equally divided between vanilla and cherry. If the manager's belief is correct and 300 cupcakes are sold, how many would you expect to be cherry cupcakes?
   (A) 300
   (B) 200
   (C) 150
   (D) 100
   (E) 75

9. Each person in a random sample of patrons of a local mall was surveyed regarding a public smoking area outside one of the mall entrances. Each person was asked if they approved of the idea of a public smoking area in the mall. The resulting data are summarized in the table below. The mall management would like to know if there is a relationship between gender and approval of the smoking area. What would be an appropriate set of hypotheses?

Public Smokers	Approve	Do Not Approve
Males	28	57
Females	39	31

   (A) H_0: Gender and approval are not independent.
   H_a: Gender and approval are independent.
   (B) H_0: Gender and approval are independent.
   H_a: Gender and approval are not independent.
   (C) H_0: Knowing a person does not approve of a public smoking area indicates their gender.
   H_a: Knowing a person does not approve of a public smoking area does not indicate their gender.
   (D) H_0: There is no difference in gender distribution based on approval.
   H_a: There is a difference in gender distribution based on approval.
   (E) H_0: There is an association between gender and approval.
   H_a: There is no association between gender and approval.

10. A local bagel shop makes six types of bagels and eight types of cream cheese toppings. Suppose that all customers order one type of bagel and one type of cream cheese. If customers are classified according to the type of bagel and type of cream cheese, how many degrees of freedom would be appropriate for a test to determine if there is an association between type of bagel and type of cream cheese purchased?
    (A) 7
    (B) 12
    (C) 14
    (D) 35
    (E) 48

11. In a recent opinion poll, likely voters were asked if they would continue to support health care reform if the cost per taxpaying citizen was increased by $800 per year. Political preference was also recorded. The P-value for a chi-square test of independence is 0.001.

    Which of the following is a correct interpretation of this result at a 0.10 level? Assume conditions for inference are met.

	Democrat	Republican	Independent	Libertarian
Support	125	87	99	48
Don't Support	75	113	101	52

    (A) Since $P < \alpha$, there is strong evidence that political preference and support are independent of each other. In other words, knowing their political preference gives no insight into their support of the increase.
    (B) Since $P < \alpha$, there is strong evidence that political preference and support are not independent of each other. In other words, knowing their political preference gives insight into their support of the increase.
    (C) Since $P < \alpha$, there is strong evidence that political preference and support are independent of each other. Since they are independent, there is no association between the two variables.
    (D) Since $P < \alpha$, there is no evidence that political preference and support are independent of each other. Since they are not independent, there is no association between the two variables.
    (E) Since $P < \alpha$, there is no evidence that political preference and support are not independent of each other. In this case, knowing their political preference would not help in knowing their support.

12. Two different cereal companies each make a bran cereal, a corn cereal, and a rice cereal. Each person in a random sample of 300 potential customers tasted all six cereals and selected their favorite. The choice was then classified according to type of cereal and the company that made the cereal. What type of test would be appropriate?
    (A) Chi-square goodness-of-fit test
    (B) Chi-square test of independence
    (C) Chi-square test of homogeneity
    (D) Either a chi-square test for independence or homogeneity is appropriate
    (E) A chi-square test is not appropriate in this situation

13. Which is not true for all chi-square tests?
    (A) The test is based on categorical data.
    (B) df is calculated using $k - 1$, where k = the number of categories.
    (C) The test is an upper-tailed test.
    (D) The χ^2 distributions are right skewed.
    (E) All of the above are true.

Questions 14–15 refer to the following set of data:

A movie theater recorded the type of snack item purchased and the type of movie the customer was attending for each person in a random sample of theater customers who made a snack bar purchase. The resulting data are given in the table below.

	Soda	Popcorn	Candy
Children's Movie	70	83	47
Action Movie	61	49	20

14. If the manager wanted to determine if there is an association between the type of movie and type of snack sold, which type test would be appropriate?
    (A) Chi-square goodness-of-fit
    (B) Chi-square test for homogeneity
    (C) Chi-square test for independence
    (D) Two-sample proportions test
    (E) Multiple sample proportions test

15. Using the data in the table above, the value of the chi-square test statistic is 5.66. Which of the following is a correct statement about the P-value for this test? Assume conditions for inference are met.
    (A) P-value > 0.10
    (B) $0.05 < P$-value < 0.10
    (C) $0.01 < P$-value < 0.05
    (D) $0.001 < P$-value < 0.01
    (E) P-value < 0.001

FREE-RESPONSE PROBLEMS

1. Regina is worried that the color of her new backpack will attract the attention of killer bees in southern California where she is going to hike. To settle her nerves she looks at the American Killer Bee Association website. It shows that these bees are highly agitated by various colors. They have found that 75% of bees are agitated by green, 9% by blue, 6% by purple or pink, and the remaining 10% by other colors. A recent study of 120 randomly selected people stung by killer bees last year found the individuals were wearing the colors shown in the table below. Do these data provide convincing evidence that the color distribution of colors worn by people stung by killer bees is different from the percentages given on the website?

Color Worn by Individual Stung by Killer Bees			
Green	Blue	Purple/Pink	Other
86	21	6	7

2. A restaurant offers both dine-in and take-out service. Customers can pay for their meal in cash, by credit card, or by debit card. The restaurant owner wonders if there is an association between the method of payment and the type of service. To investigate, a random sample is selected from the orders placed during the last year and the method of payment and the type of service is recorded for each of these orders. The data are summarized in the table below.

	Cash	Credit	Debit
Dine-in	34	122	32
Take-out	70	95	47

(a) Should the restaurant owner carry out a test of homogeneity or a test of independence to answer his question?

(b) Carry out a test to answer the question of interest to the owner. Use a significance level of 0.05 for your test.

Answers

MULTIPLE-CHOICE QUESTIONS

1. **(D)** The calculation would be found as follows:
$$\chi^2 = \frac{(60-50)^2}{50} + \frac{(80-50)^2}{50} + \frac{(30-50)^2}{50} + \frac{(10-50)^2}{50} = 2+18+18+32 = 70$$
(*Statistics: Learning from Data*, AP Edition, 1st ed. pages 694–705 / 2nd ed. pages 702–714).

2. **(E)** The χ^2 distribution is right skewed with all of its area associated with positive values. The mean of a chi-square distribution can't be 0 (*Statistics: Learning from Data*, AP Edition, 1st ed. pages 694–705 / 2nd ed. pages 702–714).

3. **(D)** There are four surgical methods and three pain levels. $df = (r-1)(c-1) = (4-1)(3-1) = 6$ (*Statistics: Learning from Data*, AP Edition, 1st ed. pages 708–718 / 2nd ed. pages 716–728).

4. **(D)** The expected counts in a two-way table are found using
$$\frac{(\text{row total} \times \text{column total})}{\text{table total}}$$
(*Statistics: Learning from Data*, AP Edition, 1st ed. pages 708–718 / 2nd ed. pages 716–728).

5. **(C)** In a two-way table, degrees of freedom are calculated by $(r-1)(c-1) = (3-1)(6-1) = 10$ (*Statistics: Learning from Data*, AP Edition, 1st ed. pages 708–718 / 2nd ed. pages 716–728).

6. **(C)** This is a χ^2 test of homogeneity. Three populations are being compared on the basis of a categorical variable (color) (*Statistics: Learning from Data*, AP Edition, 1st ed. pages 708–718 / 2nd ed. pages 716–728).

7. **(E)** $\chi^2 = 22.9$ and $df = 10$, gives a P-value = 0.01 that is less than 0.05. This means there is strong evidence to conclude that the color distributions are not all the same (*Statistics: Learning from Data*, AP Edition, 1st ed. pages 708–718 / 2nd ed. pages 716–728).

8. **(E)** The expected count calculated is $300(0.25) = 75$ (*Statistics: Learning from Data*, AP Edition, 1st ed. pages 694–705 / 2nd ed. pages 702–714).

9. **(B)** A χ^2 test of independence between the variables would be used to answer the question of interest (*Statistics: Learning from Data*, AP Edition, 1st ed. pages 708–718 / 2nd ed. pages 716–728).

10. **(D)** $df = (6-1)(8-1) = 5(7) = 35$ (*Statistics: Learning from Data*, AP Edition, 1st ed. pages 708–718 / 2nd ed. pages 716–728).

11. **(B)** The *P*-value is smaller than the significance level, so the null hypothesis would be rejected. This means there is an association and knowing people's political party provides information about their support of this issue (*Statistics: Learning from Data*, AP Edition, 1st ed. pages 708–718 / 2nd ed. pages 716–728).

12. **(B)** Because a single sample is classified on the basis of two categorical variables, the appropriate test is a χ^2 test for independence (*Statistics: Learning from Data*, AP Edition, 1st ed. pages 708–718 / 2nd ed. pages 716–728).

13. **(B)** The degrees of freedom for a χ^2 goodness-of-fit test is calculated using $k-1$. However, for a chi-square test of independence or homogeneity, $df = (r-1)(c-1)$ (*Statistics: Learning from Data*, AP Edition, 1st ed. pages 694–705 / 2nd ed. pages 702–714).

14. **(C)** This is a χ^2 test of independence since we are trying to see if knowing the type of movie provides any information about type of snack purchased (*Statistics: Learning from Data*, AP Edition, 1st ed. pages 708–718 / 2nd ed. pages 716–728).

15. **(B)** With $df = 2$, the *P*-value is 0.059 (*Statistics: Learning from Data*, AP Edition, 1st ed. pages 708–718 / 2nd ed. pages 716–728).

FREE-RESPONSE PROBLEMS

1. **HYPOTHESES**

    H_0: The proportions of bee stings by color is as specified on the website ($p_{green} = 0.75$, $p_{blue} = 0.09$, $p_{purple/pink} = 0.06$, $p_{other} = 0.10$)

    H_a: At least one of the color proportions is different from what is specified on the website

    $\alpha = 0.05$

    TEST: Chi-square goodness-of-fit test

    ASSUMPTIONS

    1. The individuals in the sample were randomly selected from all people stung by killer bees.

    2. The expected counts are shown in the table below. All expected counts are greater than 5, so the sample size is large enough.

Expected Counts for 120 Stings			
Green	Blue	Purple/Pink	Other
(90.0)	(10.8)	(7.2)	(12.0)

TEST STATISTIC

$$\chi^2 = \frac{(86-90)^2}{90} + \frac{(21-10.8)^2}{10.8} + \frac{(6-7.2)^2}{7.2} + \frac{(7-12)^2}{12} = 12.09$$

where $df = 3$

$p = 0.007$

CONCLUSION Since $0.007 < 0.05$, we to reject the null hypothesis. Therefore, there is reason to say the proportions of bee stings by killer bees are not all the same as reported on the website (*Statistics: Learning from Data*, AP Edition, 1st ed. pages 694–705 / 2nd ed. pages 702–714).

2. (a) This is a χ^2 test of independence. There was only one sample and each individual in the sample was classified according to two categorical variables.

    (b) HYPOTHESES

    H_o: method of payment and order type are independent.

    H_a: method of payment and order type are not independent.

    $\alpha = 0.05$

    ASSUMPTIONS

    1. The sample was a random sample of orders placed in the last year.

    2. The expected counts are given in the table below. All expected counts are greater than 5, so the sample size is large enough.

Expected Counts	Cash	Credit	Debit
Dine-in	$48.88	$101.99	$37.13
Take-out	$55.12	$115.01	$41.87

    TEST STATISTIC

    $$\chi^2 = \frac{(34-48.88)^2}{48.88} + \frac{(122-101.99)^2}{101.99} + \ldots + \frac{(47-41.87)^2}{41.87} = 17.291$$

    with $df = 2$

    $p = 0.00018$

    CONCLUSION With a test statistic so extreme, our *P*-value is approximately 0.000. This is smaller than any reasonable significance level, so we reject the null hypothesis. There is strong evidence that there is an association between method of payment and order type.

(*Statistics: Learning from Data*, AP Edition, 1st ed. pages 708–718 / 2nd ed. pages 716–728)

12

INFERENCE FOR LINEAR REGRESSION AND CORRELATION

In chapter 3 of this text (and chapter 9 of the textbook), you learned how to describe and summarize bivariate data. You might wonder if the sample provides evidence that the two variables are associated in the population from which the sample was selected. In this section, you will learn inference techniques for bivariate numerical data.

OBJECTIVES

- Understand a simple regression model.
- Construct a confidence interval for the slope of the population regression line.
- Perform a test of significance for the slope of the population regression line.
- Interpret and communicate the results of the statistical analysis.

SIMPLE LINEAR REGRESSION MODEL

(*Statistics: Learning from Data*, AP Edition, 1st ed. pages 736–745 / 2nd ed. pages 742–751)

Recall that we use one variable x (the explanatory variable) to help explain or shed light on the variability of another variable y (the response variable).

The simple linear regression model is the linear model that is assumed to describe the relationship between x and y in the population data. It is written as

$$y = \alpha + \beta x + e$$

where α is the population intercept and β is the population slope.

The relationship between two variables will not usually be perfectly linear, so the error e accounts for the random variability that exists. Think of the residuals as a sample from the population of errors. If a data point from the population lies above the regression line, e is positive and likewise, e is negative when a data point from the population lies below the regression line.

Our goal is to take a sample from a population and, using the data from our sample, be able to infer something about the population. In order to perform any inference procedures in the linear regression setting, we need to make four assumptions about the population and the associated errors.

The first assumption is that the mean of all the errors at any particular x value is equal to zero for each and every value of x.

Below is a scatterplot to illustrate this idea; notice that the mean of the errors is zero (remember zero is the point on the line since we are talking about errors that are directed distances above and below the line). We are assuming that the population appears like this for each and every value of x.

The second assumption we must make is that the spread of the distribution of e is the same for any particular value of x. This means that the standard deviation of e is the same for each and every value of x. The standard deviation of e is denoted σ_e.

Below is a scatterplot of what the population might look like for two specific x values; notice that the spread of the errors for each x is about the same. We are assuming that the population appears like this for each and every value of x.

The third assumption we must make is that the distribution of e is normal for any particular value of x. Below is a scatterplot of what the population might look like for two specific x's; notice that the errors appear to be normally distributed about the regression line for each x. Assessing normality can be difficult. Remember, we are assuming that the population appears like this for each and every value of x.

The fourth and final assumption is that each error that corresponds to an observation is independent of each and every error that corresponds to another observation.

Now, let's put all four conditions together. The observations must be independent and for every value of x the errors must be normally distributed with a mean of zero and the same standard deviation. Below is a picture illustrating all of these ideas together.

$y = \alpha + \beta x$, the population regression line (line of mean values)

Mean value $\alpha + \beta x_3$
Standard deviation σ
Normal curve

Mean value $\alpha + \beta x_2$
Standard deviation σ
Normal curve

Mean value $\alpha + \beta x_1$
Standard deviation σ
Normal curve

Three different x values

EXAMPLE The following data set gives the number of nights in a 3-week time frame that students completed their homework and their quiz grade on the material taught during those 3 weeks. Is it reasonable to assume that the four assumptions of the linear regression model are true?

Number of Nights	11	12	8	12	7	6	11	7	10	6	10	11	7	9	8
Quiz Grade	81	88	76	88	66	70	80	75	85	68	76	86	71	77	75

First, we look at a scatterplot and residual plot for the data to confirm that a linear model is appropriate.

Nights Completing Homework

Based on the scatterplot and the residual plot, it appears that a linear model is appropriate. Now focus on the residual plot for assumptions 1–3.

Assumption 1: The mean of e at any given x value is equal to 0. This assumption is for each and every value of x. This assumption cannot be checked; the least-squares regression line will always have residuals that have a mean of zero. We must assume that the mean of the errors is zero for the population. This assumption is reasonable when the pattern in the scatterplot is linear and there is no obvious pattern in the residual plot.

Assumption 2: σ_e is the same for each and every value of x. The scatter about the regression line does not appear to be much larger for some x values than for others, so this assumption seems reasonable.

Assumption 3: The distribution of e is normal for any particular value of x. For this assumption to be reasonable, points should tend to cluster near the line, with fewer points as you move away from the line. This appears to be the case here, so this assumption seems reasonable.

Assumption 4: The observations are independent. If no students worked together on the homework assignments or on the quiz, it seems reasonable to assume that students' homework and quiz grades are independent.

Since all four assumptions are reasonable, it makes sense to use a linear regression model.

Notice that all of the assumptions are about the population where the population is the collection of all students' number of nights of homework preparation and their corresponding quiz grade. Usually, we only have information from a sample taken from the desired population. Using a least-squares regression line, we can estimate the population parameters from sample data.

The estimated regression line for the population is

$$\hat{y} = a + bx$$

where a is a point estimate for α and b is a point estimate for β.

Let x^* be a specific value of x. Then, $a + bx^*$ has two different meanings:

1. It is an estimate of the mean y for all observations when $x = x^*$
2. It is the predicted y when $x = x^*$

EXAMPLE Refer to the previous example about number of nights a student completed their homework and their quiz grade. Estimate α and β for the population regression model.

```
NORMAL FLOAT AUTO REAL RADIAN MP
          LinReg
 y=a+bx
 a=50.18541667
 b=3.03125
 r²=0.8332644531
 r=0.9128332011
```

The least-squares regression line for our sample data is

$$\hat{y} = 50.185 + 3.031x$$

where x is the number of nights that a student completed his or her homework and y is the student's predicted quiz grade.

Therefore, our estimate for α is 50.185 points and our estimate for β is 3.031 points per night of homework completed.

SAMPLE PROBLEM 1 Data on outside temperature at 9 a.m. and number of students absent from school are given for 9 randomly selected days during the school year. Is a linear regression model reasonable? If so, estimate the equation of the population regression line. Find y when and interpret this value in context.

Outside Temperature (°F)	60	62	63	65	67	71	72	74	75
Number of Students Absent	1	0	2	5	6	5	8	7	8

SOLUTION TO PROBLEM 1 First, look at a scatterplot and a residual plot for the data.

A linear model seems appropriate for this data. Now, we must check the four assumptions.

Assumption 1: $\mu_e = 0$ for each and every value of x. This assumption is reasonable when the pattern in the scatterplot is linear and there is no obvious pattern in the residual plot, which appears to be the case here.

Assumption 2: σ_e is the same for each and every value of x. The scatter about the regression line does not appear to be much larger for some x values than for others, so this assumption seems reasonable.

Assumption 3: The distribution of e is normal for any particular value of x. For this assumption to be reasonable, points should tend to cluster near the line, with fewer points as you move away from the line. This appears to be the case here, so this assumption seems reasonable.

Assumption 4: The observations are independent. Because the days were randomly selected, it is reasonable to assume that the observations are independent.

```
NORMAL FLOAT AUTO REAL RADIAN MP

           LinReg
 y=a+bx
 a=-28.61202186
 b=0.4918032787
 r²=0.8196721311
 r=0.9053574604
```

The least-squares regression line for our sample data is

$$\hat{y} = -28.612 + 0.492x$$

where x is the outside temperature and y is the predicted number of students absent from class. This equation is the estimate of the population regression line.

When $x = 68$,

$$\hat{y} = -28.612 + 0.492(68) = -28.612 + 33.443 = 4.831$$

There are two ways to correctly interpret this value:

1. The average number of students absent on days when it is 68°F outside is 4.831 students.

2. Our model predicts that 4.831 students will be absent on an individual day where it is 68°F.

This example highlights what happens on most problems when we check the four assumptions—we did not have sufficient evidence to doubt the assumptions, so we assumed they were true and proceeded.

INFERENCES ABOUT THE SLOPE OF THE REGRESSION LINE

(*Statistics: Learning from Data*, AP Edition, 1st ed. pages 748–756 / 2nd ed. pages 754–763)

Remember that the slope of the least-squares regression line is the average change in y for a one-unit change in x. We now are concerned with β, the slope of the population regression line. It is interpreted the same way—only we are talking about the population, not a sample.

When the four assumptions for a linear regression model are met, the following is true for the slope of the sample regression line, b:

1. The mean value of b for all possible random samples is β. This means that b is an unbiased estimator of β.

2. The standard deviation of b for all possible random samples is
$$\sigma_b = \frac{\sigma}{\sqrt{s_{xx}}} \text{ where } s_{xx} = \sum x^2 - \frac{(\sum x)^2}{n}.$$

3. The sample statistic b has a normal distribution.

Since the sample statistic b has a normal distribution, the test statistic will have a standard normal distribution.

Just as before, this presents a problem. We rarely, if ever, know the value of σ. We use s_e to estimate σ and use a t interval/test instead of a z interval/test. The distribution of $t = \dfrac{b - \beta}{\dfrac{s_e}{\sqrt{s_{xx}}}}$ has a t distribution with $df = n - 2$.

EXAMPLE A teacher is interested in determining if there is a relationship between GPA and the number of minutes each day a student spends on social networking websites. She selects a random sample of nine students. Use the data given below to construct an interval, estimate the slope of the population regression line relating GPA and the number of minutes spent on social networking websites.

Minutes Spent	20	60	15	30	0	30	0	2	30
Grade Point Average	3.70	3.41	3.10	3.90	3.80	3.67	3.80	3.85	3.83

We are interested in knowing about β (the true mean change in GPA per additional minutes spent on social networking websites). The question asks for an estimate—this signals to us that we should find a confidence interval.

Name Of Interval: t interval for the slope of the population regression line

Conditions: First, look at a scatterplot and a residual plot of the sample data (shown below). A linear model seems appropriate for this data.

Websites

[Scatterplot of GPA vs Minutes with regression line, and residual plot below]

Assumption 1: $\mu_e = 0$ for each and every value of x. This assumption is reasonable when the pattern in the scatterplot is linear and there is no obvious pattern in the residual plot, which appears to be the case here.

Assumption 2: σ_e is the same for each and every value of x. The scatter about the regression line does not appear to be much larger for some x values than for others, but it appears we may have one outlier at 15 minutes, so this assumption seems reasonable.

Assumption 3: The distribution of e is normal for any particular value of x. For this assumption to be reasonable, points should tend to cluster near the line, with fewer points as you move away from the line. This appears to be the case here, so this assumption seems reasonable.

Assumption 4: Because the sample was a random sample, the observations are independent.

CALCULATIONS

Model of Websites — Simple Regression

Response attribute (numeric): GPA
Predictor attribute (numeric): Minutes

```
Sample count:     9
Equation:         GPA = -0.00397999 Minutes + 3.7560
r:                -0.299352
r-squared:        0.089612
Slope:            -0.00397999 +/- 0.0113378
SE Slope:         0.00479474
```

For a confidence level of 95% and $df = 9 - 2 = 7$, the appropriate t critical value is 2.365. From the given output, $b = 0.00398$ and $SE_b = 00479$. The interval is then

$$b \pm t^* (SE_b)$$

$$-0.00398 \pm (2.365)(0.00479)$$

$$(-0.0153, 0.0074)$$

CONCLUSION We are 95% confident that the true mean change in GPA for each additional minute spent on social networking sites each day is between -0.0153 and 0.0074.

EXAMPLE Airlines are interested in knowing if there is a relationship between number of times people travel in a year and the weight of their luggage. A random sample of adult Americans who took at least one trip in the last year was used to produce the Minitab computer output below. Suppose it is reasonable to believe that the assumptions for inference are met. Does the sample provide evidence of a relationship between number of trips and luggage weight?

Regression Analysis: Weight Of Luggage versus Number Of Times

The regression equation is
Weight Of Luggage = 35.3 − 0.157 Number Of Times   ← Equation of the estimated regression line

Predictor	Coef	SE Coef	T	P
Constant	35.2813	0.5244	67.28	0.000
Registrations	−0.15698	0.03879	−4.05	0.002

↑ Coef   ↑ Estimated SE_b ← p-value   ← Test statistic

$S = 0.768322$ (S_e)   R−Sq = 62.1%   R−Sq(adj) = 58.3%

Analysis of Variance $n - 2$

Source	DF	SS	MS	F	P
Regression	1	9.6660	9.6660	16.37	0.002
Residual Error	10	5.9032	0.5903		
Total	11	15.5692			

We are interested in knowing about β (the true mean change in baggage weight per additional trip). The question asked for a decision is in the form of a yes or no answer—is there enough evidence to show that there is a relationship between number of times a person travels in a year and the weight of his or her luggage? To answer this question, we will perform a hypothesis test about the slope of the regression line.

NAME OF TEST Linear regression t test (two tailed)

HYPOTHESES

$H_0: \beta = 0$

$H_a: \beta \neq 0$

β = the true mean change in baggage weight per additional trip

$\alpha = 0.05$

CONDITIONS The problem states that the conditions for inference are met.

CALCULATIONS From the given computer output, $t = -4.05$, P-value = 0.002, and $df = 10$.

CONCLUSION If it were true that $\beta = 0$, we would get a sample result or one more extreme than this less than 0.2% of the time. Since this P-value is less than $\alpha = 0.05$, we reject the null hypothesis. We have sufficient evidence to conclude that there is a linear relationship between the number of times people travel and the weight of their luggage.

> ## AP® Tip
>
> Be sure to know how to read a computer output. Know where you can find the statistics to answer the questions you might be asked. Some of the information on these outputs is extraneous and you will not need this information nor are you expected to know what it means. Be sure to practice finding the statistics you will need to know!

SAMPLE PROBLEM 2 Each year, most students take a test that measures their reading achievement. The score reports this in terms of the grade level at which the child is reading. The following scores are for a random sample of six children in a particular U.S. public school. Suppose it is reasonable to believe that the assumptions for inference are met. Is there convincing evidence that mean grade level score increases by more than 1 with each additional year of school?

Grade Level	1	3	4	7	9	12
Grade Level Equivalence	0.83	3.2	4.1	6.7	9.1	12.2

SOLUTION TO PROBLEM 2

NAME OF TEST t test (one tailed) for slope of regression line

HYPOTHESES

$H_0: \beta = 1$

$H_a: \beta > 1$

β = the true mean change in grade level per additional year of school

$\alpha = 0.05$

CONDITIONS The problem states that the conditions for inference are met.

AP® is a trademark registered by the College Board, which is not affiliated with, and does not endorse, this product.

CALCULATIONS Computer regression output is shown here, or a graphing calculator can be used.

```
The regression equation is
Grade Level Reading Score = - 0.068 + 1.01 Grade in
School

Predictor        Coef       SE Coef      T          P
Constant        -0.0676     0.1714      -0.39      0.713
Grade in School 1.01488     0.02424     41.86      0.000

S = 0.222195        R-Sq = 99.8%    R-Sq(adj) = 99.7%
```

Remember that the hypothesized value of the slope is 1. From the computer output, we can compute the value of the test statistic and then find the associated *P*-value (the values of the test statistic and the *P*-value aren't the ones shown in the computer output; the default computer output is for a null hypothesis of β = 0).

$$t = \frac{b - \beta}{SE_b} = \frac{1.01488 - 1}{0.024} = \frac{.015 - 1}{0.024} = 0.625$$

where *df* = 4

P-value = 0.283

CONCLUSION If it were true that β = 1, we would see a result like this or one more extreme than this about 28.3% of the time. Since this *P*-value is larger than α = 0.05, we fail to reject the null hypothesis. We do not have evidence that the mean increase in grade level score for each additional year of school is greater than one.

INTERPRETATION OF RESULTS OF HYPOTHESIS TESTING

Linear regression is often a useful way to summarize bivariate data. Researchers use linear regression hypothesis tests to make inferences about the way the two variables are related. You should ask yourself the following questions when you evaluate research that involves relating two variables.

1. Which variable is the response variable? Is it quantitative?

2. If the research uses a sample to make inferences about the population, is it reasonable to assume the conditions were met?

3. Does the model appear to be useful? Are the results of the hypothesis test given? What is the *P*-value of the test?

4. Has the linear model been used in an appropriate way? Has the research avoided extrapolation?

5. If a correlation coefficient is given, is it in the context of a test of significance? Are the results interpreted accurately?

Keep in mind the following limitations of linear regression inference:
- Small samples can show a weak linear pattern due to chance not due to a relationship in the population parameters.
- As with all inference, linear regression inference is not appropriate if the sample is not a random sample.
- As with all inference, linear regression inference procedures are not reasonable if the necessary conditions are not met.

INFERENCE FOR LINEAR REGRESSION AND CORRELATION: STUDENT OBJECTIVES FOR THE AP® EXAM

- You should be able to find a point estimate b.
- You should be able to construct a confidence interval to estimate the slope of the population regression line.
- You should be able to perform a hypothesis test for the slope of a population regression line.

MULTIPLE-CHOICE QUESTIONS

Questions 1–7 refer to the following information:

Data on x = number of powerboat registrations in Florida and y = number of manatee deaths in Florida for 31 randomly selected years were used to produce the following computer output. You can assume that all conditions needed for inference are met.

```
Regression Analysis: Manatees versus Registrations

    Predictor      Coef      SE Coef        T         P
     Constant    -40.641       5.840      -6.96     0.000
Registrations   0.125006    0.007867     15.89     0.000

S = 7.87985      R-Sq = 89.7%     R-Sq(adj) = 89.3%

Analysis of Variance

       Source   DF      SS         MS         F        P
   Regression    1    15677      15677     252.48   0.000
     Residual   29     1801
        Error                       62
        Total   30    17477
```

1. The estimate for the population regression line is
   (A) predicted manatees = −40.641 + 5.84 (registrations)
   (B) predicted manatees = 0.125 + 0.007867 (registrations)
   (C) predicted manatees = 5.840 + 0.007867 (registrations)
   (D) predicted manatees = −40.641 + 0.125006 (registrations)
   (E) predicted manatees = 7.87985 + 0.125006 (registrations)

2. The standard error of the slope is shown to be 0.0079. Interpret this value in context.
   (A) The standard deviation of the number of powerboat registrations is 0.0079.
   (B) The standard deviation of the number of manatees killed is 0079.
   (C) If many samples were taken and the slope of each least-squares regression line was recorded, the estimated standard deviation of these slopes is 0.0079.
   (D) If many samples were taken and the slopes of each least-squares regression line were recorded, the difference in the estimated change in number of manatees killed per powerboat registration and the true change in number of manatees killed per powerboat registration is on average 0.0079.
   (E) The distance between the true change in number of manatees killed per powerboat registration and the sample change in number of manatees killed per powerboat registration is 0.0079.

3. Which of the following is a confidence interval for the mean change in number of manatee deaths associated with an increase of one powerboat registration?
   (A) $-40.641 \pm t^* (5.84)$
   (B) $0.125 \pm t^* (0.0079)$
   (C) $0.125 \pm t^* (15.89)$
   (D) $0.125 \pm t^* \left(\dfrac{0.0079}{\sqrt{31}} \right)$
   (E) $0.125 \pm t^* \left(\dfrac{0.0079}{\sqrt{30}} \right)$

4. The value of the t test statistic is
   (A) 7.87985
   (B) −6.96
   (C) 15.89
   (D) 252.48
   (E) 89.3

5. For a test of $H_0: \beta = 0$, what is the value of degrees of freedom?
   (A) 1
   (B) 28
   (C) 29
   (D) 30
   (E) 32

6. In a test of $H_0: \beta = 0$ versus $H_a: \beta \neq 0$ with a significance level of 05, the decision would be to
   (A) accept H_0
   (B) fail to reject H_a
   (C) fail to reject H_0
   (D) reject H_0
   (E) reject H_a

7. The estimated standard deviation of the residuals is
   (A) 5.84
   (B) 7.87985
   (C) 0.0079
   (D) 1801
   (E) 89.7

Questions 8–13 refer to the following information:

Each person in a random sample of adults was asked to estimate the average number of minutes of television watched per day and his or her yearly salary. The following data resulted.

Minutes of TV Watched	36	57	60	62	70	76	101
Annual Salary (in thousands)	89	45	30	50	55	67	30

These data were used to produce the following regression output.

```
Regression Analysis: Salary versus TV

The regression equation is
Salary = 94.4 - 0.638 TV

Predictor        Coef      SE Coef         T          P
Constant        94.40        25.60      3.69      0.014
TV             -0.6382       0.3736    -1.71      0.148

S = 18.2023    R-Sq = 36.9%      R-Sq(adj) = 24.2%
```

The researcher wishes to determine if these data provide evidence of a linear relationship between the number of minutes spent watching television each day and annual salary. You can assume that all conditions required for inference are met.

8. The appropriate hypotheses are
   (A) $H_0: \beta = 0$; $H_a: \beta \neq 0$
   (B) $H_0: b = 0$; $H_a: b \neq 0$
   (C) $H_0: \beta \neq 0$; $H_a: \beta = 0$
   (D) $H_0: \beta = 0$; $H_a: \beta < 0$
   (E) $H_0: \beta = 0$; $H_a: \beta > 0$

9. What is the value of the correlation coefficient for these data?
   (A) −0.369
   (B) −0.607
   (C) 0.148
   (D) 0.369
   (E) 0.607

10. What proportion of variability in salary can be explained by the linear relationship between TV watched and salary?
    (A) 0
    (B) 0.148
    (C) 0.369
    (D) 0.374
    (E) 18.202

11. The P-value for the test of H_0: $\beta = 0$ versus H_a: $\beta \neq 0$ is 0.148. Which of the following is the correct interpretation of this value in context?
    (A) The probability that we committed a type I error is 0.149.
    (B) The probability that we committed a type I or type II error is 0.149.
    (C) If we were to take many samples of people and ask their TV viewing habits and their salary, 14.9% of the tests would yield different results.
    (D) If minutes watching TV and salary are not linearly related, we would get samples like this one or more extreme 14.9% of the time just by chance.
    (E) If minutes watching TV and salary are associated, we would detect the relationship only 14.9% of the time.

12. Using a significance level of 0.05, which of the following is the correct conclusion for the test of H_0: $\beta = 0$ versus H_a: $\beta \neq 0$ in context?
    (A) Since P-value $> \alpha$, we accept the null hypothesis. We have evidence that minutes watching TV and salary are linearly related.
    (B) Since P-value $> \alpha$, we reject the null hypothesis. We have evidence that minutes watching TV and salary are not linearly related.
    (C) Since P-value $> \alpha$, we fail to reject the null hypothesis. We have evidence that minutes watching TV and salary are not linearly related.
    (D) Since P-value $> \alpha$, we fail to reject the null hypothesis. We have evidence that minutes watching TV and salary are linearly related.
    (E) Since P-value $> \alpha$, we reject the null hypothesis. We have evidence that minutes watching TV and salary are linearly related.

13. Which of the following is a correct description of a type II error?
    (A) We conclude that minutes watching TV and salary are not linearly related when, in fact, they are linearly related.
    (B) We conclude that minutes watching TV and salary are linearly related when, in fact, they are not linearly related.
    (C) We conclude that minutes watching TV and salary are not linearly related when, in fact, they are not linearly related.
    (D) We conclude that minutes watching TV and salary are linearly related when, in fact, they are linearly related.
    (E) A type II error happens 5% of the time when we run similar tests on similar samples.

14. Which of the following is not a necessary condition for inference about the slope of the population regression line?
    (A) The observations must be independent of one another.
    (B) The residuals for every value of x must have a mean of zero.
    (C) The residuals must be normally distributed at each x value.
    (D) The residuals have the same standard deviation for each value of x.
    (E) The sample size must be large.

15. Which of the following is true of all significance tests for the slope of a population regression line?
    (A) The alternative hypothesis is that there is a linear relationship between x and y.
    (B) The degrees of freedom for this test is one less than the sample size.
    (C) We always assume the four necessary assumptions are true no matter what the residual plot displays.
    (D) If the slope of the sample regression line is small, then we know we will have a small P-value.
    (E) The null hypothesis assumes no linear relationship between x and y.

FREE-RESPONSE PROBLEMS

1. Each person in a random sample of 42 students at a large university was asked how much they paid per month for housing and how far from campus they lived (in miles). The resulting data were used to produce the following regression output. Assume that any conditions needed for inference are met.

   ```
   The regression equation is
   Housing cost = 452 - 9.25 Distance

   Predictor          Coef          SE           T           P
   Constant          452.1         178.1        2.54        0.039
   Distance         -9.2472        0.2145      -43.11       0.000

   S = 221.098     R-Sq = 99.6%     R-Sq(adj) = 99.6%
   ```

   (a) Estimate the slope of the population regression line using a 90% confidence interval.

   (b) A recent news report stated that students pay a premium to live near campus. Evaluate this statement based on the interval from part (a).

2. Each person in a random sample of adult males with children was asked his height and the height of his first full grown child, resulting in the following data.

Height of Father (inches)	68	68	73	72	74	71	73	73	71	70
Height of Child (inches)	61	65	65	73	61	64	65	70	66	63

   Is there convincing evidence of a linear relationship between the height of fathers and the height of their child?

Answers

MULTIPLE-CHOICE QUESTIONS

1. **(D)** The first column of the regression analysis indicates the a and b values for the regression equation $\hat{y} = a + bx$. From the output, $a = -40.641$ and $b = 0.125006$ (*Statistics: Learning from Data*, AP Edition, 1st ed. pages 736–745 / 2nd ed. pages 742–751).

2. **(C)** This follows from the definition of standard error of slope (*Statistics: Learning from Data*, AP Edition, 1st ed. pages 736–745 / 2nd ed. pages 742–751).

3. **(B)** A confidence interval on slope (β) : $b \pm t *$ (*standard error of slope*) (*Statistics: Learning from Data*, AP Edition, 1st ed. pages 748–756 / 2nd ed. pages 754–763).

4. **(C)** This is found in the regression output in the "*T*" column in the row associated with slope (*Statistics: Learning from Data*, AP Edition, 1st ed. pages 748–756 / 2nd ed. pages 754–763).

5. **(C)** Degrees of freedom for inference on slope is $n - 2$, so $31 - 2 = 29$ (*Statistics: Learning from Data*, AP Edition, 1st ed. pages 748–756 / 2nd ed. pages 754–763).

6. **(D)** The *P*-value in the regression analysis is 0.000, which is less than 0.05. Therefore, we reject the null hypothesis (*Statistics: Learning from Data*, AP Edition, 1st ed. pages 748–756 / 2nd ed. pages 754–763).

7. **(B)** This is the value of S in the regression analysis output (*Statistics: Learning from Data*, AP Edition, 1st ed. pages 736–745 / 2nd ed. pages 742–751).

8. **(A)** For all inference problems on slope, the null hypothesis is that there is no linear relationship H_0: $\beta = 0$. The researcher is testing if a linear relationship exists, so H_a: $\beta \neq 0$ (*Statistics: Learning from Data*, AP Edition, 1st ed. pages 748–756 / 2nd ed. pages 754–763).

9. **(B)** The value of *R*-squared is given in the regression analysis as 36.9%, or 0.369. To find r, we take the square root and get 0.607. The value of r should be negative since the slope is negative ($b = -0.6382$) (*Statistics: Learning from Data*, AP Edition, 1st ed. pages 736–745 / 2nd ed. pages 742–751).

10. **(D)** This is the critical value associated with 1% of the area in each tail in a t distribution with 5 degrees of freedom (*Statistics: Learning from Data*, AP Edition, 1st ed. pages 748–756 / 2nd ed. pages 754–763).

11. **(D)** A *P*-value tells us the likelihood of an event as or more extreme than what we witnessed occurring by random chance assuming the null hypothesis is true (*Statistics: Learning from Data*, AP Edition, 1st ed. pages 748–756 / 2nd ed. pages 754–763).

12. **(C)** The *P*-value is 0.148, which is greater than 0.05 (*Statistics: Learning from Data*, AP Edition, 1st ed. pages 748–756 / 2nd ed. pages 754–763).

13. **(A)** This follows from the definition of a type II error, failing to reject the null hypothesis when it should have been rejected (*Statistics: Learning from Data*, AP Edition, 1st ed. pages 748–756 / 2nd ed. pages 754–763).

14. **(E)** The residuals must be normally distributed for each and every *x* (*Statistics: Learning from Data*, AP Edition, 1st ed. pages 748–756 / 2nd ed. pages 754–763).

15. **(E)** The null hypothesis for any significance test on slope is that there exists no linear relationship between *x* and *y* (*Statistics: Learning from Data*, AP Edition, 1st ed. pages 748–756 / 2nd ed. pages 754–763).

FREE-RESPONSE QUESTIONS

1. (a) The question states that the conditions for inference are met, so it is okay to use a *t* confidence interval to estimate the population slope. With $n = 42$, $df = 40$ and the *t* critical value for a 90% confidence interval is 1.68. The confidence interval is then

    $-9.2472 \pm (1.68)(0.2145)$

    -9.2472 ± 0.3604

    $(-9.6076, -8.8868)$

    On average, the mean housing cost decreases by somewhere between $8.89 and $9.61 with each additional mile from campus.

    (b) Housing costs do tend to decrease as you move farther away from campus. A student who chose to live 5 miles from campus might expect to pay about $45 less per month than someone who lives adjacent to the campus, and a student who lives 10 miles from campus would expect to pay about $90 less per month.

    (*Statistics: Learning from Data*, AP Edition, 1st ed. pages 748–756 / 2nd ed. pages 754–763)

2. **NAME OF TEST** t test for slope of regression line

   HYPOTHESES

   H_0: $\beta = 0$

   H_a: $\beta \neq 0$

   β = the true mean change in child's height per additional inch of father's height

   $\alpha = 0.05$

   CONDITIONS

   First, look at a scatterplot and a residual plot of the sample data (shown below). A linear model seems appropriate for this data.

   Assumption 1: $\mu_e = 0$ for each and every value of x. This assumption is reasonable when the pattern in the scatterplot is linear and there is no obvious pattern in the residual plot, which appears to be the case here.

   Assumption 2: σ_e is the same for each and every value of x. The scatter about the regression line does not appear to be much larger for some x values than for others, so this assumption seems reasonable.

   Assumption 3: The distribution of e is normal for any particular value of x. For this assumption to be reasonable, points should tend to cluster near the line, with fewer points as you move away from the line. This appears to be the case here, so this assumption seems reasonable.

   Assumption 4: Because the sample was a random sample, the observations are independent.

   CALCULATIONS

   ```
   NORMAL FLOAT AUTO REAL RADIAN MP
          LinRegTTest
   y=a+bx
   β≠0 and ρ≠0
   t=0.7886941423
   p=0.4530268714
   df=8
   a=31.33915212
   b=0.4763092269
   ↓s=3.824305391
   ```

   ```
   NORMAL FLOAT AUTO REAL RADIAN MP
          LinRegTTest
   y=a+bx
   β≠0 and ρ≠0
   ↑df=8
   a=31.33915212
   b=0.4763092269
   s=3.824305391
   r²=0.0721451724
   r=0.2685985338
   ```

   $t = 0.79$ with 8 degrees of freedom, P-value $= 0.453$

CONCLUSION

Since the *P*-value of 0.453 is greater than any reasonable alpha level, we fail to reject the null hypothesis. There is not convincing evidence that the father's height and the child's height are linearly related.

(*Statistics: Learning from Data*, AP Edition, 1st ed. pages 748–756 / 2nd ed. pages 754–763)

Part III

Practice Tests

PRACTICE TEST 1

This test will give you some indication of how you might score on the AP® Statistics Exam. Of course, the exam changes every year, so it is never possible to predict a student's score with certainty. This test will also pinpoint your strengths and weaknesses on the key content areas covered by the exam.

AP® STATISTICS EXAMINATION
Section I: Multiple-Choice Questions
Time: 90 minutes
Number of Questions: 40

DIRECTIONS: Each of the following questions or incomplete statements is accompanied by five suggested answers or completions. Select the one that best answers the question or completes the statement.

1. In a *USA* TODAY/Gallup poll taken shortly after the game, 64% of respondents who described themselves as baseball fans said Major League Baseball should overturn the umpire's safe call that cost pitcher Armando Gallaraga a perfect game. The poll based on 470 respondents has a margin of error of 6%. Which of the following statements best describes what is meant by the 6% margin of error?
   (A) About 6% of the baseball fans agreed with the umpire's call.
   (B) About 6% of those polled were not actually baseball fans.
   (C) The difference between the sample percentage and the population percentage is likely to be less than 6%.
   (D) About 6% of the sample should not be included in the population.
   (E) The difference between the percentage of people in favor of overturning the call in this survey and in a second similar survey would be less than 6%.

2. A university has 12,000 female students and 8,000 male students. Fifty percent of the women use the student gym and 40% of the men use the student gym. A simple random sample of 100 students is selected. What is the expected number of students in the sample who use the gym?
   (A) 47
   (B) 46
   (C) 45
   (D) 44
   (E) 43

3. A manufacturer of batteries claims they have a shelf life of one year. The manufacturer contends that 99.5% of the batteries will function after sitting without use for one year. If the company's claim is true, what is the expected number of batteries in a random sample of 5,000 one-year- old batteries that will function?
   (A) 4,750
   (B) 4,925
   (C) 4,950
   (D) 4,975
   (E) 4,995

AP® is a trademark registered by the College Board, which is not affiliated with, and does not endorse, this product.

GO ON TO NEXT PAGE

4. A fertilizer company is trying to convince corn farmers currently using a particular fertilizer that their new product Cornplosion will lead to an increase in yield. To determine which fertilizer re7sults in a higher yield of corn, 10 one-acre fields are split into halves. The current fertilizer is used on one-half of each field and Cornplosion on the other half. The fertilizer that goes on the east half of the field is determined by coin flip. The yield of corn is measured in bushels per acre. The data are given below:

Field	Generic Fertilizer	Cornplosion
1	15	21
2	12	16
3	8	7
4	22	30
5	14	12
6	25	33
7	11	14
8	12	21
9	20	22
10	18	16

What is the number of degrees of freedom associated with the appropriate *t* test for testing to see if there is a difference between the mean corn yield for the two types of fertilizer?

(A) 9
(B) 10
(C) 13
(D) 18
(E) 20

5. A certain library has 10,000 books. Two thousand of these books are nonfiction books and the rest are fiction. It is thought that nonfiction books contain more pages than fiction books. In order to estimate the total number of pages in their library, two plans are proposed.

Plan I:

Sample 50 books at random. Estimate the mean number of pages per book using a confidence interval. Multiply both ends of the interval by 10,000 to get an interval estimate of the total.

Plan II:

Identify the 2,000 nonfiction books. Sample 10 nonfiction books at random. Estimate the mean number of pages for nonfiction books using a confidence interval. Multiply both ends of the interval by 2,000 to get an interval estimate of the total. Similarly, identify the 8,000 fiction books. Sample 40 fiction books at random. Estimate the mean number of pages for fiction books using a confidence interval. Multiply both ends of the interval by 8,000 to get an interval estimate of the total. Finally, add the lower ends from the two confidence intervals and the two higher ends from the confidence intervals to get an estimate for the total number of pages in the library.

On the basis of the information given, which of the following is the better method for estimating the total number of pages in nonfiction books in the library?

(A) Choose plan I over plan II.
(B) Choose plan II over plan I.
(C) Choose either plan, since both are good and will produce equivalent results.
(D) Choose neither plan, since neither estimates the total number of pages.
(E) The plans cannot be evaluated from the information given.

6. To check the effect of wet road conditions on automobile stopping distances, five economy-size cars from automaker A and five economy-size cars from automaker B are tested. The same driver is used to test all cars. The driver accelerates to 50 miles per hour and then brings the vehicle to a complete stop when it reaches a white line. The cars from automaker A are tested on a dry straightaway. The cars from automaker B are tested on the same track, but the track is hosed down with water before testing. The distance between the white line and where the car comes to a stop is measured for each car and the mean for the cars stopping on the dry road is compared to the mean for the cars stopping on the wet road. Is this a good experimental design?
   (A) No, because the means are not proper statistics for comparison.
   (B) No, because more than two brands should be used.
   (C) No, because road conditions are confounded with brand.
   (D) No, because the experiment should not be limited to economy-sized cars.
   (E) Yes

7. The boxplots above summarize two data sets, A and B. Which of the following statement must be true?
   (A) Set B has a higher median than set A.
   (B) Set B contains more data than set A.
   (C) The data in set B have a larger range than the data in set A.
   (D) The data in set A have a larger IQR than the data in set B.
   (E) None of the above must always be true.

8. Splatastic Paintball Range sells paintballs in bulk at wholesale prices, as well as individually at retail prices. Next year's sales will depend on market conditions, but company executives believe that the following probability distributions describe wholesale and retail sales for next year.

Wholesale Sales				
Number Sold	50,000	100,000	150,000	200,000
Probability	0.2	0.3	0.4	0.1

Retail Sales			
Number Sold	10,000	20,000	30,000
Probability	0.2	0.5	0.3

What is the expected profit for the next year if the profit from each paintball sold is $1 for wholesale and $2 for retail?
(A) $141,000
(B) $144,000
(C) $162,000
(D) $282,000
(E) $341,000

9. D'Andre and Claire are both going to a Chinese buffet. Based on their previous visits to the buffet, the probability distributions of the number of plates of food they will eat are given below.

Number of plates D'Andre will eat	1	2	3
Probability	0.1	0.2	0.7
Number of plates Claire will eat	1	2	3
Probability	0.4	0.5	0.1

Assuming D'Andre and Claire make their decisions independently, what is the probability that they will eat six plates of food combined?
(A) 0.04
(B) 0.07
(C) 0.10
(D) 0.70
(E) 0.80

10. A survey of 84 randomly selected military officers was conducted to determine whether or not they participated in high school athletics. The two-way table shows the numbers of officers by varsity status (varsity athlete, not varsity athlete) and branch of service (Navy, Air Force). Which of the following best describes the relationship between varsity status and branch of service?

	Varsity Athlete	Not Varsity Athlete	Total
Navy	32	16	48
Air Force	24	12	36
Total	56	28	84

(A) There appears to be an association, since more Navy officers than Air Force officers were varsity athletes.
(B) There appears to be an association, since twice as many officers were varsity athletes.
(C) There appears to be no association, since the proportion of officers that were varsity athletes was the same for both Navy and Air Force.
(D) There appears to be no association, since there are fewer Air Force officers who were not varsity athletes but more Navy officers who were varsity athletes.
(E) There is not enough information to decide whether or not an association exists.

11. Which is the best estimate of the standard deviation of the distribution shown below?

(A) 15 kg
(B) 20 kg
(C) 30 kg
(D) 35 kg
(E) 60 kg

12. A window manufacturer claims that its new seal-tight system will save homeowners in cold climates $100 a month on average during the winter. A consumer group is skeptical of this claim and thinks that the manufacturer may be overstating the savings. If μ represents the true mean savings for this new window system, which of the following gives the null and alternative hypotheses that the consumer group should test?

(A) H_0: $\mu \leq \$100$
    H_a: $\mu > \$100$
(B) H_0: $\mu = \$100$
    H_a: $\mu \neq \$100$
(C) H_0: $\mu < \$100$
    H_a: $\mu \geq \$100$
(D) H_0: $\mu = \$100$
    H_a: $\mu < \$100$
(E) H_0: $\mu = \$100$
    H_a: $\mu > \$100$

GO ON TO NEXT PAGE

13. Stanley's boss told him that he did not deserve a raise and that Stanley was making an amount similar to other accountants with his experience. Stanley gathered some data and found that the z-score for his salary as compared to other accountants with the same level of experience is -1.25. Which of the following is the best interpretation of this z-score?
    (A) Stanley makes 1.25% less than other accountants with his experience level.
    (B) Stanley makes 1.25% more than other accountants with his experience level.
    (C) Stanley makes $1.25 less per pay period than the average for accountants with his experience level.
    (D) Stanley's salary is 1.25 standard deviations above the mean salary of other accountants with his experience level.
    (E) Stanley's salary is 1.25 standard deviations below the mean salary of other accountants with his experience level.

14. Uncle Hugo's Electronics decided to see whether a local music CD section would be profitable at its stores nationwide. It decided to set up local music displays at its 100 biggest locations. In this study, Uncle Hugo's marketing department found that sales of local artists were significantly greater in stores with the local music display. Which of the following statements explains why it would *not* be appropriate to recommend that all of the stores should add a local music section?
    I. The study only targeted Uncle Hugo's largest locations and there may not be as much good local music available in smaller locations.
    II. Only 100 stores had a local display while 900 stores did not have a local display.
    III. The sample consisted of more than 5% of the population.
    (A) I only
    (B) II only
    (C) III only
    (D) I and II only
    (E) I, II, and III

Questions 15–16 refer to the following information:

Every Wednesday Burgerville has a "discount deck day." A customer who comes in with a child may choose to pick two cards from a standard deck of playing cards. If the two cards are the same number then the child's junior burger is free with the purchase of a megaburger. If the two cards are the same suit, then the child's junior burger is half price with the purchase of a megaburger. The menu price for a junior burger is $2.00 and a megaburger is $4.00. Let X represent the amount paid by a customer with a child for a junior burger and a megaburger. The expected value of X is $5.65 and the standard deviation is $0.59.

15. If a customer with a child picks from the discount deck and purchases both a junior burger and a megaburger every Wednesday for 12 consecutive weeks, what is the total amount that the customer would expect to pay for all of the burgers?
    (A) $5.65
    (B) $56.50
    (C) $65.50
    (D) $67.80
    (E) $70.00

16. If a customer with a child picks from the discount deck every Wednesday and buys both a junior burger and a megaburger for 5 consecutive weeks, what is the standard deviation of the total amount paid for all of the burgers?
    (A) $0.26
    (B) $0.35
    (C) $1.32
    (D) $1.74
    (E) $2.95

17. Which of the following is not a property of all normal distributions?
    (A) The distribution is symmetric.
    (B) The distribution is centered at 0.
    (C) The median and the mean are equal.
    (D) The IQR is about 1.35 standard deviations.
    (E) About 95% of all observations fall within 2 standard deviations above or below the mean.

18. Before going to college, Chelsea wanted to see if she could get some pocket money by selling her old car online. She selected a sample of the bid prices on 25 similar cars sold online in the past month. Later Chelsea realized that the lowest-priced car in the sample was mistakenly recorded as half the price it actually sold for. However, after correcting the error, the corrected price was still less than or equal to any other car price in her sample. Which of the following sample statistics must have remained the same after the correction was made?
    (A) Mean
    (B) Median
    (C) Mode
    (D) Range
    (E) Variance

GO ON TO NEXT PAGE

19. The back-to-back stem-and-leaf display below gives the growth in millimeters of 23 onion bulbs planted by students in Mrs. Shelton's third grade class.

After One Week		After Two Weeks
6	0	
9 8 8 7 6 6 6 5 4	1	7
4 2 1 1 0	2	
8 6 5 5 3 3 2	2	5 6 6 6 7 9
4	3	0 0 0 0 1 2 3 3 5 6
	4	2 2 3 6 8

Which of the following statements is *not* justified by the data?
(A) For the plants shown, most of them grew less than 25 millimeters per week.
(B) In general, plants grew at the same rate in the first week as they did in the second.
(C) The spread between the shortest and tallest plant did not change much between the two weeks.
(D) The size of every plant increased from week one to week two.
(E) The median size of the plants increased from week one to week two.

20. A carnival game requires you to make three baskets in a row to win a prize. Andre is a basketball player who normally makes 80% of his shots, but because of the trick rim he estimates that he can only make the shot 60% of the time. Assuming that successive shots are independent, what is the probability that Andre wins a prize if he decides to play the game once?
(A) 0.2
(B) 0.216
(C) 0.4
(D) 0.512
(E) 0.6

21. Laws have been proposed in some border states that would allow police officers to ask motorists to prove that they are U.S. citizens during routine traffic stops. If it is determined that these motorists are not in the United States legally then they will be deported. Putting this in terms of a hypothesis test, H_0 is that the motorist is in the United States legally and H_a is that the motorist is not in the United States legally. Which of the following is an example of a Type I error?
(A) A motorist is in the country legally but does not have the paperwork to prove it in his or her vehicle and so the motorist is thought to not be in the country legally.
(B) A motorist is not in the country legally but has counterfeit paperwork that fools the police and so the motorist is thought to be in the country legally.
(C) A motorist is not in the country legally but when stopped gets deported.
(D) A motorist is not in the country legally but never gets stopped by the police.
(E) A motorist is in the country legally and is not stopped by the police.

22. The number of people in a gym at noon on each of 60 randomly selected days produces a mean of 34.7 people and a standard deviation of 8.1 people. Which of the following is an approximate 90% confidence interval for the mean number of people in the gym at noon? Assume conditions for inference are met.
(A) (26.70, 42.70)
(B) (32.95, 36.45)
(C) (32.65, 36.75)
(D) (33.65, 35.75)
(E) (34.48, 34.92)

23. Mr. Branch and his son Dennis both played on their college basketball teams. Mr. Branch scored an average of 12.5 points per game at a time when the average number of points scored by a player in college was 11 points a game and the standard deviation was 3.8 points. Dennis scored an average of 15.8 points a game when the average number of points scored by a player in college was 14 points a game and the standard deviation was 6.1 points. Mr. Branch contends that while he's proud of his son, he was a better scorer compared to the players of his day than his son was compared to his contemporaries. Dennis claims that he is the better scorer. Who is correct in saying that he did better when compared to his peers?
   (A) Mr. Branch is correct.
   (B) Dennis is correct.
   (C) Neither is correct, they both did equally well.
   (D) There is no basis for comparison, since they played in different eras for different teams.
   (E) There is not enough information for comparison, because the number of players in each era is not known.

24. A die is rolled six times, and the number of times a 3 is rolled is counted. This procedure of six dice rolls is repeated 100 times and the results are summarized in a frequency distribution. Which of the frequency distributions below is most likely to contain the results from these 100 trials?

(A)
Number of 3s	Frequency
0	33
1	40
2	16
3	8
4	2
5	1
6	0

(B)
Number of 3s	Frequency
0	5
1	10
2	20
3	30
4	20
5	10
6	5

(C)
Number of 3s	Frequency
0	0
1	100
2	0
3	0
4	0
5	0
6	0

(D)
Number of 3s	Frequency
0	50
1	25
2	12
3	6
4	4
5	2
6	1

(E)
Number of 3s	Frequency
0	14
1	14
2	15
3	15
4	14
5	14
6	14

GO ON TO NEXT PAGE

25. An art gallery wants to conduct a survey to see what type of offerings people are most interested in purchasing. The gallery wants to begin with a simple random sample of 50 people who have previously purchased art at the gallery. Which of the following survey methods will produce a simple random sample?
    (A) Survey the 50 most recent purchasers.
    (B) Survey the 50 purchasers who have spent the most money at the gallery.
    (C) Use random numbers to choose 10 people each who have purchased watercolors, sculptures, canvas, photographs, and mixed media and survey them.
    (D) Hold a brunch for previous customers and put comment cards at 50 randomly assigned seats.
    (E) Number a list of all people who have previously made a purchase. Use random numbers to choose 50 people from this list and survey them.

26. There is a linear relationship between the amount of fat in a sandwich and the amount of calories in a sandwich. A least-squares line was fit using some data collected by a nutritionist, resulting in

    $$\hat{y} = 217.3 + 35.2x$$

    where x is the grams of fat in the sandwich and y is the estimated caloric content of the sandwich. What is the estimated increase in calories that corresponds to an increase of 8 grams of fat?
    (A) 35.2
    (B) 217.3
    (C) 281.6
    (D) 498.9
    (E) 1738.4

27. In a test of the null hypothesis $H_0: \mu = 23$ against the alternative hypothesis $H_a: \mu > 23$, a random sample from a normal population with a known standard deviation produces a mean of 28.9. The z test statistic is 2.48 and the P-value is 0.0066. Based on these statistics, which of the following conclusions could be drawn?
    (A) There is convincing evidence that $\mu > 23$.
    (B) There is convincing evidence that $\mu = 23$.
    (C) 0.66% of the time, rejecting the alternative hypothesis is an error.
    (D) 0.66% of the time, the mean is above 23.
    (E) 99.34% of the time, the mean is below 23.

28. The weights of watermelons are approximately normally distributed about a mean of 90 ounces and a standard deviation of 15 ounces. If a watermelon is in the 96th percentile for weight, then its weight, in ounces, is closest to which of the following?
    (A) 26
    (B) 105
    (C) 116
    (D) 126
    (E) 262

29. Ten golf carts were selected at random from a country club to be outfitted with an engine modification designed to increase their maximum speed. The time needed to complete 18 holes was recorded for a group using the upgraded golf carts and a group using golf carts that had not been modified. The difference in means for the time needed to complete 18 holes was 24 minutes. With μ_U denoting the mean time for unmodified carts and μ_M denoting the mean time for modified carts, a 95% confidence interval estimate of the true difference in mean time, $\mu_U - \mu_M$, is (16, 32). Which of the following statements is a correct decision based on this confidence interval? Assume conditions for inference are met.

(A) We have evidence that μ_U is around 16 and μ_M is around 32.
(B) The country club should not change to modified carts because we have evidence that μ_U is less than μ_M.
(C) The country club should change to modified carts because we have evidence that μ_U is greater than μ_M.
(D) The country club should not change to modified carts because we have evidence there is no difference between μ_U and μ_M.
(E) The country club should convert the modified carts back to the original engines because we do not have evidence that the modified carts are better.

30. Tree seedlings grow at a predictable rate. The equation of the least-squares regression line to model this growth is $\hat{y} = 0.68 + 1.21x$ where x is number of years since the seed was planted and y is height in feet. What is the residual for a tree that was planted 3 years ago and is 4 feet tall?

(A) −0.31
(B) −0.68
(C) −1.52
(D) −3.63
(E) −4.31

31. The distribution of the number of empty seats on the APlus airlines route between Boston and Philadelphia follows approximately a normal distribution. Based on a very large sample, it was found that 10% of the flights had more than 20 empty seats, and 20% of the flights had 5 seats or fewer available. What are the mean and standard deviation of the distribution of the number of seats available on the APlus route between Boston and Philadelphia?

(A) $\mu = 15$; $\sigma = 5$
(B) $\mu = 11$; $\sigma = 5$
(C) $\mu = 15$; $\sigma = 7$
(D) $\mu = 11$; $\sigma = 7$
(E) $\mu = 7$; $\sigma = 15$

GO ON TO NEXT PAGE

32. Which of the following represents a distribution where the mean is greater than the median?

(A) [symmetric mound shape]

(B) [right-skewed shape]

(C) [strongly right-skewed shape]

(D) [bimodal shape]

(E) [U-shape]

33. The process of packaging candy corn yields bags with varying numbers of candy pieces. The candy manufacturer claims that, on average, bags of candy corn contain 350 pieces. The Consumer's Corner magazine tests a random sample of 40 bags. The mean number of pieces of candy corn for this sample is 346.8 pieces, while the standard deviation is 12.4 pieces. Which of the following describes the approximate P-value for a test to determine if there is evidence that the mean number of candies per bag is less than the candy maker claims? Assume conditions for inference are met.
(A) P-value < 0.001
(B) $0.001 < P$-value < 0.01
(C) $0.01 < P$-value < 0.05
(D) $0.05 < P$-value < 0.10
(E) P-value > 0.10

34. A survey was conducted to estimate the proportion of California workers who would rather live in a different state. In a random sample of 100 California workers, 28% indicated that they would rather live in another state. Find a 95% confidence interval for the proportion of all Californian workers who would rather live in another state. Assume conditions for inference are met.
(A) (0.192, 0.368)
(B) (0.207, 0.353)
(C) (0.230, 0.330)
(D) (0.234, 0.326)
(E) (0.255, 0.305)

35. Sally realizes that all of her professors are going to give an exam of some kind in the half week that leads up to Thanksgiving break. Sally takes four classes, and each class is equally likely to place its exam on either the Monday, Tuesday, or Wednesday before Thanksgiving break. Each exam is scheduled independently of the other exams. What is the probability that Sally has all four of her exams on one day?
(A) 0
(B) 0.012
(C) 0.037
(D) 0.250
(E) 0.333

36. A study was conducted by psychologists to determine at what age children develop their first crush. They asked college freshman to select from one of four age categories, and the results are listed below:

	Age 0–8	Age 9–12	Age 13–16	Age 16+
Male	2	11	35	10
Female	7	19	23	4

According to the two-way table, what percentage of males had their first crush before the age of 13?
(A) 3.4
(B) 18.9
(C) 22.4
(D) 34.5
(E) 49.1

37. Which of the following is least likely to be a potential confounding variable in a study of the effect of diet on weight loss in pounds?
(A) Gender
(B) Beginning weight
(C) Time spent exercising
(D) Name
(E) Time spent watching TV

38. The periodic table provides an atomic mass for each element, but these figures do not prove accurate for certain isotopes of some elements. Because isotopes are likely to contain a different mix of neutrons and electrons, the weights of some isotopes can be significantly more or less than the weight of the general element. Such isotopes occur much more rarely than the general element. If you were to plot the weights of the element and its isotopes, the isotopes could be clearly identified as falling far away from the accepted mean. The best word to describe the isotopes as they relate to such a plot in statistics would be
(A) outlier.
(B) residual.
(C) deviation.
(D) quartile.
(E) minimum.

39. The 23 members of the math club decide to hold the "random awards" in which they use a random number table to award 1st, 2nd, and 3rd prizes. Each member is given a two-digit number from 01 to 23, then the prizes are drawn in reverse order with 3rd prize being the first member who appears in the random number table below when digits are read two at a time:

92646 90110 79361 04891 39174 39823

Which numbered members of the math club won the three prizes?
(A) 11, 04, 17
(B) 9, 2, 6
(C) 01, 10, 17
(D) 01, 11, 10
(E) 01, 10, 10

40. Sales of jelly (X) and sales of peanut butter (Y) at a local store are recorded weekly. The correlation between X and Y is 0.9. Which is the best explanation of what this correlation means?
    (A) 90% of customers either buy peanut butter or jelly.
    (B) 90% of the time, when a customer buys peanut butter, they also buy the jelly.
    (C) 90% of the variability in peanut butter sales can be explained by variability in jelly sales.
    (D) 81% of the variability in peanut butter sales can be explained by variability in jelly sales.
    (E) 90% of the time when the price of peanut butter goes up, so does the price of jelly.

STOP

END OF SECTION I

IF YOU FINISH BEFORE TIME IS CALLED, YOU MAY CHECK YOUR WORK ON THIS SECTION. DO NOT GO ON TO SECTION II UNTIL YOU ARE TOLD TO DO SO.

SECTION II: FREE-RESPONSE QUESTIONS

Part A
Questions 1–5
Spend about 65 minutes on this part of the exam
Percent of Section II grade—75

DIRECTIONS: Show all your work. Clearly indicate the methods you use, as you will be graded on the correctness of the methods as well as the accuracy of your results and explanation.

1. The table below provides the cumulative proportions for times in the Men's 200-meter freestyle Olympic race. Cumulative proportions for the 2004 and 2008 Olympics are shown below.

Cumulative Proportions for Men's 200-Meter Freestyle Olympic Entry Times						
Time	2004	2008	Time	2004	2008
1:43	0.125	0	1:48	0.875	0.625
1:44	0.125	0	1:49	1	0.750
1:45	0.25	0.125	1:50	1	0.875
1:46	0.5	0.25	1:51	1	1
1:47	0.875	0.375	1:52	1	1

The cumulative proportions are graphed below:

(a) Use the cumulative proportions graph to approximate the median finishing time for each year. Show supporting work on the graph.
(b) Use the cumulative proportion graph to approximate the interquartile range for each year.
(c) Using the results from parts (a) and (b), write a sentence or two for a newspaper column comparing the two distributions of times.

GO ON TO NEXT PAGE

2. A cereal manufacturer wants to investigate if having a display at the end of an aisle in a grocery store would increase sales of a new cereal compared to having the new cereal shelved with the rest of the cereals that the store carries. Sixteen grocery stores have agreed to participate in the study, which will last two weeks. For each store, the cereal can be placed on a display at the end of an aisle or with the rest of the cereals. In any particular store, different locations can be used for week 1 and for week 2 if desired, but the cereal can only be in one of the two locations in any given week.

   The marketing manager proposes that 8 of the 16 stores be selected at random. These 8 stores will display the cereal at the end of an aisle and the other 8 stores will display the cereal with the rest of the cereals that the store sells. At the end of the two-week period, mean sales for stores with aisle displays will be compared to mean sales for stores that did not have aisle displays.
   (a) Describe an alternate way to carry out the study that would improve on the study design proposed by the marketing manager.
   (b) Given the design you proposed in part (a) and assuming that any conditions for inference are met, what hypothesis test would be appropriate to determine if the data from the study supports the statement that mean sales are higher when an end-of-aisle display is used?

3. Mrs. Murdock gives her statistics students a mock exam before the real AP® exam. In her class, all students are required to take both the mock exam and the AP® Statistics exam. Ten percent of the students who pass the AP® exam did not pass the mock exam and 7% of the students who do not pass the AP® test passed the mock exam. Overall, 58% of her students pass the AP® test.
   (a) What is the probability that a student selected at random from Mrs. Murdock's students passed the mock exam? Show your work.
   (b) What is the probability that a student selected at random from Mrs. Murdock's students who passed the mock exam also passes the AP® exam?

4. In a large urban school with over 6,000 students, a random sample of 375 parents were interviewed at the start of a new school year. Of the 375 parents, 280 said that they thought the principal was doing an excellent job. However, when she implemented a stricter grading policy a month into the school year, it was thought that the proportion of parents who thought the principal was doing an excellent job decreased. To investigate, a new random sample of 523 parents was selected, and 358 thought the principal was doing an excellent job.
   (a) Do these data support the conclusion that there was a decrease in the proportion of parents who thought the principal was doing an excellent job after the new grading policy was implemented?
   (b) The school board wants to use this information to freeze the principal's salary if there is evidence that the principal's support has declined. Using the information from part (a), describe the error that could be made in the context of this problem. What would be a consequence of making this error?

5. The percentage of high school teachers who have taken advanced course work after receiving a teaching credential was recorded for both science teachers and mathematics teachers for 12 randomly selected school districts in California. The resulting data are given in the table below.

School District	Percentage Math Teachers	Percentage Science Teachers
1	41	36
2	38	34
3	44	37
4	30	32
5	21	30
6	24	32
7	33	36
8	40	38
9	48	40
10	41	37
11	35	35
12	30	36

With μ_M denoting the mean percentage of math teachers with advanced course work for school districts in California and μ_S denoting the mean percentage of science teachers with advanced course work for school districts in California, a researcher used a two-sample t test to test $H_0 : \mu_M - \mu_S = 0$ versus $H_a : \mu_M - \mu_S > 0$.

This resulted in a test statistic of $t = 0.07$ and a P-value of 0.474.
(a) What conclusion did the researcher find based on these results?
(b) Explain why the two-sample t test is not an appropriate choice for testing these hypotheses.
(c) What conditions are needed to perform a paired t test? Would it be reasonable to perform this test?

SECTION II
Part B
Question 6
Spend about 25 minutes on this part of the exam
Percent of Section II grade—25

DIRECTIONS: Show all your work. Clearly indicate the methods you use, as you will be graded on the correctness of the methods as well as the accuracy of your results and explanation.

6. A high school counselor at a large public high school is interested in developing a model to predict SAT® math scores. He takes a random sample of 50 seniors at the school who took the SAT® exam and recorded SAT® math score, the number of math courses completed at the high school and the number of science courses completed at the high school for each of the students in the sample. Computer output resulting from fitting a linear regression model with
   y = SAT® math score (an integer between 200 and 800)
   and
   x = number of math courses completed is given below.

```
Regression Analysis: SAT® math score versus math courses

The regression equation is
SAT® math score = 505 + 47.4 math courses

Predictor              Coef         SE Coef           T             P
Constant              505.14         13.54         37.32         0.000
math courses           47.436         3.595        13.20         0.000

S = 29.6836            R-Sq = 78.4%          R-Sq(adj) = 77.9%
```

(a) Construct and interpret a 90% confidence interval for the slope of the population regression line. You may assume that the conditions for inference are met.
(b) Use the least squares regression line to predict the SAT® math score of a student who has taken four math courses in high school.
(c) Interpret the value of r^2 in context.
(d) A multiple regression model is one that incorporates more than one predictor variable. The regression output below resulted from fitting a multiple regression model that incorporates both number of math courses and number of science courses as predictors. Use the regression equation to predict the SAT® math score of a student who has taken four math courses and three science courses. How does this prediction compare to the prediction in part (b)?

```
Regression Analysis: SAT® Math Score versus Math Courses, Science
Courses
The regression equation is
SAT® math score = 515 + 47.7 math courses - 3.16 science courses

Predictor              Coef         SE Coef           T             P
Constant              514.70        18.00          28.59         0.000
math courses           47.682        3.621         13.17         0.000
science courses        -3.164        3.909         -0.81         0.422

S = 29.7907            R-Sq = 78.7%          R-Sq(adj) = 77.8%
```

(e) 4The values of s_e, r^2, and the standard deviations of the regression coefficients are interpreted in the same way as they are interpreted in linear regression. Do you think that using the multiple regression model that includes both number of math courses completed and number of science courses completed would result in predictions that are much more accurate than those produced by the linear regression model that only uses number of math courses completed? Explain your reasoning.

END OF EXAMINATION

SAT® is a trademark owned by the College Board, which is not affiliated with, and does not endorse, this product.

ANSWERS TO PRACTICE TEST 1

MULTIPLE-CHOICE ANSWERS

Using the table below, score your test.

Determine how many questions you answered correctly and how many you answered incorrectly. You will find explanations of the answers on the following pages.

1. B	9. C	17. B	25. C	33. A
2. D	10. A	18. D	26. A	34. C
3. A	11. D	19. B	27. C	35. C
4. B	12. E	20. A	28. C	36. D
5. C	13. A	21. B	29. A	37. A
6. A	14. D	22. A	30. C	38. C
7. C	15. C	23. A	31. C	39. D
8. B	16. B	24. E	32. A	40. C

ANSWERS AND EXPLANATIONS

MULTIPLE-CHOICE ANSWERS

1. **(C)** The margin of error reflects sampling variability and describes how results from a sample might differ from the underlying population. A 6% margin of error indicates that we expect the sample percentage of 64% to be within 6 percentage points of the actual population percentage (*Statistics: Learning from Data*, AP Edition, 1st ed. pages 460–465 and 467–477 and 480–481 / 2nd ed. pages 475–480 and 482–493 and 497–498).

2. **(B)** The first step is figuring out what portion of your sample is likely to be women and which portion is likely to be men. Since the campus has a 12,000/8,000 ratio, the ratio of our sample should be 60/40. Of the 60 women, 50% would likely use the gym, which is 30 students. Of the 40 men, 40% would likely use the gym, which is 16 students. Thirty students plus 16 students is a total of 46 from the sample that we expect to use the gym (*Statistics: Learning from Data*, AP Edition, 1st ed. pages 339–343 / 2nd ed. pages 353–357).

3. **(D)** Multiply the 5,000 batteries by the 0.995 percentage of functioning batteries and the result is 4,975 batteries. Looking at it another way, if 99.5% of the batteries function after a year then for every thousand batteries, five would be nonfunctional. For 5,000, this number becomes 25. 5000 − 25 gives you 4,975 functioning batteries (*Statistics: Learning from Data*, AP Edition, 1st ed. pages 339–343 / 2nd ed. pages 353–357).

4. **(A)** Because the samples are paired, the degrees of freedom is one less than the number of pairs. In this case, $df = 10 - 1 = 9$ (*Statistics: Learning from Data*, AP Edition, 1st ed. pages 633–639, 649–651, 672–674, and 679–682 / 2nd ed. pages 642–650).

5. **(B)** Plan I does not differentiate between fiction and nonfiction books, which is a problem since it is believed that nonfiction books have more pages. Plan II is an effective use of stratified sampling and outlines a way to accurately estimate the total number of pages in the library (*Statistics: Learning from Data*, AP Edition, 1st ed. pages 13–21 / 2nd ed. pages 9–20).

6. **(C)** Road conditions are confounded with brand. The stated purpose is to check the effect of road conditions on stopping distances. To correct for this, we would need to include both wet and dry conditions for brand A and brand B, or we would need to focus on only brand A or brand B but not both (*Statistics: Learning from Data*, AP Edition, 1st ed. pages 24–38 / 2nd ed. pages 23–38).

7. **(A)** The median is represented by the center line in the box. Set B's median is located further to the right than set A so set B's median larger than set A's median. It is unclear from a box and whiskers plot how many data points are being represented, so you cannot definitively say which set contains more data. The range of the data is represented by the distance between endpoints of the whiskers, and in this case the whiskers in set A extend farther than the whiskers in set B so set A has a larger range than set B (*Statistics: Learning from Data*, AP Edition, 1st ed. pages 149–156 / 2nd ed. pages 158–165).

8. **(C)** In order to find the expected profit, you need to multiply the profit per item by the number of items sold and the probability of selling that number, then total it for all possible outcomes. On wholesale sales the company is expected to make $1[50,000(0.2) + 100,000(0.3) + 150,000(0.4) + 200,000(0.1)] = (10,000 + 30,000 + 60,000 + 20,000) = $120,000. On retail sales the company is expected to make $2[10,000(0.2) + 20,000(0.5) + 30,000(0.3)] = 2(2,000 + 10,000 + 9,000) = $42,000. The total is $120,000 + $42,000 = $162,000 (*Statistics: Learning from Data*, AP Edition, 1st ed. pages 339–343 / 2nd ed. pages 353–357).

9. **(B)** The only way for the two of them to eat six plates combined is for each of them to eat three. Since both events have to occur and events are independent, the probabilities are multiplied. $(0.7)(0.1) = 07$ (*Statistics: Learning from Data*, AP Edition, 1st ed. pages 302–308 / 2nd ed. pages 318–323).

10. **(C)** There would be an association only if one of the two branches had a higher proportion of varsity athletes than the other. The proportion of varsity athletes is 32/48 = 2/3 for Navy and 24/36 = 2/3 for Air Force. Because the proportion is the same for both Navy and Air Force, there does not appear to be an association (*Statistics: Learning from Data*, AP Edition, 1st ed. pages 708–718 / 2nd ed. pages 716–728).

11. **(A)** For a normal distribution, the standard deviation is the distance from the mean to either dotted line where the dotted line shows where the normal curve changes from concave up to concave down. This distance is 15 kg (*Statistics: Learning from Data*, AP Edition, 1st ed. pages 373–387 and 395–398 / 2nd ed. pages 380–394 and 412–415).

12. **(D)** The null hypothesis is that the windows will save $100. The consumer group is not concerned with the case where the windows save more than $100, only the case where the windows save less than $100, which goes against the company's claim. If we reject the null hypothesis then we have evidence against the company's claim (*Statistics: Learning from Data*, AP Edition, 1st ed. pages 591–602 / 2nd ed. pages 614–625).

13. **(E)** The z-score describes how many standard deviations a data point is above or below the mean. A z-score of −1.25 tells us that Stanley's salary is below the mean because of the negative sign and 1.25 standard deviations his salary is away from the mean. So Stanley's salary is 1.25 standard deviations below the mean (*Statistics: Learning from Data*, AP Edition, 1st ed. pages 160–162 / 2nd ed. pages 170–173).

14. **(A)** The issue of concern is the way in which the sample was selected, not the sample size. The fact that the 100 stores that had local displays were not chosen at random introduces bias (*Statistics: Learning from Data*, AP Edition, 1st ed. pages 13–21 / 2nd ed. pages 9–20).

15. **(D)** To calculate the expected cost over 12 weeks, you take the expected cost for one week and multiply it by the number of weeks. (5.65)(12) = $67.80 (*Statistics: Learning from Data*, AP Edition, 1st ed. pages 339–343 / 2nd ed. pages 353–357).

16. **(C)** With X_1 = amount paid in week 1, X_2 = amount paid in week 2, and so on, the total amount paid is $T = X_1 + X_2 + \ldots X_5$. $Var(T) = Var(X_1) + Var(X_2) + \ldots + Var(X_5) = 0.59^2 + 0.59^2 + \ldots + 0.59^2 = 5(0.59^2) = 1.74$. $StdDev(T) = \sqrt{1.74} = 1.32$ (*Statistics: Learning from Data*, AP Edition, 1st ed. pages 339–343 / 2nd ed. pages 353–357).

17. **(B)** All normal distributions are symmetric and have mean equal to the median. While some normal distributions are centered at 0, this is not the case for all normal distributions (*Statistics: Learning from Data*, AP Edition, 1st ed. pages 373–387 and 395–398 / 2nd ed. pages 380–394 and 412–415).

18. **(B)** The median is the only number that remains unchanged because the correction was made in a place that could not be the center of the data. The mean will change because you have added no additional cars, but the total of all bid prices has changed. The mode may or may not change depending on whether there is another car in the sample that sold for the corrected price. The range must change because the data point that was corrected was an endpoint of the data. The variance also must change because the distance from that data point to the mean has changed as have all other data points' distances to the new mean. The median is the only statistic listed that could not possibly change with the given information (*Statistics: Learning from Data*, AP Edition, 1st ed. pages 133–135 and 143 / 2nd ed. pages 140–142 and 150–151).

19. **(D)** We cannot be sure that every individual plant grew from week one to week two. Since we do not know how the data points are connected, it is possible that the plant that was 26 millimeters after one week was still 26 millimeters after two weeks. Without further information about the data, we cannot be sure that each plant increased in size (*Statistics: Learning from Data*, AP Edition, 1st ed. pages 68–96 / 2nd ed. pages 70–93).

20. **(B)** To win a prize, Andre would have to make all three shots. If his probability of making each shot is 0.6 and the shots are independent, then the probability of making all three is $(0.6)(0.6)(0.6) = 0.216$ (*Statistics: Learning from Data*, AP Edition, 1st ed. pages 302–308 / 2nd ed. pages 318–323).

21. **(A)** If a motorist is in the country legally but does not have the paperwork to prove it in his or her vehicle, then we would reject the null hypothesis when the null hypothesis is actually true. This is the definition of Type I error (*Statistics: Learning from Data*, AP Edition, 1st ed. pages 502–505 / 2nd ed. pages 516–520).

22. **(B)** Because the population standard deviation is not known, a one-sample t confidence interval would be used. With a 90% confidence interval the t critical value is 1.67. The given standard deviation of the sample is 8.1 with a sample size of 60. So the margin of error is $1.67\left(\dfrac{8.1}{\sqrt{60}}\right) = 1.75$ (*Statistics: Learning from Data*, AP Edition, 1st ed. pages 578–588 / 2nd ed. pages 600–612).

23. **(A)** Mr. Branch has a z-score of $z = \dfrac{12.5 - 11}{3.8} = 0.395$. Dennis has a z-score of $z = \dfrac{15.8 - 14}{6.1} = 0.295$. Because Mr. Branch's z-score is higher than Dennis's z-score, it means Mr. Branch did better when compared to the players of his era (*Statistics: Learning from Data*, AP Edition, 1st ed. pages 160–162 / 2nd ed. pages 170–173).

24. **(A)** The frequency distribution for A correctly describes the behavior of this variable. We would expect to see about one 3 in six rolls of a die. To find the probability of rolling no 3s you would take the probability of not rolling a 3 on a single roll (5/6) to the power of the number of rolls $(5/6)^6 = 0.334$. Similarly, to find the probability of rolling 3 on all six rolls it would be $(1/6)^6 = 0.000021$. The proper frequency table should peak at the most common number of 3s rolled over the course of six rolls and taper off from there (*Statistics: Learning from Data*, AP Edition, 1st ed. pages 273–276 and 278–287 / 2nd ed. pages 285–289 and 291–301).

25. **(E)** This is the only method that results in a simple random sample. Method A only reaches the most recent clients, not the whole list. Method B may only reach the wealthiest clients. Method C is not a simple random sample because it stratifies by type of art. Method D would only sample those willing to attend the lunch (*Statistics: Learning from Data*, AP Edition, 1st ed. pages 13–21 / 2nd ed. pages 9–20).

26. **(C)** The slope of the line is the predicted increase associated with an increase of one gram of fat. For 8 grams, the approximate increase would be $(8)(35.2) = 281.6$ (*Statistics: Learning from Data*, AP Edition, 1st ed. pages 198–206 / 2nd ed. pages 209–219).

27. **(A)** This z test statistic is large and the *P*-value is very small at 0.0066. For this reason, we reject the null hypothesis and conclude that we have evidence that $\mu > 23$ (*Statistics: Learning from Data*, AP Edition, 1st ed. pages 591–602 / 2nd ed. pages 614–625).

28. **(C)** If the watermelon is in the 96th percentile, then for the standard normal distribution this occurs at 1.75 standard deviations above the mean. $90 + (15)(1.75) = 90 + 26 = 116$ ounces (*Statistics: Learning from Data*, AP Edition, 1st ed. pages 373–387 and 395–398 / 2nd ed. pages 380–394 and 412–415).

29. **(C)** Because all numbers contained in the confidence interval are positive numbers, we can be confident that the mean time for the unmodified carts is greater than the mean time for the modified carts by somewhere between 16 and 32 minutes (*Statistics: Learning from Data*, AP Edition, 1st ed. pages 618–627, 644–649, 672–674, and 679–682 / 2nd ed. pages 657–670).

30. **(A)** $\hat{y} = 0.68 + 1.21(3) = 4.31$, residual = actual height − predicted height = $y - \hat{y} = 4 - 4.31 = -0.31$ (*Statistics: Learning from Data*, AP Edition, 1st ed. 1st ed. pages 211–225 / 2nd ed. pages 223–239).

31. **(D)** Using a normal distribution table, we find that 90% occurs at a z-score of 1.28 and 20% occurs at a z-score of –0.84. By working backward through our z-score equation, we solve two equations for two variables, mean and standard deviation: $\frac{20-\mu}{\sigma}=1.28$ and $\frac{5-\mu}{\sigma}=-0.84$. Solving the first equation for μ, we get $\mu = 20 - 1.28\sigma$. Substituting this for μ in the second equation, it gives us: $\frac{5-(20-1.28\sigma)}{\sigma}=-0.84$. So, $\sigma = 7.07$. Substituting back into our $\mu = 20 - 1.28\sigma$ equation, $\mu = 10.94$. The rounded answers are 7 and 11 (*Statistics: Learning from Data*, AP Edition, 1st ed. pages 373–387 and 395–398 / 2nd ed. pages 380–394 and 412–415).

32. **(C)** When the histogram is unimodal with a longer upper tail, the outlying values in the upper tail pull the mean up. So the mean generally lies above the median (*Understandable Statistics: Concepts and Methods*, 11th ed. pages 454–462/12th ed. pages 456–464).

33. **(D)** Because the value of the population standard deviation is unknown, this would be a one-sample t test. The test statistic is $t=\frac{346.8-350}{\frac{12.4}{\sqrt{40}}}=-1.63$. The P-value is the area to the left of -1.63 under the t curve with $df = 39$. This area is 0.055 (*Statistics: Learning from Data*, AP Edition, 1st ed. pages 133–135 and 143 / 2nd ed. pages 140–142 and 150–151).

34. **(A)** To find the confidence interval you need to use the equation $\hat{p}\pm 1.96\sqrt{\frac{\hat{p}(1-\hat{p})}{n}}=0.28\pm 1.96\sqrt{\frac{(0.28)(0.72)}{100}}=0.28\pm 0.89$. The 95% confidence interval is then (0.191, 0.369) (*Statistics: Learning from Data*, AP Edition, 1st ed. pages 460–465 and 467–477 and 480–481 / 2nd ed. pages 475–480 and 482–493 and 497–498).

35. **(C)** The chance of all four exams occurring on one particular day is $(1/3)^4 = 0.0123$. When that is multiplied by the three possible days on which it could occur, you get $(0.0123)(3) = 0.037$ (*Statistics: Learning from Data*, AP Edition, 1st ed. pages 302–308 / 2nd ed. pages 318–323).

36. **(C)** First, find the total number of males who participated in the survey: $2 + 11 + 35 + 10 = 58$. Then find the total number who had their first crush before the age of 13: $2 + 11 = 13$. To find the percentage, take 13/58 and multiply by 100 to get 22.4% (*Statistics: Learning from Data*, AP Edition, 1st ed. pages 267–276 / 2nd ed. pages 280–289).

37. **(D)** While the rest of the variables could be related to weight loss, name is not related to weight loss (*Statistics: Learning from Data*, AP Edition, 1st ed. pages 24–38 / 2nd ed. pages 23–38).

38. **(A)** A data point that lies far away from the accepted mean is called an outlier (*Statistics: Learning from Data*, AP Edition, 1st ed. pages 149–156 / 2nd ed. pages 158–165).

39. **(C)** As you read across and cross off 2 numbers at a time, the first number under 23 comes after crossing out 92, 64, and 69. The next two numbers are 01, 10. Both count since both are below 23. Then after crossing out 79, 36, 10 (it is a repeat – we already picked person numbered 10), 48, 91, and 39, you come to 17 for the top prize in the random awards (*Statistics: Learning from Data*, AP Edition, 1st ed. pages 317–323 / 2nd ed. pages 333–340).

40. **(D)** The square of the correlation coefficient, r^2, is the proportion of variability in y that can be explained by variability in x (*Statistics: Learning from Data*, AP Edition, 1st ed. pages 211–225 / 2nd ed. pages 223–239).

Free-Response Answers

1. (a) The median time will be the time that corresponds to a cumulative proportion of 50. Half of the times will be smaller than this value and half larger. By finding 50 on the cumulative proportion axis of the graph, moving over to the plot for 2004, and then looking down to find the corresponding time on the time axis, you can determine that the median finishing time for 2004 is 1:46. The median finishing time for 2008 is 1:48. You should show this process on the graph.
   (b) The quartiles can be found in a way that is similar to the way you found the median by finding the times that correspond to cumulative proportions of 0.25 and 0.75. For 2004, the quartiles are 1:45 and 1:47, and the IQR is 2 seconds. For 2008, the quartiles are 1:46 and 1:49, and the IQR is 3 seconds.
   (c) The 200-meter freestyle times slowed between 2004 and 2008. However, the variability in times was a bit larger in 2008 than in 2004.

   (*Statistics: Learning from Data*, AP Edition, 1st ed. pages 68–96, 135–140, and 144–147 / 2nd ed. pages 70–93, 142–147, and 151–156)

   Scoring Question 1:

   Each part of this problem can be scored as essentially correct (E), partially correct (P), or incorrect (I).

   Part (a) is scored
      E if correct medians are given for both years and supporting work is indicated on the graph.
      P if correct medians are given for both years but no supporting work is shown on the graph.

   Part (b) is scored
      E if both IQRs are correctly computed.
      P if quartiles for both years are correctly computed but the IQR is reported as an interval rather than a single number.

Part (c) is scored
  E if the response comments on (1) times tend to be faster in 2004 than 2008 and
    (2) variability tends to be greater in 2008 than 2004.
  P if the response comments on only one of the two things required for an E.

Question 1 is scored a
  4 if all three parts are E.
  3 if two parts are E and the one is P.
  2 if two parts are E and no parts are P, OR one part is E and two parts are P, or if three parts are P.
  1 if two parts are P and one part is I OR if one part is E and no parts are P.
  0 if one OR no parts are P.

2. (a) Because some stores may have a higher volume of sales overall than other stores and this may be related to how much cereal is sold, it would be a good idea to try both locations in each store. For each store, the cereal will be displayed at the end of an aisle for one of the two weeks of the study and with the rest of the cereals for the other week. For each store, flip a coin to determine which of the two weeks will use the end-of-aisle display—if the coin lands heads, assign the end-of-aisle display to week 1 and if the coin lands tails, assign the end-of-aisle display to week 2. Record sales at each store for each of the two weeks.
   (b) The design described in part (a) will result in paired data (paired by store). A paired t test would be used.

(*Statistics: Learning from Data*, AP Edition, 1st ed. pages 24–38, 633–639, 649–651, 672–674, and 679–682 / 2nd ed. pages 23–38 and 642–650)

Scoring Question 2:

Each part of this problem can be scored as essentially correct (E), partially correct (P), or incorrect (I).

Part (a) is scored
  E if the proposed design uses both locations at each store and uses random assignment to determine which of the two weeks will have the end-of-aisle display.
  P if the proposed design uses both locations at each store but does not explicitly state that random assignment will be used to determine which of the two weeks will have the end-of-aisle display.

Part (b) is scored
  E if a paired t test is recommended.
  P if the response fails to recognize the pairing and recommends a two-sample t test.
  I if another test is recommended.

Question 2 is scored a
  4 if both parts are E.
  3 if one part is E and the other is P.
  2 if one part is E and one part is I or if both parts are P.
  1 if one part is P and one part is I.
  0 if both parts are I.

3. A good place to start is to organize the probability information given using a tree diagram. The diagram is not required, but it makes the required computations easier to visualize.

```
                          ┌── Pass Mock Exam (0.90)
         Pass AP® Exam (0.58)
                          └── Don't Pass Mock (0.10)

                          ┌── Pass Mock Exam (0.07)
         Don't Pass AP® Exam (0.42)
                          └── Don't Pass Mock (0.93)
```

(a) Let M = event that the selected student passed the mock exam and A = the selected student passes the AP® exam. Then
$$P(M) = P(M\,|\,A)P(A) + P(M\,|\,\text{not }A)P(\text{not }A)$$
$$= (0.90)(0.58) + (0.07)(0.42)$$
$$= 0.5220 + 0.0294$$
$$= 0.5514$$

(b) $$P(A\,|\,M) = \frac{P(M\,|\,A)(P(A)}{P(M\,|\,A)P(A) + P(M\,|\,\text{not }A)P(\text{not }A)}$$
$$= \frac{0.522}{0.514}$$
$$= 0.9467$$

(*Statistics: Learning from Data*, AP Edition, 1st ed. pages 273–276, 278–287, and 290–299 / 2nd ed. pages 285–289, 291–301, and 304–314)

Scoring Question 3:

Each part of this problem can be scored as essentially correct (E), partially correct (P), or incorrect (I).

Part (a) is scored
  E if the a correct probability is computed with appropriate supporting work.
  P if a correct probability is computed but appropriate supporting work is not given OR the student computes $P(M \cap A)$ or $P(M \cap \text{not }A)$ rather than $P(M)$.

Part (b) is scored
  E if the a correct probability is computed with appropriate supporting work.
  P if a correct probability is computed but appropriate supporting work is not given OR the student computes $P(M\,|\,A)$ rather than $P(A\,|\,M)$.

Question 3 is scored a
    4 if both parts are E.
    3 if one part is E and the other is P.
    2 if one part is E and one part is I OR if both parts are P.
    1 if one part is P and one part is I.
    0 if both parts are I.

4. (a) **Hypotheses:**

    $H_0: p_B - p_A = 0$

    $H_a: p_B - p_A > 0$

    where p_B is the true proportion of all parents who thought the principal was doing an excellent job before the change and p_A is the true proportion of all parents who thought the principal was doing an excellent job after the change.
    $\alpha = 0.05$

    Test: two-sample z-test for difference in proportions.

    Assumptions:

    The two samples are independent random samples from the populations of all parents before and after the change in grading policy. We are told that there are more than $10(375) = 3750$ and $10(523) = 5230$ parents in the school.

    $\hat{p}_B = \dfrac{280}{375} = 0.75 \qquad \hat{p}_A = \dfrac{358}{523} = 0.68$

    $n_B \hat{p}_B = 375(0.75) > 10 \qquad$ and $\qquad n_A \hat{p}_A = 523(0.68) > 10$

    $n_B(1 - \hat{p}_B) = 375(0.25) > 10 \quad b_A(1 - \hat{p}_A) = 523(0.32) > 10$

    So, the sample sizes are large enough.

    Calculations:

    $p_c = \dfrac{280 + 358}{375 + 523} = 0.71$

    $z = \dfrac{(0.75 - 0.68) - 0}{\sqrt{\dfrac{0.71(1-0.71)}{375} + \dfrac{0.71(1-0.71)}{523}}} = 2.025$

    P-value $= 0.021$

    Conclusion: Since the P-value is less than α, we reject the null hypothesis. There is strong evidence that the proportion who think the principal is doing an excellent job decreased after the new policy was implemented.

    (b) Since we rejected the null hypothesis, a Type I error could have been made. A Type I error is when we reject the null hypothesis when it's true. In this context, this means believing that the proportion who think the principal is doing an excellent job has decreased when in fact it has not. So the school board will freeze the principal's salary when they shouldn't. The principal is losing out on any pay raise that he/she should be getting.

(*Statistics: Learning from Data*, AP Edition, 1st ed. pages 502–505, 542–548, 550–557, 674–676, and 682–684 / 2nd ed. pages 516–520, 556–562, 564–572, and 573–580)

Scoring Question 4:

Each part is scored as essentially correct (E), partially correct (P), or incorrect (I). There are three parts to the hypothesis test in part (a): hypotheses and assumptions, test and calculations, and conclusion. Each of these parts can be scored as essentially correct (E), partially correct (P), or incorrect (I).

For Part (a)
  Hypotheses and assumptions are scored as
  E if (1) the correct hypotheses are given and notation is defined and (2) all three assumptions for the test are adequately addressed.
  P if the response includes only one of the two components required for an E.

  Calculations are scored as
  E if (1) the correct test is identified either by name or by formula and (2) correct values of the test statistic and P-value are given.
  P if the correct test is identified either by name or by formula but either the value of the test statistic or the P-value is omitted or incorrect. Note: Calculations should be consistent with the hypothesized values given in the null hypothesis.

  Conclusion is scored as
  E if a correct conclusion is given in context and the conclusion is linked to the P-value.
  P if a correct decision to reject or fail to reject the null hypothesis is given but the conclusion is not in context or the conclusion is not linked to the P-value.

Part (b) is scored as
  E if a Type I error is identified, correctly described in context, and a logical consequence is described.
  P if Type II error is chosen and correctly defined in context with a consequence described consistent with a Type II error OR Type I error is identified but not correctly described in context or a logical consequence is not described.

Question 4 is scored a
  4 if four parts are E.
  3 if three parts are E and one is P OR three parts are E and one is I OR two parts are E and two parts are P.
  2 if two parts are E and one part is P and one part is I OR two parts are E and two parts are I OR one part is E and three parts are P OR one part is E and two parts are P and one part is I OR if four parts are P.
  1 if one part is E and one part is P and two parts are I OR one part is E and three parts are I OR three parts are P and one part is I OR two parts are P and two parts are I.
  0 if one part is P and three parts are I OR four parts are I.

5. (a) Based on this test, the researcher failed to reject the null hypothesis and concluded that there was no evidence that the mean percentage of teachers who have taken advanced course work for school districts in California is greater for math teachers than for science teachers.
   (b) The two samples are paired by school district. A two-sample t test is only appropriate for independent samples.
   (c) **Assumptions:**
   The school districts were selected at random.
   The number of pairs is not large, so we need to be willing to assume that the population distribution of differences is approximately normal. The differences are

   5   4   7   −2   −9   −8   −3   2   8   4   0   −6

   A boxplot of these differences is given here:

   The boxplot is approximately symmetric and there are no outliers, so it is reasonable to assume that the difference distribution is approximately normal.
   Since the conditions are met, it would be reasonable to perform a paired t test for population means.

(*Statistics: Learning from Data*, AP Edition, 1st ed. pages 633–639, 649–651, 672–674, and 679–682 / 2nd ed. pages 642–650).

Scoring Question 5:

Part (a) is scored as essentially correct (E), partially correct (P), or incorrect (I).

Part (a) is scored as
  E if a correct conclusion is given in context and the conclusion is linked to the P-value.
  P if a correct decision to reject or fail to reject the null hypothesis is given but the conclusion is not in context or the conclusion is not linked to the P-value.

Part (b) is scored as
  E if the response states that the two-sample t test is only appropriate for independent samples and notes that these samples are paired.
  P if the response does not include context OR the response does not give a sketch of the sample data to justify normality.

Then Question 5 is scored a
- 4 if all three parts are E.
- 3 if two parts are E and the one is P.
- 2 if two parts are E and no parts are P OR one part is E and two parts are P OR if three parts are P.
- 1 if two parts are P and one part is I OR if one part is E and no parts are P.
- 0 if one or no parts are P.

6. (a) We will use a t confidence interval for the slope. With $n = 50$, $df = 50 - 2 = 48$. The appropriate t critical value is 1.68. Using values from the computer output, the confidence interval is then

   $47.436 \pm (1.68)(3.595) = 47.436 \pm 6.040 = (41.396, 53.476)$

   Based on the sample data, we think that, on average, SAT® math score increases by somewhere between 41 and 53 points with each additional math course taken.

   (b) $\hat{y} = 505 + 47.4(4) = 694.6$. Because SAT® math scores must be integers, we would round this to 695. We would predict an SAT® math score of 695 for a student who had completed 4 math courses.

   (c) From the computer output, $r^2 = 0.784$. This means that about 78% of the variability in SAT math scores can be explained by the number of math courses taken.

   (d) $\hat{y} = 515 + 47.7(4) - 3.16(3) = 696.32$. Because SAT® math scores must be integers, we would round this to 696. We would predict an SAT® math score of 696 for a student who had completed four math courses and three science courses. This prediction is not much different from the prediction in part (b).

   (e) In the linear model, the value of the standard deviation s_e provides information about what we can expect for predictions based on the regression line. Since we are told that s_e is interpreted in a similar way for multiple regression, we would want to compare the values of s_e for the two models. For the linear model, $s_e = 29.6836$ and for the multiple regression model $s_e = 29.7907$. Since these two standard deviations are nearly equal, we would not expect predictions based on the multiple regression model to be more accurate than those based on the linear model.

(*Statistics: Learning from Data*, AP Edition, 1st ed. pages 198–206, 211–225, and 748–756 / 2nd ed. pages 209–219, 223–239, and 754–763)

Scoring Question 6:

Parts (b) and (c) are scored together. Parts (a) (b and c), (d) and (e) are each scored as essentially correct (E), partially correct (P), or incorrect (I).

Part (a) is scored
  E if the confidence interval is correctly computed and interpreted in context.
  P if an incorrect t critical value or standard deviation is used in the calculation of the confidence interval OR if the interpretation is missing or not in context.

Part (b and c) is scored
  E if a correct prediction is made in Part (b) and a correct interpretation is given in context in Part (c).
  P if the calculation of the prediction in Part (b) is not correct OR if the interpretation in Part (b) is missing, incorrect or not in context.

Part (d) is scored
   E if a correct predicted value is computed and a comparison to the prediction from Part (b) is made.
   P if the prediction is incorrectly computed and this prediction is compared to the prediction in Part (b) OR if the prediction is correctly computed but no comparison is made.

Part (e) is scored
   E if the response says that the predictions based on the multiple regression model will not be much more accurate than those based on the linear model and justifies this by appealing either to the values of s_e for both models.
   P if the response says that the predictions based on the multiple regression model will not be much more accurate than those based on the linear model but the explanation is weak or is not linked to the value of s_e.

Question 6 is scored a
   4 if four parts are E.
   3 if three parts are E and one is P OR three parts are E and one is I OR two parts are E and two parts are P.
   2 if two parts are E and one part is P and one part is I OR two parts are E and two parts are I OR one part is E and three parts are P OR one part is E and two parts are P and one part is I OR if four parts are P.
   1 if one part is E and one part is P and two parts are I OR one part is E and three parts are I OR three parts are P and one part is I OR two parts are P and two parts are I.
   0 if one part is P and three parts are I OR four parts are I.

Calculating Your Score

Section I: Multiple-Choice Questions

[_____] × 1.25 = _____
Number Correct   Weighted Section I Score
(out of 40)   (do not round)

Section II: Free-Response Questions

Question 1 _____ × (1.875) = _____
         (out of 4)   (Do not round)

Question 2 _____ × (1.875) = _____
         (out of 4)   (Do not round)

Question 3 _____ × (1.875) = _____
         (out of 4)   (Do not round)

Question 4 _____ × (1.875) = _____
         (out of 4)   (Do not round)

Question 5 _____ × (1.875) = _____
         (out of 4)   (Do not round)

Question 6 _____ × (3.1255) = _____
         (out of 4)   (Do not round)

Sum = _____
Weighted Section II Score
(Do not round)

Composite Score

_____ + _____ = _____
Weighted   Weighted   Composite Score
Section I Score   Section II Score (Round to nearest
                                                         whole number)

Composite Score Range	Approximate AP® Grade
68–100	5
53–67	4
40–52	3
29–39	2
0–28	1

PRACTICE TEST 2

This test will give you some indication of how you might score on the AP® Statistics Exam. Of course, the exam changes every year, so it is never possible to predict a student's score with certainty. This test will also pinpoint your strengths and weaknesses on the key content areas covered by the exam.

AP® STATISTICS EXAMINATION
Section I: Multiple-Choice Questions
Time: 90 minutes
Number of Questions: 40

DIRECTIONS: Each of the following questions or incomplete statements is accompanied by five suggested answers or completions. Select the one that best answers the question or completes the statement.

1. John thinks that whenever he takes the late bus home after school, he is hungrier than when he takes the regular bus home. He decides to record whether or not he goes back for seconds at the dinner table each night and cross-references those data with which bus he took home from school. He found that he had seconds at dinner eight of the nine recorded days in which he took the late bus as compared to having seconds at dinner only seven of the twenty-one times he took the early bus. John turned in a paper to his statistics teacher that stated that the late bus was causing his hunger. When John's paper was returned to him, the professor had written, "Were the days you took the late bus the same days you played afterschool sports?" What potential problem is his professor is trying to point out?
   (A) The possibility of a confounding variable
   (B) The low power of a test with small sample sizes
   (C) The lack of blinding
   (D) The unequal sample sizes
   (E) The lack of a control group

2. Four statistics are being considered for estimating a population characteristic. The statistics are as follows. Which of these statistics would be the best one to use?

   Statistic 1: unbiased with a standard deviation of 0.03

   Statistic 2: biased with a standard deviation of 0.03

   Statistic 3: biased with a standard deviation of 0.5

   Statistic 4: unbiased with a standard deviation of 1.3
   (A) Statistic 1
   (B) Statistic 2
   (C) Statistic 3
   (D) Statistic 4
   (E) Either Statistic 1 or 4 would be a good choice.

3. When determining which students will represent their high school in a local competition, the principal selected two students at random from a list of all freshmen at the school, two students at random from all sophomores, two students at random from all juniors and two students at random from all seniors. This is an example of
   (A) Simple random sampling
   (B) Cluster sampling
   (C) Systematic sampling
   (D) Stratified sampling
   (E) Convenience sampling

4. A security watch group insists that the least secure area of the United States is its ports. To justify this claim, the group surveyed members of the dockworkers' unions in various cities to ask whether or not they thought a terrorist shipment would be intercepted using current inspection procedures. Of the 457 dockworkers surveyed, only 114 felt confident that a shipment would be intercepted. Which of the following represents a 95% confidence interval for the true proportion of dockworkers that think that a terrorist shipment would be intercepted? Assume all conditions for inference are met.
   (A) (0.17, 0.33)
   (B) (0.25, 0.25)
   (C) (0.19, 0.31)
   (D) (0.23, 0.27)
   (E) (0.21, 0.29)

5. It is sometimes stated that the American judicial system is built on the idea that it is better to let 100 guilty men go free than to lock up one innocent man. If it is assumed from the saying "presumed innocent" that the null hypothesis of a criminal trial is that the accused did not commit the crime, which type of error is represented in the two situations that began this question?

   Situation 1: A guilty man is found innocent.

   Situation 2: An innocent man is convicted.
   (A) Both represent Type I error.
   (B) Both represent Type II error.
   (C) Situation 1 represents Type I error, Situation 2 represents Type II error.
   (D) Situation 1 represents Type II error, Situation 2 represents Type I error.
   (E) Both represent both types of error.

6. Herman has applied for three jobs. He believes that the probability that he gets a job offer is 0.20 for each of the three jobs and that whether or not he gets an offer for one of the jobs is independent of whether or not he gets an offer for either of the other two jobs. What is the probability that Herman gets at least one job offer?
   (A) 0.008
   (B) 0.488
   (C) 0.512
   (D) 0.600
   (E) 0.800

7. A researcher focusing on Native American studies wants to determine the current attitude of Native Americans toward the U.S. government. The researcher creates a survey of five statements that respondents can mark with a number 1 to 5 indicating how strongly they agree or disagree with each statement. Some of these sampling methods described below would introduce the potential for bias. Which of the following sampling methods would produce potential selection bias within this sample?
   (A) The researcher posts his survey to a popular Native American website and allows any Native American to take the survey.
   (B) Federal government employees administer the survey on reservations while wearing badges that are fully visible to the respondents.
   (C) All members from the three largest tribes still existing in America are given the survey.
   (D) The researcher accesses a list of all of the Native Americans living in the United States from the U.S. Census department and randomly selects 100 people from that list to take the survey.
   (E) The survey is given to all Americans.

8. While attending his 10-year high school reunion, Chester ran into his old friend Gary who immediately began talking about the new job he landed in New York City. Even though Gary and Chester both became accountants, Gary makes more money. Gary said his salary was $100,000 and Chester felt embarrassed by his salary of $80,000. Chester's wife, a statistician, tells Chester that he is doing better compared to the people in his town than Gary is compared to the people in New York. She did some research and found that the average salary for an accountant in New York was $80,000 with a standard deviation of $8,000 while the average salary for an accountant in Chester's home town was $60,000 with a standard deviation of $5,000. What are the associated z-scores for Chester and Gary?
   (A) Chester's z-score = 1.25, Gary's z-score = 4
   (B) Chester's z-score = 2.5, Gary's z-score = 4
   (C) Chester's z-score = 4, Gary's z-score = 4
   (D) Chester's z-score = 1.25, Gary's z-score = 2.5
   (E) Chester's z-score = 4, Gary's z-score = 2.5

GO ON TO NEXT PAGE

9. Thomas has $1,000 that he wants to invest in a mutual fund. After some research, he has narrowed down his choices to one of three mutual funds. He plans to hold on to the fund for five years, and his research gives him the following probabilities and payouts based on his $1,000 investment five years later.

Payout:	500	1000	2000
Fund X	0.5	0	0.5
Fund Y	0.33	0.33	0.34
Fund Z	0.25	0.5	0.25

Order the funds from highest expected value to lowest expected value.
(A) Fund X, Fund Y, Fund Z
(B) Fund Y, Fund Z, Fund X
(C) Fund Z, Fund X, Fund Y
(D) Fund Y, Fund X, Fund Z
(E) Fund X, Fund Z, Fund Y

10. The distribution of the weights of fish in a lake is approximately normal with a mean of 2 pounds. It is known that 15% of the fish in the lake are larger than 3 pounds. What is the standard deviation of the weights of fish in the lake?
(A) 0.15
(B) 0.67
(C) 0.85
(D) 0.96
(E) 1.00

Questions 11–12 refer to the following information:

The State of Virginia wants to determine how many more people would use the Chesapeake Bay Bridge if the price were lowered from $12 to $10 with a valid Virginia ID. At first it was suggested that the Department of Motor Vehicles survey a random sample of people in the state if they had used the bridge in the past and how likely they would be to use it in the future should the rate remain the same and should the rate decrease. But objections were raised that a majority of Virginians do not live close enough to the bridge to be likely to use the bridge regardless of the price. It was then suggested that the survey be conducted at the tollbooth to the bridge. Again, there were objections. This time, the complaint was that you would not reach those who had decided not to use the bridge. Finally, someone suggested that the 10 counties closest to the bridge be identified and the survey be conducted by selecting a random sample of drivers in these counties. Everyone agreed that this was the preferable method to use in order to gauge increased traffic that would be generated by a reduction in rate.

11. For the final sampling method used, what is the population, and what is the sample?
    (A) Sample: All drivers in Virginia, Population: All drivers who consider using the bridge
    (B) Sample: All drivers who use the Chesapeake Bay Bridge, Population: All drivers in Virginia
    (C) Sample: Selected drivers in the counties closest to the bridge, Population: All drivers in the counties closest to the bridge
    (D) Sample: Selected drivers in the counties closest to the bridge, Population: All drivers in Virginia
    (E) Sample: All drivers who do not currently use the bridge, Population: All drivers in Virginia

12. In switching from the first sampling method where people were randomly chosen from all drivers in Virginia to the final sampling method, the state researchers were attempting to address the problem of people who live far from the bridge not using it. In this circumstance, what is the best description of how proximity to the bridge impacts this study?
    (A) It creates nonresponse bias.
    (B) It is a variable that could influence the response.
    (C) It defines the sampling frame.
    (D) It creates outliers.
    (E) It is used for clustering.

13. To illustrate the danger of using a regression equation to make predictions that are outside the range of the data, an AP® Statistics teacher used data on $x =$ year and $y =$ median house price for years from 1997 to 2007 to fit a least-squares regression line. During this time period, the median price increased from each year to the next. The line was then used to predict median house price for the years 2008, 2009, 2010, and 2011. During this time period, however, housing prices declined significantly. Which of the following best describes how the predicted median prices compare to the actual median prices for 2008, 2009, 2010, and 2011?
    (A) Some of the predictions would be greater than the actual median price and some would be less than the actual median price.
    (B) The predictions would tend to be less than the actual values and would be closer to the actual value in 2011 than 2008.
    (C) The predictions would tend to be less than the actual values and would be closer to the actual value in 2008 than 2011.
    (D) The predictions would tend to be greater than the actual values and would be closer to the actual value in 2011 than 2008.
    (E) The predictions would tend to be greater than the actual values and would be closer to the actual value in 2008 than 2011.

14. Environmental scientists enlisted to help with a beach erosion problem in a coastal community studied the accumulation of sand along the shoreline. They took measurements from a sample of randomly selected sand dunes, recording the distance from the top of the dune to the highest point of water at high tide. One month later they come back to the same locations and measure again. The following table summarizes the measurements at each of the two times.

	n	$\bar{x}$	s
June measurement	135	14.2	1.8
July measurement	135	13.8	2.1
Difference (June – July)	135	0.4	0.2

Using the null hypothesis that there is no difference between mean distance in June and mean distance in July, what is the value of the t test statistic associated with a test to determine if the mean distance from dune to ocean was smaller in July than it was in June? Assume all conditions for inference are met.

(A) $t = 0.10$
(B) $t = 1.68$
(C) $t = 2.00$
(D) $t = 17.74$
(E) $t = 23.24$

15. In a population of cigarette smokers, 26% quit smoking in 2005. Of those who quit, 41% have not had a single cigarette in the five years after quitting. If a person is selected at random from the original population of cigarette smokers, what is the probability that the selected person quit smoking in 2005 and did not have a single cigarette in the 5 years after quitting?

(A) 0.88
(B) 0.83
(C) 0.43
(D) 0.17
(E) 0.11

16. Researchers at a prestigious medical school were asked how they could be sure that their own biases toward the drug they were studying were not influencing their observations of patient behavior. The researchers responded that their study had been structured in a way that neither the patients nor the people measuring the response knew who was being given the drug and who was being given a placebo. What term describes this aspect of the study?

(A) Replication
(B) Direct control
(C) Blocking
(D) Single blind
(E) Double blind

17. An apple producer owns a large orchard that is pesticide free. The producer contends that 98.2% of the apples will be worm free after ripening on the tree. If the company's claim is true, what is the expected number of worm-infested apples in a random sample of 25,000 apples from the pesticide free orchard?
    (A) 24,550
    (B) 24,500
    (C) 24,450
    (D) 550
    (E) 450

18. A study was done to estimate the amount of time spent exercising by residents of a nursing home. Investigators recorded the number of minutes per week spent exercising by each of 26 randomly selected residents. The sample had a mean of 42 minutes and a standard deviation of 15 minutes. Assuming exercise times have a distribution that is approximately normal, which of the following is a 95% confidence interval for the mean time spent exercising per week by the nursing home residents? Assume all conditions for inference are met.
    (A) (40, 44)
    (B) (36, 48)
    (C) (30, 54)
    (D) (39, 45)
    (E) (27, 57)

19. Wheelchairs have braking mechanisms that minimize speeds as they go down hills. In order to test how long it takes different wheelchairs to come to a complete stop after going down a hill, a consumer group tests 20 different wheelchair models on a ramp at their facility. The testers roll down the ramp and then apply the brake when they reach a white line at the base of the ramp. The distance from the white line to where the wheelchair came to a complete stop is measured and recorded. A relative frequency histogram of the stopping times is shown below.

    What proportion of wheelchairs tested were able to stop in 3.5 feet or less?
    (A) 0.05
    (B) 0.15
    (C) 0.40
    (D) 0.60
    (E) 0.70

GO ON TO NEXT PAGE

20. The air conditioner in Bob's apartment is broken. This is the third time it has malfunctioned since Bob moved in 6 months ago. After speaking with his neighbors, Bob realized that the air conditioning is a consistent problem throughout his apartment complex. Bob wants to collect data to determine if there is evidence that the mean time between malfunctions is less than 90 days. He plans to test a null hypothesis that says the mean time between malfunctions is equal to 90 days against the alternative hypothesis that says that the mean time between malfunctions is less than 90. Which of the following represents the conclusion that there insufficient evidence to conclude that the mean time between malfunctions is less than 90 days?
    (A) Reject H_0
    (B) Fail to reject H_0
    (C) Reject H_a
    (D) Fail to reject H_a
    (E) Accept H_a

21. Data on the number of pounds of tuna caught by selected fisheries has been recorded each year. For a particular fishery, the sampling distribution of the sample mean pounds of tuna for random samples of 9 years has a mean of 350 and a standard deviation of 63. What are the mean and standard deviation of the population?
    (A) $\mu = 117, \sigma = 21$
    (B) $\mu = 350, \sigma = 21$
    (C) $\mu = 350, \sigma = 63$
    (D) $\mu = 350, \sigma = 189$
    (E) $\mu = 3{,}150\ \sigma = 567$

22. In trying to describe the weight of dinosaurs to her fifth-grade class, Mrs. Crofton decides to put dinosaur weights in terms the children can understand. She researches weights of Tryannosaurs and finds out that the weights were approximately normally distributed with a mean of 7.5 tons and a standard deviation of 0.5 tons. Which of the following is a correct statement about Tryannosaur weights?
    (A) About 70% of the Tryannosaurs were between 4.45 and 4.95 tons.
    (B) About that 70% of the Tryannosaurs were between 6.5 and 8.5 tons.
    (C) About 70% of the Tryannosaurs were between 7.0 and 7.5 tons.
    (D) About 70% of the Tryannosaurs were between 7.0 and 8.0 tons.
    (E) About 70% of the Tryannosaurs were between 7.5 and 8.0 tons.

23. Below is a relative frequency distribution for the number of cars per household from a study of 50 families from suburban Boston.

Number of Cars	Frequency	Relative Frequency
0	8	0.16
1	17	0.34
2	15	0.30
3	7	0.14
4 or more	3	0.06

    According to the table, what percentage of families in this study had more than two cars?
    (A) 6
    (B) 14
    (C) 20
    (D) 30
    (E) 80

24. Gym of the Jungle is a fitness center focusing on unique class offerings beyond the customary classes offered at rival gyms. The schedule of classes and their registration numbers are given in the chart below:

	1 PM	6 PM	9 PM	Total
Rope Swinging	14	32	12	58
Stump Jump	18	23	21	62
Saunastenics	12	17	15	44
Total	44	72	48	164

What is the probability that someone registered to take a class at 6 PM is in Saunastenics?
(A) 0.104
(B) 0.170
(C) 0.236
(D) 0.386
(E) 0.439

25. Meat Market sandwich shop offers five different kinds of bread, four different kinds of meat, and seven different sauces on their sandwiches. Each sandwich contains one bread, one sauce, and two different meats. How many different sandwiches are possible?
(A) 16
(B) 19
(C) 140
(D) 420
(E) 560

26. A church choir wants to attract more members between the ages of 16 and 30. The current choir members believe that early Sunday morning practices may be a problem for this group, so they decided to take a simple random sample of 30 church members in the targeted age group to determine a convenient time to hold practices. Each person in the sample was sent a survey. Ten people responded to the survey, and half of the responses identified Friday nights as their best practice time. If the choir used this information to make a decision to change the practice time to Friday nights, which type of bias might be impacting their decision?
(A) Selection bias
(B) Measurement or response bias
(C) Nonresponse bias
(D) Sampling frame bias
(E) Replacement bias

GO ON TO NEXT PAGE

27. A video game manufacturer noticed that most of its competitors set the retail price of their new games at $60 and then wait a number of months before lowering the prices. The marketing department feels this might not be the best price for maximum profit. They are considering a price of $50 for their next new game. The company knows that most new purchases are made by people who have previously purchased a game from the company. With the $60 price for new games, about 50% of those who have made a previous purchase also buy a new game when it is released with a price of $60. The company believes that a price of $50 would result in a higher profit if more than 5% of those who have made a previous purchase would buy the new game with a $50 price but not with a $60 price. The company plans to survey a large random sample selected from those who have made a previous purchase to see what proportion would purchase with a $50 price but not with a $60 price. What hypotheses should the company test?

(A) $H_0: \mu = 50$; $H_a: \mu \neq 50$
(B) $H_0: p = 0.50$; $H_a: p > 0.50$
(C) $H_0: p = 0.05$; $H_a: p > 0.05$
(D) $H_0: p = 50$; $H_a: p = 60$
(E) $H_0: \mu = 50$; $H_a: \mu > 50$

28. As part of an adult education statistics class, the professor asked the students in each of her two sections to report their ages. She then constructed a back-to-back stem-and-leaf display to compare the two sections. This display is reproduced below:

Section 1		Section 2
9	1	7 9
9 9 7 6 2 2 2	2	3 5 8 9
8 6 3 3 1	3	0 0 0 2 3 3 7 8
6 5 2	4	2 7 7
9 3	5	9

If the two sections were combined into a single data set, what is the mode of this data set?
(A) 0
(B) 9
(C) 29
(D) 30
(E) 33

29. A game is played in which two players (player A and player B) each toss a fair coin. If both tosses result in heads or both tosses result in tails, the players will toss again. If the tosses result in one head and one tail, the player whose toss was the head is the winner. What is the probability that each player must toss exactly three times before a winner is declared and that player A is the winner?

(A) $\dfrac{1}{4}$

(B) $\dfrac{1}{2}$

(C) $\left(\dfrac{1}{2}\right)^3$

(D) $\left(\dfrac{1}{2}\right)^2 \left(\dfrac{1}{4}\right)$

(E) $\left(\dfrac{1}{4}\right)^3$

30. Below is one possibility for a standard BINGO card.

B	I	N	G	O
3	28	32	56	66
15	18	45	48	67
12	22	FREE	51	70
8	20	41	53	73
9	17	38	47	68

In the game of BINGO, there are 75 balls numbered 1–75 placed in a cylinder and selected at random. What is the probability that the first ball selected matches one of the numbers on the bingo card above?
(A) 0.66
(B) 0.50
(C) 0.33
(D) 0.32
(E) 0.07

31. Which of the scatter diagrams below represents a negative linear relationship between two variables?

(A)

(B)

(C)

(D)

(E)

32. After being randomly selected for a prize at a concert, you are told that you can choose between two options. Option one is that you take a $25 gift card. Option two is that you draw a slip of paper from a hat that has two slips, one that says zero and one that says 100. If you get one of the zeros, you get nothing. If you get the 100, then you get a $100 gift card. Which of the following best compares the expected value and standard deviation of the amount won for the two options?
    (A) Option one has a larger expected value and larger standard deviation than option two.
    (B) Option one has a larger expected value and smaller standard deviation than option two.
    (C) Option one has a smaller expected value and smaller standard deviation than option two.
    (D) Option one has a smaller expected value and larger standard deviation than option two.
    (E) They both have equal expected values and standard deviations.

33. A shoe company wants to determine the effect of factory layoffs on production. After compiling data, they determine that a regression line that relates number of employees to factory shoe output is a good fit. The equation of the least-squares regression line is $\hat{y} = 3000 + 140x$, where $\hat{y}$ is the predicted number of shoes produced in a day and x is the number of employees working at the factory. If the company is considering firing 10 employees, how much does the regression line predict that shoe output would drop?
    (A) 140 shoes
    (B) 700 shoes
    (C) 1,400 shoes
    (D) 3,000 shoes
    (E) 30,000 shoes

34. A vaccine has been developed that is designed to reduce the chance of catching a cold during the winter months. In an experiment to evaluate the effectiveness of this vaccine, 500 volunteers were randomly assigned to one of two groups. Those in one group received the vaccine and those in the other group received an injection with no active ingredients. The no active ingredient injection is an example of
    (A) blinding.
    (B) a confounding variable.
    (C) a blocking factor.
    (D) a volunteer treatment.
    (E) a placebo.

35. Suppose that the number of dandelions in a one-acre grassland plot is approximately normally distributed with a mean of 750 and a standard deviation of 80. Approximately what percentage of one-acre grassland plots between 590 and 910 dandelions?
    (A) 50%
    (B) 68%
    (C) 75%
    (D) 95%
    (E) 99.7%

36. Danny's friend Joe claims that he is the best coin flipper in the history of coins. When Danny asks what he means, Joe says he can get heads flipping a coin 75% of the time. To prove his point, Joe flips a coin four times and gets three heads. Danny explains that this is not that unusual with only four tosses, but that if Joe were to continue to toss the coin a large number of times, the percentage of heads would get close to 50%. What statistical principle is Danny describing?
    (A) Central Limit Theorem
    (B) Law of Large Numbers
    (C) Law of Total Probability
    (D) Law of Small Numbers
    (E) Empirical Rule

37. At Studytown International Airport, customers have their choice of three airlines for both international and domestic travel. The table below lists the number of travelers on each airline on July 1, 2010.

Airline	International	Domestic	Total
Skyway	114	361	475
Avian Air	45	212	257
Patriot Air	0	845	845
Total	159	1418	1577

What is the probability that a randomly selected passenger traveling domestically from Studytown on the first of July would have flown on Patriot Air?
(A) 0.254
(B) 0.404
(C) 0.536
(D) 0.596
(E) 0.899

38. A printer company believes that its printers use less ink than a competitor's printer. To support this claim, the company plans to test 50 printers made by the company and 50 printers made by the competitor. Each printer will print the same page over and over and the number of pages printed before running out of ink will be recorded. The resulting data will be used to carry out a hypothesis test to determine if there is evidence that the mean number of pages printed before running out of ink differs for the two brands of printers. They plan to use a significance level of 0.05. Which of the following would increase the power of the test?
   I. Use 25 printers of each brand instead of 50.
   II. Use 100 printers of each brand instead of 50.
   III. Use a significance level of 0.01 instead of 0.05.
   IV. Use a significance level of 0.10 instead of 0.05.

(A) II only
(B) I and III only
(C) I and IV only
(D) II and III only
(E) II and IV only

39. After showing up late for work again, Lafayette is called into his boss's office. The boss presents him with a cumulative relative frequency distribution of Lafayette's arrival times. In each case it is based on the time that the system clocked him in. The system records the time rounded to the next 15-minute interval, so if Lafayette clocked in at 8:51 it would record his arrival as 9:00. The chart is displayed below:

Time of Day	Cumulative Relative Frequency
8:45	0.04
9:00	0.15
9:15	0.27
9:30	0.61
9:45	0.83
10:00	1

According to the chart, what time is Lafayette most likely to clock into work?
(A) 8:46 to 9:00
(B) 9:01 to 9:15
(C) 9:16 to 9:30
(D) 9:31 to 9:45
(E) 9:46 to 10:00

40. In 2010, the proportion of all cars on the Tony T's Toyotas lot that were hybrids was 0.08. Suppose that a new government program significantly reduced the cost of production on these vehicles. In 2011, the lot at Tony T's has 300 vehicles and 32 of them are hybrids. In trying to establish whether or not the government program was effective in increasing the availability of hybrid vehicles, statisticians are asked to use the sample on Tony's lot to determine if this program has led to a statistically significant increase in the proportion of hybrids. Assuming that the conditions for inference are met, what is the z test statistic for the proper test?
(A) 0.11
(B) 0.27
(C) 0.68
(D) 1.70
(E) 5.10

STOP

END OF SECTION I

IF YOU FINISH BEFORE TIME IS CALLED, YOU MAY CHECK YOUR WORK ON THIS SECTION. DO NOT GO ON TO SECTION II UNTIL YOU ARE TOLD TO DO SO.

Section II: Free-Response Questions

Part A
Questions 1–5
Spend about 65 minutes on this part of the exam
Percent of Section II grade—75

DIRECTIONS: Show all your work. Clearly indicate the methods you use, as you will be graded on the correctness of the methods as well as the accuracy of your results and explanation.

1. Rolling Hills Country Club wants to hold a charity golf tournament to benefit a cancer foundation. Thirty-two players will be divided into eight teams of four that will then compete to win prizes. The tournament director would like to create the teams of four in a way that doesn't tend to favor any one team.

    (a) One possibility for creating teams is to let people that usually play together during the year play together on the same team for the tournament. Is this a good idea? Explain why or why not.

    (b) Two other possibilities for creating teams are

    Method 1 (random assignment): Assign the 32 golfers to the eight teams at random.

    Method 2: Order the golfers by ability using their average score for the past 12 months. Create four groups of golfers, with the first group consisting of the golfers ranked 1–8 (the eight best golfers), the second group consisting of the golfers ranked 9–16, the third group consisting of the golfers ranked 17–24, and the fourth group consisting of the golfers ranked 25–32 (the eight worst golfers). Form the one team of four by selecting one golfer at random from each of the four groups. Form the second team by selecting one golfer at random from the remaining golfers in each group, and so on.

    Which of these two methods is more likely to create teams that are comparable in terms of ability? Explain your reasoning.

    (c) Describe how you would use a table of random numbers or a random number generator to create the teams using the method you selected in part (b).

GO ON TO NEXT PAGE

2. A spinner at a carnival is divided into 20 segments of equal size, as shown below.

Ten of the segments are labeled "0", five are labeled "$1", three are labeled "$2", and two are labeled "$5". If the spinner is fair, each of the 20 segments is equally likely to be the one that comes to rest at the top of the wheel on any given spin. In order to decide if there is evidence that the spinner is not fair, an investigator records the outcomes of 500 spins, resulting in the data summarized in the following table:

Outcome	0	$1	$2	$5
Frequency	280	140	55	25

Do these data provide convincing evidence that the spinner is not fair?

3. In order to assess the effect of boxing on hearing loss, researchers conducted a study using a large number of retired boxers over age 50 and a large number of adults over 50 who had never boxed. Five distinct tones used in hearing tests were played and the number of these tones that a person was able to hear was recorded. These data were used to obtain the approximate probability distribution for the number of tones heard for boxers and for non-boxers.

Retired Boxers

Tones heard	0	1	2	3	4	5
Probability	0.10	0.20	0.20	0.25	0.15	0.10

Non-boxers

Tones heard	0	1	2	3	4	5
Probability	0.05	0.10	0.10	0.25	0.20	0.30

(a) Based on these probability distributions, what is the expected value of the number of tones heard for retired boxers over 50?

(b) Suppose that a randomly selected retired boxer identifies two tones and a randomly selected non-boxer identifies four. The difference (retired boxer − nonboxer) in the scores is −2. List all combinations of possible scores for a retired boxer and a non-boxer that will produce a difference of −2.

(c) Find the probability that the difference in the scores for a randomly selected boxer and a randomly selected non-boxer (retired boxer – boxer) is –2.
(d) Based on this hearing test, 30% of retired boxers over 50 and 15% of non-boxers over 50 were classified as having severe hearing loss. How many of the five tones would someone need to hear in order to be classified as not having severe hearing loss?

4. The television game show "Jeopardy" has contestants compete for prize money by answering bits of trivia in the form of a question. After many years on TV with the same dollar values for each question, "Jeopardy" producers decided to double the dollar value of each question. Below are comparative boxplots of the winning contestant's prize money before and after the change in dollar values:

(a) In a few sentences, describe the similarities and differences in the distributions of amount won before and after the change.
(b) Did doubling the dollar value of questions tend to result in greater amounts won? Provide a justification based on the given boxplots.
(c) If doubling the dollar value of the questions tended to produce prize amounts that were twice as large as before the dollar values were doubled, what could you have expected the "after" boxplot to like? Answer by sketching in an "after" boxplot in the figure below.

GO ON TO NEXT PAGE

5. After Mrs. Simmons' middle school students learned that Native Americans used to wake themselves for battle by drinking a lot of water the night before their battle, they wanted to conduct an experiment to see if this really works. Eighty students who volunteered to be a part of the experiment and who received parental approval to participate were the subjects in the experiment. Subjects were assigned at random to one of two treatment groups. Those assigned to the "water" treatment drank 24 ounces of water between 7:30 and 8:00 p.m. Those assigned to the "no water" treatment group did not drink any water after 7:30 p.m. All subjects were instructed to go to bed at 9:00 p.m. and then to record the time when they first woke up. The next day, each subject computed the number of minutes of sleep before waking. The resulting data are summarized below.

Group	n	Mean	Standard deviation
Water	40	289	56
No water	40	406	53

Do the data in the table provide evidence that sleep time for the water treatment is shorter than for the no water treatment?

Section II
Part B
Question 6
Spend about 25 minutes on this part of the exam
Percent of Section II grade—25

DIRECTIONS: Show all your work. Clearly indicate the methods you use, as you will be graded on the correctness of the methods as well as the accuracy of your results and explanation.

6. A film executive believes that the days of the epic film are returning and that it is becoming more profitable to create longer movies. To investigate this theory, he recorded the length (in minutes) and the amount of money the movie made (domestic gross, in millions of dollars) for the 12 most profitable movies made between 2001 and 2005 and for the 12 most profitable movies made between 2006 and 2010. The resulting data are shown in the tables below:

2001–2005

Movie	Year	Domestic Gross (millions of dollars)	Length (minutes)
Shrek 2	2004	436	93
Spider-Man	2002	403	121
Star Wars Episode 3: Revenge of the Sith	2005	380	140
The Lord of the Rings: The Return of the King	2003	377	201
Spider-Man 2	2004	373	127
Passion of the Christ	2004	370	127
The Lord of the Rings: The Two Towers	2002	340	179
Finding Nemo	2003	339	100
Harry Potter and the Sorcerer's Stone	2001	317	152
The Lord of the Rings: The Fellowship of the Ring	2001	313	178
Star Wars Episode 2: Attack of the Clones	2002	310	142
The Pirates of the Caribbean: The Curse of the Black Pearl	2003	305	143

2006–2010

Movie	Year	Domestic Gross (millions of dollars)	Length (minutes)
Avatar	2009	754	162
The Dark Knight	2008	533	152
Pirates of the Caribbean: Dead Man's Chest	2006	423	151
Toy Story 3	2010	405	103
Transformers: Revenge of the Fallen	2009	402	150
Spider-Man 3	2007	336	139
Alice in Wonderland	2010	334	108
Shrek the Third	2007	320	93
Transformers	2007	318	144
Iron Man	2008	318	126
Indiana Jones and the Kingdom of the Crystal Skull	2008	317	122
Iron Man 2	2010	312	124

GO ON TO NEXT PAGE

(a) Construct two dotplots, one for 2001–2005 and one for 2006–2010, that would allow you to compare the length distributions of the top 12 movies in each time period.
(b) Based on the dotplots in part (a), write a few sentences comparing the two movie length distributions. Do the dotplots support the statement that top 12 movies tended to be longer for the time period 2006–2010 than for the time period 2001–2005?
(c) Below are a scatter diagram and linear regression output for each of the two time periods separately and for the data set that consists of all 24 films from 2001 to 2010 combined. Does there appear to be a relationship between domestic gross and length? Do you think the relationship between domestic gross and length is the same in each of the two time periods? Support your answer by providing an explanation based on the scatter diagrams and computer output.

All Years (2001–2010)

```
The regression equation is
Domestic Gross = 297 + 0.583 length

Predictor           Coef        SE Coef        T           P
Constant            296.8       103.4          2.87        0.009
Length              0.5834      0.7428         0.79        0.441

S = 97.7172         R-Sq = 2.7%        R-Sq(adj) = 0.0%
```

2001–2005

```
The regression equation is
Domestic Gross 2001-2005 = 431 - 0.535 Length
2001-2005

Predictor              Coef    SE Coef          T         P
Constant             431.17      53.76       8.02     0.000
Length 2001-2005    -0.5350     0.3703      -1.44     0.179


S = 39.3706         R-Sq = 17.3%      R-Sq(adj) = 9.0%
```

Scatterplot of Domestic Gross 2006–2010 vs Length 2006–2010

```
The regression equation is
Domestic Gross 2006-2010 = - 69 + 3.56 Length 2006-
2010

Predictor              Coef    SE Coef          T         P
Constant              -69.0      199.1      -0.35     0.736
Length 2006-2010      3.558      1.499       2.37     0.039


S = 109.203         R-Sq = 36.0%      R-Sq(adj) = 29.6%
```

(d) Would you recommend using any of the three regression models in part (c) to predict the domestic gross for a new movie coming out this year that was 215 minutes long? If so, which model and why? If not, explain why not.

END OF EXAMINATION

Answers to Practice Test 2

Multiple-Choice Answers

Using the table below, score your test.

Determine how many questions you answered correctly and how many you answered incorrectly. You will find explanations of the answers on the following pages.

1. A	9. A	17. E	25. D	33. C
2. A	10. D	18. B	26. C	34. E
3. D	11. C	19. D	27. C	35. D
4. E	12. B	20. B	28. E	36. B
5. D	13. E	21. D	29. D	37. D
6. B	14. E	22. D	30. D	38. E
7. C	15. E	23. C	31. D	39. C
8. E	16. E	24. C	32. C	40. D

Answers and Explanations

Multiple-Choice Answers

1. **(A)** Because John did not randomly assign days to the early bus and late bus, there is a potential for a confounding variable. While he might conclude that there is an association, he cannot conclude that the lateness was the cause of his hunger; the sports may have contributed to why he was hungrier on the days he takes the late bus (*Statistics: Learning from Data*, AP Edition, 1st ed. pages 24–38 / 2nd ed. pages 23–38).

2. **(A)** When you have a choice between unbiased statistics, the best statistic is the one with the smallest standard deviation (*Statistics: Learning from Data*, AP Edition, 1st ed. pages 135–140 and 144–147 / 2nd ed. pages 142–147 and 151–156).

3. **(D)** Because the population of students was divided into four subgroups and a random sample was selected from each subgroup, this is an example of stratified sampling (*Statistics: Learning from Data*, AP Edition, 1st ed. pages 13–21 / 2nd ed. pages 9–20).

4. **(E)** In order to construct the 95% confidence interval, you must first determine the sample proportion. $\hat{p} = \dfrac{114}{457} = .25$. Using the large sample confidence interval method with a z critical value of 1.96 for a 95% confidence level, you get $0.25 \pm 1.96\sqrt{\dfrac{0.25(1-0.25)}{457}} = (0.21, 0.29)$ (*Statistics: Learning from Data*, AP Edition, 1st ed. pages 460–465 and 467–477 and 480–481 / 2nd ed. pages 475–480 and 482–493 and 497–498).

5. **(D)** Type I error occurs when you reject the null hypothesis, even though the null hypothesis is actually true. If the null hypothesis is that a man is innocent, then in this case we reject that hypothesis and find him guilty even though he was actually innocent. Situation 2 represents this Type I error. Type II error occurs when you fail to reject the null hypothesis even though it is false. If the null hypothesis is that a man is innocent, failing to reject this hypothesis means that you continue to believe he's innocent. If you have made a Type II error, then you continue to believe the man is innocent even though he is actually guilty, the situation described in situation 1 (*Statistics: Learning from Data*, AP Edition, 1st ed. 1st ed. pages 502–505 / 2nd ed. pages 516–520).

6. **(B)** In order to determine the probability that Herman gets at least one job offer, the best option is to first look at the probability that he does not get any offers and then subtract that from 1. For each of his new applications, there is a probability of 0.80 that he does not get the job. Taking into account that he applied for 3 jobs, the probability that he does not get an offer from any of the three is $(0.8)(0.8)(0.8) = 0.512$. The probability of at least one offer is $1 - 512 = 0.468$ (*Statistics: Learning from Data*, AP Edition, 1st ed. pages 273–276 and 278–287 / 2nd ed. pages 285–289 and 291–301).

7. **(C)** By limiting the survey to only the three largest tribes, you systematically exclude all the remaining tribes. This is selection bias. Answer A is an example of nonresponse bias. Answer B is an example of measurement or response bias. Answer D would be a viable sampling method. Answer E includes respondents who are not in the desired population (*Statistics: Learning from Data*, AP Edition, 1st ed. pages 13–21 / 2nd ed. pages 9–20).

8. **(E)** To calculate the z-scores, we use the formula $z = \dfrac{x - \mu}{\sigma}$. Chester's z-score is $z = \dfrac{80000 - 60000}{5000} = 4$. Gary's z-score is $z = \dfrac{100000 - 80000}{8000} = 2.5$ (*Statistics: Learning from Data*, AP Edition, 1st ed. pages 160–162 / 2nd ed. pages 170–173).

9. **(A)** To find expected value, you multiply payout by probability and then add. E(Fund X) = 0.5(500) + 0.5(2,000) = 1,250. E(Fund Y) = 0.33(500) + 0.33(1,000) + 0.34(2,000) = 1175. E(Fund Z) = 0.25(500) + 0.50(1,000) + 0.25(2,000) = 1125. The order from highest to lowest expected value is therefore X, Y, Z (*Statistics: Learning from Data*, AP Edition, 1st ed. pages 352–361 / 2nd ed. pages 367–378).

10. **(D)** For a standard normal distribution, about 15% of the area is to the right of 1.04. This means that 3 pounds must be 1.04 standard deviations above the mean. Solving $1.04\sigma = 1$ gives $\sigma = 0.96$ (*Statistics: Learning from Data*, AP Edition, 1st ed. pages 373–387 and 395–398 / 2nd ed. pages 380–394 and 412–415).

11. **(C)** The sample was selected from all drivers in the counties closest to the bridge, so this is the population. The sample is those drivers in these counties that are actually selected for the survey (*Statistics: Learning from Data*, AP Edition, 1st ed. pages 13–21 / 2nd ed. pages 9–20).

12. **(B)** Proximity to the bridge could influence the response since those far from the bridge will probably not use the bridge no matter what the cost is (*Statistics: Learning from Data*, AP Edition, 1st ed. pages 13–21 / 2nd ed. pages 9–20).

13. **(E)** Because prices were increasing from 1997 to 2007, the slope of the regression line will be positive. This means the predicted value will increase each year. Because prices actually declined from 2008 to 2011, the predictions would be too large and the prediction would be farther from the actual value in 2011 than in 2008 (*Statistics: Learning from Data*, AP Edition, 1st ed. pages 198–206 / 2nd ed. pages 209–219).

14. **(E)** Because the samples are paired, the paired t test would be used. The value of the test statistic is $t = \dfrac{\bar{x}_d - 0}{\dfrac{s_d}{\sqrt{n}}} = \dfrac{0.4}{\dfrac{0.2}{\sqrt{135}}} = 23.24$ (*Statistics: Learning from Data*, AP Edition, 1st ed. pages 633–639, 649–651, 672–674, and 679–682 / 2nd ed. pages 642–650).

15. **(E)** This question asks for P(quits smoking and no cigarette for five years). This probability can be computed as P(quits smoking and no cigarette for five years) = P(no cigarette for five years | quits smoking) P(quits smoking) = (0.41)(0.26) (*Statistics: Learning from Data*, AP Edition, 1st ed. pages 290–299 / 2nd ed. pages 304–314).

16. **(E)** Because neither the people measuring the response nor the patients know who is in the drug group and who is in the placebo group, the study is double blind (*Statistics: Learning from Data*, AP Edition, 1st ed. pages 24–38 / 2nd ed. pages 23–38).

17. **(E)** In order to find the number of worm-infested apples, you take the percentage of worm-free apples and multiply it by the number of apples in the sample. 25,000(0.982) = 24,550. Subtract this number from the total apples and you get 25,000 − 24,550 = 450 (*Statistics: Learning from Data*, AP Edition, 1st ed. pages 339–343 / 2nd ed. pages 353–357).

18. **(B)** To calculate the *t* confidence interval, you use the *t* critical value of 2.06 for a 95% $42 \pm 2.06\left(\frac{15}{\sqrt{26}}\right) = (36, 48)$ confidence interval. (*Statistics: Learning from Data*, AP Edition, 1st ed. pages 578–588 / 2nd ed. pages 600–612).

19. **(D)** To find the proportion of wheelchairs that stop within 3.5 feet, add together the relative frequencies corresponding to stopping distances in the first three bins of the histogram. 0.05 + 0.15 + 0.40 = 0.60 (*Statistics: Learning from Data*, AP Edition, 1st ed. pages 68–96 / 2nd ed. pages 70–93).

20. **(B)** If statistical analysis shows that the air conditioners are lasting 90 days or more before needing to be serviced, then the null hypothesis has not been rejected. We therefore fail to reject the null hypothesis (*Statistics: Learning from Data*, AP Edition, 1st ed. pages 511–513 / 2nd ed. pages 526–529).

21. **(D)** The population mean is the same as the mean of the sampling distribution of $\bar{x}$. The standard deviation of the sampling distribution of $\bar{x}$ is $\frac{\sigma}{\sqrt{n}}$ so σ = (standard deviation of sampling distribution) $(\sqrt{n}) = (63)(\sqrt{9}) = 189$ (*Statistics: Learning from Data*, AP Edition, 1st ed. pages 568–576 / 2nd ed. pages 590–598).

22. **(D)** Because dinosaur weights are approximately normally distributed, we can use the Empirical Rule. This says that approximately 68% (which is about 70%) of the weights will be within one standard deviation of the mean weight (*Statistics: Learning from Data*, AP Edition, 1st ed. pages 160–162 / 2nd ed. pages 170–173).

23. **(C)** The families that have more than two cars are the ones that have been listed as either having three cars or four or more cars. 0.14 + 0.06 = 0.20. Converting this decimal to a percentage gives you a final answer of 20% (*Statistics: Learning from Data*, AP Edition, 1st ed. pages 273–276 and 278–287 / 2nd ed. pages 285–289 and 291–301).

24. **(C)** There are 72 total people registered for 6 PM classes. Of those 72, 17 are in Saunastenics. $\frac{17}{72} = 0.236$ (*Statistics: Learning from Data*, AP Edition, 1st ed. pages 267–276 / 2nd ed. pages 280–289).

25. **(D)** The total number of possible sandwiches can be found by multiplying. (5)(7)(4)(3) = 420 (*Statistics: Learning from Data*, AP Edition, 1st ed. pages 273–276 and 278–287 / 2nd ed. pages 285–289 and 291–301).

26. **(C)** Because the choir only received 10 responses to the 30 surveys that were sent out, the sample may differ from the corresponding population because the 20 that did not respond may differ in some profound way that is related to time to hold practice. Data were not obtained from all the individuals in the simple random sample, thus this is an example of nonresponse bias (*Statistics: Learning from Data*, AP Edition, 1st ed. pages 13–21 / 2nd ed. pages 9–20).

27. **(C)** With p denoting the proportion of previous purchasers who would buy the new game with a price of $50 but not with a price of $60, the question of interest is whether $p > 0.05$ (*Statistics: Learning from Data*, AP Edition, 1st ed. pages 496–500 / 2nd ed. pages 510–515).

28. **(E)** The mode is the most frequently occurring number. In this case, the number 33 occurs twice in each class for a total of four times between the two classes (*Statistics: Learning from Data*, AP Edition, 1st ed. pages 133–135 and 143 / 2nd ed. pages 140–142 and 150–151).

29. **(D)** For this outcome to occur, we must have two tosses where both players toss heads or both players toss tails followed by a toss where player A tosses a head and player B tosses a tail. The probability of HH or TT is $\frac{1}{2}$ and the probability of HT is $\frac{1}{4}$, so the probability of interest is $\left(\frac{1}{2}\right)^2\left(\frac{1}{4}\right)$ (*Statistics: Learning from Data*, AP Edition, 1st ed. pages 273–276 and 278–287 / 2nd ed. pages 285–289 and 291–301).

30. **(D)** In order to calculate the probability of one of the numbers being selected, you take the total number of numbers on the card (24 because you do not count the free space) and divide it by the total number of balls that could be selected. $\frac{24}{75} = 0.32$ (*Statistics: Learning from Data*, AP Edition, 1st ed. pages 267–276 / 2nd ed. pages 280–289).

31. **(D)** This scatter diagram slopes down and to the right, and the pattern is linear. Answer choice C also shows a negative relationship, but it is curved rather than linear (*Statistics: Learning from Data*, AP Edition, 1st ed. pages 182–193 / 2nd ed. pages 192–204).

32. **(C)** There is only one possible outcome under option one, so expected value for option one is 25. For option two it is $0(2/3) + 100(1/3) = 33.3$. So, option one has a smaller expected value. The standard deviation of option one is equal to zero because the amount won is always 25. Option two has a standard deviation that is larger than 0 because there will be variability in the amount won. So, option one has a smaller standard deviation (*Statistics: Learning from Data*, AP Edition, 1st ed. pages 352–361 / 2nd ed. pages 367–378).

33. **(C)** By firing 10 employees, you would be making a change in x of -10. Multiplying this by the slope we get a change in output of $(140)(-10) = -1{,}400$. The regression line predicts that shoe production would fall by 1,400 shoes (*Statistics: Learning from Data*, AP Edition, 1st ed. pages 198–206 / 2nd ed. pages 209–219).

34. **(E)** Those in the no vaccine group still received an injection. This is an example of a placebo treatment (*Statistics: Learning from Data*, AP Edition, 1st ed. pages 24–38 / 2nd ed. pages 23–38).

35. **(D)** With a mean of 750, 590, and 910 are each 160 away from the mean. That is two times the standard deviation of 80. According to the Empirical Rule, approximately 95% of the observations are within two standard deviations of the mean (*Statistics: Learning from Data*, AP Edition, 1st ed. pages 160–162 / 2nd ed. pages 170–173).

36. **(B)** The law of large numbers states that as the number of repetitions of a chance experiment increases, the chance that the relative frequency of occurrence for an event will differ from the true probability of the event by more than any small number approaches zero. What this is saying that in the long run, the relative frequency will be very close to the true probability (*Statistics: Learning from Data*, AP Edition, 1st ed. pages 267–276 / 2nd ed. pages 280–289).

37. **(D)** To find the probability from this table, you need to find $P(\text{patriot} \mid \text{domestic})$. Look first at the total of the domestic category, and the table entry is 1,418. Then look for how many of those domestic travelers flew on Patriot Air. $\frac{845}{1418} = 0.596$ (*Statistics: Learning from Data*, AP Edition, 1st ed. pages 290–299 / 2nd ed. pages 304–314).

38. **(E)** Two ways to increase the power of a test are to increase the significance level of the test and to increase the sample size (*Statistics: Learning from Data*, AP Edition, 1st ed. pages 526–530 / 2nd ed. pages 543–547).

39. **(C)** To find the relative frequency for 9:00 from a cumulative relative frequency distribution, $0.15 - 0.04 = 0.11$. Similarly, for 9:15: $0.27 - 0.15 = 0.12$, for 9:30: $0.61 - 0.27 = 0.34$, for 9:45: $0.83 - 0.61 = 0.22$, and for 10:00: $1 - 0.83 = 0.17$. Of those numbers, 0.34 is the largest and thus the most likely time for Lafayette to clock in is between 9:16 and 9:30 (*Statistics: Learning from Data*, AP Edition, 1st ed. pages 68–96 / 2nd ed. pages 70–93).

40. **(D)** $\hat{p} = \frac{32}{300} = 0.1067$. The z test statistic is
$$z = \frac{0.1067 - 0.08}{\sqrt{\frac{(0.08)(1-0.08)}{300}}} = \frac{0.0267}{0.0157} = 1.70$$
(*Statistics: Learning from Data*, AP Edition, 1st ed. pages 514–523 / 2nd ed. pages 530–539).

Free-Response Answers

1. (a) This is not a good idea. People who usually play golf together may be similar in ability and so with this method of creating teams, one team might have all very good golfers and other teams might not have any very good golfers.
   (b) The second method is more likely to create comparable teams because each team will consist of a golfer with a high ranking, a golfer with a low ranking, and two golfers ranked near the middle. With random assignment in the first option, it is possible that one team might contain two or more highly ranked golfers.
   (c) Number the golfers from 1 to 32 based on their ranking. Generate a random number between 1 and 8 and assign the corresponding player to Team 1. Generate a random number between 9 and 16 and assign the corresponding player to Team 1. Generate a random number between 17 and 24 and assign the corresponding player to Team 1. Generate a random number between 25 and 32 and assign the corresponding player to Team 1. Team 1 is now complete. Next, follow the same procedure to create Team 2. If any of the random numbers generated correspond to a golfer who has already been assigned to a team, continue to generate random numbers in the appropriate range until a number corresponding to an unassigned golfer is obtained. Continue this process until all teams have been formed.

(*Statistics: Learning from Data*, AP Edition, 1st ed. pages 24–38 / 2nd ed. pages 23–38)

Scoring Question 1:

Each part of this problem can be scored as essentially correct (E), partially correct (P), or incorrect (I).

Part (a) is scored
  E if the response states that this is not a good idea and gives a plausible explanation for why this method might not create comparable teams.
  P if the response gives a plausible explanation for why this method might not create comparable teams, but fails to answer the question about whether or not this is a good idea.

Part (b) is scored
  E if the student chooses Method 2 and provides a clear explanation of why this method is more likely to result in comparable teams.
  P if the student chooses Method 2 but the explanation is weak or poorly communicated.

Part (c) is scored
  E if a correct method is clearly described.
  Note: If Method 1 is chosen in part (b), the description in part (c) should be consistent with that selection. A correct method for random assignment that is clearly described would then be scored as E for part (c).
  P if a correct method is implied, but the description is not complete or is not clearly communicated.

Question 1 is scored a
  4 if all three parts are E.
  3 if two parts are E and the one is P.
  2 if two parts are E and no parts are P, OR one part is E and two parts are P, OR if three parts are P.
  1 if two parts are P and one part is I OR if one part is E and no parts are P.
  0 if one OR no parts are P.

2. This question can be answered using a chi-square goodness-of-fit test. In the long run, if the spinner is fair, it should land on a segment labeled 0 about 10/20 of the time, a segment labeled $1 about 5/20 of the time, a segment labeled $5 about 3/20 of the time and a segment labeled $5 about 2/20 of the time.

   Hypotheses:

   $H_0 : p_1 = 0.50, p_2 = 0.25, p_3 = 0.15, p_4 = 0.10$

   H_a : at least one of the p_i's is different from the value specified in H_0

   where

   p_1 = the true proportion of the time that the spinner lands on a 0

   p_2 = the true proportion of the time that the spinner lands on a $1

   p_3 = the true proportion of the time that the spinner lands on a $2

   p_4 = the true proportion of the time that the spinner lands on a $5

   Test statistic:

   The test is a chi-square goodness of fit, with test statistic

   $$X^2 = \sum \frac{(\text{observed} - \text{expected})^2}{\text{expected}}$$

   Assumptions:
   (1) Spins are independent, so it is reasonable to regard the 500 observations as if it were a random sample of spins of this spinner.
   (2) Large sample. The expected counts are 500(0.50) = 250, 500(0.25) = 125, 500(0.15) = 75 and 500(0.10) = 50. All expected counts are greater than 5, so the sample size is large enough.

   Calculations:

   $$X^2 = \frac{(280-250)^2}{250} + \frac{(140-125)^2}{125} + \frac{(55-75)^2}{75} + \frac{(25-50)^2}{50} = 23.23$$

   $df = 4 - 1 = 3$

   P-value = 0.000

   Conclusion:
   Because the P-value is so small (smaller than any reasonable alpha level), we reject the null hypothesis and conclude that there is convincing evidence that the spinner is not fair.

   (*Statistics: Learning from Data*, AP Edition, 1st ed. pages 694–705 / 2nd ed. pages 702–714).

Scoring Question 2:

There are four parts to this hypothesis test: hypotheses, test and assumptions, calculations, and conclusion. Each of these parts can be scored as essentially correct (E), partially correct (P), or incorrect (I).

Hypotheses are scored as
　E if a correct pair of hypotheses is given and the parameters used in the null hypothesis are defined.
　P if hypotheses are correct but parameters are not defined OR if the form of the hypotheses is correct but hypothesized proportions other than 0.50, 0.25, 0.15, and 0.10 are specified in the null hypothesis.

Test and assumptions are scored as
　E if (1) the correct test is identified either by name or by formula and (2) both assumptions for the test are adequately addressed. P if the response includes only one of the two components required for an E.

Calculations are scored as
　E if correct values of the test statistic and P-value are given.
　P if either the value of the test statistic or the P-value is omitted or incorrect.
Note: Calculations should be consistent with the hypothesized values given in the null hypothesis of part (a).

Conclusion is scored as
　E if a correct conclusion is given in context and the conclusion is linked to the P-value.
　P if a correct decision to reject or fail to reject the null hypothesis is given but the conclusion is not in context or the conclusion is not linked to the P-value.

Then Question 2 is scored a
　4 if four parts are E.
　3 if three parts are E and one is P OR three parts are E and one is I OR two parts are E and two parts are P.
　2 if two parts are E and one part is P and one part is I OR two parts are E and two parts are I OR one part is E and three parts are P OR one part is E and two parts are P and one part is I OR if four parts are P.
　1 if one part is E and one part is P and two parts are I OR one part is E and three parts are I OR three parts are P and one part is I OR two parts are P and two parts are I.
　0 if one part is P and three parts are I OR four parts are I.

3. (a) The expected number of tones heard for boxers over 50 is $E(\text{tones}) = 0(0.10) + 1(0.20) + 2(0.20) + 3(0.25) + 4(0.15) + 5(0.10) = 2.45$ tones.

   (b) Combinations of scores that result in a difference (boxer − nonboxer) of −2 are

Boxer	Non-boxer
3	5
2	4
1	3
0	2

   (c) To find the probability that the difference between a randomly selected boxer and a randomly selected non-boxer is −2, we need to compute the probability of observing each of the pairs listed in part (b) and then add these probabilities. Since the selection of the boxer and the selection of the non-boxer are independent, $P(3,5) = P(\text{boxer} = 3 \text{ and non-boxer} = 5) = (0.25)(0.30) = 0.075$. Similarly, $P(2,4) = (0.20)(0.25) = 0.50$, $P(1, 3) =$

(0.20)(0.25) = 0.05, and $P(0, 2) = (0.10)(0.10) = 0.010$. This gives $P(\text{difference} = -2) = 0.75 + 0.050 + 0.050 + 0.010 = 0.185$

(d) For boxers, 30% heard only 0 or 1 tone. For non-boxers, 15% heard only 0 or 1 tone. This means that those with severe hearing loss heard only 0 or 1 tone. It follows that someone who heard two or more tones was not classified as having severe hearing loss.

(*Statistics: Learning from Data*, AP Edition, 1st ed. pages 273–276, 278–287, and 352–361 / 2nd ed. pages 285–289, 291–301, and 367–378)

Scoring Question 3:

Each part (a), (b), (c), and (d) are each scored as essentially correct (E), partially correct (P), or incorrect (I).

Part (a) is scored
  E if the expected value is correctly computed with supporting work shown.
  P if the expected value is correctly computed with no supporting work shown.

Part (b) is scored
  E if all four pairs of scores that result in a difference of –2 are specified.
  P if two or three pairs of scores that result in a difference of –2 are specified.

Part (c) is scored
  E if a correct probability is given with appropriate supporting work.
  P if a correct probability is given but there is no supporting work OR if the probability is incorrect because some but not all of the four possible combinations of scores that result in a difference of –2 were considered.

Part (d) is scored
  E if the response identifies 2 or more tones (or equivalently more than 1 tone or 2, 3, 4, or 5 tones) as the description of someone who does not have severe hearing loss.
  P if the response only describes sever hearing loss as 0 or 1 tones heard, but does not explicitly describe NOT severe hearing loss.

Question 3 is scored a
  4 if four parts are E.
  3 if three parts are E and one is P OR three parts are E and one is I OR two parts are E and two parts are P.
  2 if two parts are E and one part is P and one part is I OR two parts are E and two parts are I OR one part is E and three parts are P OR one part is E and two parts are P and one part is I OR if four parts are P.
  1 if one part is E and one part is P and two parts are I OR one part is E and three parts are I OR three parts are P and one part is I OR two parts are P and two parts are I.
  0 if one part is P and three parts are I OR four parts are I.

4. (a) Both distributions appear to be approximately symmetric. The most noticeable difference is in variability, with prize amounts more variable after the change than before the change. The median prize amount is greater after the change, and there do not appear to be unusual prize amounts before or after the change.
   (b) Overall, prize amounts tended to be greater after the dollar amounts were doubled. From the boxplot, we can see that the median prize amount was greater after the change and that the upper quartile after the change is greater than the maximum prize before the change. This means that more than 25% of the prizes won after the change were greater than any prize won before the change.
   (c) A boxplot should be consistent with the following: approximate minimum = 4; approximate lower quartile = 14; approximate median = 42; approximate upper quartile = 78; approximate maximum = 90.

   (*Statistics: Learning from Data*, AP Edition, 1st ed. pages 149–156 / 2nd ed. pages 158–165)

Scoring Question 4:

Each part of this problem can be scored as essentially correct (E), partially correct (P), or incorrect (I).

Part (a) is scored
   E if the two distributions are compared on the basis of all three of shape, center, and spread.
   P if the distributions are compared on only 2 of shape, center, and spread OR
   I if shape, center and spread are described for both distributions, but no comparative statements are made.

Part (b) is scored
   E if the response says that doubling did tend to result in greater amounts won and provides an appropriate justification based on the given boxplots.
   P if the response says that doubling did tend to result in greater amounts won but the justification is weak or is not tied to characteristics of the boxplot.

Part (c) is scored
   E if a boxplot is drawn that is consistent with doubling. The drawn boxplot should be drawn so that the approximate values used to construct the plot are: Minimum ≈ 4, lower quartile ≈ 14, median ≈ 42, upper quartile ≈ 78, and maximum ≈ 90.
   P if a boxplot is drawn that has similar variability to the boxplot in part (a) but is shifted to the right so that the median of the after boxplot is approximately twice the median of the before boxplot.

Question 4 is scored a
   4 if all three parts are E.
   3 if two parts are E and the one is P.
   2 if two parts are E and no parts are P, OR one part is E and two parts are P, OR if three parts are P.
   1 if two parts are P and one part is I OR if one part is E and no parts are P.
   0 if one OR no parts are P.

5. **Hypotheses:**

$H_0: \mu_W - \mu_N = 0$ $\quad\quad\quad$ $H_0: \mu_W = \mu_N$
$\quad\quad\quad\quad\quad\quad$ or
$H_a: \mu_W - \mu_N < 0$ $\quad\quad\quad$ $H_a: \mu_W < \mu_N$

where μ_W denotes the true mean sleep time (in minutes) for the water treatment and μ_N denotes the true mean sleep time for the no water treatment

Test: two-sample t test

Assumptions:
(1) Random assignment: The question states that subjects were assigned to the treatment groups at random.
(2) Large samples or sleep time distributions approximately normal: both sample sizes were 40, which is larger than 30. The sample sizes are large enough to proceed.

Calculations:

$$t = \frac{\bar{x}_W - \bar{x}_N}{\sqrt{\frac{s_W^2}{n_W} + \frac{s_N^2}{n_N}}} = \frac{(289 - 406)}{\sqrt{\frac{(56)^2}{40} + \frac{(53)^2}{40}}} = \frac{117}{12.19} = 9.598$$

$df = 77$

P-value ≈ 0

Note: $df = 40 - 1 = 39$ may also be used.

Conclusion:
Because the P-value is so small (smaller than any reasonable alpha level), we reject the null hypothesis. There is convincing evidence that the mean sleep time for the water treatment is less than the mean sleep time for the no water treatment.

(*Statistics: Learning from Data*, AP Edition, 1st ed. pages 618–627, 644–649, 672–674, and 679–682 / 2nd ed. pages 657–670)

Scoring Question 5:

There are four parts to this hypothesis test: hypotheses, test and assumptions, calculations, and conclusion. Each of these parts can be scored as essentially correct (E), partially correct (P), or incorrect (I).

Hypotheses are scored as
  E if both hypotheses are correctly specified.
  P if only one of the hypotheses is correctly specified.

Test and assumptions are scored as
  E if (1) the correct test is identified either by name or by formula and (2) both assumptions for the test are adequately addressed.
  P if the response includes only one of the two components required for an E.

Calculations are scored as
  E if correct values of the test statistic and P-value are given.
  P if either the value of the test statistic or the P-value is omitted or incorrect.

Conclusion is scored as
- E if a correct conclusion is given in context and the conclusion is linked to the *P*-value.
- P if a correct decision to reject or fail to reject the null hypothesis (based on the *P*-value in the response) is given but the conclusion is not in context or the conclusion is not linked to the *P*-value.

Question 5 is scored a
- 4 if four parts are E.
- 3 if three parts are E and one is P OR three parts are E and one is I OR two parts are E and two parts are P.
- 2 if two parts are E and one part is P and one part is I OR two parts are E and two parts are I OR one part is E and three parts are P OR one part is E and two parts are P and one part is I OR if four parts are P.
- 1 if one part is E and one part is P and two parts are I OR one part is E and three parts are I OR three parts are P and one part is I OR two parts are P and two parts are I.
- 0 if one part is P and three parts are I OR four parts are I.

6. (a)

   (b) There is more variability in movie length for the 2001–2005 movies than for the 2006–2010 movies. There were a few unusually long movies in the 2001–2005 data, and so the mean length was probably greater for this group of movies than the movies in the 2006–2010 data set. The data do not support the statement that the top 12 movies tended to be longer for the 2006–2010 time period.

   (c) For the data set that consists of all 24 films, there does not appear to be any strong relationship between domestic gross and length. Although there is an outlier in the scatter diagram (*Avatar,* with a domestic gross of 754 million) there is no apparent pattern and the r^2 value is only 0.027, indicating that very little of the variability in domestic gross is explained by length.

   Looking at the two time periods separately, there is no evidence of a linear relationship for the 2001–2005 time period, and the r^2 value for this time period is only 0.173. For the 2006–2010 time period, the scatter diagram does show an interesting pattern, with the most profitable movies having the greatest lengths. r^2 is higher here at 0.360. However, a nonlinear equation would be a better choice for describing the relationship between domestic gross and length.

   So, it appears that the relationship between domestic gross and length is not the same for the most profitable movies in these two time periods.

   (d) No, it would not be a good idea to use any of the three regression equations to make a prediction. There are two key reasons why this is not a good idea. First, the data sets consisted only of the 12 most profitable movies in each time period and are not representative of all movies made in that time period. Second, using any of these regression equations to make a prediction for a movie made outside the time period 2001–2010 is not a good idea because there is no reason to think that the relationship between domestic gross and length would be the same for a different time period.

(*Statistics: Learning from Data,* AP Edition, 1st ed. pages 182–193, 198–206, and 211–225 / 2nd ed. pages 192–204, 209–219, and 223–239)

Scoring Question 6:

Each part of this problem can be scored as essentially correct (E), partially correct (P), or incorrect (I).

Part (a) is scored
  E if correct dotplots are provided, the dotplots are labeled by time period, a scale is indicated, and the same scale is used for both dotplots.
  P if correct dotplots are given with scales indicated, but the dotplots are not labeled by time period and/or different scales are used for the two dotplots.

Part (b) is scored
  E if the two distributions are compared on the basis of center and spread, and the response states that the dotplots do not support the statement that top 12 movies tended to be longer in the 2006–2010 time period.
  P if the distributions are compared on only one center and spread OR if the distributions are compared on both center and spread but the response does not explicitly address the question of support for the statement that top 12 movies tended to be longer in the 2006–2010 time period.

Part (c) is scored
  E if the response (1) indicates that the relationship is not the same for the two time periods, (2) an appropriate justification based on the scatter diagrams and regression output is provided, and (3) the response makes note of the nonlinear pattern in the 2006–2010 scatter diagram.
  Note: Because the movies are not a random sample from some population of movies, inference about the slope is not meaningful. Regression is merely being used here as a descriptive tool. If the response appeals to the t test for slope, this can be overlooked as long as this is not the only justification provided.
  P if only 2 of the 3 components required for an E are included in the response.

Part (d) is scored
  E if the response states that it is not a good idea to use any of the regression equations to make the prediction and gives at least two valid reasons to support this statement.
  P if E if the response states that it is not a good idea to use any of the regression equations to make the prediction but only gives at least one valid reason to support this statement.

Question 6 is scored a
  4 if four parts are E.
  3 if three parts are E and one is P OR three parts are E and one is I OR two parts are E and two parts are P.
  2 if two parts are E and one part is P and one part is I OR two parts are E and two parts are I OR one part is E and three parts are P OR one part is E and two parts are P and one part is I OR if four parts are P.
  1 if one part is E and one part is P and two parts are I OR one part is E and three parts are I OR three parts are P and one part is I OR two parts are P and two parts are I.
  0 if one part is P and three parts are I OR four parts are I.

Calculating Your Score

Section I: Multiple-Choice Questions

[_____] × 1.25 = _____
Number Correct   Weighted Section I Score
(out of 40)   (do not round)

Section II: Free-Response Questions

Question 1 _____ × (1.875) = _____
        (out of 4)   (Do not round)

Question 2 _____ × (1.875) = _____
        (out of 4)   (Do not round)

Question 3 _____ × (1.875) = _____
        (out of 4)   (Do not round)

Question 4 _____ × (1.875) = _____
        (out of 4)   (Do not round)

Question 5 _____ × (1.875) = _____
        (out of 4)   (Do not round)

Question 6 _____ × (3.1255) = _____
        (out of 4)   (Do not round)

                                                  Sum = _____
                                                              Weighted Section II Score
                                                              (Do not round)

Composite Score

_____ + _____ = _____
Weighted   Weighted   Composite Score
Section I Score Section II Score (Round to nearest
                                 whole number)

Composite Score Range	Approximate AP® Grade
68–100	5
53–67	4
40–52	3
29–39	2
0–28	1

Part IV

Equations and Constants

Descriptive Statistics

$$\bar{x} = \frac{\sum x_i}{n}$$

$$s_x = \sqrt{\frac{1}{n-1}\sum(x_i - \bar{x})^2}$$

$$s_p = \sqrt{\frac{(n_1-1)s_1^2 + (n_2-1)s_2^2}{(n_1-1)+(n_2-1)}}$$

$$\hat{y} = b_0 + b_1 x$$

$$b_1 = \frac{\sum(x_i - \bar{x})(y_i - \bar{y})}{\sum(x_i - \bar{x})^2}$$

$$b_0 = \bar{y} - b_1 \bar{x}$$

$$r = \frac{1}{n-1}\sum\left(\frac{x_i - \bar{x}}{s_x}\right)\left(\frac{y_i - \bar{y}}{s_y}\right)$$

$$b_1 = r\frac{s_y}{s_x}$$

$$s_{b_1} = \frac{\sqrt{\frac{\sum(y_i - \hat{y}_i)^2}{n-2}}}{\sqrt{\sum(x_i - \bar{x})^2}}$$

Probability

$$P(A \cup B) = P(A) + P(B) - P(A \cap B)$$

$$P(A|B) = \frac{P(A \cap B)}{P(B)}$$

$$E(X) = \mu_x = \sum x_i p_i$$

$$Var(X) = \sigma_x^2 = \sum(x_i - \mu_i)^2 p_i$$

If X has a binomial distribution with parameters n and p, then:

$$P(X = k) = \binom{n}{k} p^k (1-p)^{n-k}$$

$$\mu_x = np$$

$$\sigma_x = \sqrt{np(1-p)}$$

$$\mu_{\hat{p}} = p$$

$$\sigma_{\hat{p}} = \sqrt{\frac{p(1-p)}{n}}$$

If $\bar{x}$ is the mean of a random sample of size n from an infinite population with μ and standard deviation σ, then:

$$\mu_{\bar{x}} = \mu$$

$$\sigma_{\bar{x}} = \frac{\sigma}{\sqrt{n}}$$

Iferential Statistics

Standardized test statistic: $\dfrac{\text{statistic} - \text{parameter}}{\text{standard deviation of statistic}}$

Confidence interval: statistic $\pm$ (critical value) $\cdot$ (standard deviation of statistic)

Single-Sample

Statistic	Standard Deviation of Statistic
Sample Mean	$\dfrac{\sigma}{\sqrt{n}}$
Sample Proportion	$\sqrt{\dfrac{p(1-p)}{n}}$

Two-Sample

Statistic	Standard Deviation of Statistic
Difference of sample means	$\sqrt{\dfrac{\sigma_1^2}{n_1} + \dfrac{\sigma_2^2}{n_2}}$ Special case when $\sigma_1 = \sigma_2$ $\sigma\sqrt{\dfrac{1}{n_1} + \dfrac{1}{n_2}}$
Difference of sample proportions	$\sqrt{\dfrac{p_1(1-p_1)}{n_1} + \dfrac{p_2(1-p_2)}{n_2}}$ Special case when $p_1 = p_2$ $\sqrt{p(1-p)}\sqrt{\dfrac{1}{n_1} + \dfrac{1}{n_2}}$

Chi-square test statistic $= \sum \dfrac{(\text{observed} - \text{expected})^2}{\text{expected}}$

TABLE A: STANDARD NORMAL PROBABILITIES

Table entry for z is probability lying below z.

z	.00	.01	.02	.03	.04	.05	.06	.07	.08	.09
−3.4	.0003	.0003	.0003	.0003	.0003	.0003	.0003	.0003	.0003	.0002
−3.3	.0005	.0005	.0005	.0004	.0004	.0004	.0004	.0004	.0004	.0003
−3.2	.0007	.0007	.0006	.0006	.0006	.0006	.0006	.0005	.0005	.0005
−3.1	.0010	.0009	.0009	.0009	.0008	.0008	.0008	.0008	.0007	.0007
−3.0	.0013	.0013	.0013	.0012	.0012	.0011	.0011	.0011	.0010	.0010
−2.9	.0019	.0018	.0018	.0017	.0016	.0016	.0015	.0015	.0014	.0014
−2.8	.0026	.0025	.0024	.0023	.0023	.0022	.0021	.0021	.0020	.0019
−2.7	.0035	.0034	.0033	.0032	.0031	.0030	.0029	.0028	.0027	.0026
−2.6	.0047	.0045	.0044	.0043	.0041	.0040	.0039	.0038	.0037	.0036
−2.5	.0062	.0060	.0059	.0057	.0055	.0054	.0052	.0051	.0049	.0048
−2.4	.0082	.0080	.0078	.0075	.0073	.0071	.0069	.0068	.0066	.0064
−2.3	.0107	.0104	.0102	.0099	.0096	.0094	.0091	.0089	.0087	.0084
−2.2	.0139	.0136	.0132	.0129	.0125	.0122	.0119	.0116	.0113	.0110
−2.1	.0179	.0174	.0170	.0166	.0162	.0158	.0154	.0150	.0146	.0143
−2.0	.0228	.0222	.0217	.0212	.0207	.0202	.0197	.0192	.0188	.0183
−1.9	.0287	.0281	.0274	.0268	.0262	.0256	.0250	.0244	.0239	.0233
−1.8	.0359	.0351	.0344	.0336	.0329	.0322	.0314	.0307	.0301	.0294
−1.7	.0446	.0436	.0427	.0418	.0409	.0401	.0392	.0384	.0375	.0367
−1.6	.0548	.0537	.0526	.0516	.0505	.0495	.0485	.0475	.0465	.0455
−1.5	.0668	.0655	.0643	.0630	.0618	.0606	.0594	.0582	.0571	.0559
−1.4	.0808	.0793	.0778	.0764	.0749	.0735	.0721	.0708	.0694	.0681
−1.3	.0968	.0951	.0934	.0918	.0901	.0885	.0869	.0853	.0838	.0823
−1.2	.1151	.1131	.1112	.1093	.1075	.1056	.1038	.1020	.1003	.0985
−1.1	.1357	.1335	.1314	.1292	.1271	.1251	.1230	.1210	.1190	.1170
−1.0	.1587	.1562	.1539	.1515	.1492	.1469	.1446	.1423	.1401	.1379
−0.9	.1841	.1814	.1788	.1762	.1736	.1711	.1685	.1660	.1635	.1611
−0.8	.2119	.2090	.2061	.2033	.2005	.1977	.1949	.1922	.1894	.1867
−0.7	.2420	.2389	.2358	.2327	.2296	.2266	.2236	.2206	.2177	.2148
−0.6	.2743	.2709	.2676	.2643	.2611	.2578	.2546	.2514	.2483	.2451
−0.5	.3085	.3050	.3015	.2981	.2946	.2912	.2877	.2843	.2810	.2776
−0.4	.3446	.3409	.3372	.3336	.3300	.3264	.3228	.3192	.3156	.3121
−0.3	.3821	.3783	.3745	.3707	.3669	.3632	.3594	.3557	.3520	.3483
−0.2	.4207	.4168	.4129	.4090	.4052	.4013	.3974	.3936	.3897	.3859
−0.1	.4602	.4562	.4522	.4483	.4443	.4404	.4364	.4325	.4286	.4247
−0.0	.5000	.4960	.4920	.4880	.4840	.4801	.4761	.4721	.4681	.4641

TABLE A: STANDARD NORMAL PROBABILITIES (CONTINUED)

Table entry for z is the probability lying below z.

z	.00	.01	.02	.03	.04	.05	.06	.07	.08	.09
0.0	.5000	.5040	.5080	.5120	.5160	.5199	.5239	.5279	.5319	.5359
0.1	.5398	.5438	.5478	.5517	.5557	.5596	.5636	.5675	.5714	.5753
0.2	.5793	.5832	.5871	.5910	.5948	.5987	.6026	.6064	.6103	.6141
0.3	.6179	.6217	.6255	.6293	.6331	.6368	.6406	.6443	.6480	.6517
0.4	.6554	.6591	.6628	.6664	.6700	.6736	.6772	.6808	.6844	.6879
0.5	.6915	.6950	.6985	.7019	.7054	.7088	.7123	.7157	.7190	.7224
0.6	.7257	.7291	.7324	.7357	.7389	.7422	.7454	.7486	.7517	.7549
0.7	.7580	.7611	.7642	.7673	.7704	.7734	.7764	.7794	.7823	.7852
0.8	.7881	.7910	.7939	.7967	.7995	.8023	.8051	.8078	.8106	.8133
0.9	.8159	.8186	.8212	.8238	.8264	.8289	.8315	.8340	.8365	.8389
1.0	.8413	.8438	.8461	.8485	.8508	.8531	.8554	.8577	.8599	.8621
1.1	.8643	.8665	.8686	.8708	.8729	.8749	.8770	.8790	.8810	.8830
1.2	.8849	.8869	.8888	.8907	.8925	.8944	.8962	.8980	.8997	.9015
1.3	.9032	.9049	.9066	.9082	.9099	.9115	.9131	.9147	.9162	.9177
1.4	.9192	.9207	.9222	.9236	.9251	.9265	.9279	.9292	.9306	.9319
1.5	.9332	.9345	.9357	.9370	.9382	.9394	.9406	.9418	.9429	.9441
1.6	.9452	.9463	.9474	.9484	.9495	.9505	.9515	.9525	.9535	.9545
1.7	.9554	.9564	.9573	.9582	.9591	.9599	.9608	.9616	.9625	.9633
1.8	.9641	.9649	.9656	.9664	.9671	.9678	.9686	.9693	.9699	.9706
1.9	.9713	.9719	.9726	.9732	.9738	.9744	.9750	.9756	.9761	.9767
2.0	.9772	.9778	.9783	.9788	.9793	.9798	.9803	.9808	.9812	.9817
2.1	.9821	.9826	.9830	.9834	.9838	.9842	.9846	.9850	.9854	.9857
2.2	.9861	.9864	.9868	.9871	.9875	.9878	.9881	.9884	.9887	.9890
2.3	.9893	.9896	.9898	.9901	.9904	.9906	.9909	.9911	.9913	.9916
2.4	.9918	.9920	.9922	.9925	.9927	.9929	.9931	.9932	.9934	.9936
2.5	.9938	.9940	.9941	.9943	.9945	.9946	.9948	.9949	.9951	.9952
2.6	.9953	.9955	.9956	.9957	.9959	.9960	.9961	.9962	.9963	.9964
2.7	.9965	.9966	.9967	.9968	.9969	.9970	.9971	.9972	.9973	.9974
2.8	.9974	.9975	.9976	.9977	.9977	.9978	.9979	.9979	.9980	.9981
2.9	.9981	.9982	.9982	.9983	.9984	.9984	.9985	.9985	.9986	.9986
3.0	.9987	.9987	.9987	.9988	.9988	.9989	.9989	.9989	.9990	.9990
3.1	.9990	.9991	.9991	.9991	.9992	.9992	.9992	.9992	.9993	.9993
3.2	.9993	.9993	.9994	.9994	.9994	.9994	.9994	.9995	.9995	.9995
3.3	.9995	.9995	.9995	.9996	.9996	.9996	.9996	.9996	.9996	.9997
3.4	.9997	.9997	.9997	.9997	.9997	.9997	.9997	.9997	.9997	.9998

TABLE B: t DISTRIBUTION CRITICAL VALUES

Table entry for p and C is the point t^* with probability p lying above it and probability C lying between $-t^*$ and t^*.

df	Tail probability p											
	.25	.20	.15	.10	.05	.025	.02	.01	.005	.0025	.001	.0005
1	1.000	1.376	1.963	3.078	6.314	12.71	15.89	31.82	63.66	127.3	318.3	636.6
2	.816	1.061	1.386	1.886	2.920	4.303	4.849	6.965	9.925	14.09	22.33	31.60
3	.765	.978	1.250	1.638	2.353	3.182	3.482	4.541	5.841	7.453	10.21	12.92
4	.741	.941	1.190	1.533	2.132	2.776	2.999	3.747	4.604	5.598	7.173	8.610
5	.727	.920	1.156	1.476	2.015	2.571	2.757	3.365	4.032	4.773	5.893	6.869
6	.718	.906	1.134	1.440	1.943	2.447	2.612	3.143	3.707	4.317	5.208	5.959
7	.711	.896	1.119	1.415	1.895	2.365	2.517	2.998	3.499	4.029	4.785	5.408
8	.706	.889	1.108	1.397	1.860	2.306	2.449	2.896	3.355	3.833	4.501	5.041
9	.703	.883	1.100	1.383	1.833	2.262	2.398	2.821	3.250	3.690	4.297	4.781
10	.700	.879	1.093	1.372	1.812	2.228	2.359	2.764	3.169	3.581	4.144	4.587
11	.697	.876	1.088	1.363	1.796	2.201	2.328	2.718	3.106	3.497	4.025	4.437
12	.695	.873	1.083	1.356	1.782	2.179	2.303	2.681	3.055	3.428	3.930	4.318
13	.694	.870	1.079	1.350	1.771	2.160	2.282	2.650	3.012	3.372	3.852	4.221
14	.692	.868	1.076	1.345	1.761	2.145	2.264	2.624	2.977	3.326	3.787	4.140
15	.691	.866	1.074	1.341	1.753	2.131	2.249	2.602	2.947	3.286	3.733	4.073
16	.690	.865	1.071	1.337	1.746	2.120	2.235	2.583	2.921	3.252	3.686	4.015
17	.689	.863	1.069	1.333	1.740	2.110	2.224	2.567	2.898	3.222	3.646	3.965
18	.688	.862	1.067	1.330	1.734	2.101	2.214	2.552	2.878	3.197	3.611	3.922
19	.688	.861	1.066	1.328	1.729	2.093	2.205	2.539	2.861	3.174	3.579	3.883
20	.687	.860	1.064	1.325	1.725	2.086	2.197	2.528	2.845	3.153	3.552	3.850
21	.686	.859	1.063	1.323	1.721	2.080	2.189	2.518	2.831	3.135	3.527	3.819
22	.686	.858	1.061	1.321	1.717	2.074	2.183	2.508	2.819	3.119	3.505	3.792
23	.685	.858	1.060	1.319	1.714	2.069	2.177	2.500	2.807	3.104	3.485	3.768
24	.685	.857	1.059	1.318	1.711	2.064	2.172	2.492	2.797	3.091	3.467	3.745
25	.684	.856	1.058	1.316	1.708	2.060	2.167	2.485	2.787	3.078	3.450	3.725
26	.684	.856	1.058	1.315	1.706	2.056	2.162	2.479	2.779	3.067	3.435	3.707
27	.684	.855	1.057	1.314	1.703	2.052	2.158	2.473	2.771	3.057	3.421	3.690
28	.683	.855	1.056	1.313	1.701	2.048	2.154	2.467	2.763	3.047	3.408	3.674
29	.683	.854	1.055	1.311	1.699	2.045	2.150	2.462	2.756	3.038	3.396	3.659
30	.683	.854	1.055	1.310	1.697	2.042	2.147	2.457	2.750	3.030	3.385	3.646
40	.681	.851	1.050	1.303	1.684	2.021	2.123	2.423	2.704	2.971	3.307	3.551
50	.679	.849	1.047	1.299	1.676	2.009	2.109	2.403	2.678	2.937	3.261	3.496
60	.679	.848	1.045	1.296	1.671	2.000	2.099	2.390	2.660	2.915	3.232	3.460
80	.678	.846	1.043	1.292	1.664	1.990	2.088	2.374	2.639	2.887	3.195	3.416
100	.677	.845	1.042	1.290	1.660	1.984	2.081	2.364	2.626	2.871	3.174	3.390
1000	.675	.842	1.037	1.282	1.646	1.962	2.056	2.330	2.581	2.813	3.098	3.300
∞	.674	.841	1.036	1.282	1.645	1.960	2.054	2.326	2.576	2.807	3.091	3.291
	50%	60%	70%	80%	90%	95%	96%	98%	99%	99.5%	99.8%	99.9%
	Confidence level C											

TABLE C: χ^2 CRITICAL VALUES

Table entry for p is the point (χ^2) with probability lying above it

df	Tail probability p										
	.25	.20	.15	.10	.05	.025	.02	.01	.005	.0025	.001
1	1.32	1.64	2.07	2.71	3.84	5.02	5.41	6.63	7.88	9.14	10.83
2	2.77	3.22	3.79	4.61	5.99	7.38	7.82	9.21	10.60	11.98	13.82
3	4.11	4.64	5.32	6.25	7.81	9.35	9.84	11.34	12.84	14.32	16.27
4	5.39	5.99	6.74	7.78	9.49	11.14	11.67	13.28	14.86	16.42	18.47
5	6.63	7.29	8.12	9.24	11.07	12.83	13.39	15.09	16.75	18.39	20.51
6	7.84	8.56	9.45	10.64	12.59	14.45	15.03	16.81	18.55	20.25	22.46
7	9.04	9.80	10.75	12.02	14.07	16.01	16.62	18.48	20.28	22.04	24.32
8	10.22	11.03	12.03	13.36	15.51	17.53	18.17	20.09	21.95	23.77	26.12
9	11.39	12.24	13.29	14.68	16.92	19.02	19.68	21.67	23.59	25.46	27.88
10	12.55	13.44	14.53	15.99	18.31	20.48	21.16	23.21	25.19	27.11	29.59
11	13.70	14.63	15.77	17.28	19.68	21.92	22.62	24.72	26.76	28.73	31.26
12	14.85	15.81	16.99	18.55	21.03	23.34	24.05	26.22	28.30	30.32	32.91
13	15.98	16.98	18.20	19.81	22.36	24.74	25.47	27.69	29.82	31.88	34.53
14	17.12	18.15	19.41	21.06	23.68	26.12	26.87	29.14	31.32	33.43	36.12
15	18.25	19.31	20.60	22.31	25.00	27.49	28.26	30.58	32.80	34.95	37.70
16	19.37	20.47	21.79	23.54	26.30	28.85	29.63	32.00	34.27	36.46	39.25
17	20.49	21.61	22.98	24.77	27.59	30.19	31.00	33.41	35.72	37.95	40.79
18	21.60	22.76	24.16	25.99	28.87	31.53	32.35	34.81	37.16	39.42	42.31
19	22.72	23.90	25.33	27.20	30.14	32.85	33.69	36.19	38.58	40.88	43.82
20	23.83	25.04	26.50	28.41	31.41	34.17	35.02	37.57	40.00	42.34	45.31
21	24.93	26.17	27.66	29.62	32.67	35.48	36.34	38.93	41.40	43.78	46.80
22	26.04	27.30	28.82	30.81	33.92	36.78	37.66	40.29	42.80	45.20	48.27
23	27.14	28.43	29.98	32.01	35.17	38.08	38.97	41.64	44.18	46.62	49.73
24	28.24	29.55	31.13	33.20	36.42	39.36	40.27	42.98	45.56	48.03	51.18
25	29.34	30.68	32.28	34.38	37.65	40.65	41.57	44.31	46.93	49.44	52.62
26	30.43	31.79	33.43	35.56	38.89	41.92	42.86	45.64	48.29	50.83	54.05
27	31.53	32.91	34.57	36.74	40.11	43.19	44.14	46.96	49.64	52.22	55.48
28	32.62	34.03	35.71	37.92	41.34	44.46	45.42	48.28	50.99	53.59	56.89
29	33.71	35.14	36.85	39.09	42.56	45.72	46.69	49.59	52.34	54.97	58.30
30	34.80	36.25	37.99	40.26	43.77	46.98	47.96	50.89	53.67	56.33	59.70
40	45.62	47.27	49.24	51.81	55.76	59.34	60.44	63.69	66.77	69.70	73.40
50	56.33	58.16	60.35	63.17	67.50	71.42	72.61	76.15	79.49	82.66	86.66
60	66.98	68.97	71.34	74.40	79.08	83.30	84.58	88.38	91.95	95.34	99.61
80	88.13	90.41	93.11	96.58	101.9	106.6	108.1	112.3	116.3	120.1	124.8
100	109.1	111.7	114.7	118.5	124.3	129.6	131.1	135.8	140.2	144.3	149.4